saturn
apartments 3

HISAE IWAOKA

saturn
apartments **3**

floor 18: alone in her room

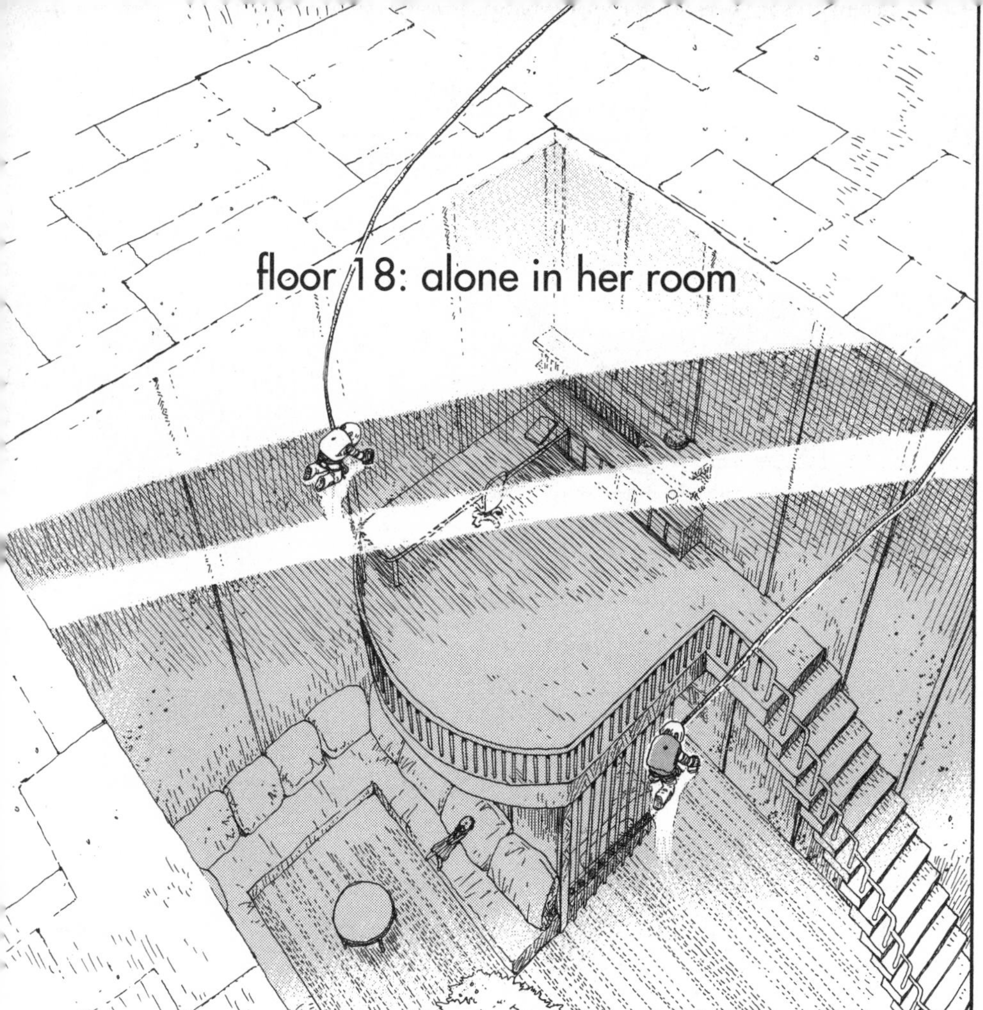

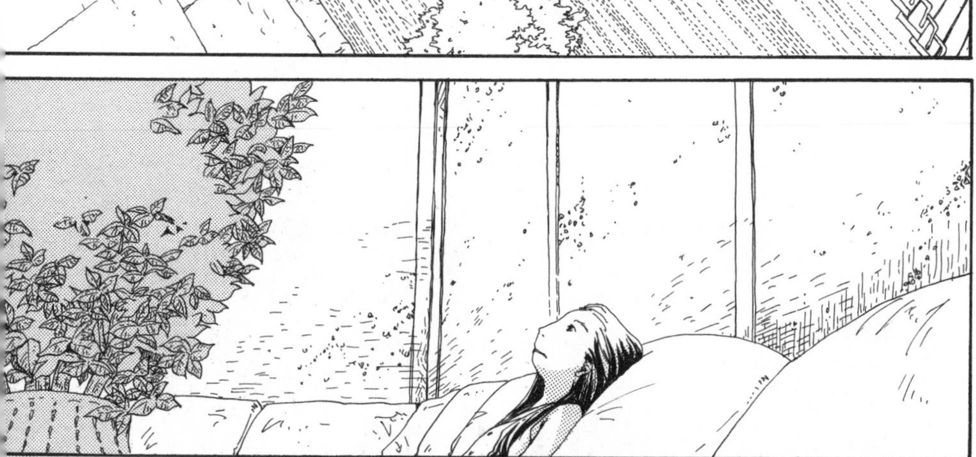

PAAH.

...

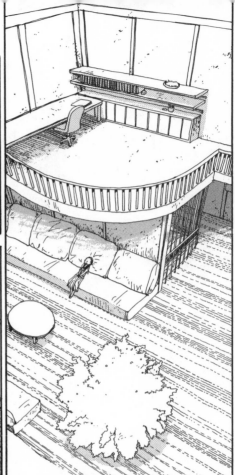

EEEK!

FUP

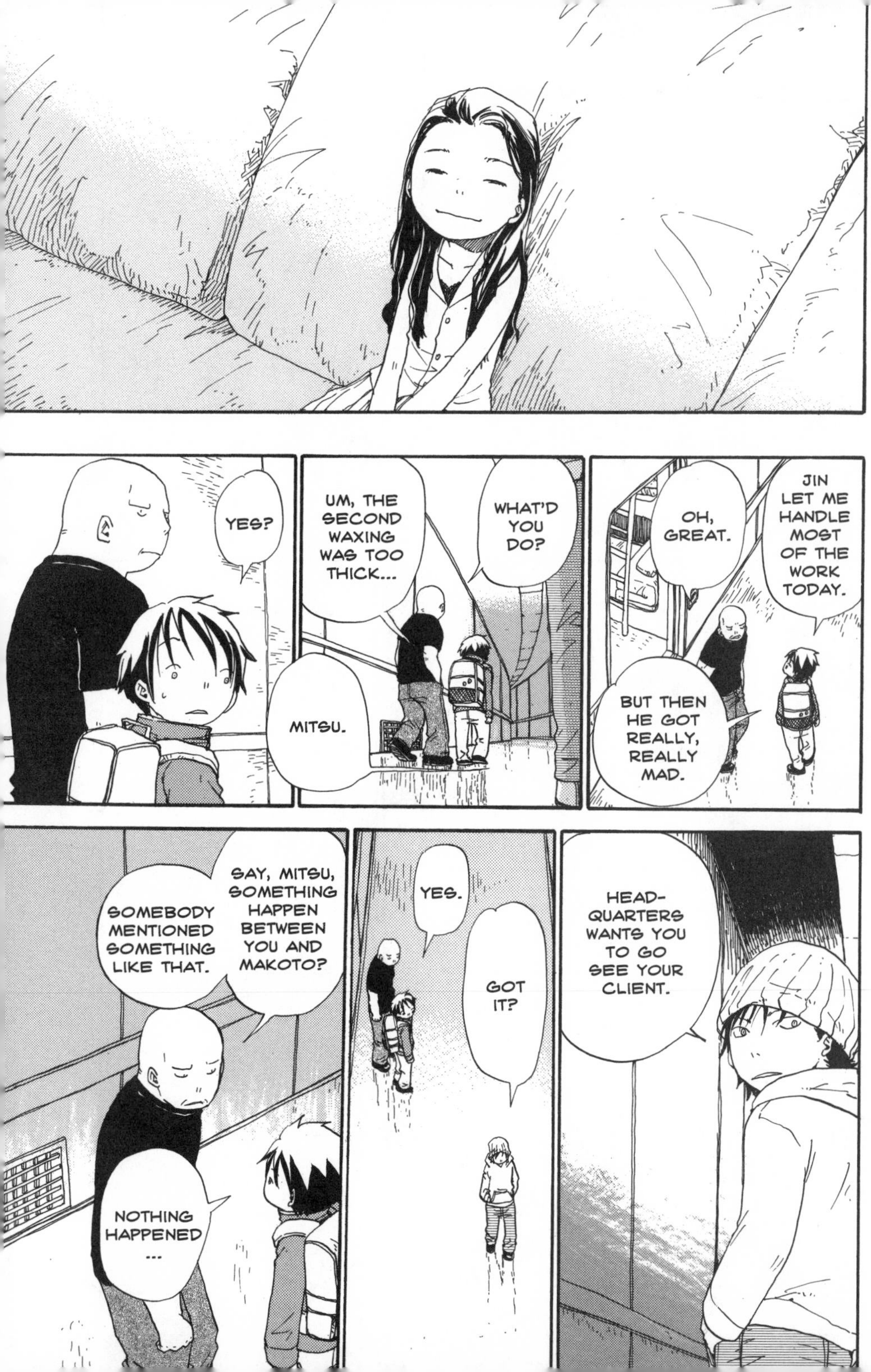

JIN LET ME HANDLE MOST OF THE WORK TODAY.
OH, GREAT.
BUT THEN HE GOT REALLY, REALLY MAD.
WHAT'D YOU DO?
UM, THE SECOND WAXING WAS TOO THICK...
MITSU.
YES?
HEAD-QUARTERS WANTS YOU TO GO SEE YOUR CLIENT.
YES.
GOT IT?
SAY, MITSU, SOMETHING HAPPEN BETWEEN YOU AND MAKOTO?
SOMEBODY MENTIONED SOMETHING LIKE THAT.
NOTHING HAPPENED ...

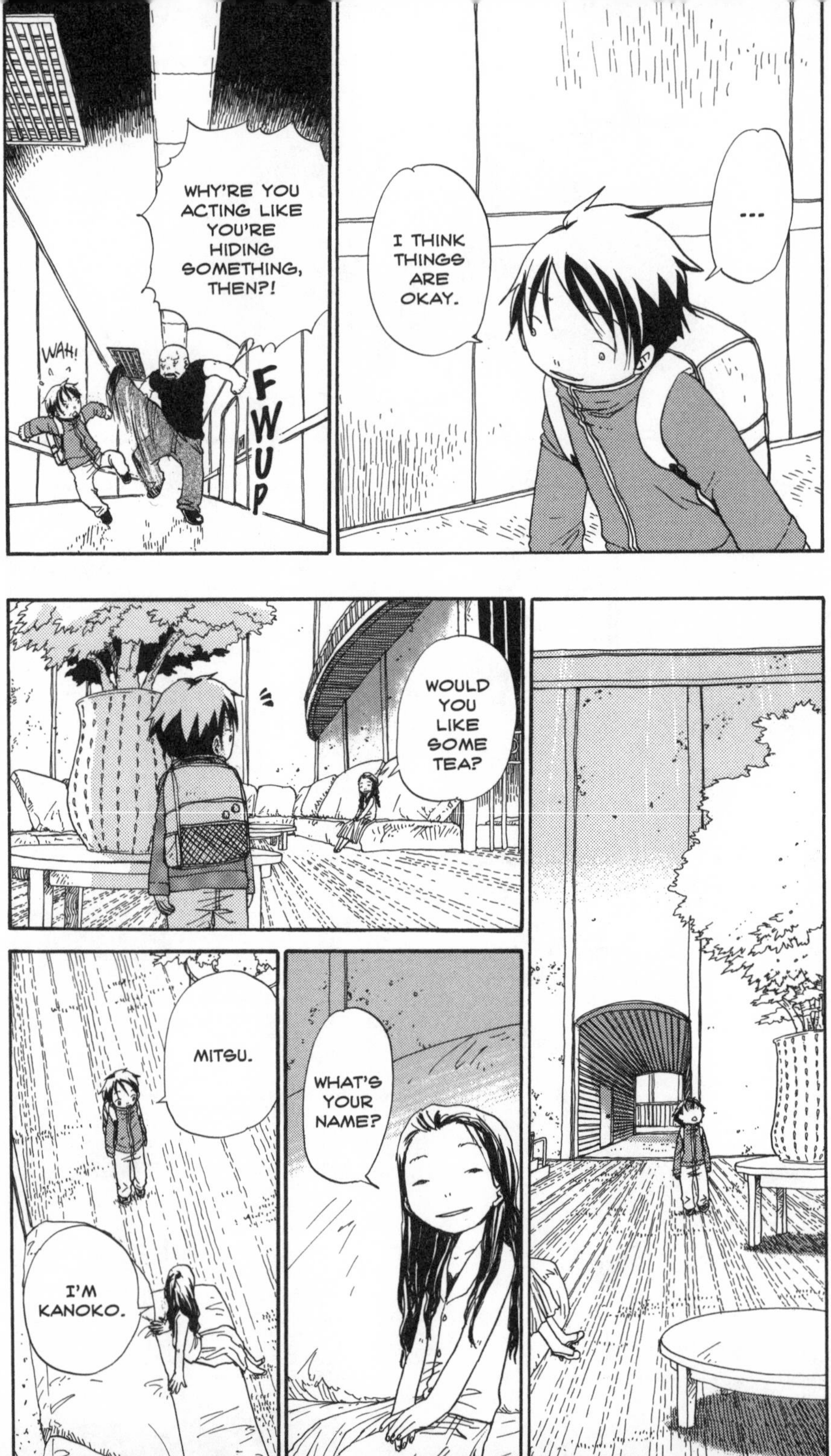
...
I THINK THINGS ARE OKAY.
WHY'RE YOU ACTING LIKE YOU'RE HIDING SOMETHING, THEN?!
FWUP
WAH!
WOULD YOU LIKE SOME TEA?
WHAT'S YOUR NAME?
MITSU.
I'M KANOKO.

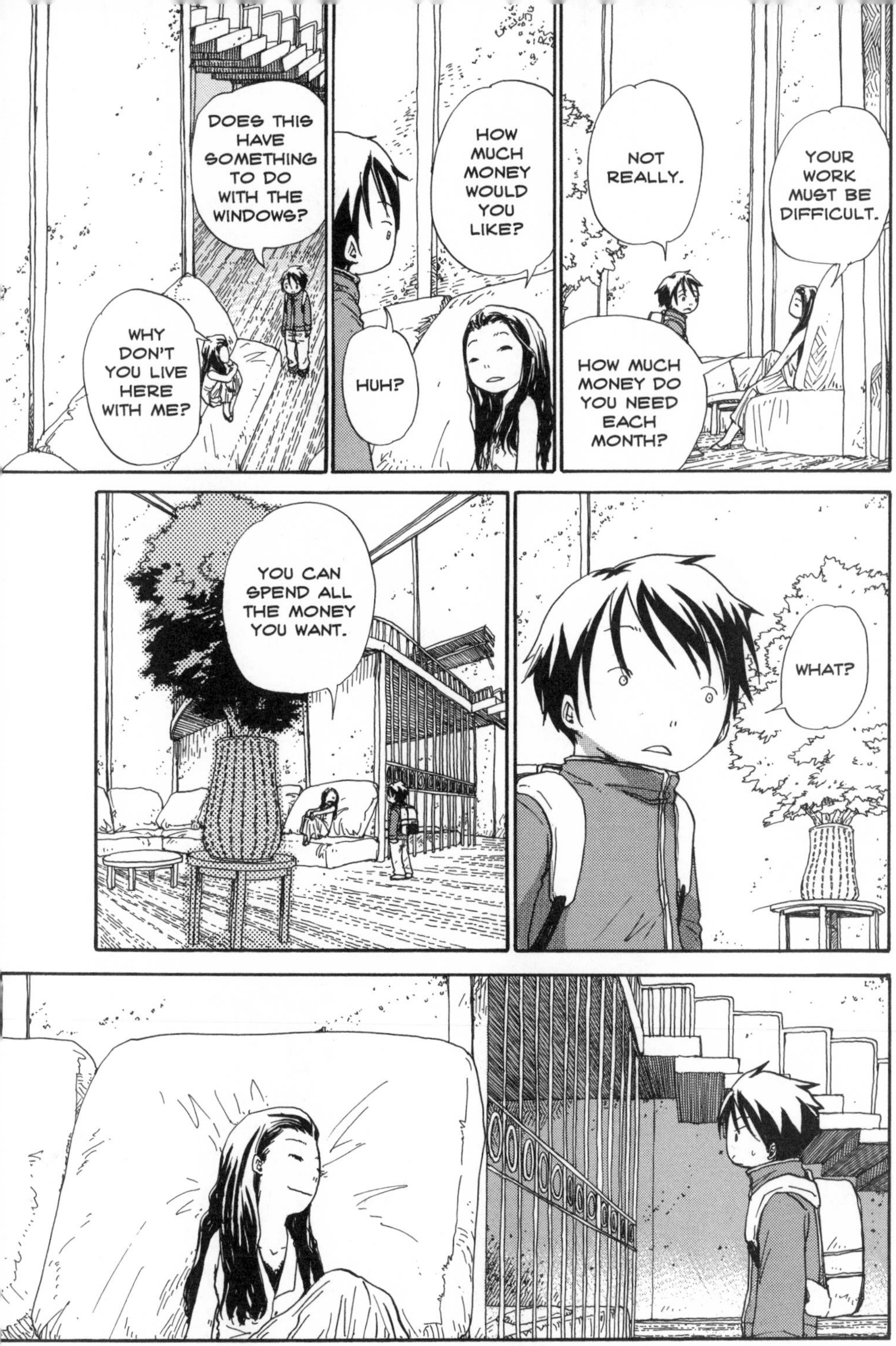
YOUR WORK MUST BE DIFFICULT.
NOT REALLY.
HOW MUCH MONEY DO YOU NEED EACH MONTH?
HOW MUCH MONEY WOULD YOU LIKE?
HUH?
DOES THIS HAVE SOMETHING TO DO WITH THE WINDOWS?
WHY DON'T YOU LIVE HERE WITH ME?
WHAT?
YOU CAN SPEND ALL THE MONEY YOU WANT.

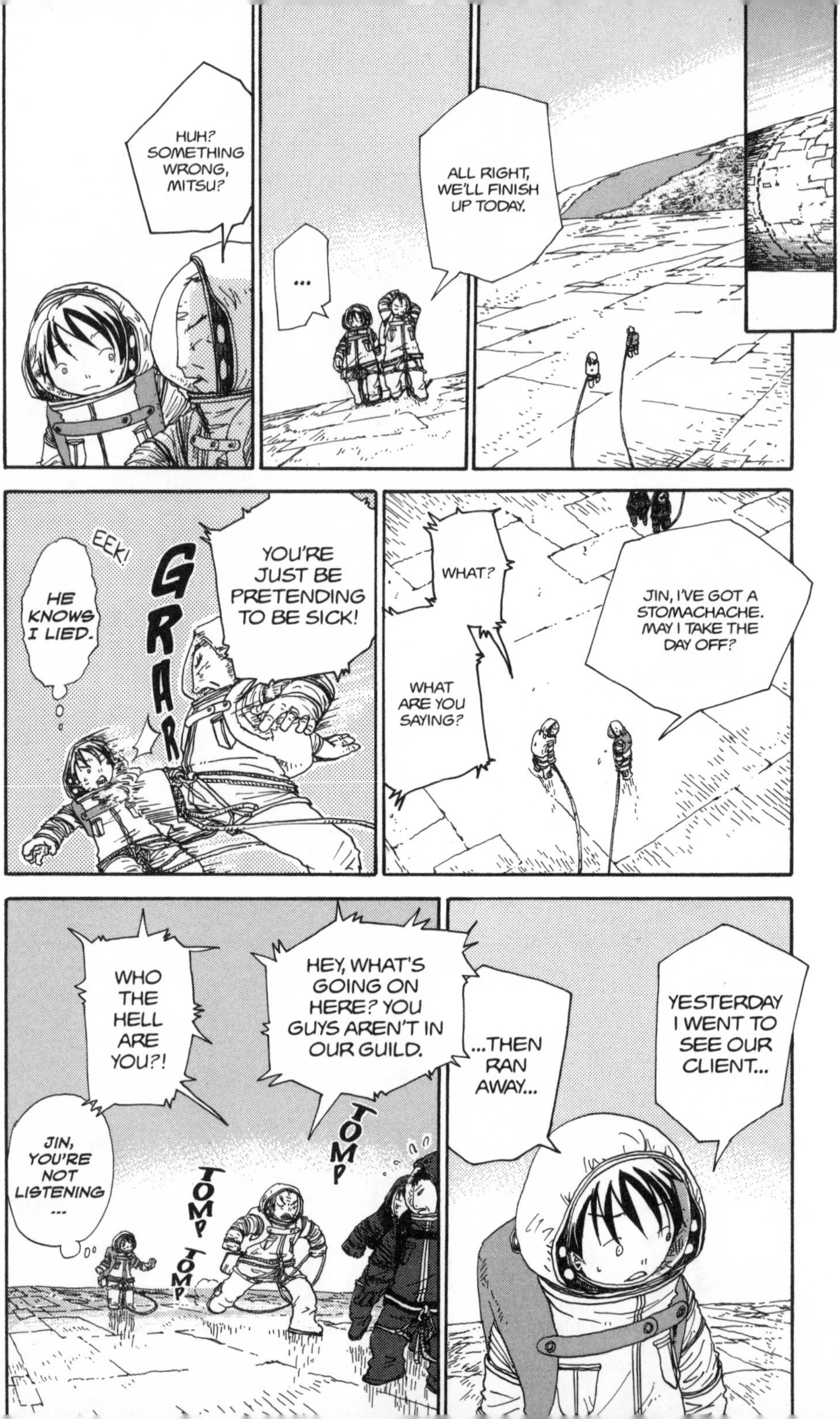
ALL RIGHT, WE'LL FINISH UP TODAY.
...
HUH? SOMETHING WRONG, MITSU?
JIN, I'VE GOT A STOMACHACHE. MAY I TAKE THE DAY OFF?
WHAT?
WHAT ARE YOU SAYING?
YOU'RE JUST BE PRETENDING TO BE SICK!
GRAR
EEK!
HE KNOWS I LIED.
YESTERDAY I WENT TO SEE OUR CLIENT...
...THEN RAN AWAY...
HEY, WHAT'S GOING ON HERE? YOU GUYS AREN'T IN OUR GUILD.
TOMP
WHO THE HELL ARE YOU?!
TOMP
TOMP
TOMP
JIN, YOU'RE NOT LISTENING ...

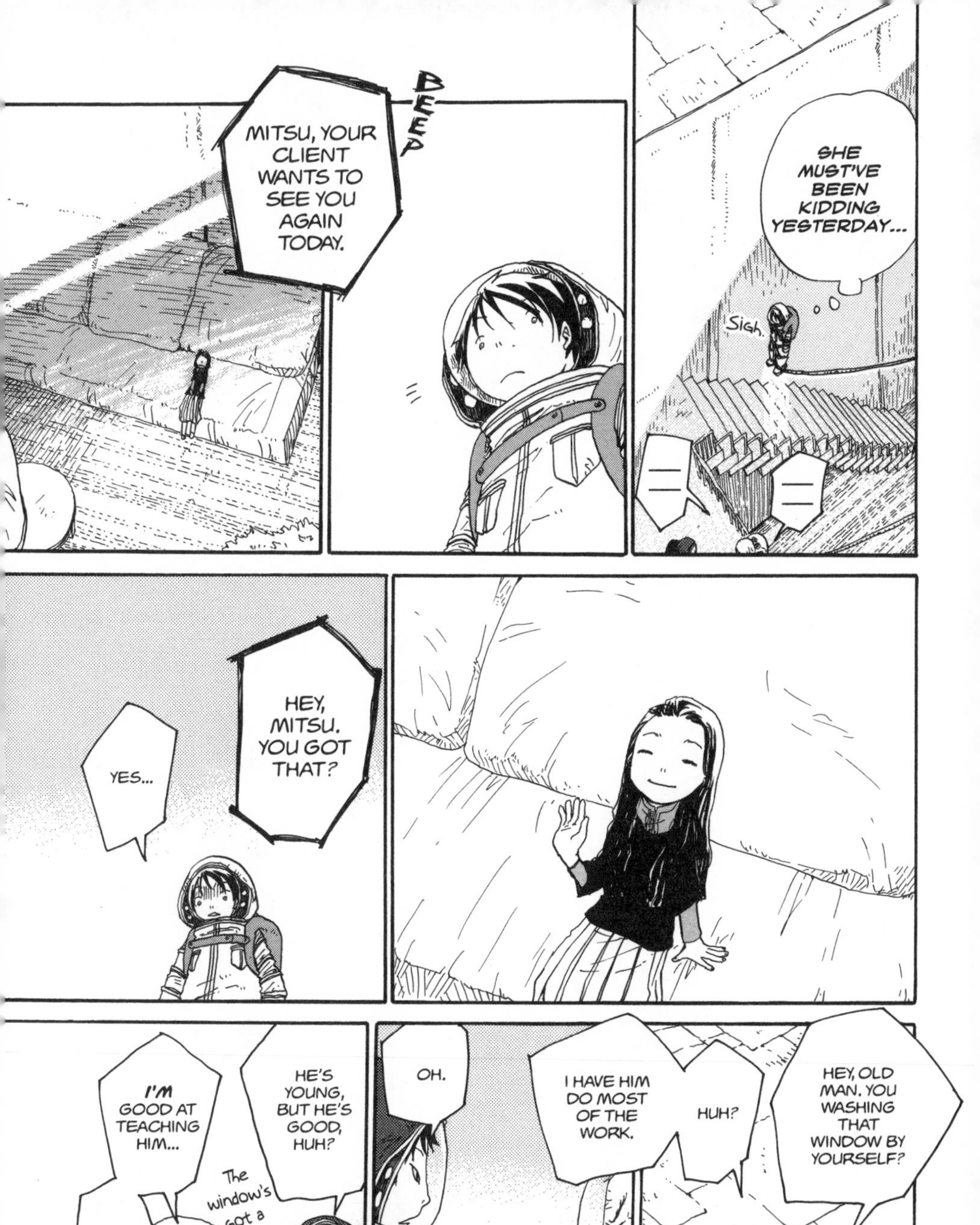
SHE MUST'VE BEEN KIDDING YESTERDAY...
Sigh.
BEEP
MITSU, YOUR CLIENT WANTS TO SEE YOU AGAIN TODAY.
HEY, MITSU. YOU GOT THAT?
YES...
HEY, OLD MAN. YOU WASHING THAT WINDOW BY YOURSELF?
HUH?
I HAVE HIM DO MOST OF THE WORK.
OH.
EEK!
HE'S YOUNG, BUT HE'S GOOD, HUH?
The window's got a nice shine.
I'M GOOD AT TEACHING HIM...
...YOU IDIOT.

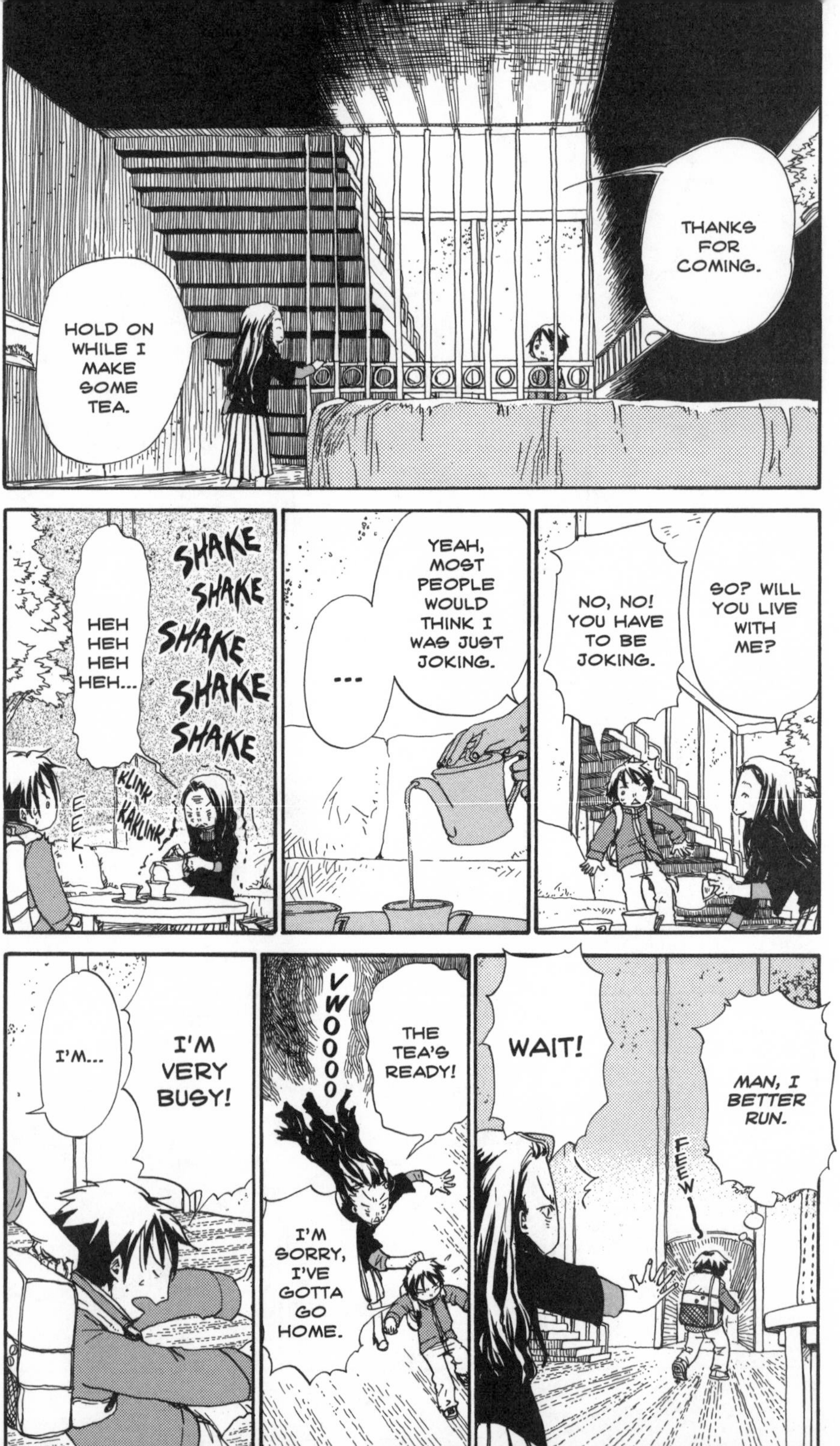
THANKS FOR COMING.
HOLD ON WHILE I MAKE SOME TEA.
SO? WILL YOU LIVE WITH ME?
NO, NO! YOU HAVE TO BE JOKING.
YEAH, MOST PEOPLE WOULD THINK I WAS JUST JOKING.
...
SHAKE SHAKE SHAKE SHAKE SHAKE
HEH HEH HEH HEH...
KLINK KAKLINK
EEK!
MAN, I BETTER RUN.
FEEW!
WAIT!
THE TEA'S READY!
VWOOOOO
I'M SORRY, I'VE GOTTA GO HOME.
I'M...
I'M VERY BUSY!

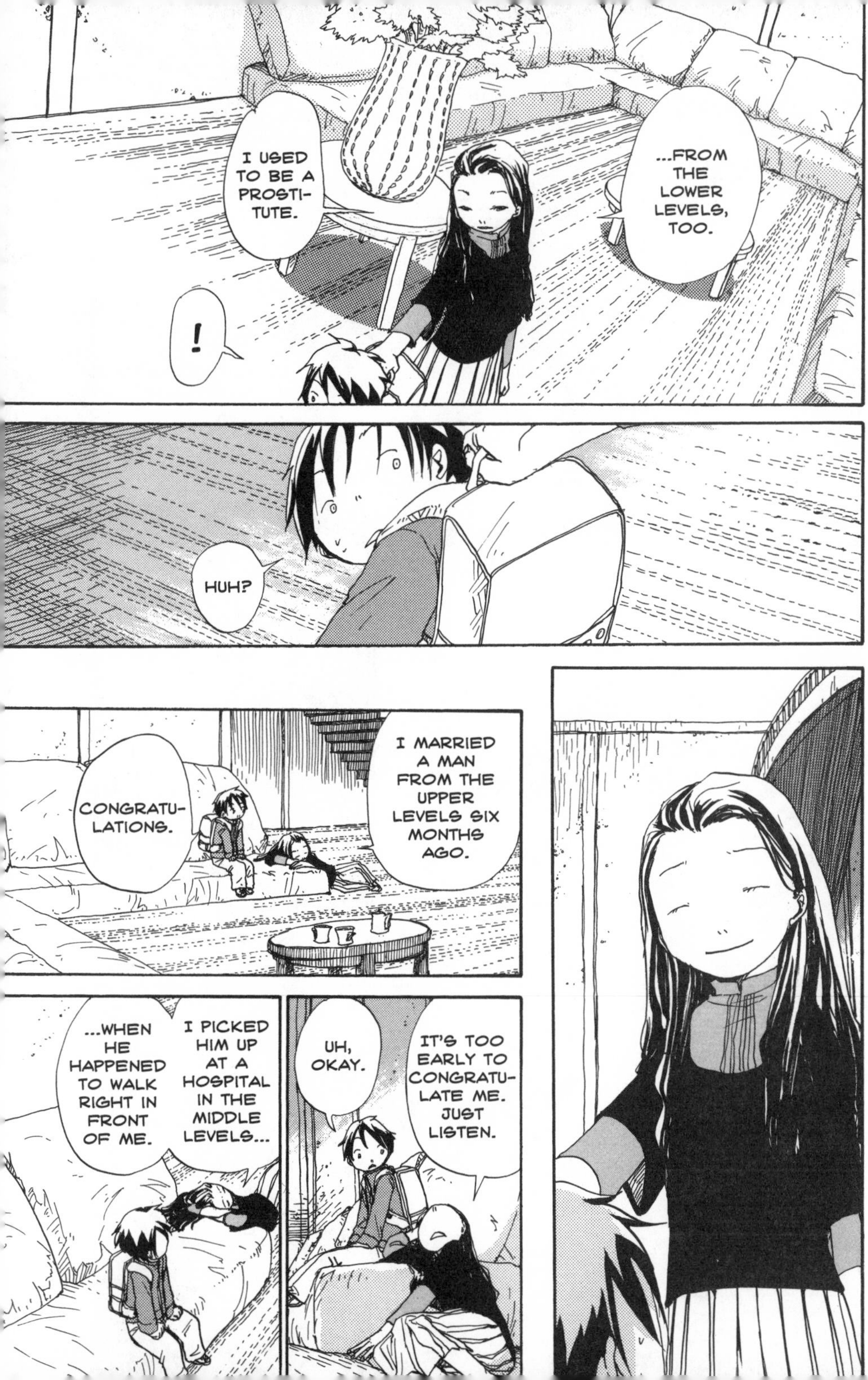
...FROM THE LOWER LEVELS, TOO.
I USED TO BE A PROSTITUTE.
!
HUH?
I MARRIED A MAN FROM THE UPPER LEVELS SIX MONTHS AGO.
CONGRATULATIONS.
IT'S TOO EARLY TO CONGRATULATE ME. JUST LISTEN.
UH, OKAY.
I PICKED HIM UP AT A HOSPITAL IN THE MIDDLE LEVELS...
...WHEN HE HAPPENED TO WALK RIGHT IN FRONT OF ME.

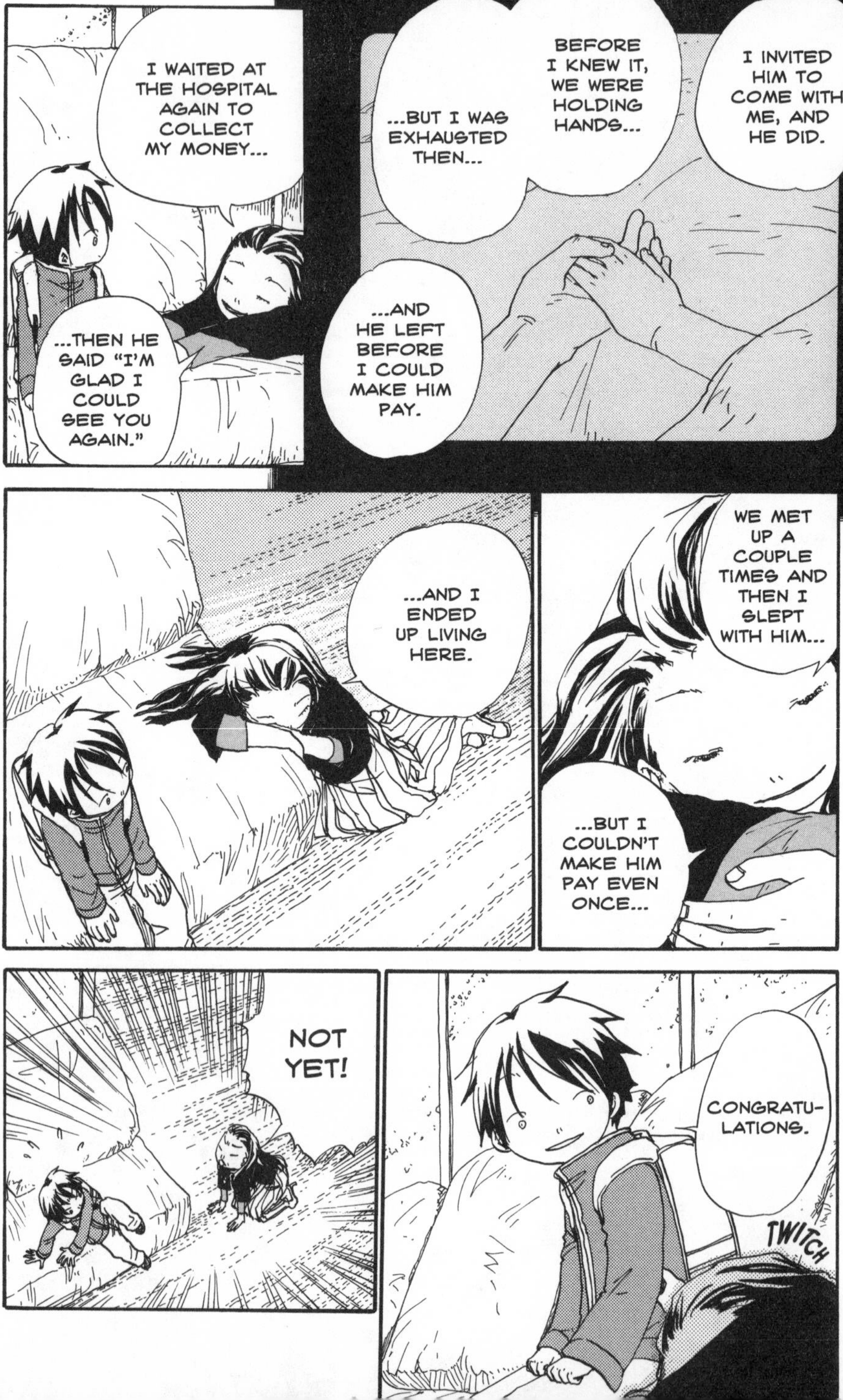
I INVITED HIM TO COME WITH ME, AND HE DID.
BEFORE I KNEW IT, WE WERE HOLDING HANDS...
...BUT I WAS EXHAUSTED THEN...
...AND HE LEFT BEFORE I COULD MAKE HIM PAY.
I WAITED AT THE HOSPITAL AGAIN TO COLLECT MY MONEY...
...THEN HE SAID "I'M GLAD I COULD SEE YOU AGAIN."
WE MET UP A COUPLE TIMES AND THEN I SLEPT WITH HIM...
...BUT I COULDN'T MAKE HIM PAY EVEN ONCE...
...AND I ENDED UP LIVING HERE.
CONGRATU-LATIONS.
TWITCH
NOT YET!

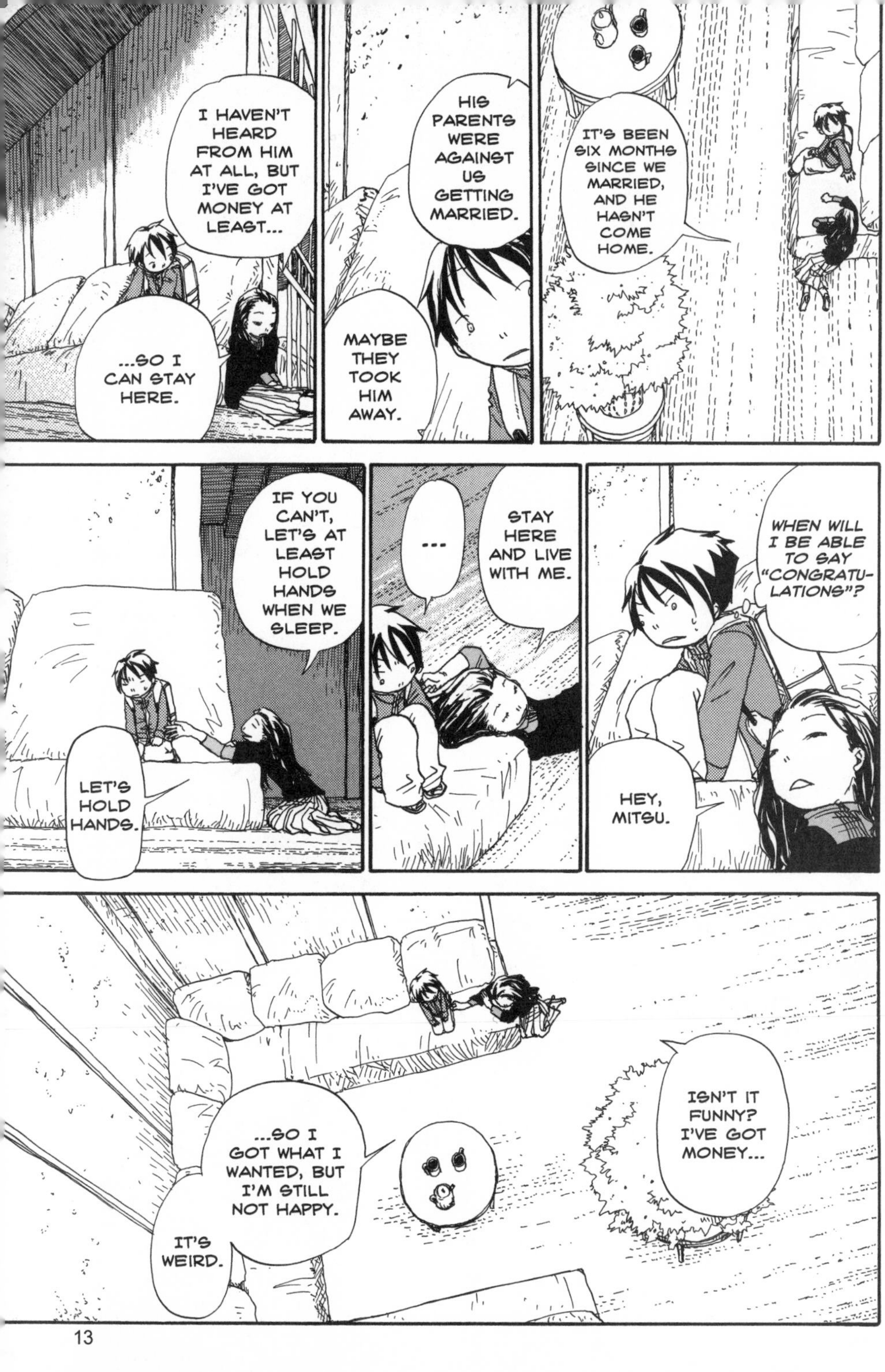
IT'S BEEN SIX MONTHS SINCE WE MARRIED, AND HE HASN'T COME HOME.
HIS PARENTS WERE AGAINST US GETTING MARRIED.
MAYBE THEY TOOK HIM AWAY.
I HAVEN'T HEARD FROM HIM AT ALL, BUT I'VE GOT MONEY AT LEAST...
...SO I CAN STAY HERE.
WHEN WILL I BE ABLE TO SAY "CONGRATULATIONS"?
HEY, MITSU.
STAY HERE AND LIVE WITH ME.
...
IF YOU CAN'T, LET'S AT LEAST HOLD HANDS WHEN WE SLEEP.
LET'S HOLD HANDS.
ISN'T IT FUNNY? I'VE GOT MONEY...
...SO I GOT WHAT I WANTED, BUT I'M STILL NOT HAPPY.
IT'S WEIRD.

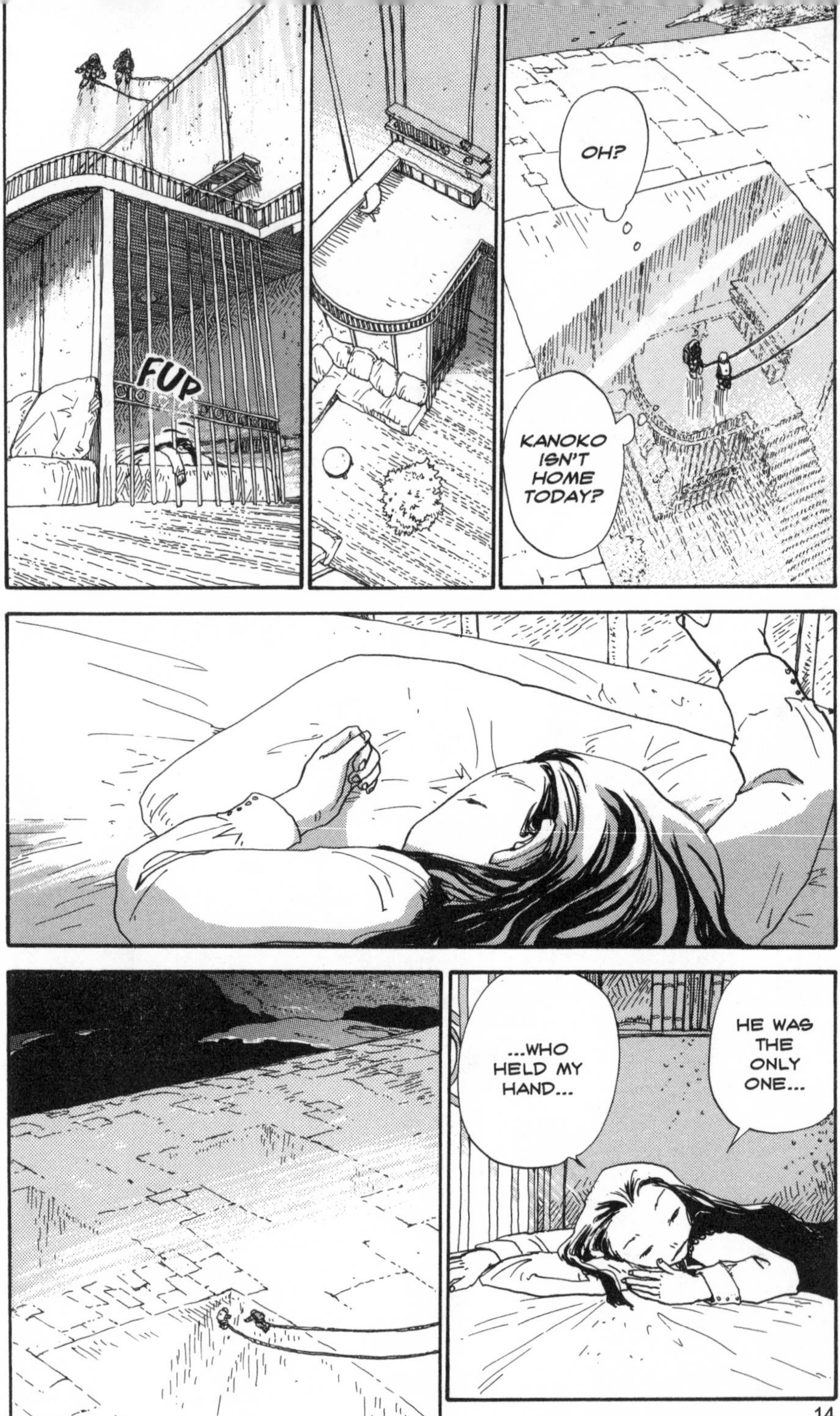
OH?
KANOKO ISN'T HOME TODAY?
FUP
HE WAS THE ONLY ONE...
...WHO HELD MY HAND...

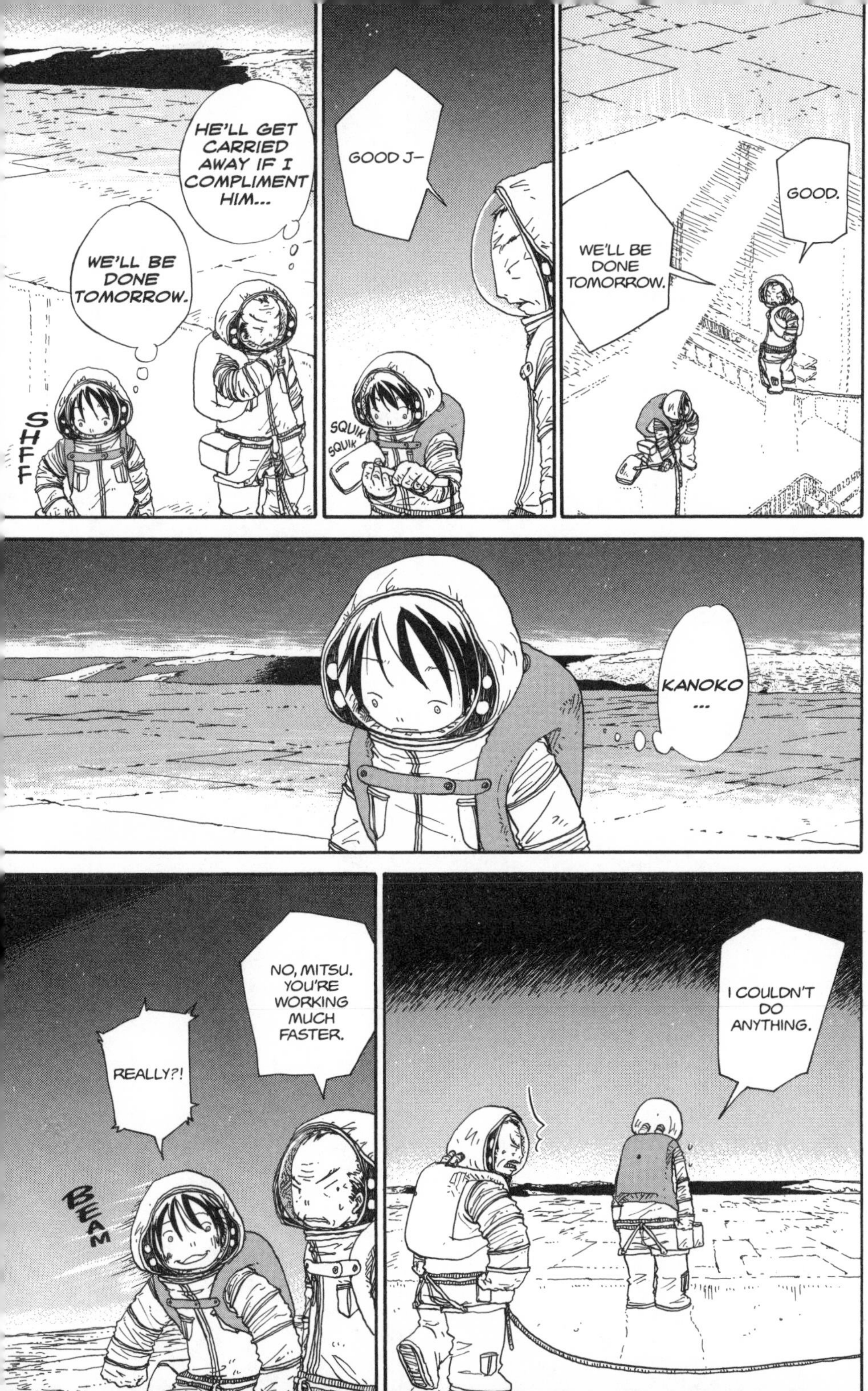
GOOD.
WE'LL BE DONE TOMORROW.
GOOD J–
SQUIK SQUIK
HE'LL GET CARRIED AWAY IF I COMPLIMENT HIM...
WE'LL BE DONE TOMORROW.
SHFF
KANOKO ...
I COULDN'T DO ANYTHING.
NO, MITSU. YOU'RE WORKING MUCH FASTER.
REALLY?!
BEAM

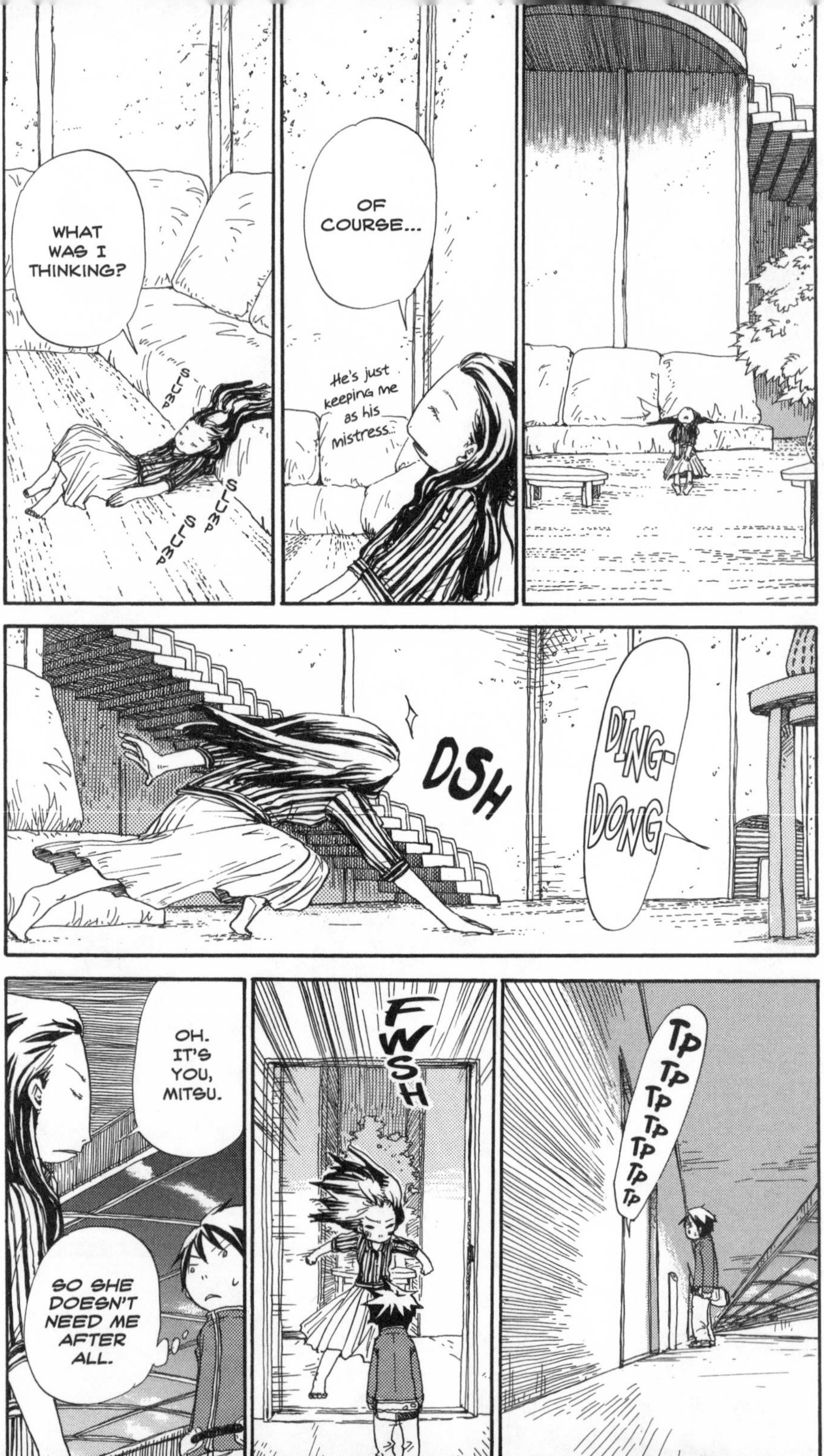
OF COURSE...
He's just keeping me as his mistress...
WHAT WAS I THINKING?
SLUMP
SLUMP
SLUMP
DING-DONG
DSH
TP TP TP TP TP TP TP
FWSH
OH. IT'S YOU, MITSU.
SO SHE DOESN'T NEED ME AFTER ALL.

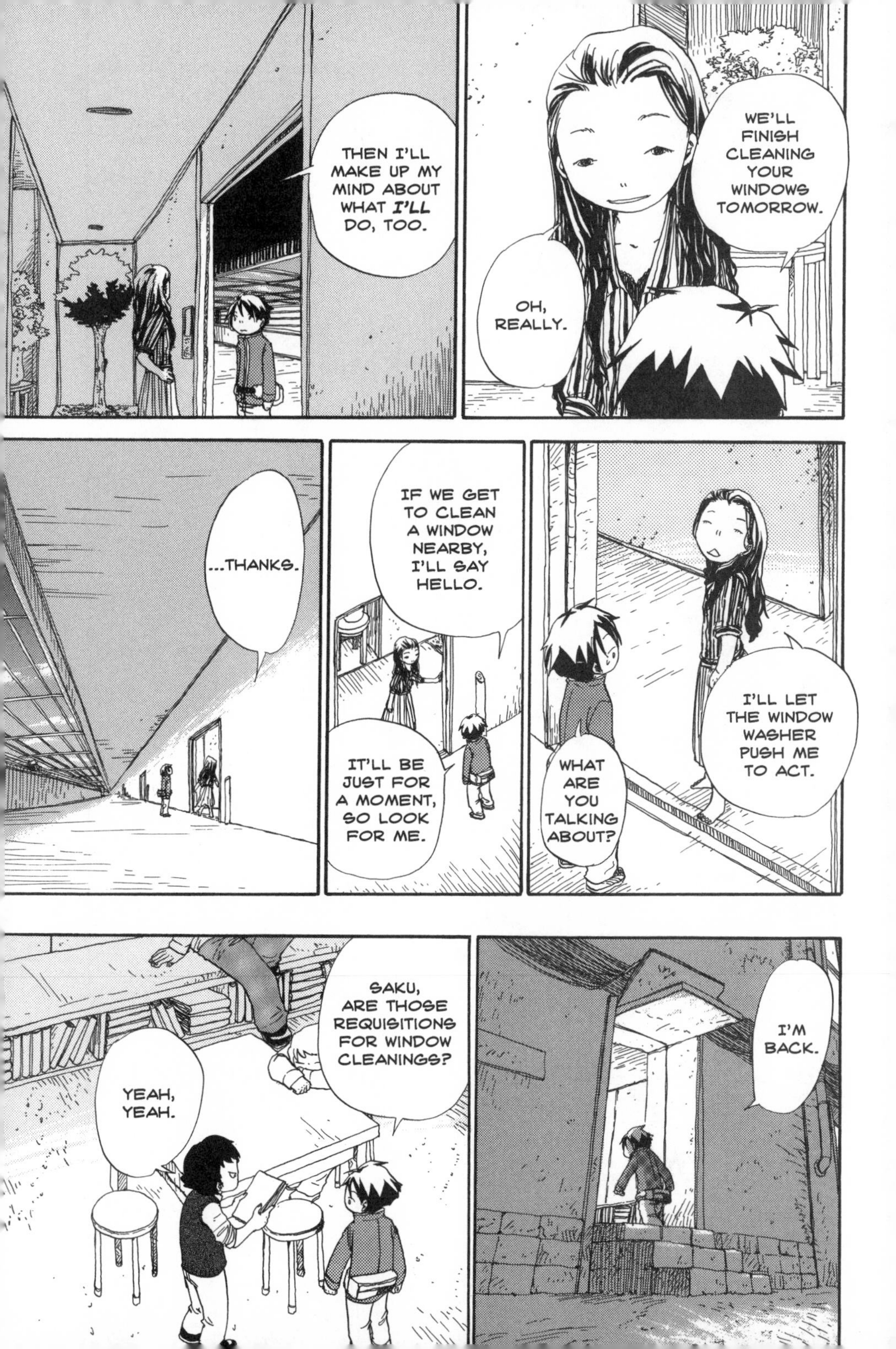
WE'LL FINISH CLEANING YOUR WINDOWS TOMORROW.
OH, REALLY.
THEN I'LL MAKE UP MY MIND ABOUT WHAT *I'LL* DO, TOO.
I'LL LET THE WINDOW WASHER PUSH ME TO ACT.
WHAT ARE YOU TALKING ABOUT?
IF WE GET TO CLEAN A WINDOW NEARBY, I'LL SAY HELLO.
IT'LL BE JUST FOR A MOMENT, SO LOOK FOR ME.
...THANKS.
I'M BACK.
SAKU, ARE THOSE REQUISITIONS FOR WINDOW CLEANINGS?
YEAH, YEAH.

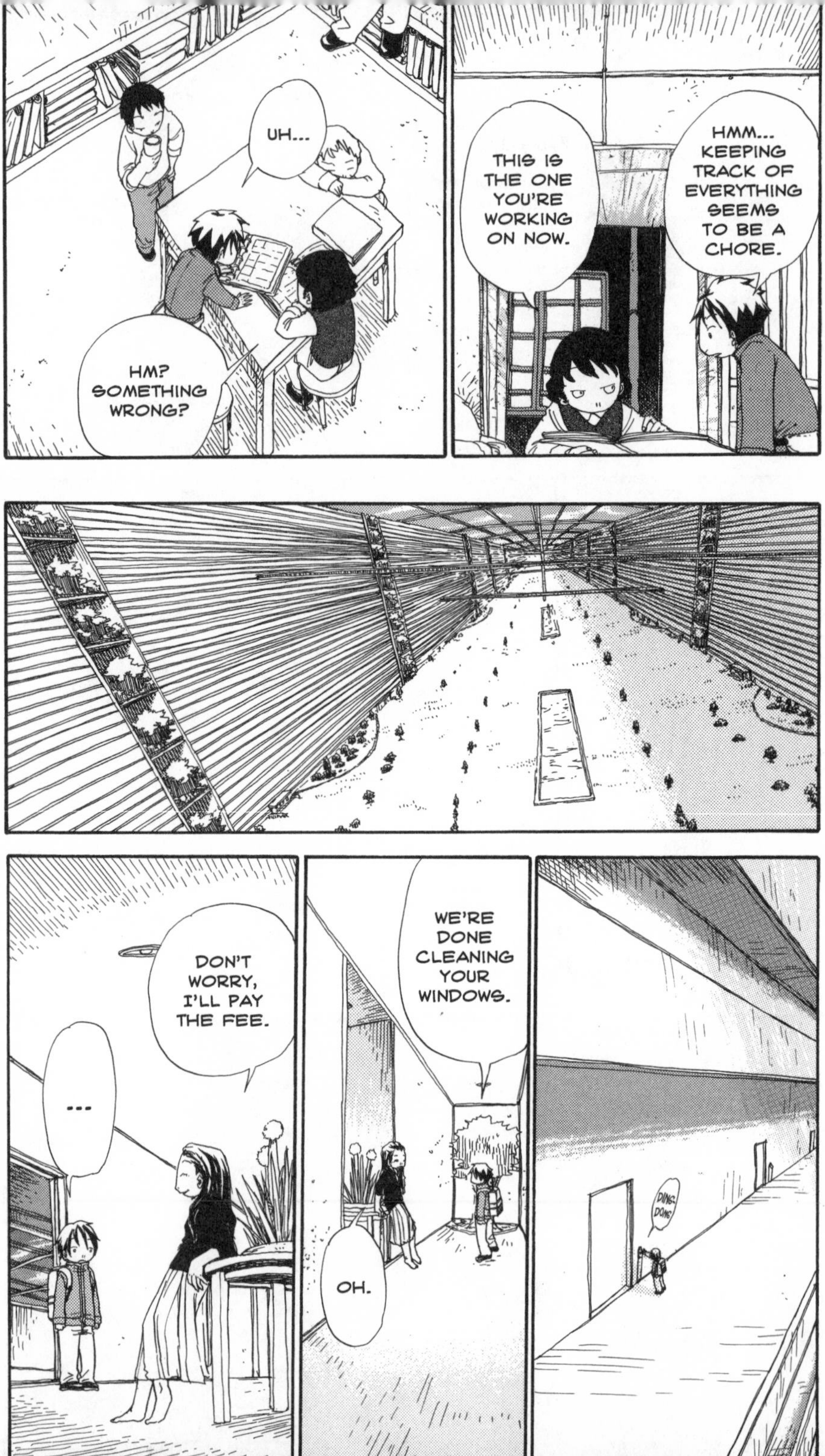
HMM... KEEPING TRACK OF EVERYTHING SEEMS TO BE A CHORE.
THIS IS THE ONE YOU'RE WORKING ON NOW.
UH...
HM? SOMETHING WRONG?
DING DONG
WE'RE DONE CLEANING YOUR WINDOWS.
OH.
DON'T WORRY, I'LL PAY THE FEE.
...

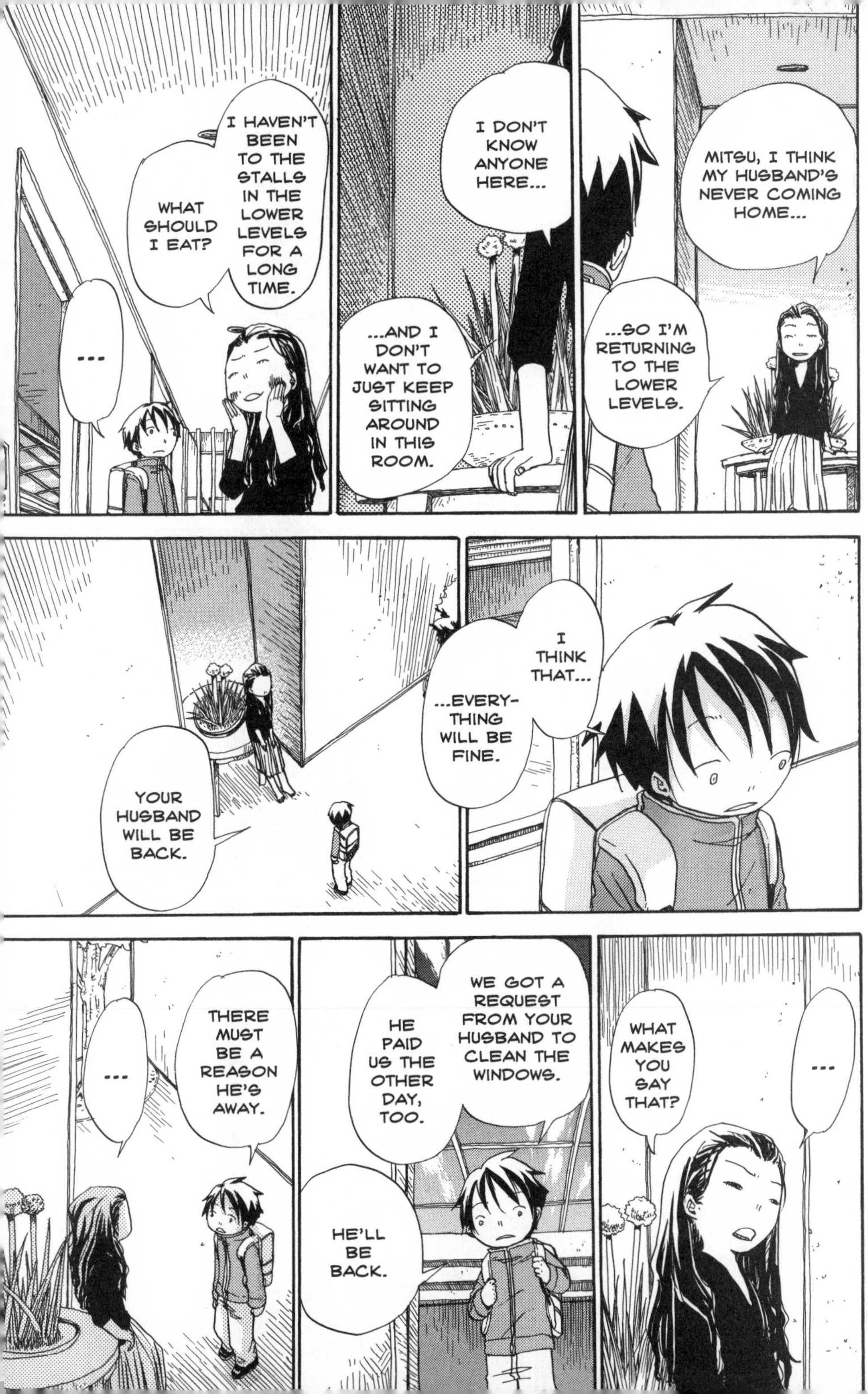
MITSU, I THINK MY HUSBAND'S NEVER COMING HOME...
...SO I'M RETURNING TO THE LOWER LEVELS.
I DON'T KNOW ANYONE HERE...
...AND I DON'T WANT TO JUST KEEP SITTING AROUND IN THIS ROOM.
I HAVEN'T BEEN TO THE STALLS IN THE LOWER LEVELS FOR A LONG TIME.
WHAT SHOULD I EAT?
...
I THINK THAT...
...EVERYTHING WILL BE FINE.
YOUR HUSBAND WILL BE BACK.
...
WHAT MAKES YOU SAY THAT?
WE GOT A REQUEST FROM YOUR HUSBAND TO CLEAN THE WINDOWS.
HE PAID US THE OTHER DAY, TOO.
HE'LL BE BACK.
THERE MUST BE A REASON HE'S AWAY.
...

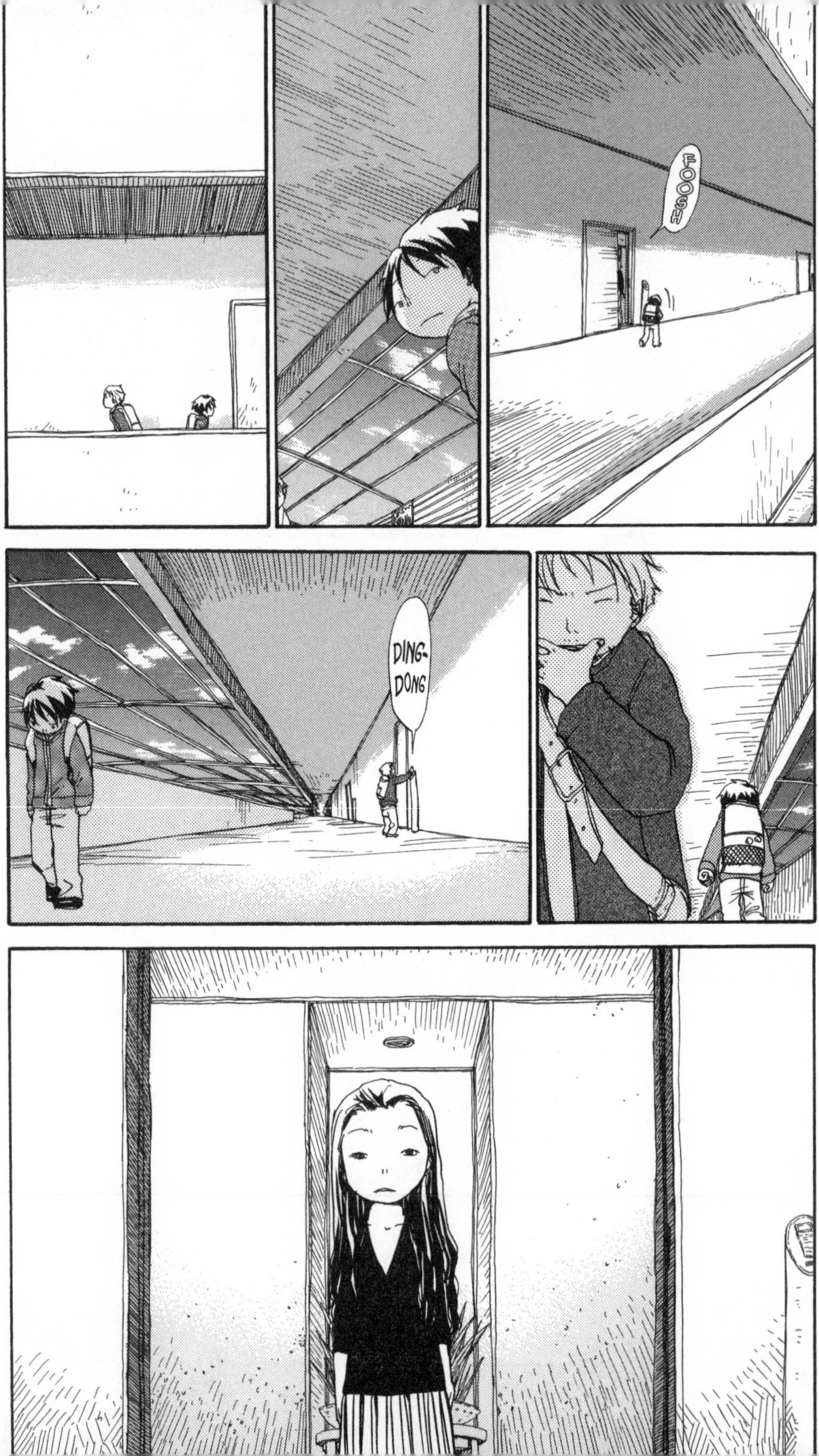
FOOSH
DING-DONG

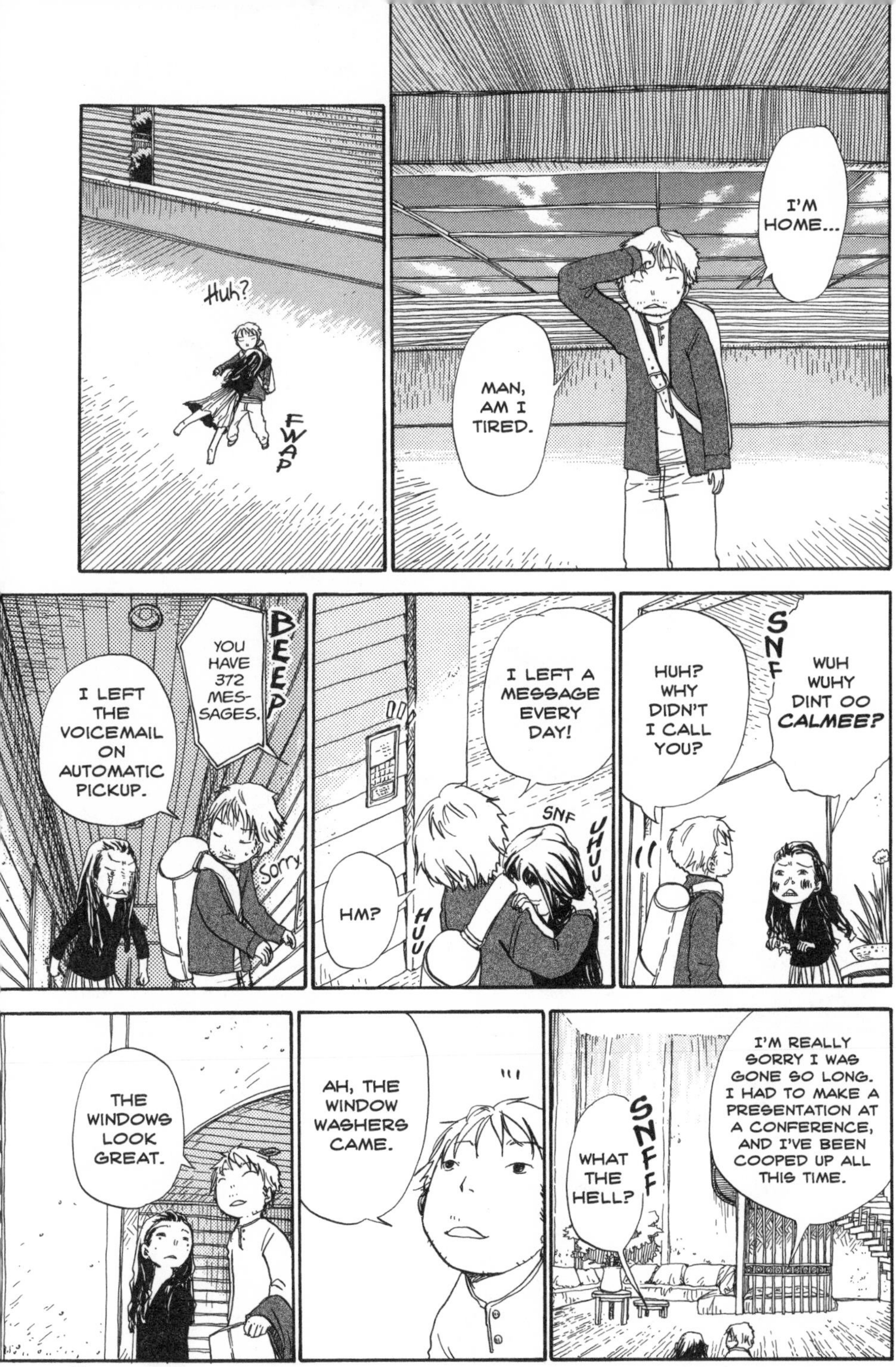
I'M HOME...
MAN, AM I TIRED.
Huh?
FWAP
SNF
WUH WUHY DINT OO CALMEE?
HUH? WHY DIDN'T I CALL YOU?
I LEFT A MESSAGE EVERY DAY!
SNF
UHUU
HM?
HUU
BEEP
YOU HAVE 372 MES-SAGES.
I LEFT THE VOICEMAIL ON AUTOMATIC PICKUP.
Sorry.
I'M REALLY SORRY I WAS GONE SO LONG. I HAD TO MAKE A PRESENTATION AT A CONFERENCE, AND I'VE BEEN COOPED UP ALL THIS TIME.
SNFF
WHAT THE HELL?
AH, THE WINDOW WASHERS CAME.
THE WINDOWS LOOK GREAT.

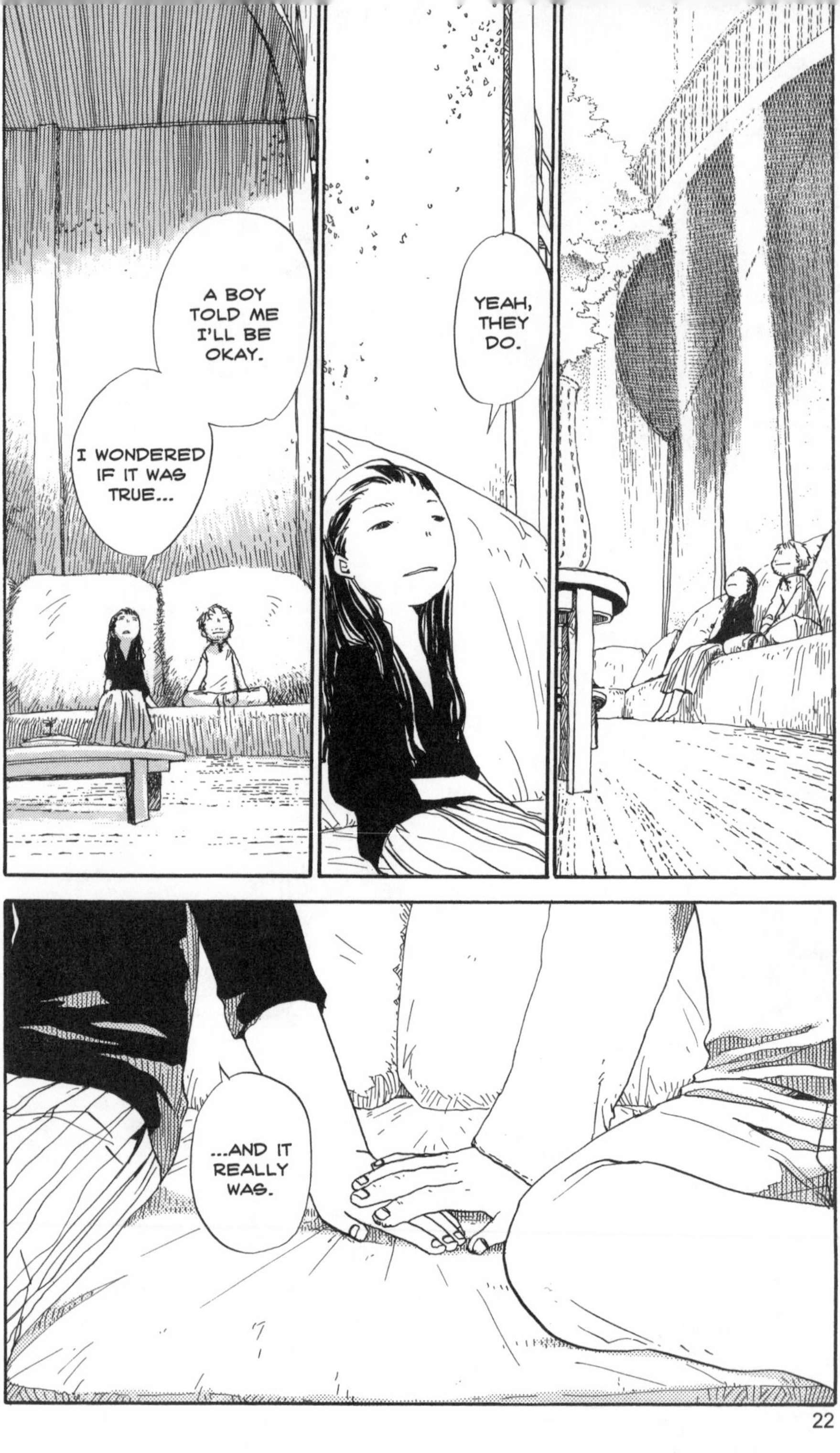
YEAH, THEY DO.
A BOY TOLD ME I'LL BE OKAY.
I WONDERED IF IT WAS TRUE...
...AND IT REALLY WAS.

floor 19: symbols

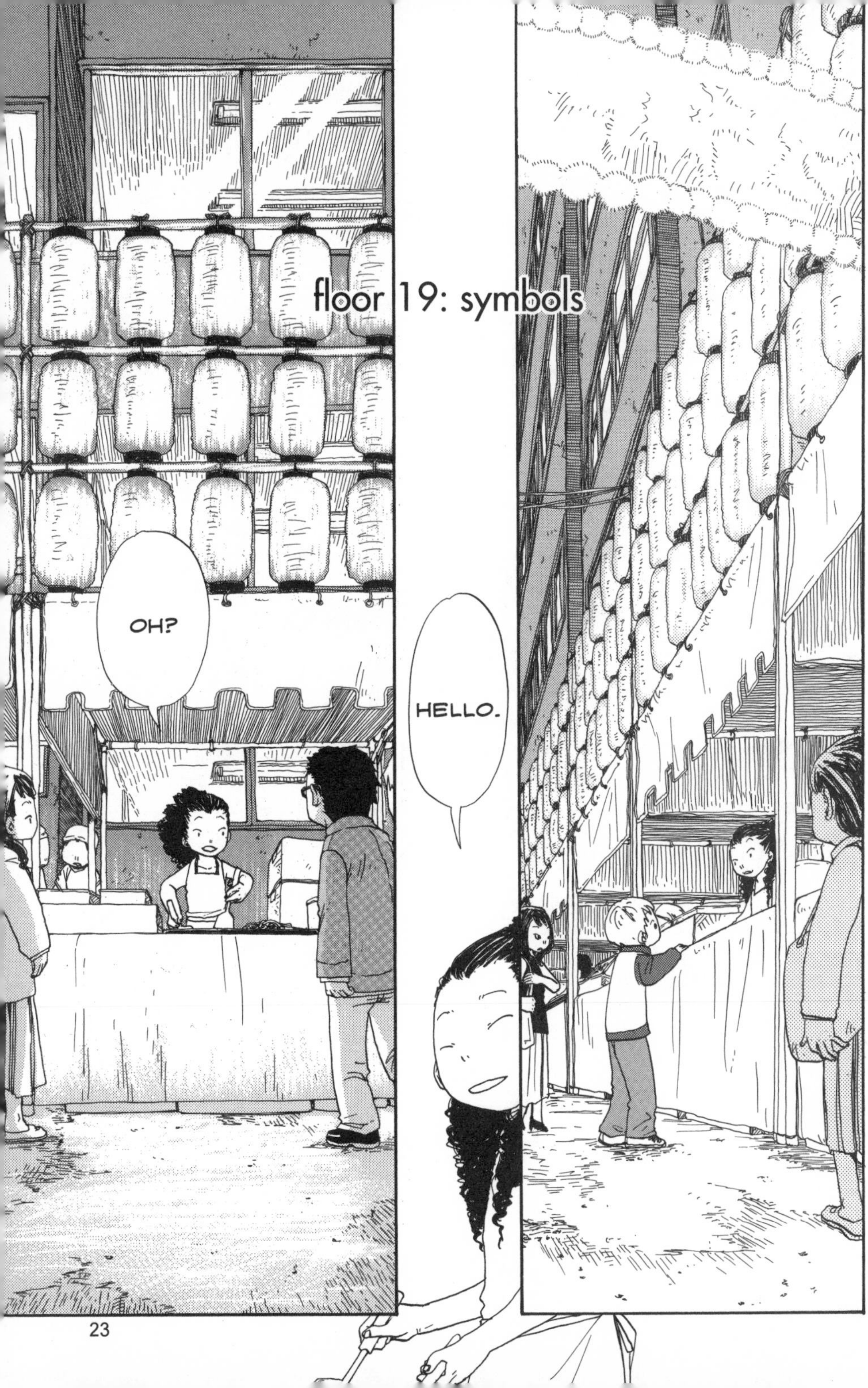
HELLO.
OH?

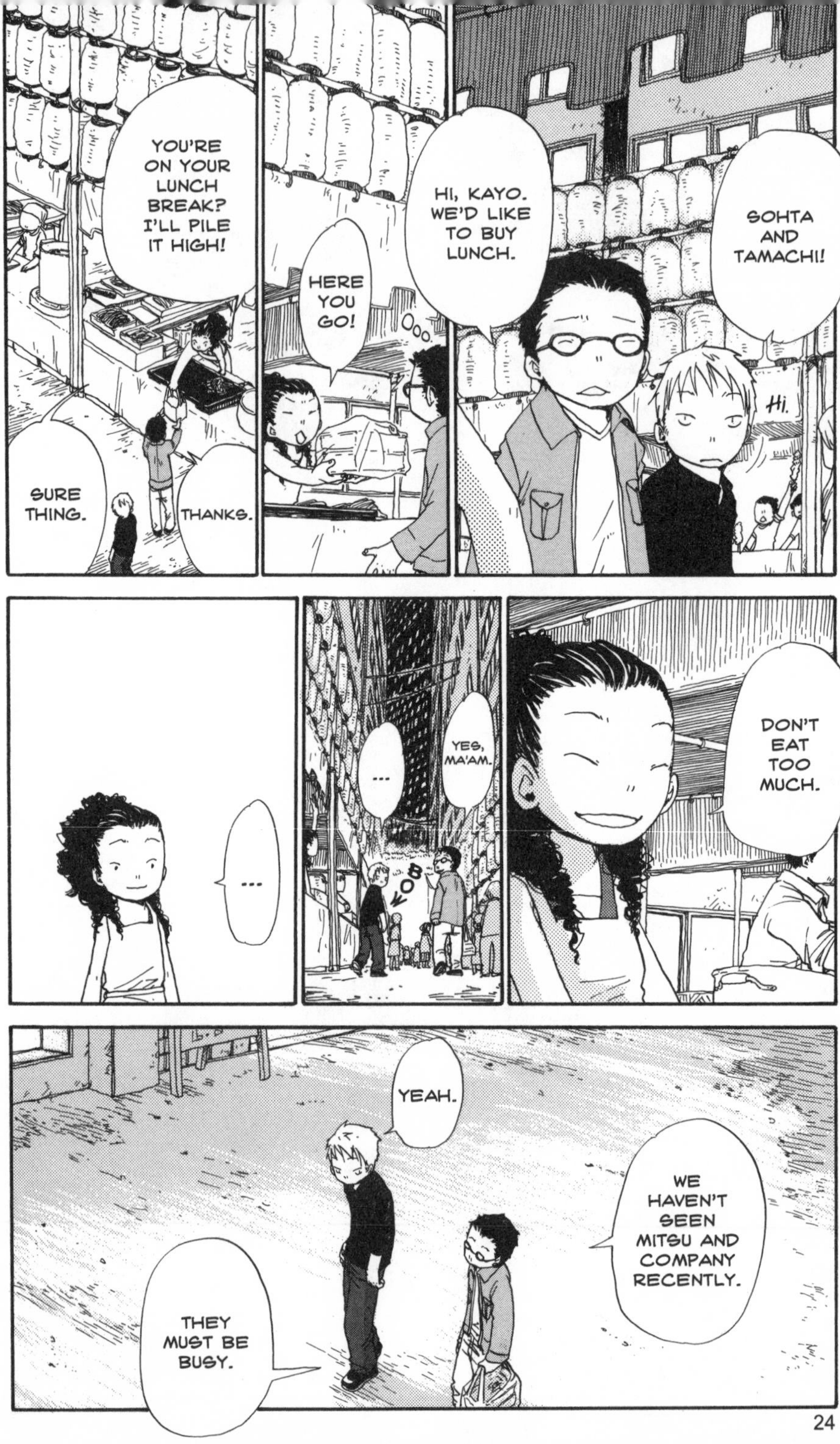
SOHTA AND TAMACHI!
HI, KAYO. WE'D LIKE TO BUY LUNCH.
Hi.
HERE YOU GO!
Ooo.
YOU'RE ON YOUR LUNCH BREAK? I'LL PILE IT HIGH!
THANKS.
SURE THING.
DON'T EAT TOO MUCH.
YES, MA'AM.
...
...
WE HAVEN'T SEEN MITSU AND COMPANY RECENTLY.
YEAH.
THEY MUST BE BUSY.

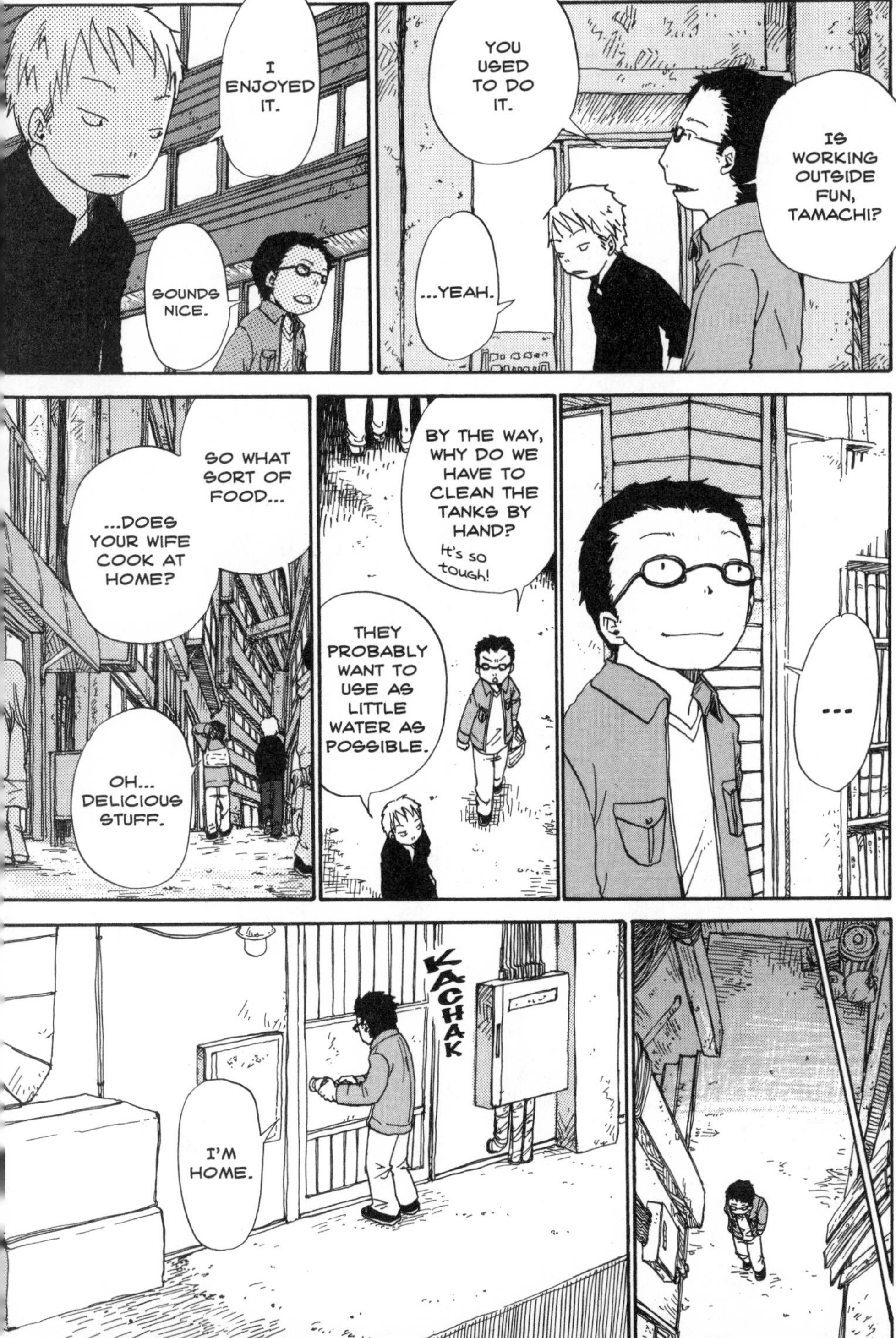
IS WORKING OUTSIDE FUN, TAMACHI?
...YEAH.
YOU USED TO DO IT.
I ENJOYED IT.
SOUNDS NICE.
...
BY THE WAY, WHY DO WE HAVE TO CLEAN THE TANKS BY HAND?
It's so tough!
THEY PROBABLY WANT TO USE AS LITTLE WATER AS POSSIBLE.
SO WHAT SORT OF FOOD...
...DOES YOUR WIFE COOK AT HOME?
OH... DELICIOUS STUFF.
KACHAK
I'M HOME.

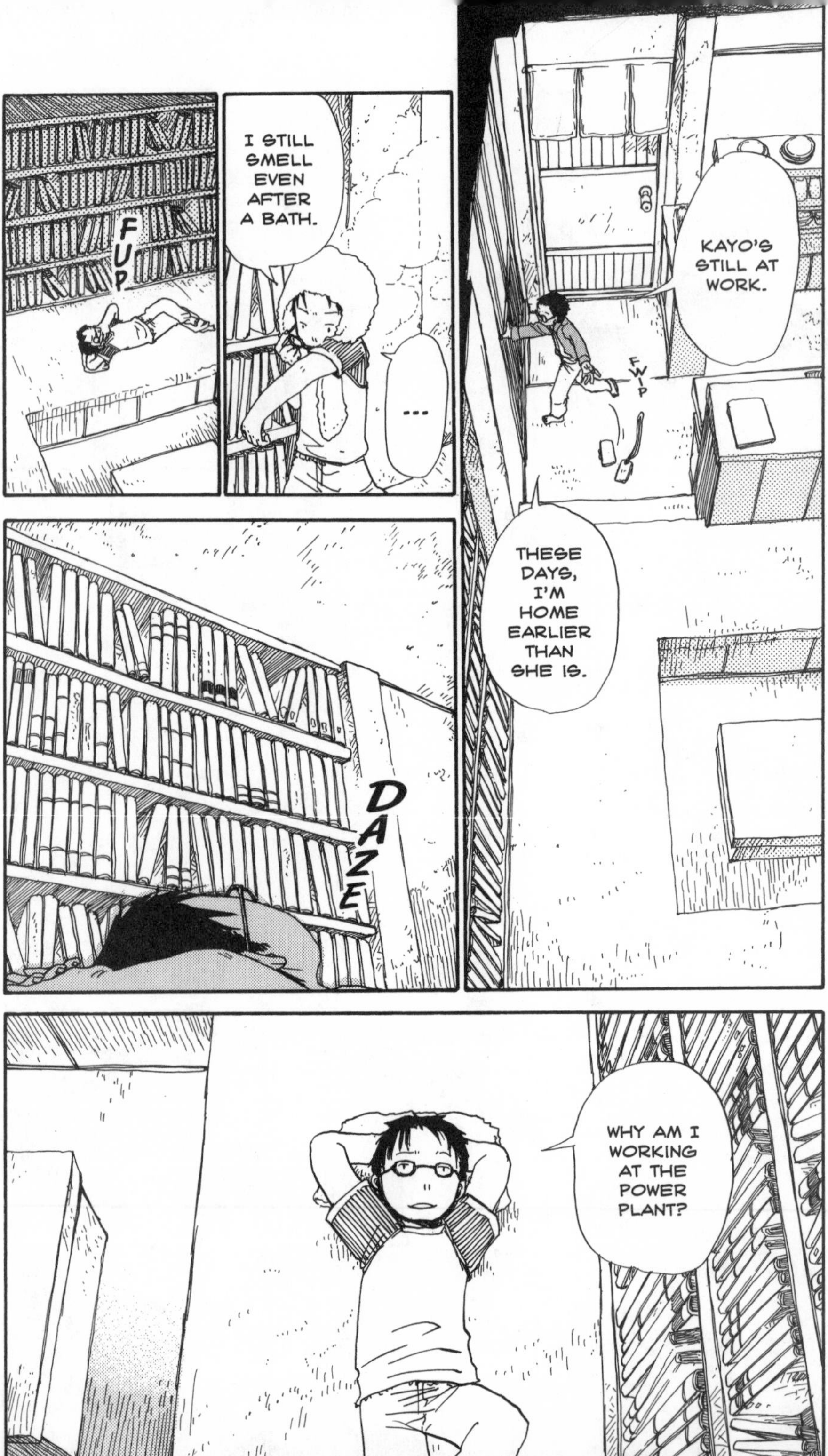
KAYO'S STILL AT WORK.
FWIP
THESE DAYS, I'M HOME EARLIER THAN SHE IS.
I STILL SMELL EVEN AFTER A BATH.
...
FUP
DAZE
WHY AM I WORKING AT THE POWER PLANT?

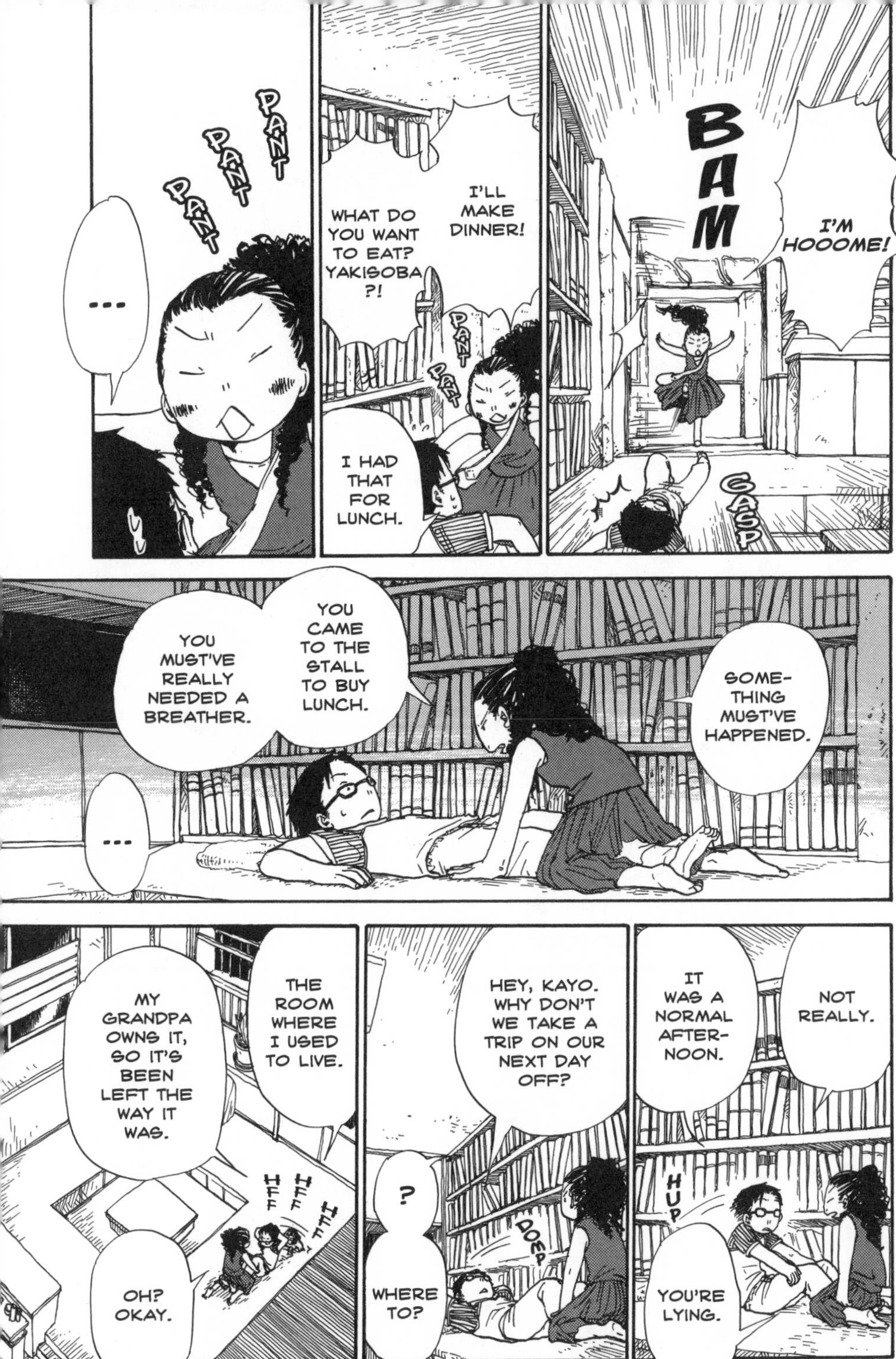
BAM
I'M HOOOME!
GASP
I'LL MAKE DINNER!
WHAT DO YOU WANT TO EAT? YAKISOBA?!
PANT PANT
I HAD THAT FOR LUNCH.
PANT PANT PANT
...
SOMETHING MUST'VE HAPPENED.
YOU CAME TO THE STALL TO BUY LUNCH.
YOU MUST'VE REALLY NEEDED A BREATHER.
...
NOT REALLY.
IT WAS A NORMAL AFTERNOON.
HUP
YOU'RE LYING.
HEY, KAYO. WHY DON'T WE TAKE A TRIP ON OUR NEXT DAY OFF?
?
DOMP
WHERE TO?
THE ROOM WHERE I USED TO LIVE.
MY GRANDPA OWNS IT, SO IT'S BEEN LEFT THE WAY IT WAS.
HFF HFF HFF
OH? OKAY.

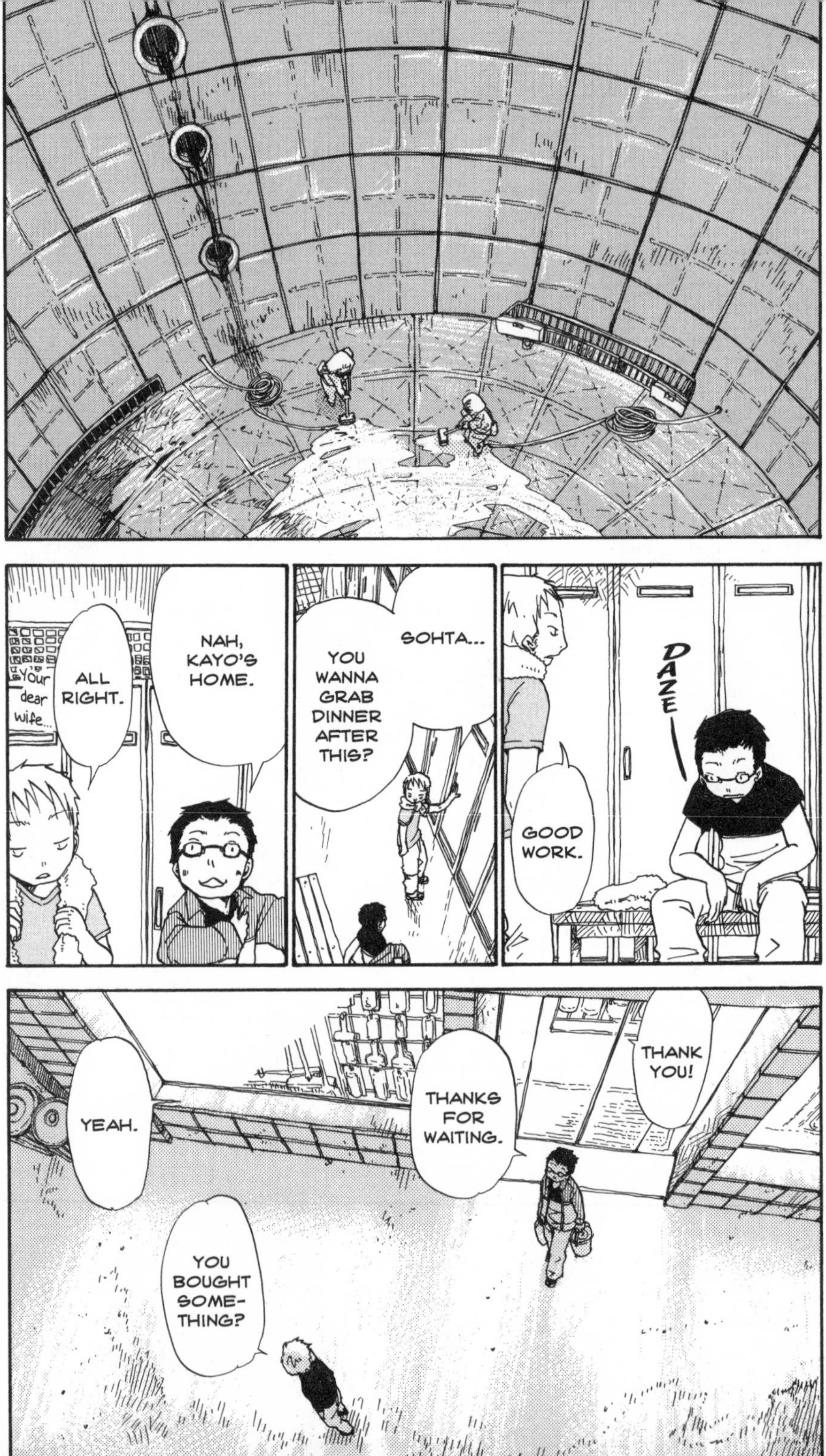
DAZE
GOOD WORK.
SOHTA...
YOU WANNA GRAB DINNER AFTER THIS?
NAH, KAYO'S HOME.
ALL RIGHT.
Your dear wife...
THANK YOU!
THANKS FOR WAITING.
YEAH.
YOU BOUGHT SOME-THING?

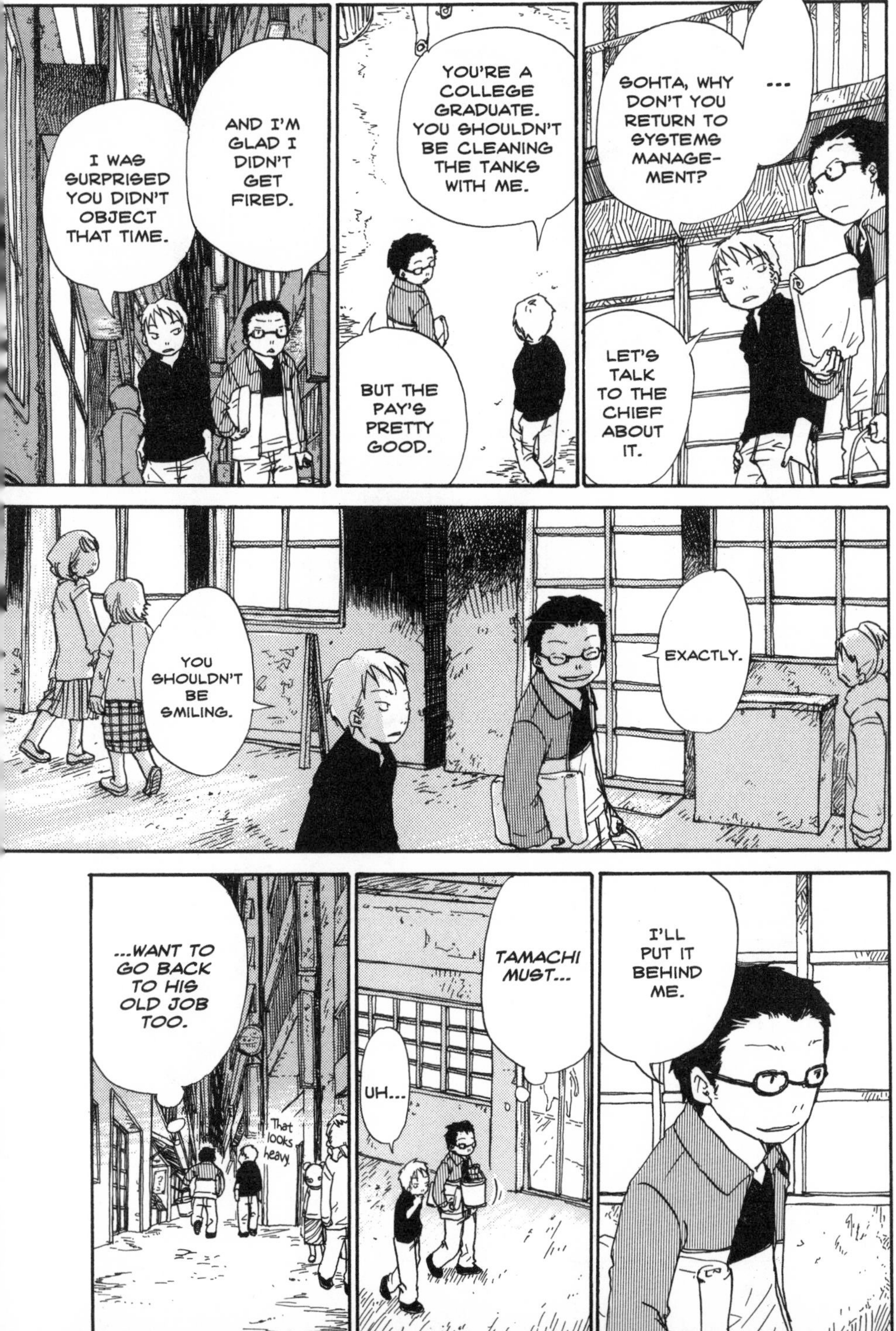
SOHTA, WHY DON'T YOU RETURN TO SYSTEMS MANAGEMENT?
...
LET'S TALK TO THE CHIEF ABOUT IT.
YOU'RE A COLLEGE GRADUATE. YOU SHOULDN'T BE CLEANING THE TANKS WITH ME.
BUT THE PAY'S PRETTY GOOD.
I WAS SURPRISED YOU DIDN'T OBJECT THAT TIME.
AND I'M GLAD I DIDN'T GET FIRED.
EXACTLY.
YOU SHOULDN'T BE SMILING.
I'LL PUT IT BEHIND ME.
TAMACHI MUST...
UH...
...WANT TO GO BACK TO HIS OLD JOB TOO.
That looks heavy.

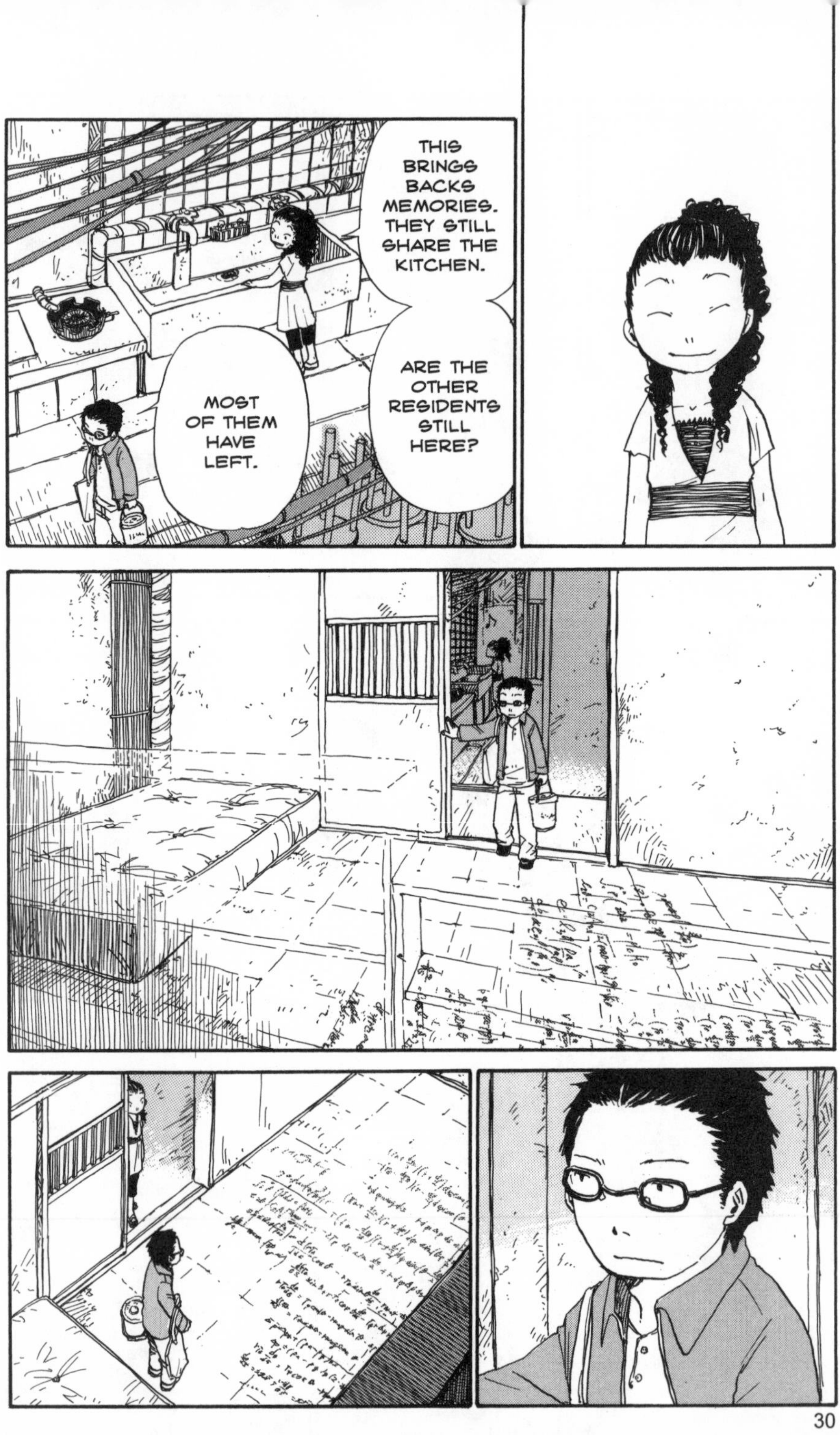
THIS BRINGS BACKS MEMORIES. THEY STILL SHARE THE KITCHEN.
ARE THE OTHER RESIDENTS STILL HERE?
MOST OF THEM HAVE LEFT.

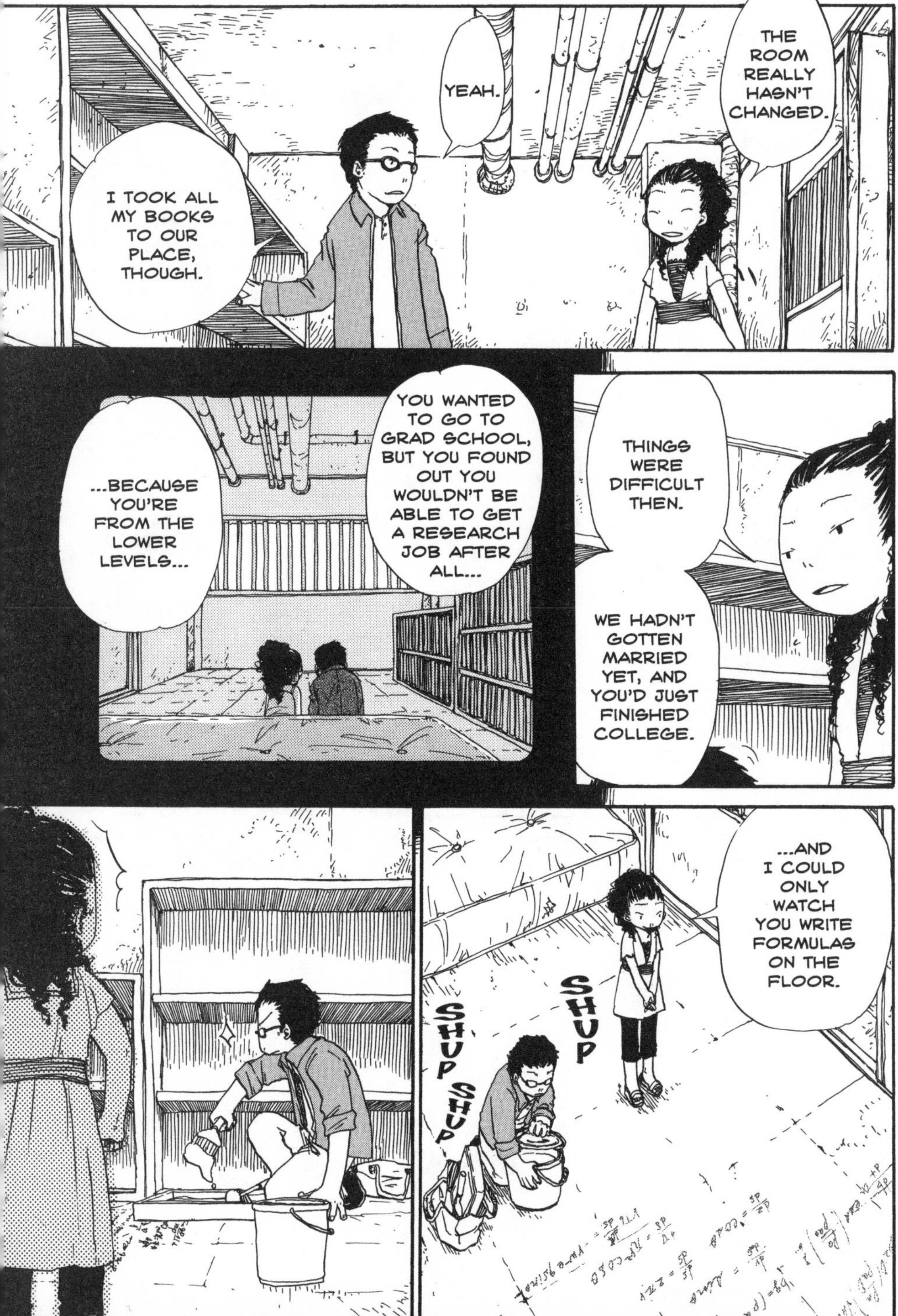
THE ROOM REALLY HASN'T CHANGED.
YEAH.
I TOOK ALL MY BOOKS TO OUR PLACE, THOUGH.
THINGS WERE DIFFICULT THEN.
WE HADN'T GOTTEN MARRIED YET, AND YOU'D JUST FINISHED COLLEGE.
YOU WANTED TO GO TO GRAD SCHOOL, BUT YOU FOUND OUT YOU WOULDN'T BE ABLE TO GET A RESEARCH JOB AFTER ALL...
...BECAUSE YOU'RE FROM THE LOWER LEVELS...
...AND I COULD ONLY WATCH YOU WRITE FORMULAS ON THE FLOOR.
SHUP
SHUP
SHUP

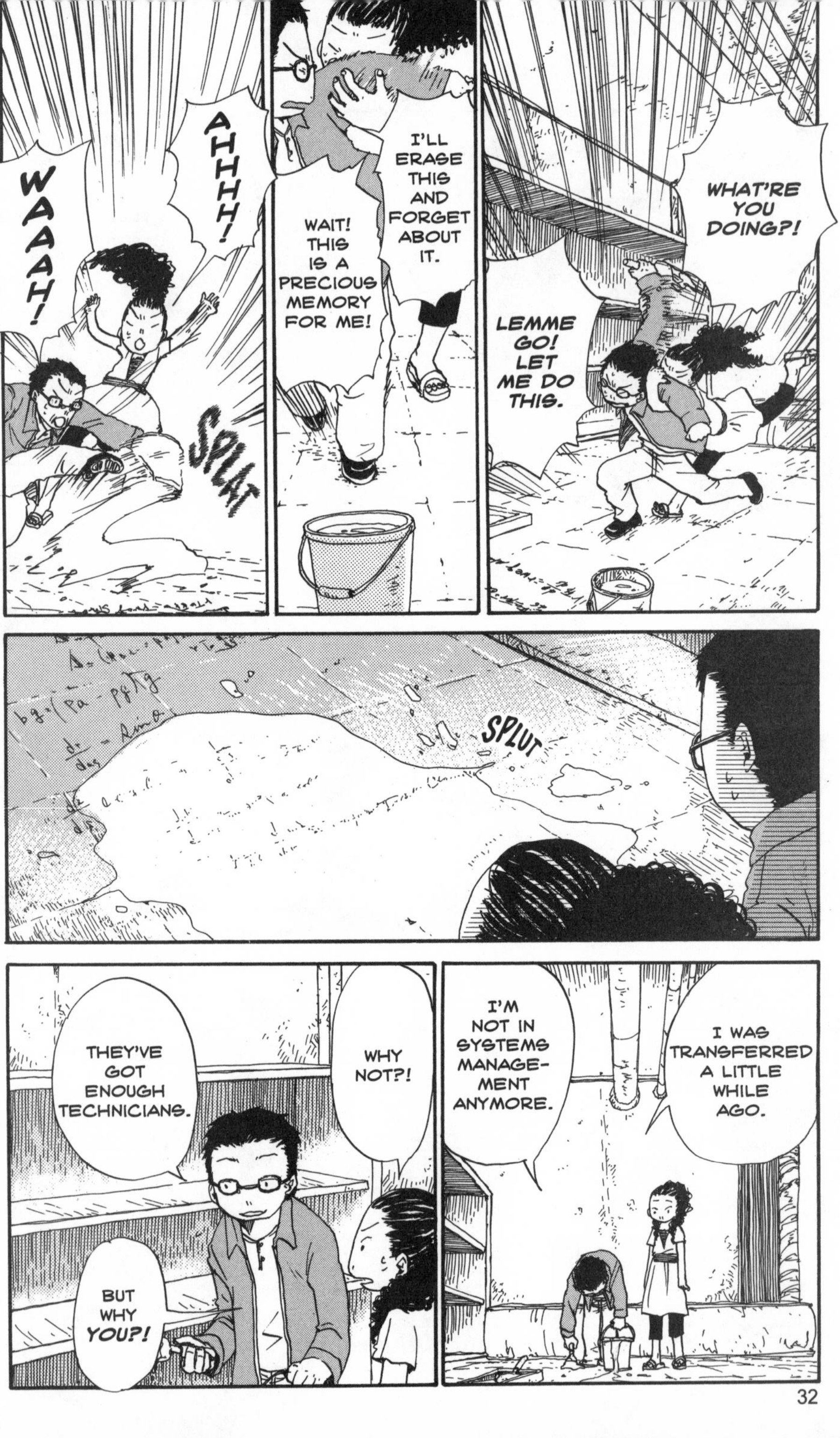
WHAT'RE YOU DOING?!
LEMME GO! LET ME DO THIS.
I'LL ERASE THIS AND FORGET ABOUT IT.
WAIT! THIS IS A PRECIOUS MEMORY FOR ME!
AHHHH!
WAAAAH!
SPLAT
SPLUT
I WAS TRANSFERRED A LITTLE WHILE AGO.
I'M NOT IN SYSTEMS MANAGE-MENT ANYMORE.
WHY NOT?!
THEY'VE GOT ENOUGH TECHNICIANS.
BUT WHY YOU?!

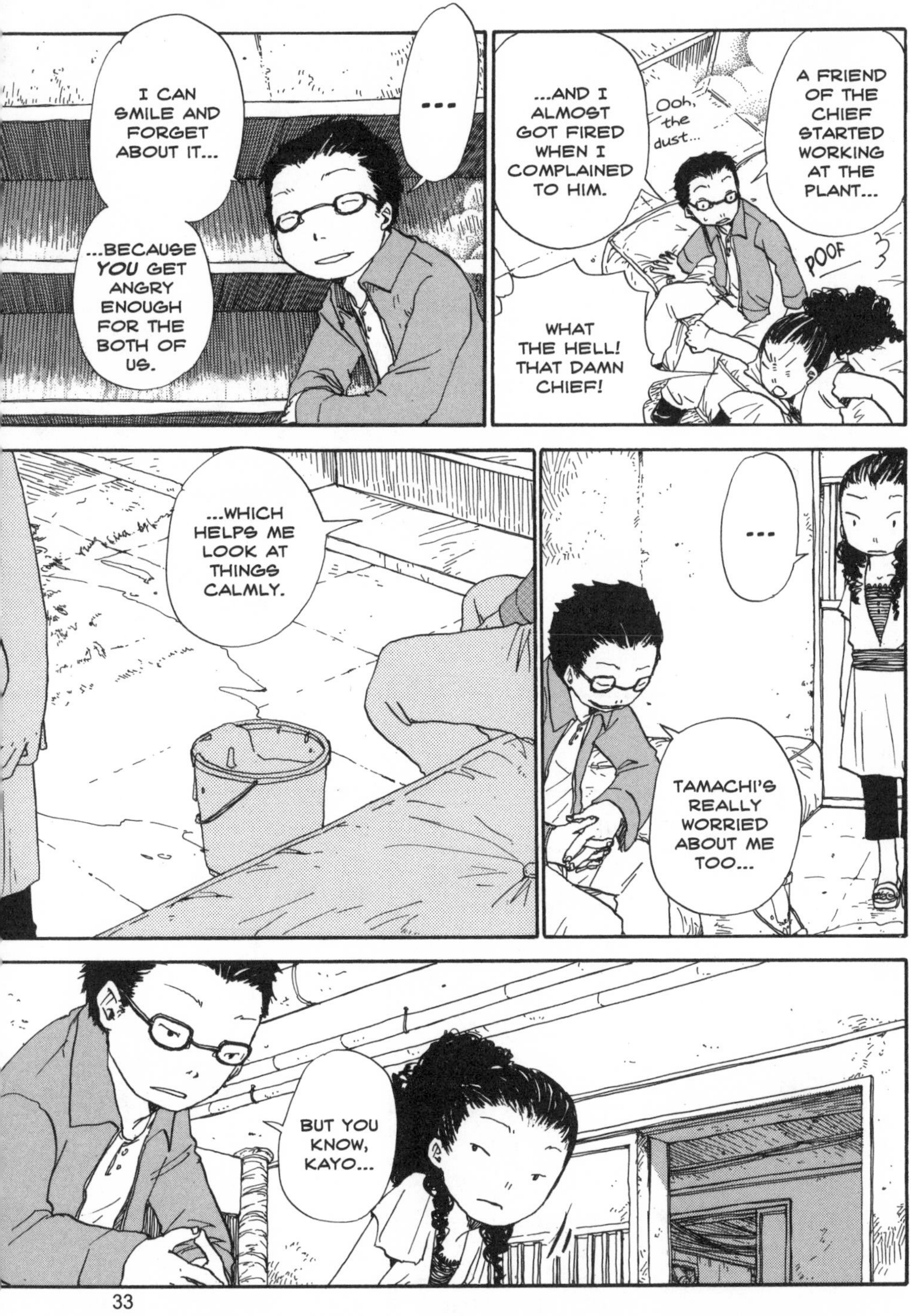
A FRIEND OF THE CHIEF STARTED WORKING AT THE PLANT...
POOF
Ooh, the dust...
...AND I ALMOST GOT FIRED WHEN I COMPLAINED TO HIM.
WHAT THE HELL! THAT DAMN CHIEF!
...
I CAN SMILE AND FORGET ABOUT IT...
...BECAUSE *YOU* GET ANGRY ENOUGH FOR THE BOTH OF US.
...
TAMACHI'S REALLY WORRIED ABOUT ME TOO...
...WHICH HELPS ME LOOK AT THINGS CALMLY.
BUT YOU KNOW, KAYO...

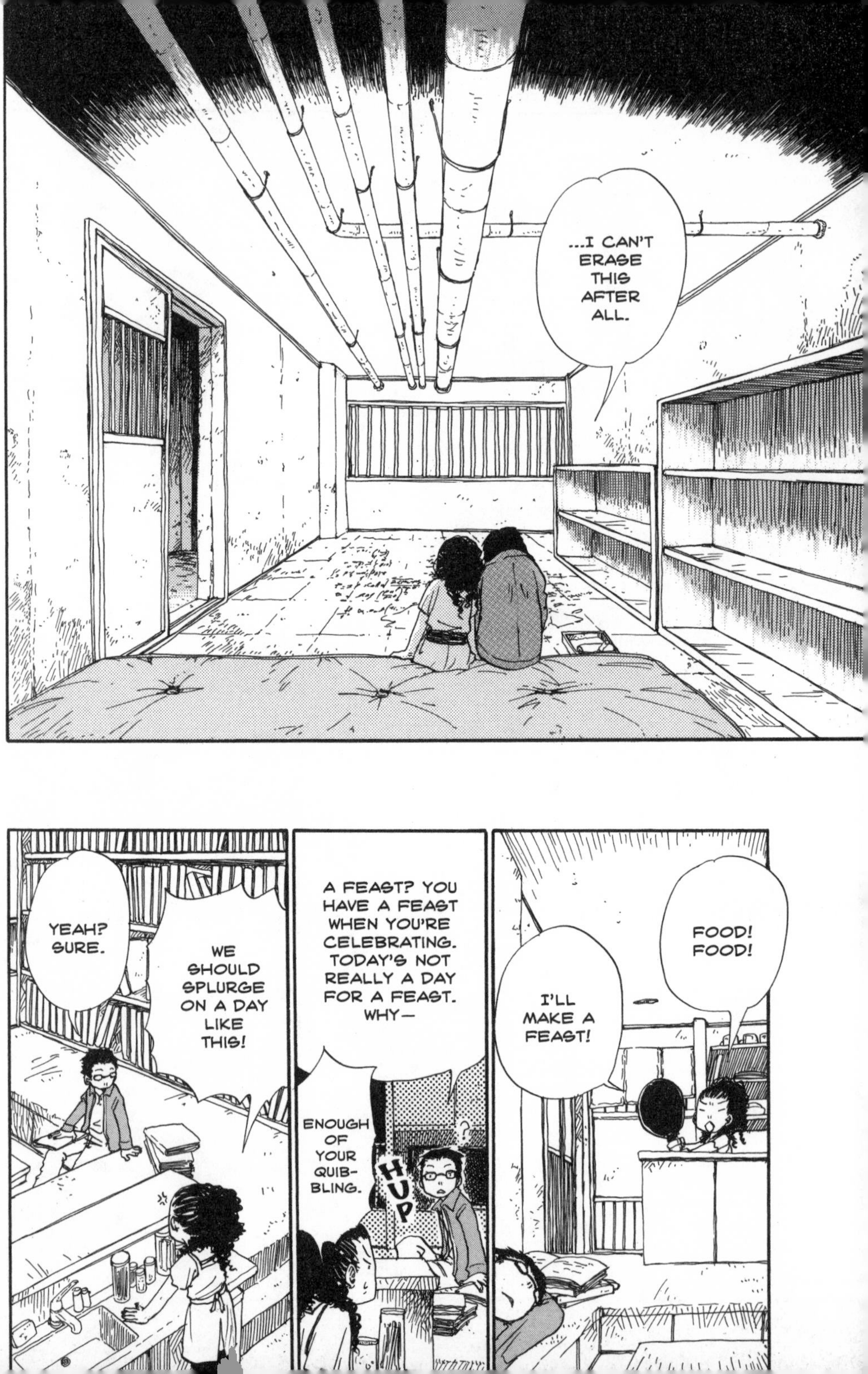
...I CAN'T ERASE THIS AFTER ALL.
FOOD! FOOD!
I'LL MAKE A FEAST!
A FEAST? YOU HAVE A FEAST WHEN YOU'RE CELEBRATING. TODAY'S NOT REALLY A DAY FOR A FEAST. WHY—
ENOUGH OF YOUR QUIB-BLING.
HUP
WE SHOULD SPLURGE ON A DAY LIKE THIS!
YEAH? SURE.

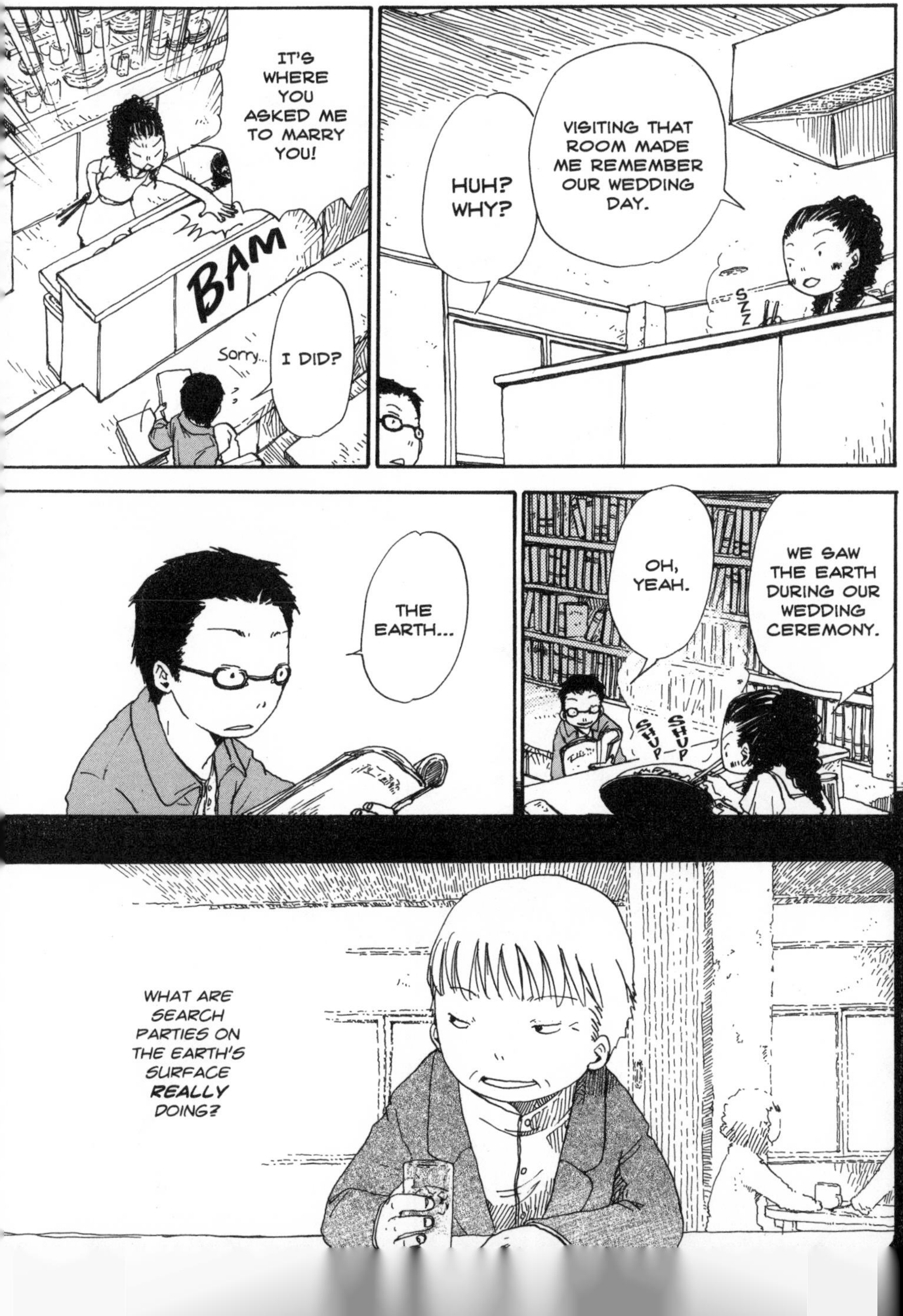
VISITING THAT ROOM MADE ME REMEMBER OUR WEDDING DAY.
HUH? WHY?
SZZ
IT'S WHERE YOU ASKED ME TO MARRY YOU!
BAM
I DID?
Sorry...
WE SAW THE EARTH DURING OUR WEDDING CEREMONY.
OH, YEAH.
SHUP SHUP
THE EARTH...
WHAT ARE SEARCH PARTIES ON THE EARTH'S SURFACE **REALLY** DOING?

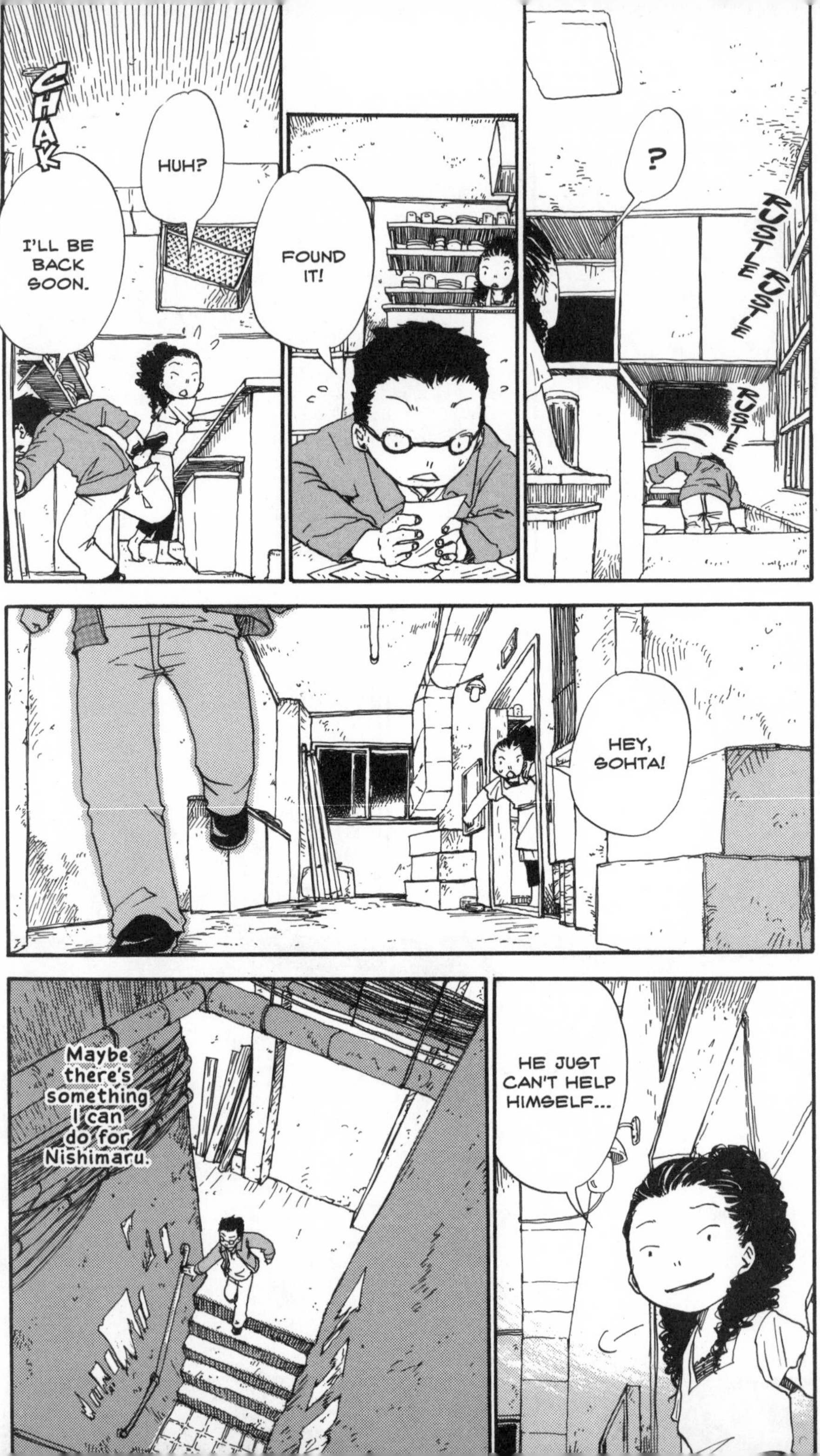
?
RUSTLE RUSTLE
RUSTLE
FOUND IT!
HUH?
CHAK
I'LL BE BACK SOON.
HEY, SOHTA!
HE JUST CAN'T HELP HIMSELF...
Maybe there's something I can do for Nishimaru.

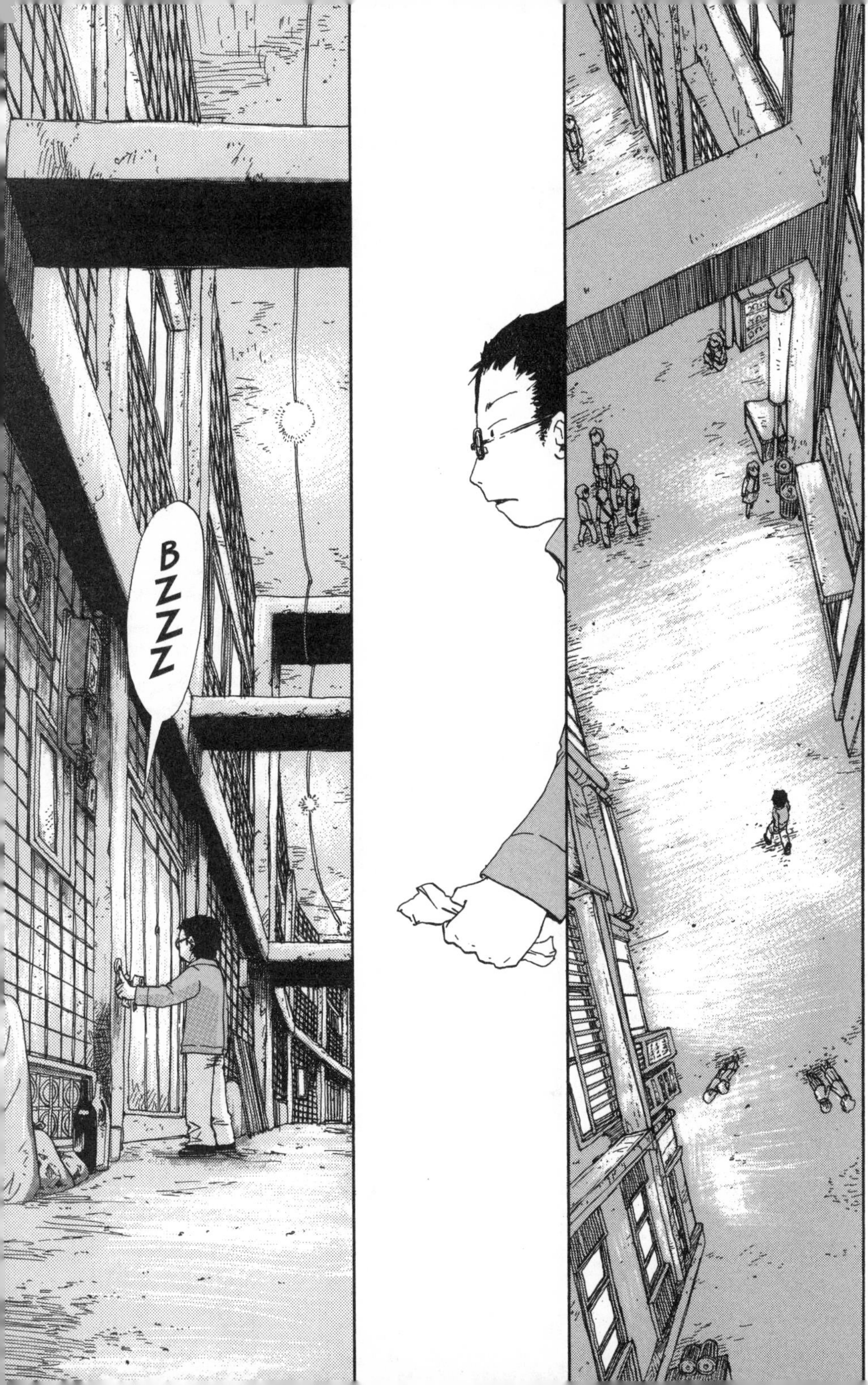
BZZZ

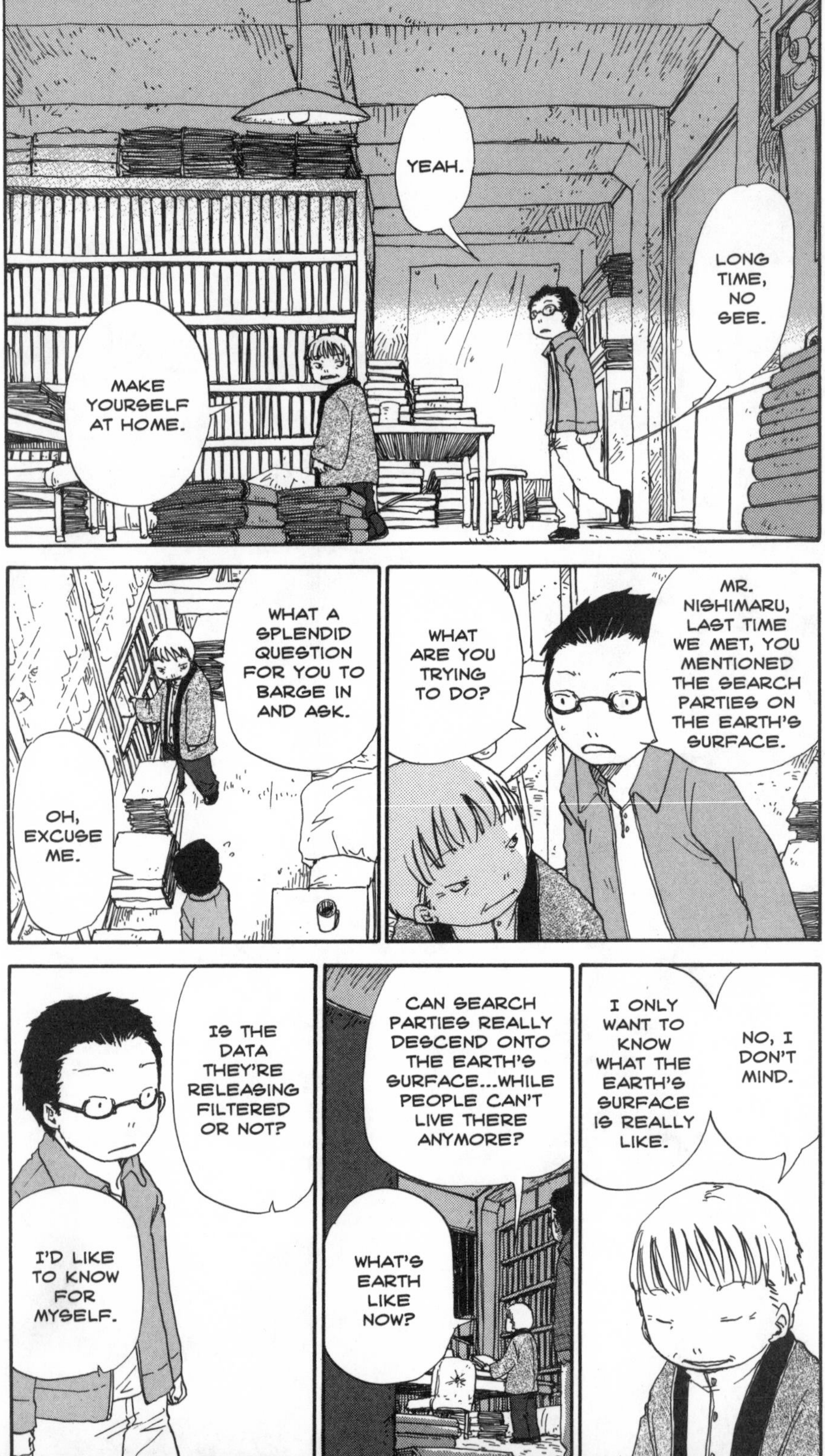
LONG TIME, NO SEE.
YEAH.
MAKE YOURSELF AT HOME.
MR. NISHIMARU, LAST TIME WE MET, YOU MENTIONED THE SEARCH PARTIES ON THE EARTH'S SURFACE.
WHAT ARE YOU TRYING TO DO?
WHAT A SPLENDID QUESTION FOR YOU TO BARGE IN AND ASK.
OH, EXCUSE ME.
NO, I DON'T MIND.
I ONLY WANT TO KNOW WHAT THE EARTH'S SURFACE IS REALLY LIKE.
CAN SEARCH PARTIES REALLY DESCEND ONTO THE EARTH'S SURFACE...WHILE PEOPLE CAN'T LIVE THERE ANYMORE?
WHAT'S EARTH LIKE NOW?
IS THE DATA THEY'RE RELEASING FILTERED OR NOT?
I'D LIKE TO KNOW FOR MYSELF.

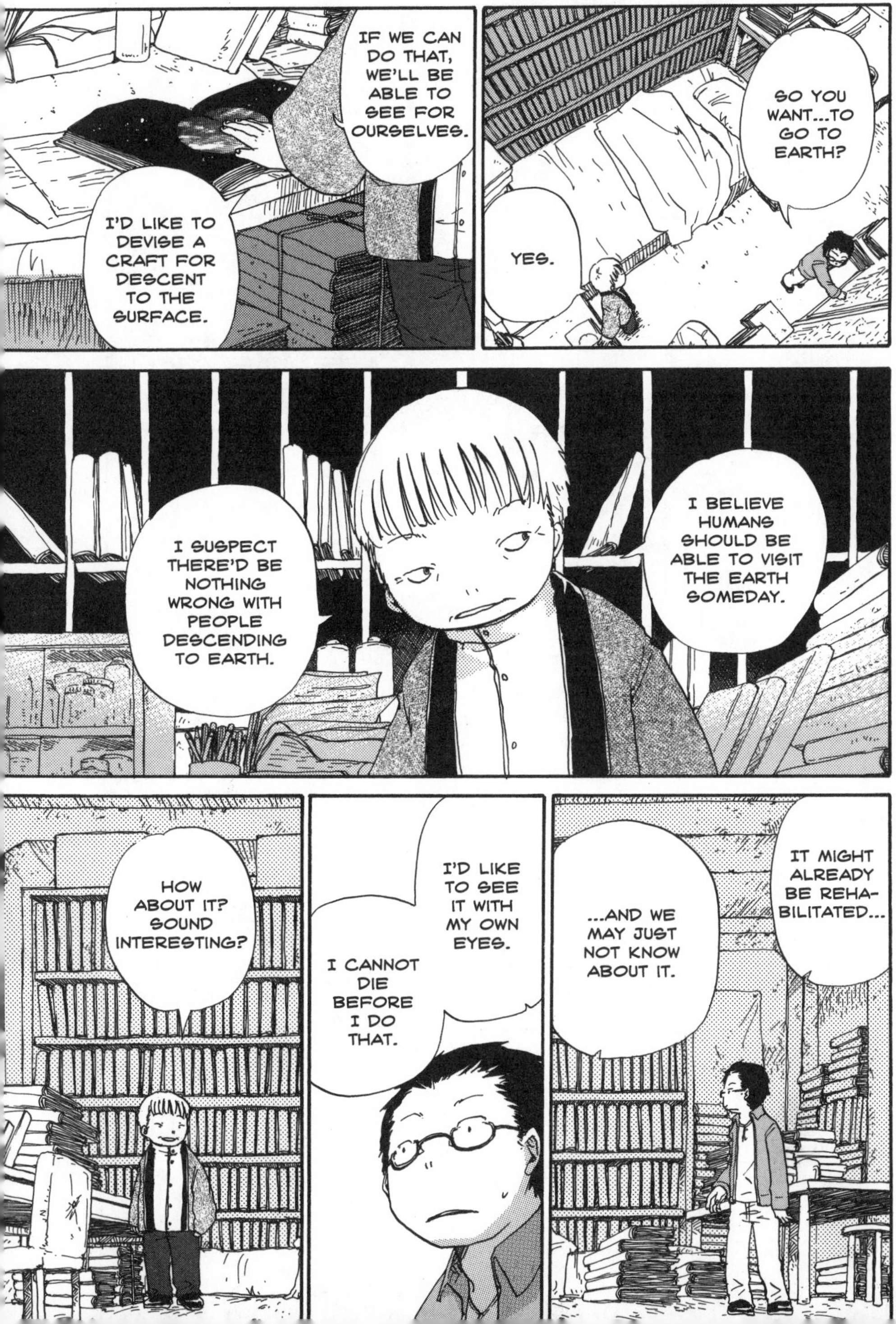
SO YOU WANT...TO GO TO EARTH?
YES.
I'D LIKE TO DEVISE A CRAFT FOR DESCENT TO THE SURFACE.
IF WE CAN DO THAT, WE'LL BE ABLE TO SEE FOR OURSELVES.
I BELIEVE HUMANS SHOULD BE ABLE TO VISIT THE EARTH SOMEDAY.
I SUSPECT THERE'D BE NOTHING WRONG WITH PEOPLE DESCENDING TO EARTH.
IT MIGHT ALREADY BE REHA-BILITATED...
...AND WE MAY JUST NOT KNOW ABOUT IT.
I'D LIKE TO SEE IT WITH MY OWN EYES.
I CANNOT DIE BEFORE I DO THAT.
HOW ABOUT IT? SOUND INTERESTING?

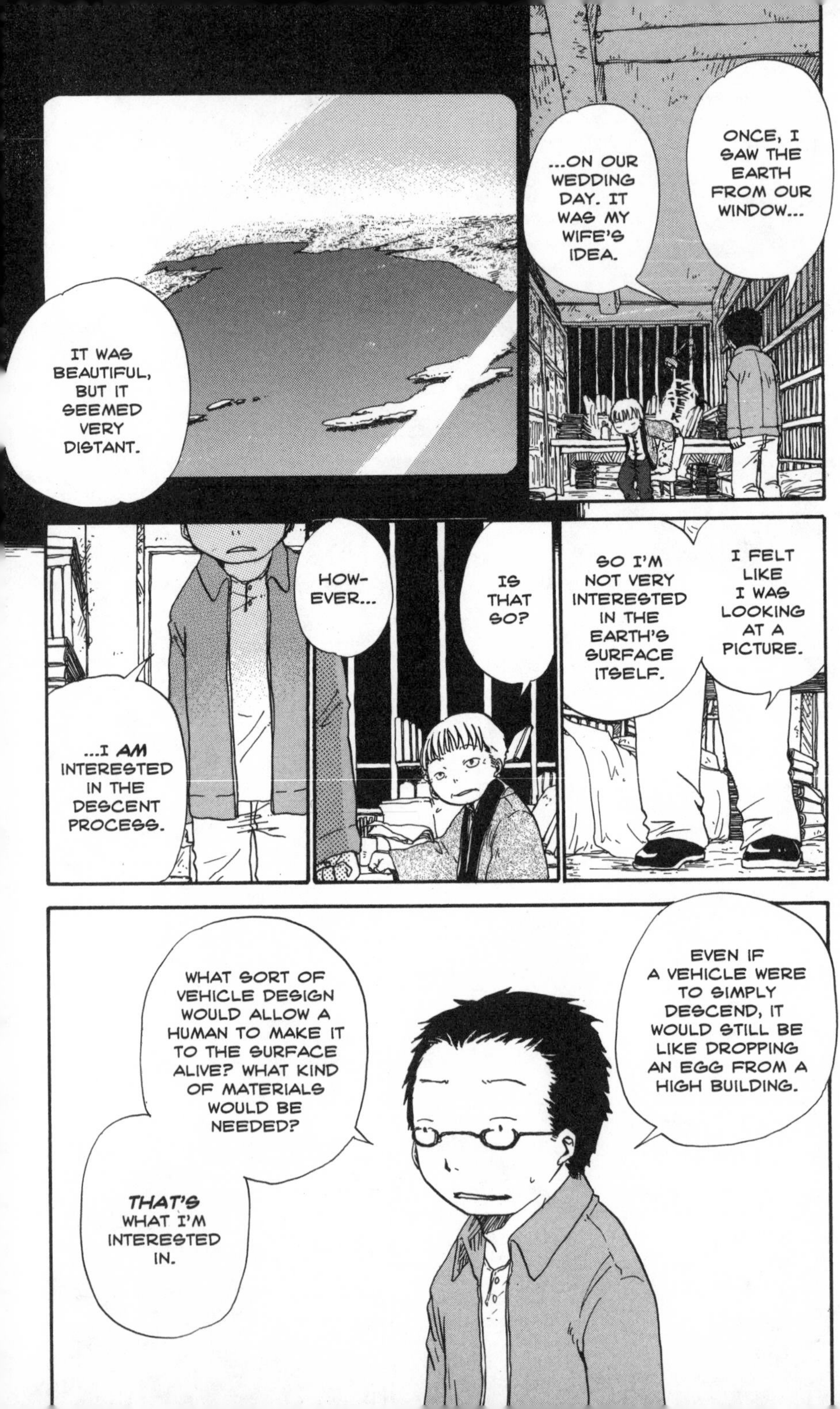
ONCE, I SAW THE EARTH FROM OUR WINDOW...
...ON OUR WEDDING DAY. IT WAS MY WIFE'S IDEA.
IT WAS BEAUTIFUL, BUT IT SEEMED VERY DISTANT.
I FELT LIKE I WAS LOOKING AT A PICTURE.
SO I'M NOT VERY INTERESTED IN THE EARTH'S SURFACE ITSELF.
IS THAT SO?
HOW-EVER...
...I *AM* INTERESTED IN THE DESCENT PROCESS.
EVEN IF A VEHICLE WERE TO SIMPLY DESCEND, IT WOULD STILL BE LIKE DROPPING AN EGG FROM A HIGH BUILDING.
WHAT SORT OF VEHICLE DESIGN WOULD ALLOW A HUMAN TO MAKE IT TO THE SURFACE ALIVE? WHAT KIND OF MATERIALS WOULD BE NEEDED?
THAT'S WHAT I'M INTERESTED IN.

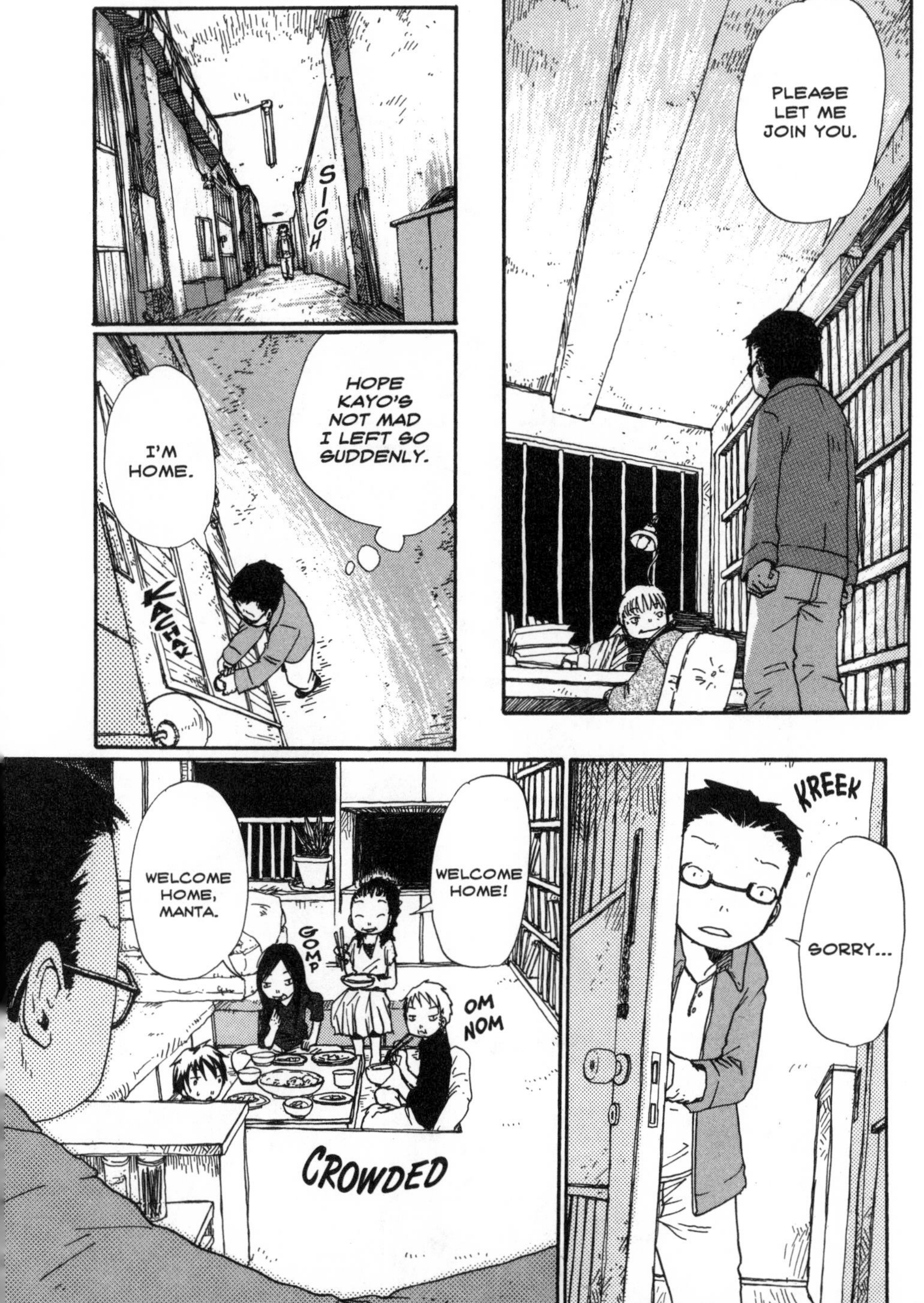
PLEASE LET ME JOIN YOU.
SIGH
HOPE KAYO'S NOT MAD I LEFT SO SUDDENLY.
I'M HOME.
KREEK
SORRY...
WELCOME HOME!
WELCOME HOME, MANTA.
GOMP
OM NOM
CROWDED

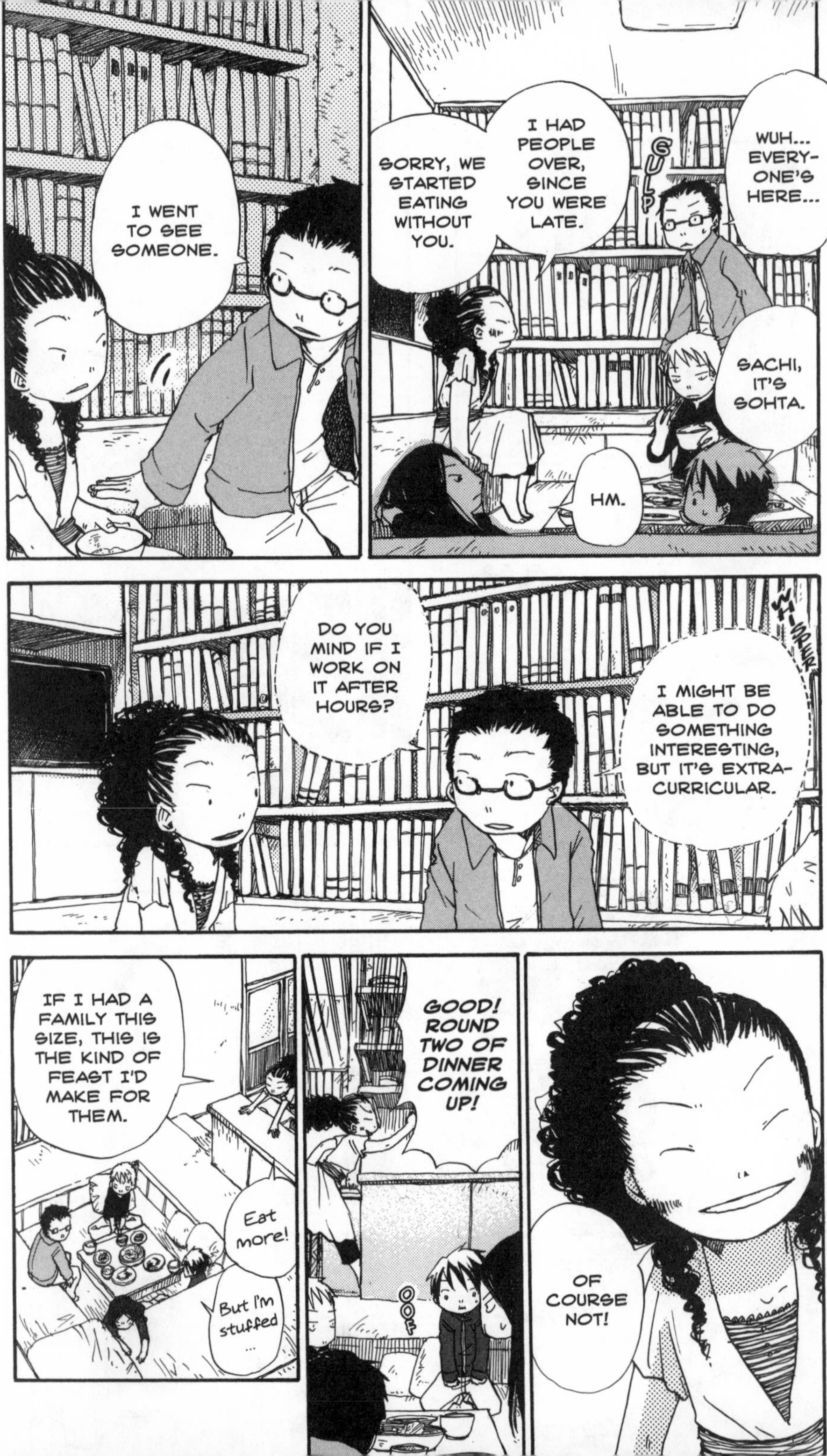
WUH... EVERY-ONE'S HERE...
GULP
I HAD PEOPLE OVER, SINCE YOU WERE LATE.
SORRY, WE STARTED EATING WITHOUT YOU.
SACHI, IT'S SOHTA.
HM.
I WENT TO SEE SOMEONE.
WHISPER
I MIGHT BE ABLE TO DO SOMETHING INTERESTING, BUT IT'S EXTRA-CURRICULAR.
DO YOU MIND IF I WORK ON IT AFTER HOURS?
OF COURSE NOT!
GOOD! ROUND TWO OF DINNER COMING UP!
OOF
IF I HAD A FAMILY THIS SIZE, THIS IS THE KIND OF FEAST I'D MAKE FOR THEM.
Eat more!
But I'm stuffed ...

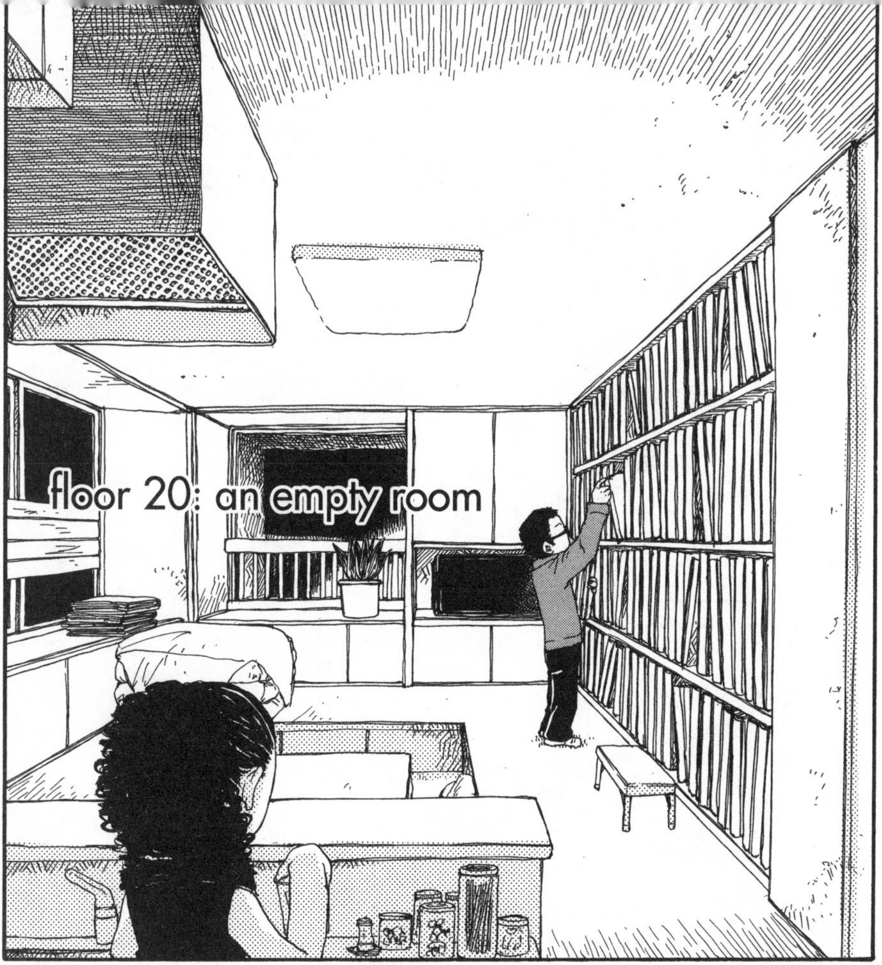
floor 20: an empty room

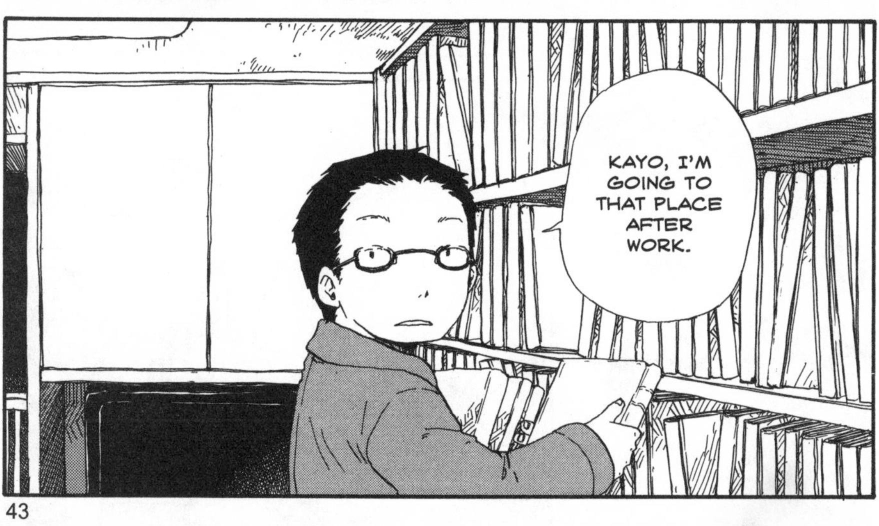
KAYO, I'M GOING TO THAT PLACE AFTER WORK.

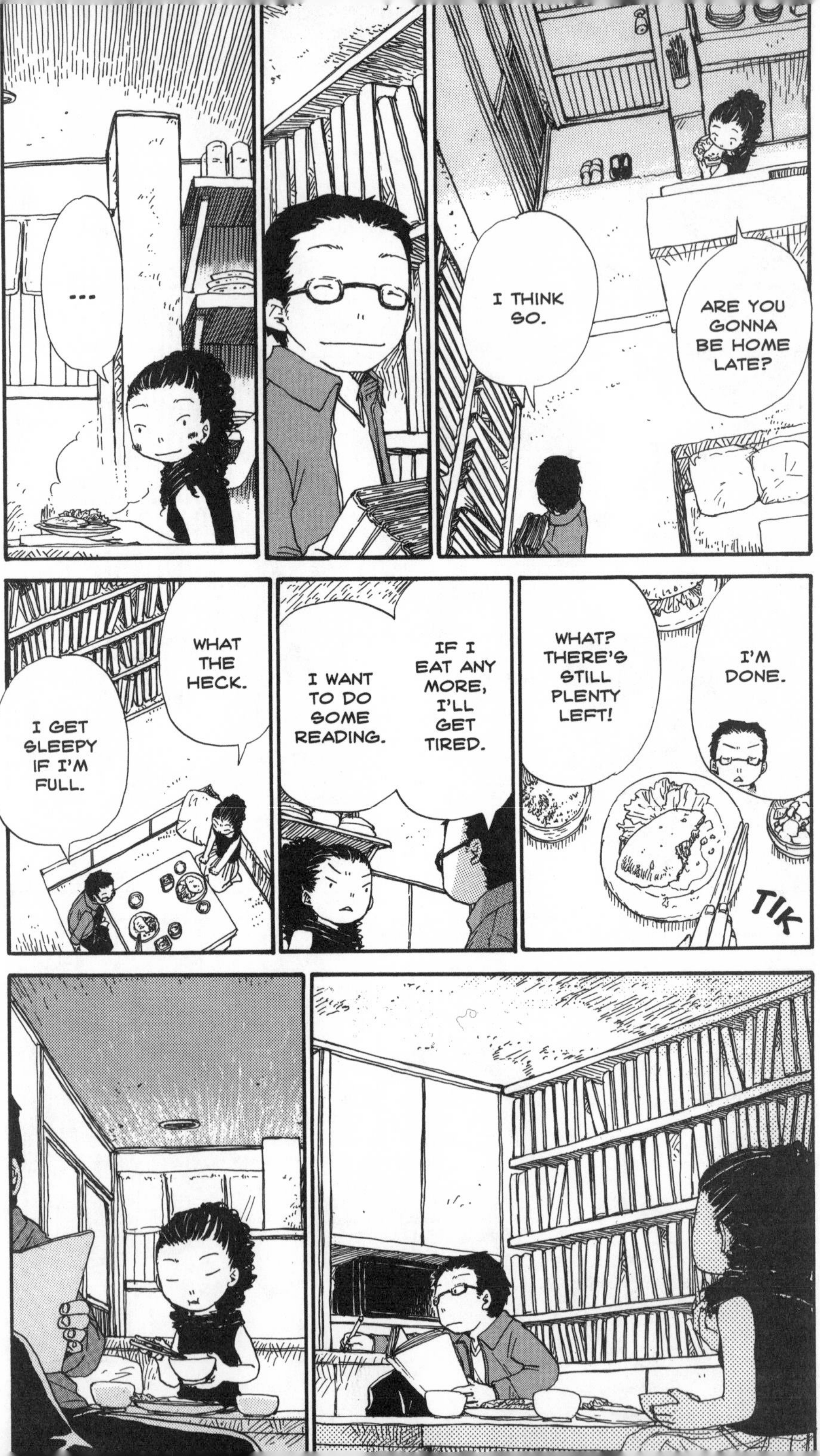
ARE YOU GONNA BE HOME LATE?
I THINK SO.
...
I'M DONE.
WHAT? THERE'S STILL PLENTY LEFT!
TIK
IF I EAT ANY MORE, I'LL GET TIRED.
I WANT TO DO SOME READING.
WHAT THE HECK.
I GET SLEEPY IF I'M FULL.

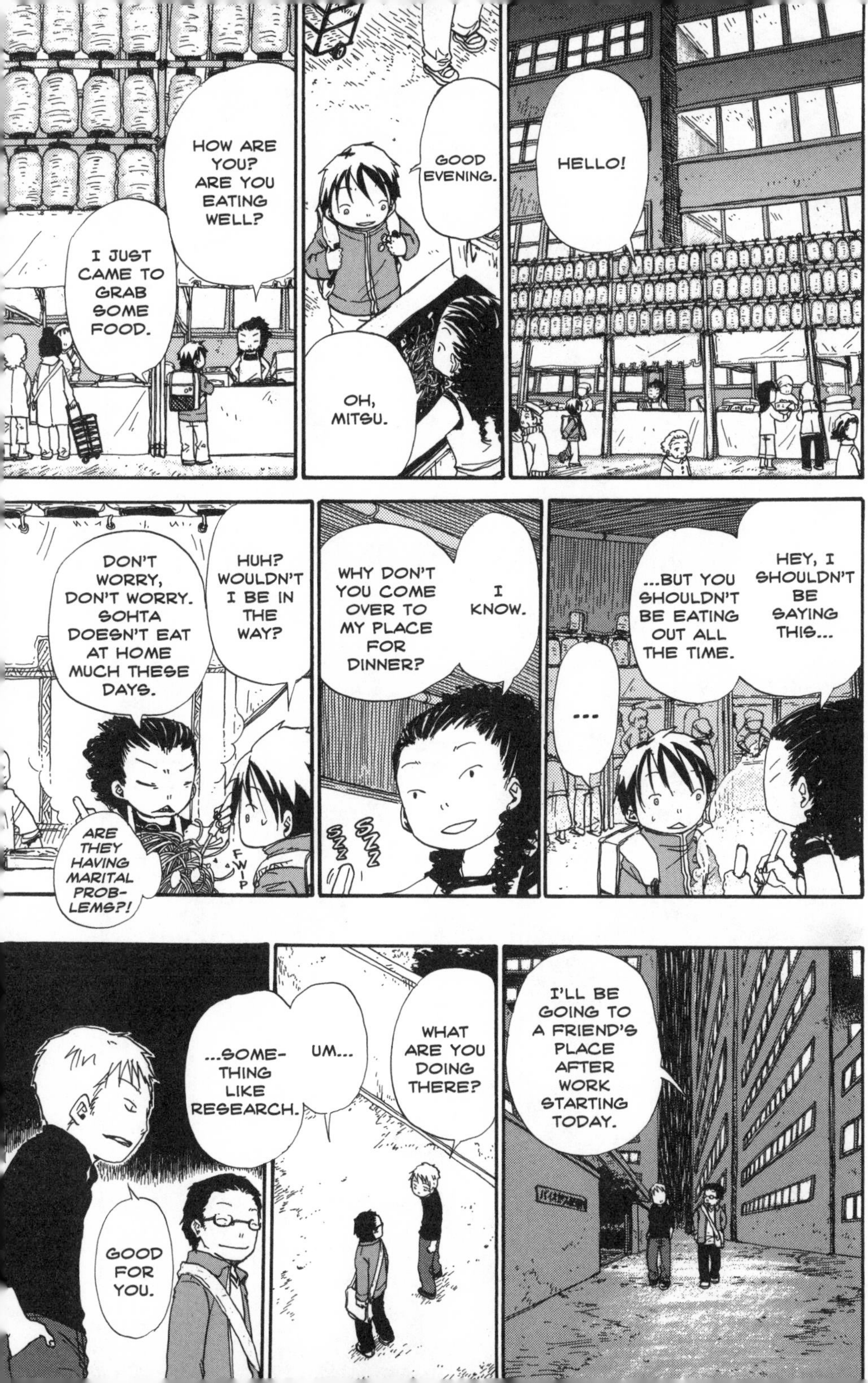
HELLO!
GOOD EVENING.
OH, MITSU.
HOW ARE YOU? ARE YOU EATING WELL?
I JUST CAME TO GRAB SOME FOOD.
HEY, I SHOULDN'T BE SAYING THIS...
...BUT YOU SHOULDN'T BE EATING OUT ALL THE TIME.
...
I KNOW.
WHY DON'T YOU COME OVER TO MY PLACE FOR DINNER?
SZZ SZZ
HUH? WOULDN'T I BE IN THE WAY?
DON'T WORRY, DON'T WORRY. SOHTA DOESN'T EAT AT HOME MUCH THESE DAYS.
FWIP
ARE THEY HAVING MARITAL PROB-LEMS?!
I'LL BE GOING TO A FRIEND'S PLACE AFTER WORK STARTING TODAY.
WHAT ARE YOU DOING THERE?
UM...
...SOME-THING LIKE RESEARCH.
GOOD FOR YOU.

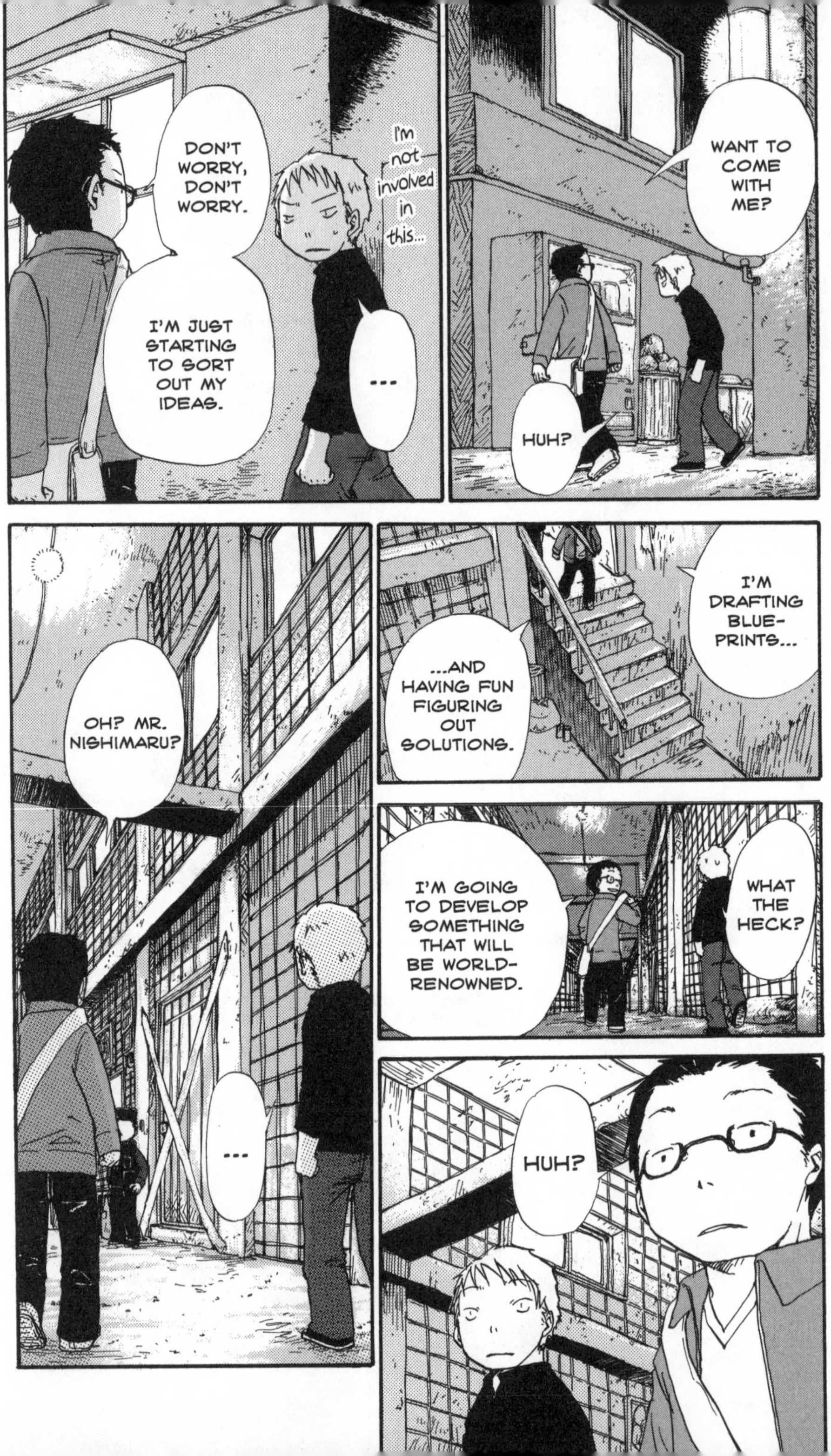
WANT TO COME WITH ME?
HUH?
DON'T WORRY, DON'T WORRY.
I'M JUST STARTING TO SORT OUT MY IDEAS.
I'm not involved in this...
...
I'M DRAFTING BLUE-PRINTS...
...AND HAVING FUN FIGURING OUT SOLUTIONS.
WHAT THE HECK?
I'M GOING TO DEVELOP SOMETHING THAT WILL BE WORLD-RENOWNED.
HUH?
OH? MR. NISHIMARU?
...

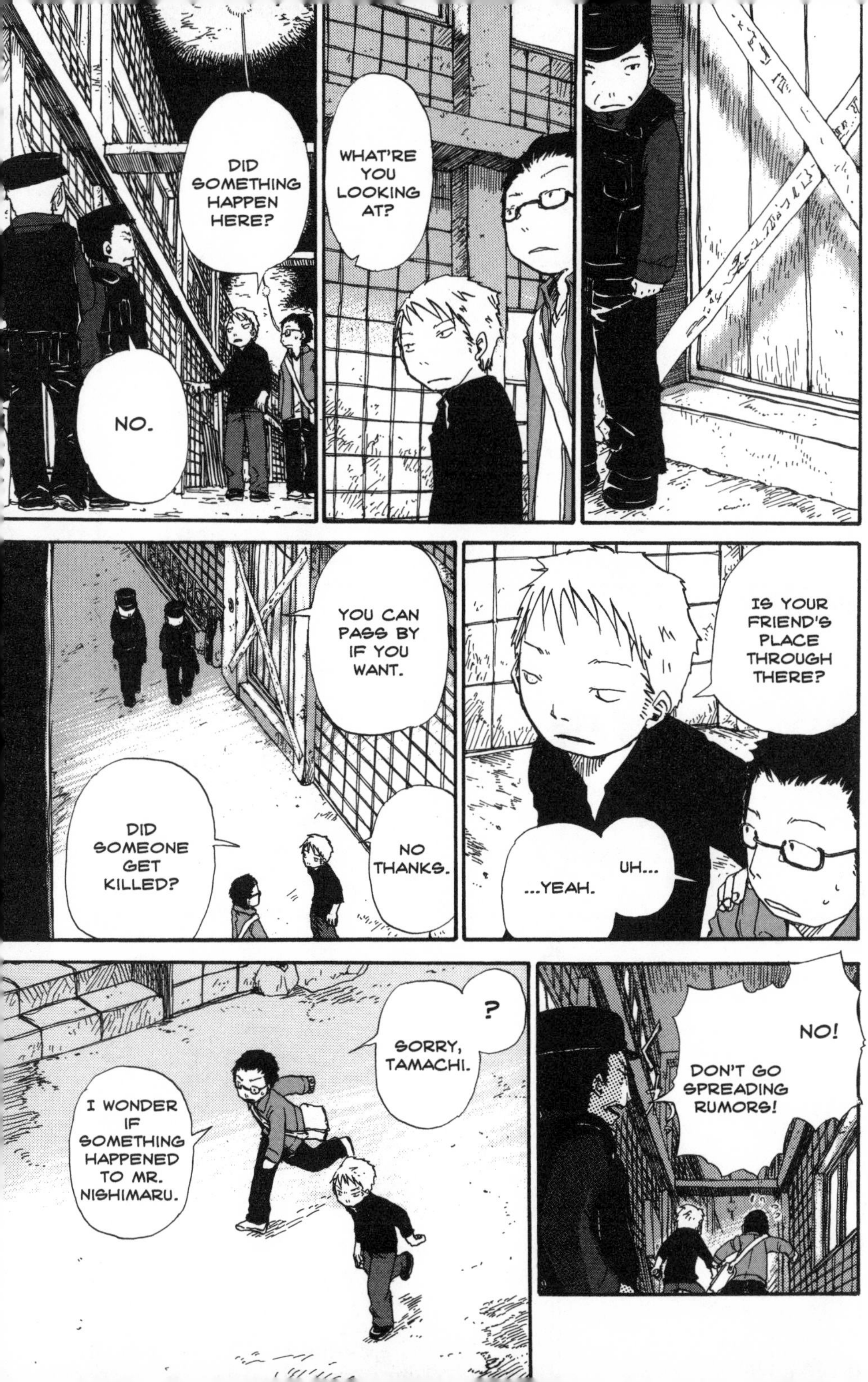
WHAT'RE YOU LOOKING AT?
DID SOMETHING HAPPEN HERE?
NO.
IS YOUR FRIEND'S PLACE THROUGH THERE?
UH...
...YEAH.
YOU CAN PASS BY IF YOU WANT.
NO THANKS.
DID SOMEONE GET KILLED?
NO!
DON'T GO SPREADING RUMORS!
?
SORRY, TAMACHI.
I WONDER IF SOMETHING HAPPENED TO MR. NISHIMARU.

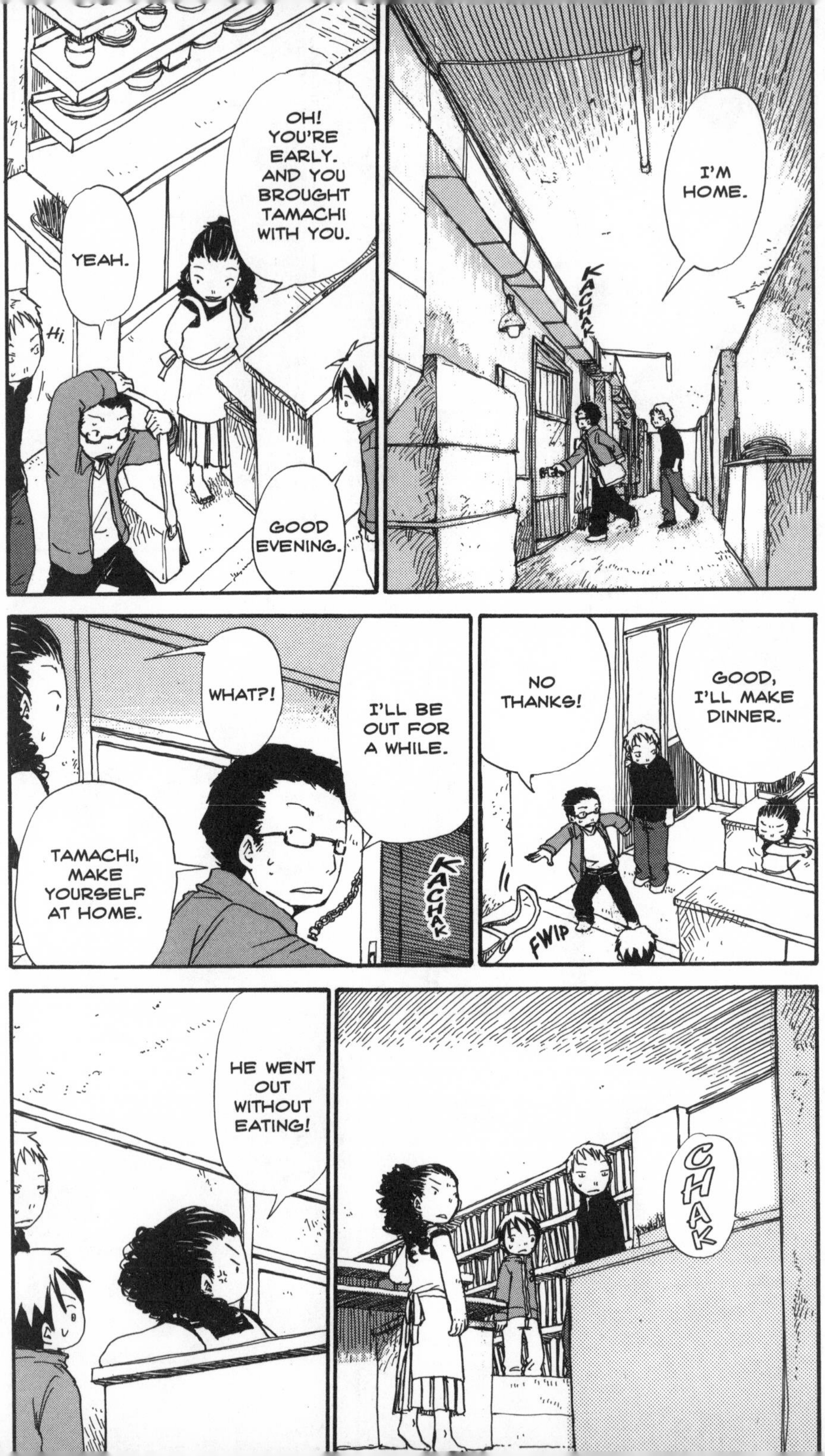
I'M HOME.
KACHAK
OH! YOU'RE EARLY. AND YOU BROUGHT TAMACHI WITH YOU.
YEAH.
Hi
GOOD EVENING.
GOOD, I'LL MAKE DINNER.
NO THANKS!
FWIP
I'LL BE OUT FOR A WHILE.
KACHAK
WHAT?!
TAMACHI, MAKE YOURSELF AT HOME.
CHAK
HE WENT OUT WITHOUT EATING!

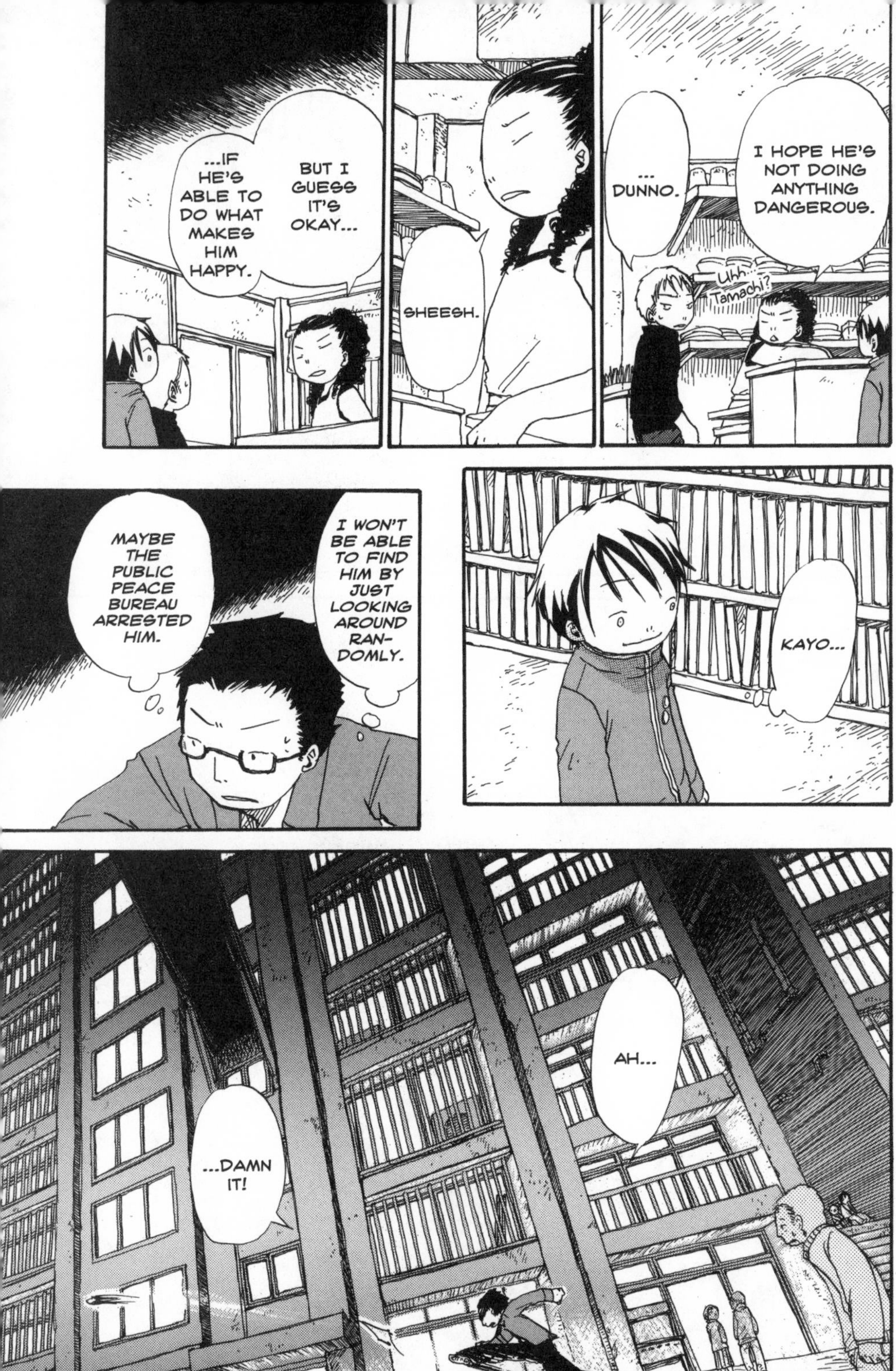
I HOPE HE'S NOT DOING ANYTHING DANGEROUS.
... DUNNO.
Uhh... Tamachi?
SHEESH.
BUT I GUESS IT'S OKAY...
...IF HE'S ABLE TO DO WHAT MAKES HIM HAPPY.
KAYO...
I WON'T BE ABLE TO FIND HIM BY JUST LOOKING AROUND RAN-DOMLY.
MAYBE THE PUBLIC PEACE BUREAU ARRESTED HIM.
AH...
...DAMN IT!

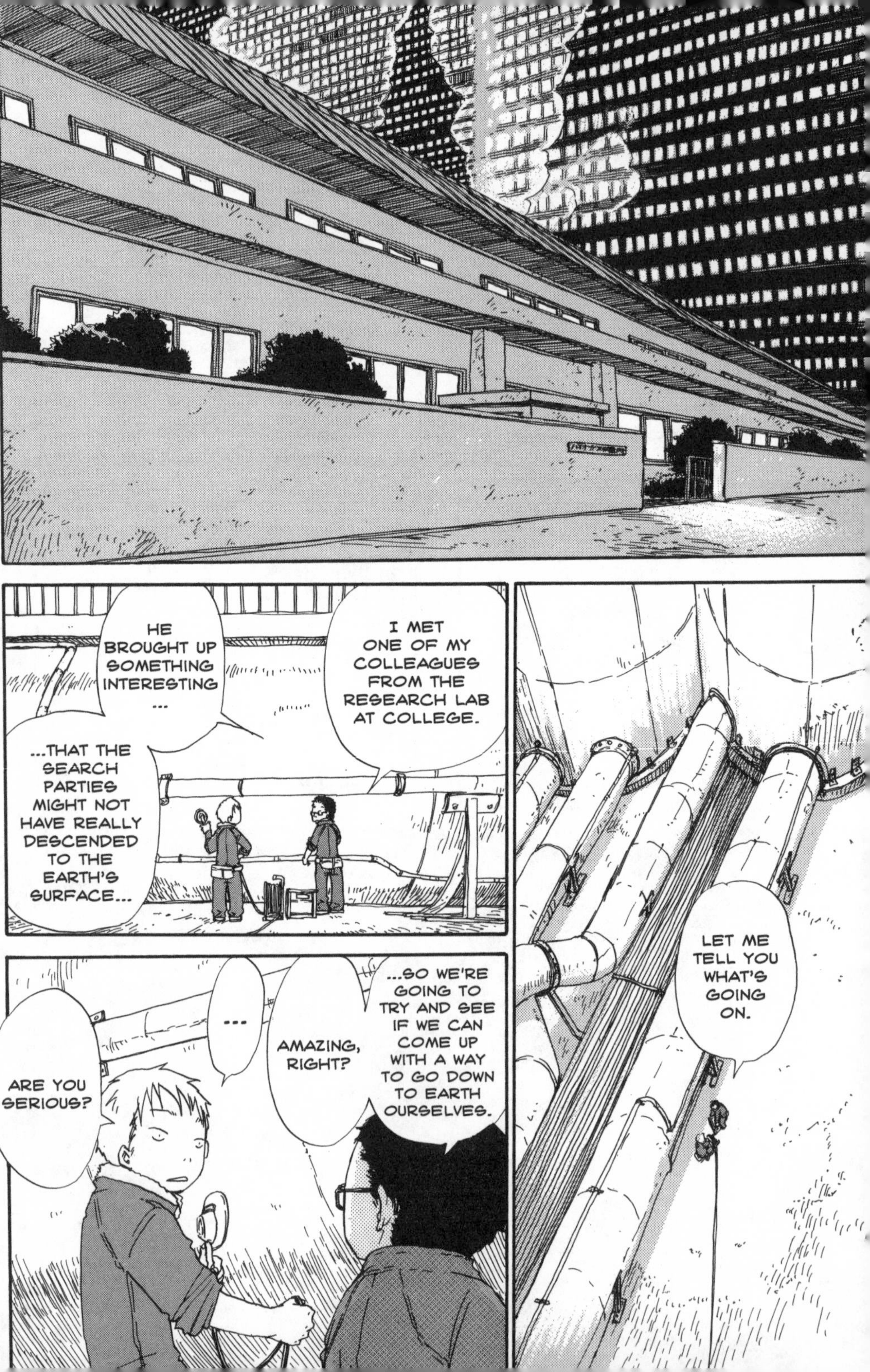
LET ME TELL YOU WHAT'S GOING ON.
I MET ONE OF MY COLLEAGUES FROM THE RESEARCH LAB AT COLLEGE.
HE BROUGHT UP SOMETHING INTERESTING...
...THAT THE SEARCH PARTIES MIGHT NOT HAVE REALLY DESCENDED TO THE EARTH'S SURFACE...
...SO WE'RE GOING TO TRY AND SEE IF WE CAN COME UP WITH A WAY TO GO DOWN TO EARTH OURSELVES.
AMAZING, RIGHT?
...
ARE YOU SERIOUS?

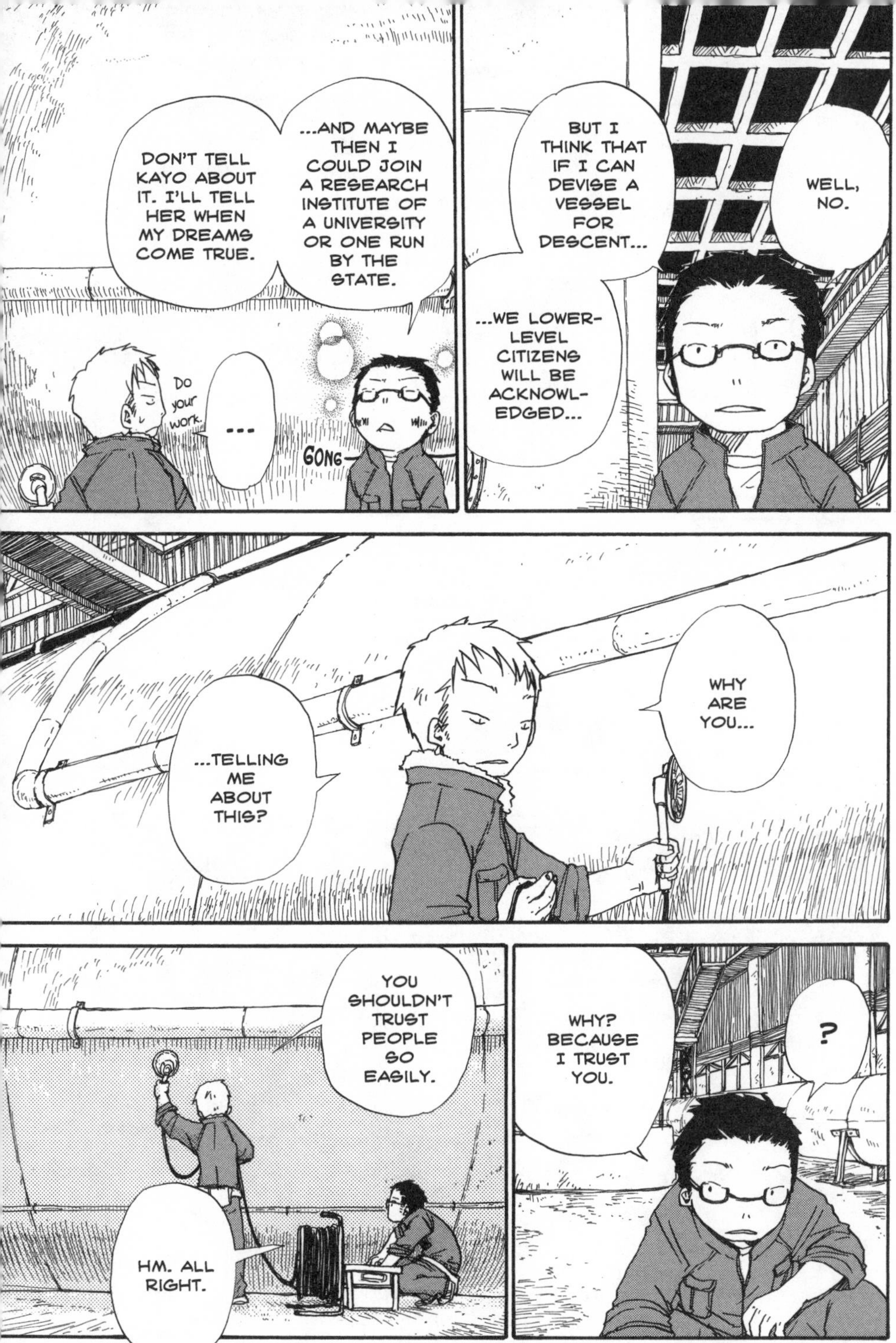
WELL, NO.
BUT I THINK THAT IF I CAN DEVISE A VESSEL FOR DESCENT...
...WE LOWER-LEVEL CITIZENS WILL BE ACKNOWLEDGED...
...AND MAYBE THEN I COULD JOIN A RESEARCH INSTITUTE OF A UNIVERSITY OR ONE RUN BY THE STATE.
DON'T TELL KAYO ABOUT IT. I'LL TELL HER WHEN MY DREAMS COME TRUE.
...
Do your work.
GONG
WHY ARE YOU...
...TELLING ME ABOUT THIS?
?
WHY? BECAUSE I TRUST YOU.
YOU SHOULDN'T TRUST PEOPLE SO EASILY.
HM. ALL RIGHT.

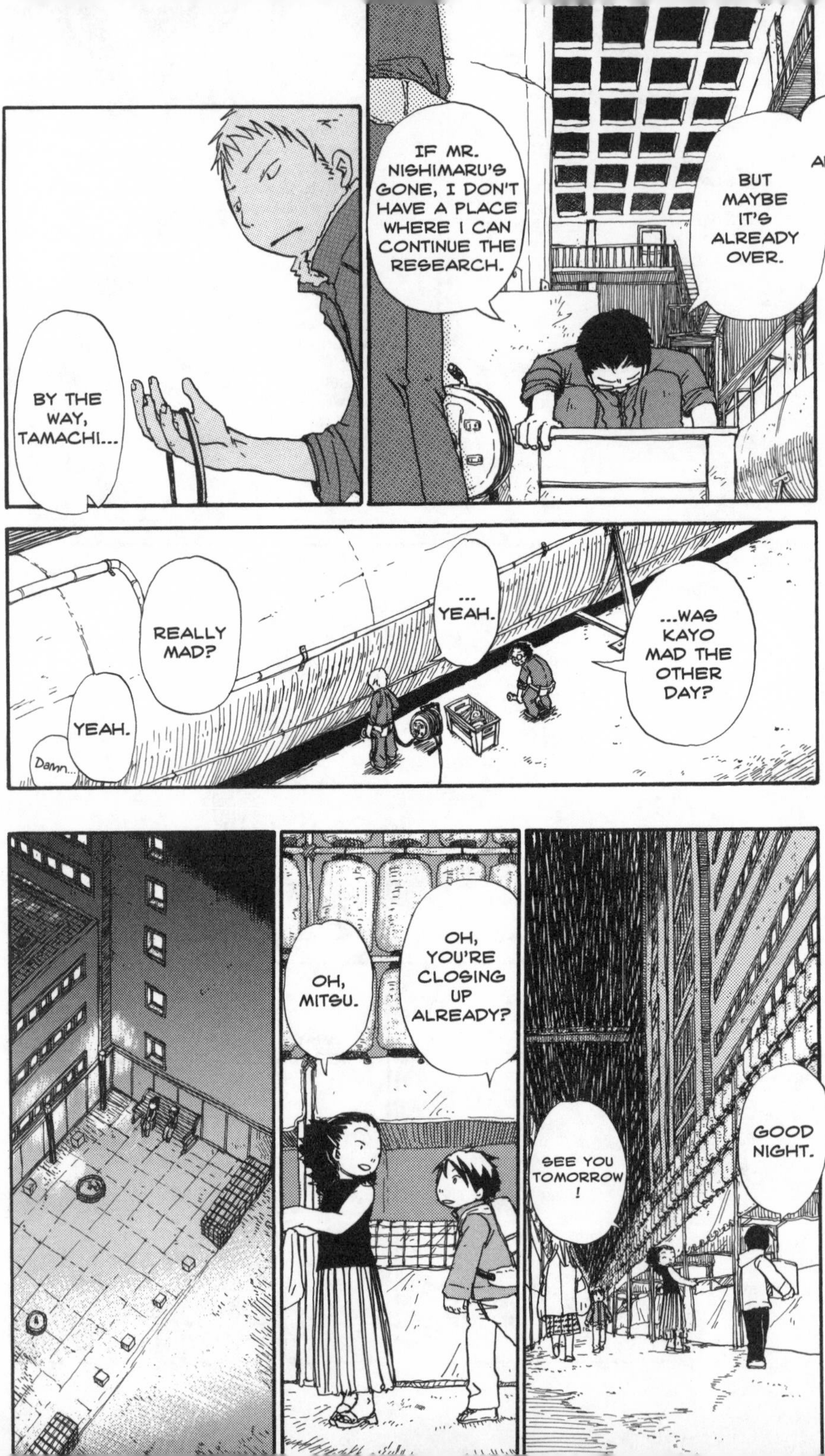
AH! BUT MAYBE IT'S ALREADY OVER.
IF MR. NISHIMARU'S GONE, I DON'T HAVE A PLACE WHERE I CAN CONTINUE THE RESEARCH.
BY THE WAY, TAMACHI...
...WAS KAYO MAD THE OTHER DAY?
... YEAH.
REALLY MAD?
YEAH.
Damn...
GOOD NIGHT.
SEE YOU TOMORROW!
OH, YOU'RE CLOSING UP ALREADY?
OH, MITSU.

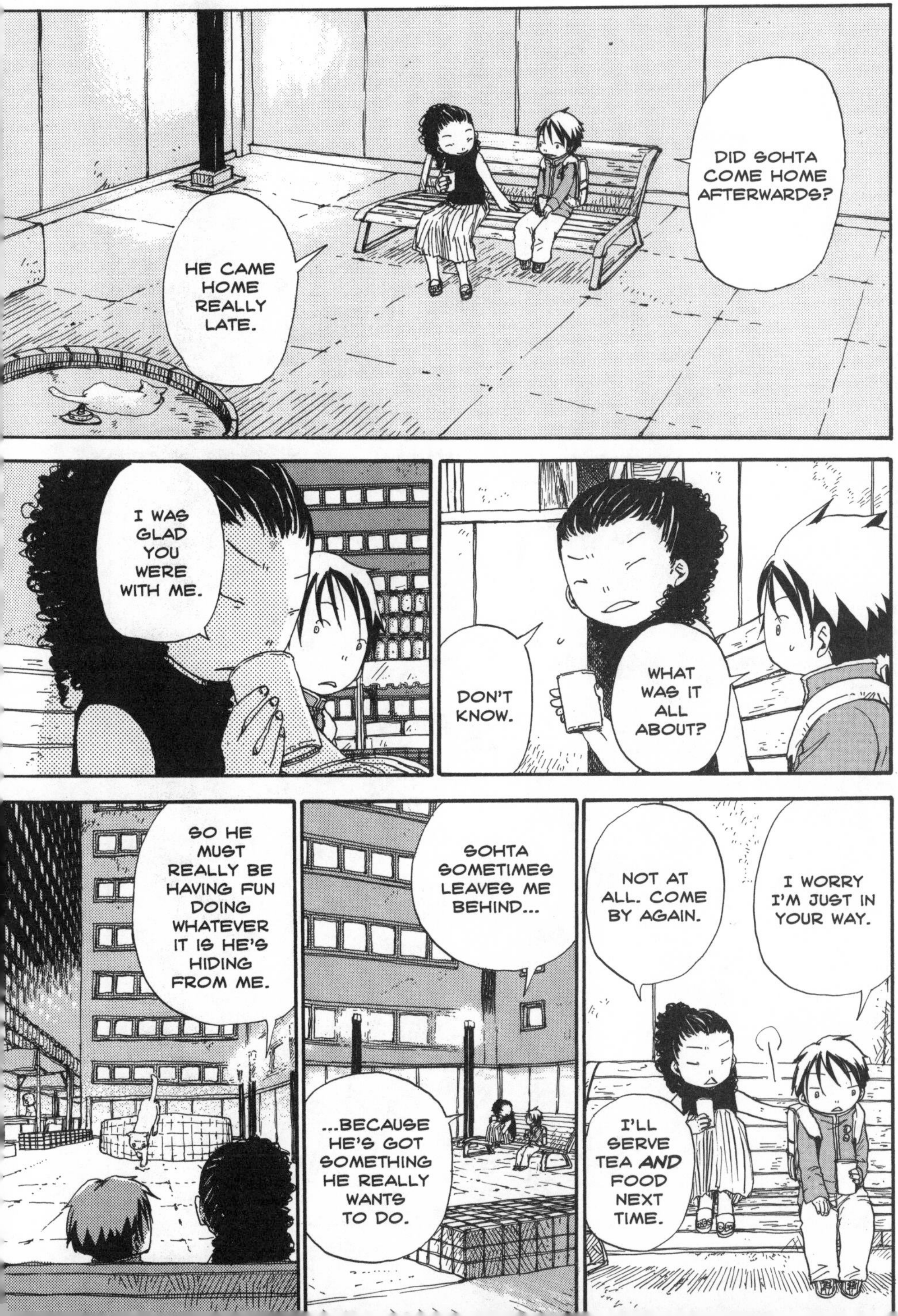
DID SOHTA COME HOME AFTERWARDS?
HE CAME HOME REALLY LATE.
WHAT WAS IT ALL ABOUT?
DON'T KNOW.
I WAS GLAD YOU WERE WITH ME.
I WORRY I'M JUST IN YOUR WAY.
NOT AT ALL. COME BY AGAIN.
I'LL SERVE TEA ***AND*** FOOD NEXT TIME.
SOHTA SOMETIMES LEAVES ME BEHIND...
...BECAUSE HE'S GOT SOMETHING HE REALLY WANTS TO DO.
SO HE MUST REALLY BE HAVING FUN DOING WHATEVER IT IS HE'S HIDING FROM ME.

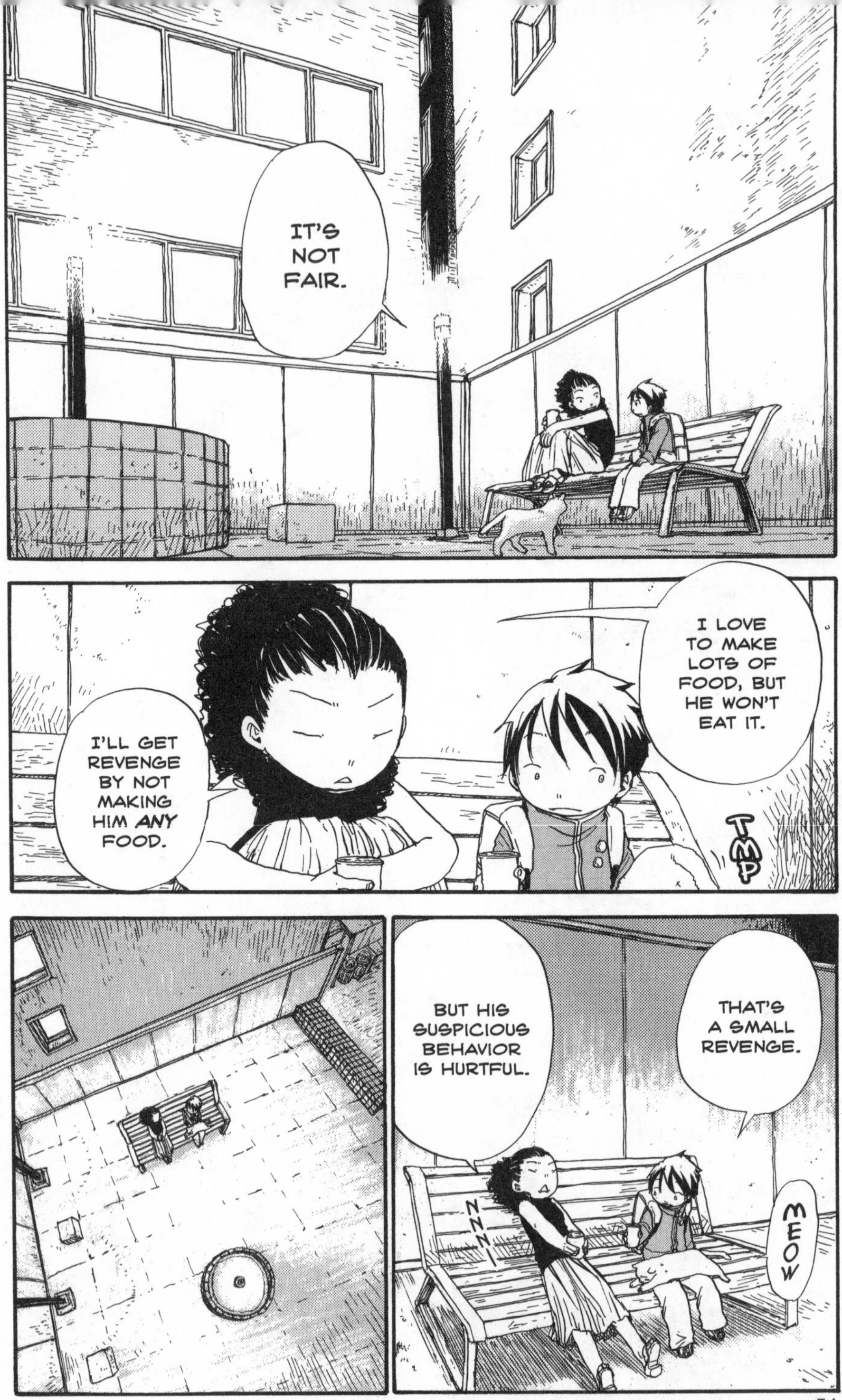
IT'S NOT FAIR.
I LOVE TO MAKE LOTS OF FOOD, BUT HE WON'T EAT IT.
TMP
I'LL GET REVENGE BY NOT MAKING HIM *ANY* FOOD.
THAT'S A SMALL REVENGE.
MEOW
BUT HIS SUSPICIOUS BEHAVIOR IS HURTFUL.
NNN

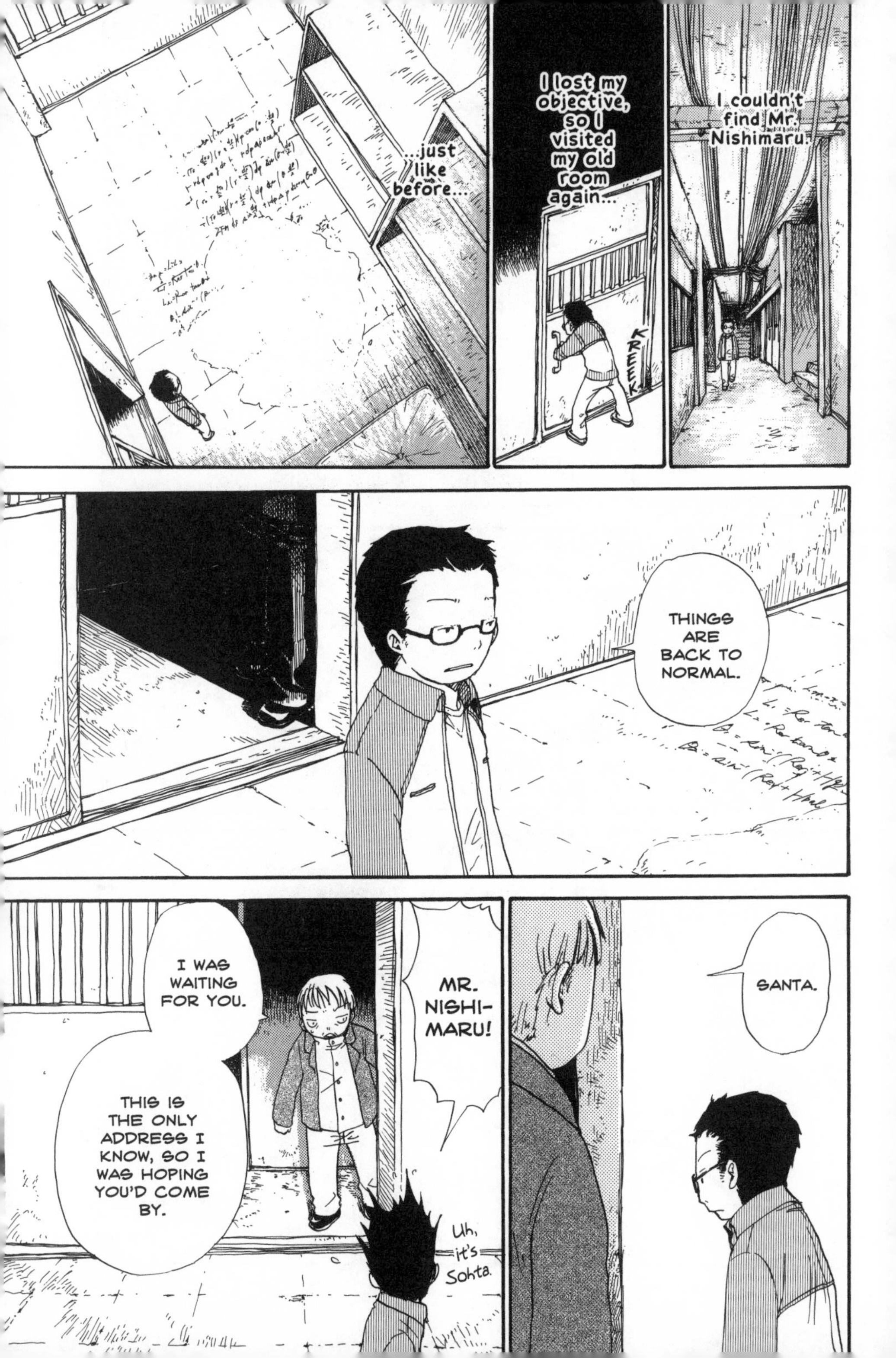
I couldn't find Mr. Nishimaru.
I lost my objective, so I visited my old room again...
KREEEK
...just like before...
THINGS ARE BACK TO NORMAL.
SANTA.
MR. NISHI-MARU!
I WAS WAITING FOR YOU.
THIS IS THE ONLY ADDRESS I KNOW, SO I WAS HOPING YOU'D COME BY.
Uh, it's Sohta.

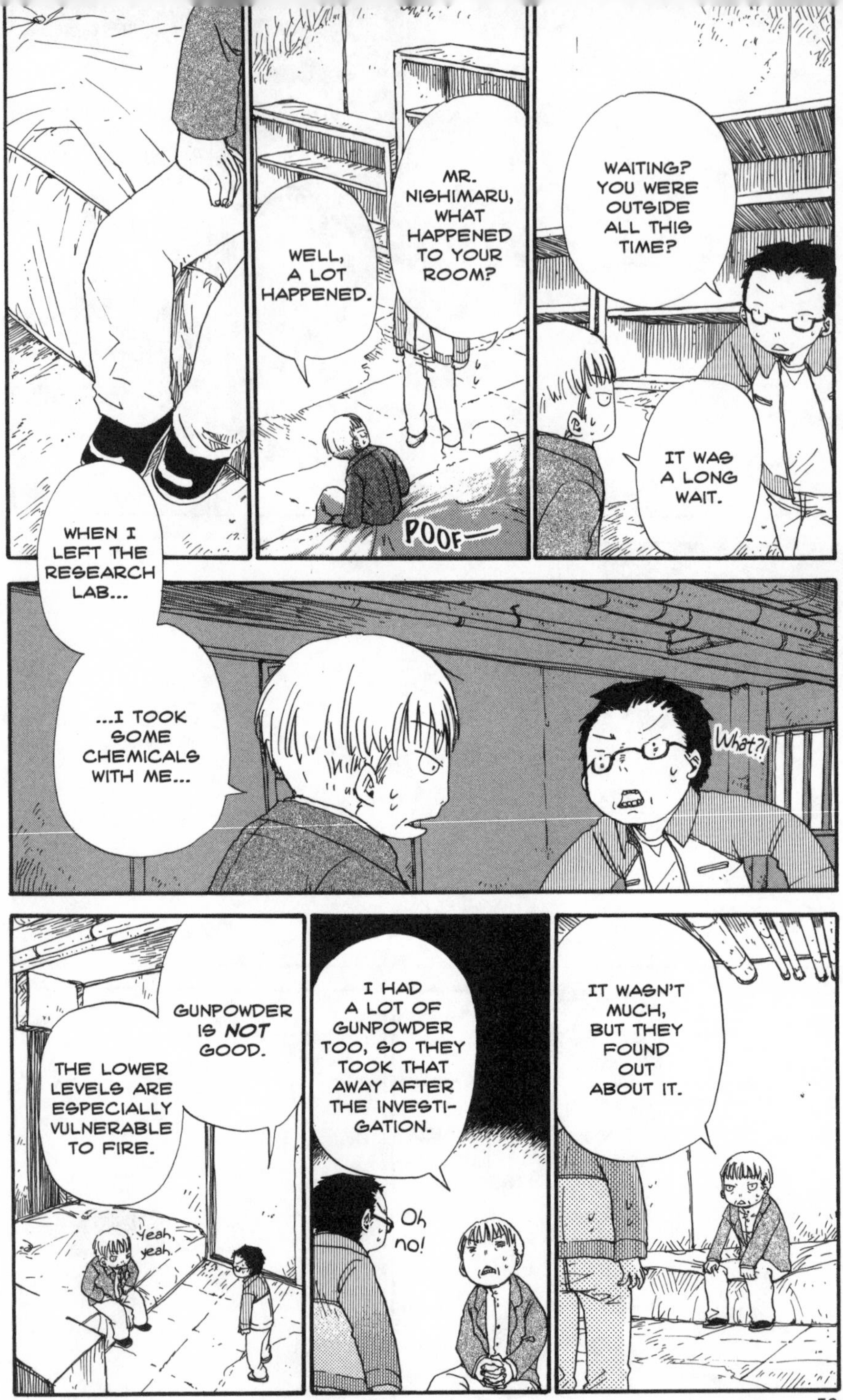
WAITING? YOU WERE OUTSIDE ALL THIS TIME?
IT WAS A LONG WAIT.
MR. NISHIMARU, WHAT HAPPENED TO YOUR ROOM?
WELL, A LOT HAPPENED.
POOF—
WHEN I LEFT THE RESEARCH LAB...
...I TOOK SOME CHEMICALS WITH ME...
What?!
IT WASN'T MUCH, BUT THEY FOUND OUT ABOUT IT.
I HAD A LOT OF GUNPOWDER TOO, SO THEY TOOK THAT AWAY AFTER THE INVESTI-GATION.
Oh no!
GUNPOWDER IS NOT GOOD.
THE LOWER LEVELS ARE ESPECIALLY VULNERABLE TO FIRE.
Yeah, yeah.

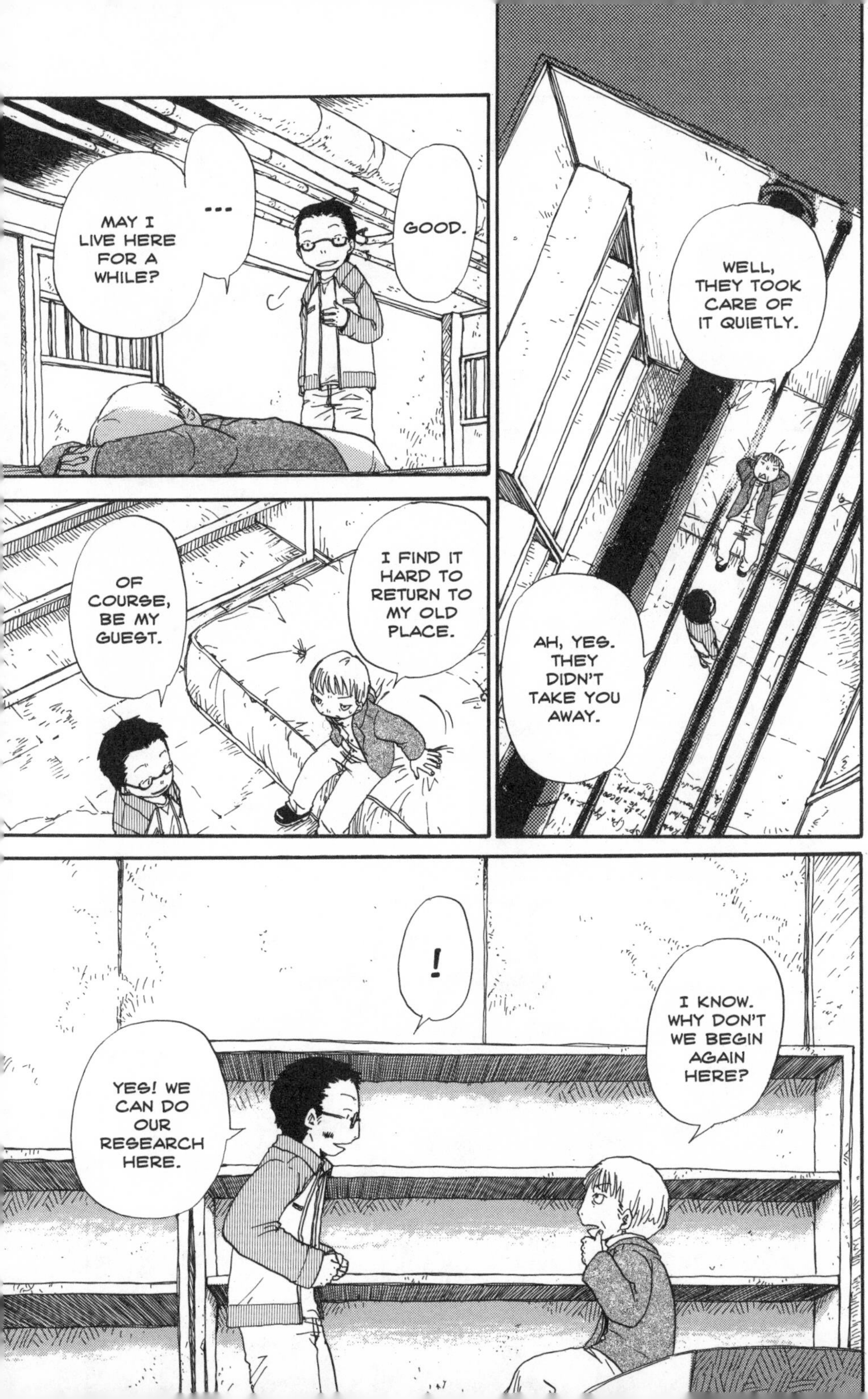
WELL, THEY TOOK CARE OF IT QUIETLY.
AH, YES. THEY DIDN'T TAKE YOU AWAY.
GOOD.
...
MAY I LIVE HERE FOR A WHILE?
I FIND IT HARD TO RETURN TO MY OLD PLACE.
OF COURSE, BE MY GUEST.
I KNOW. WHY DON'T WE BEGIN AGAIN HERE?
!
YES! WE CAN DO OUR RESEARCH HERE.

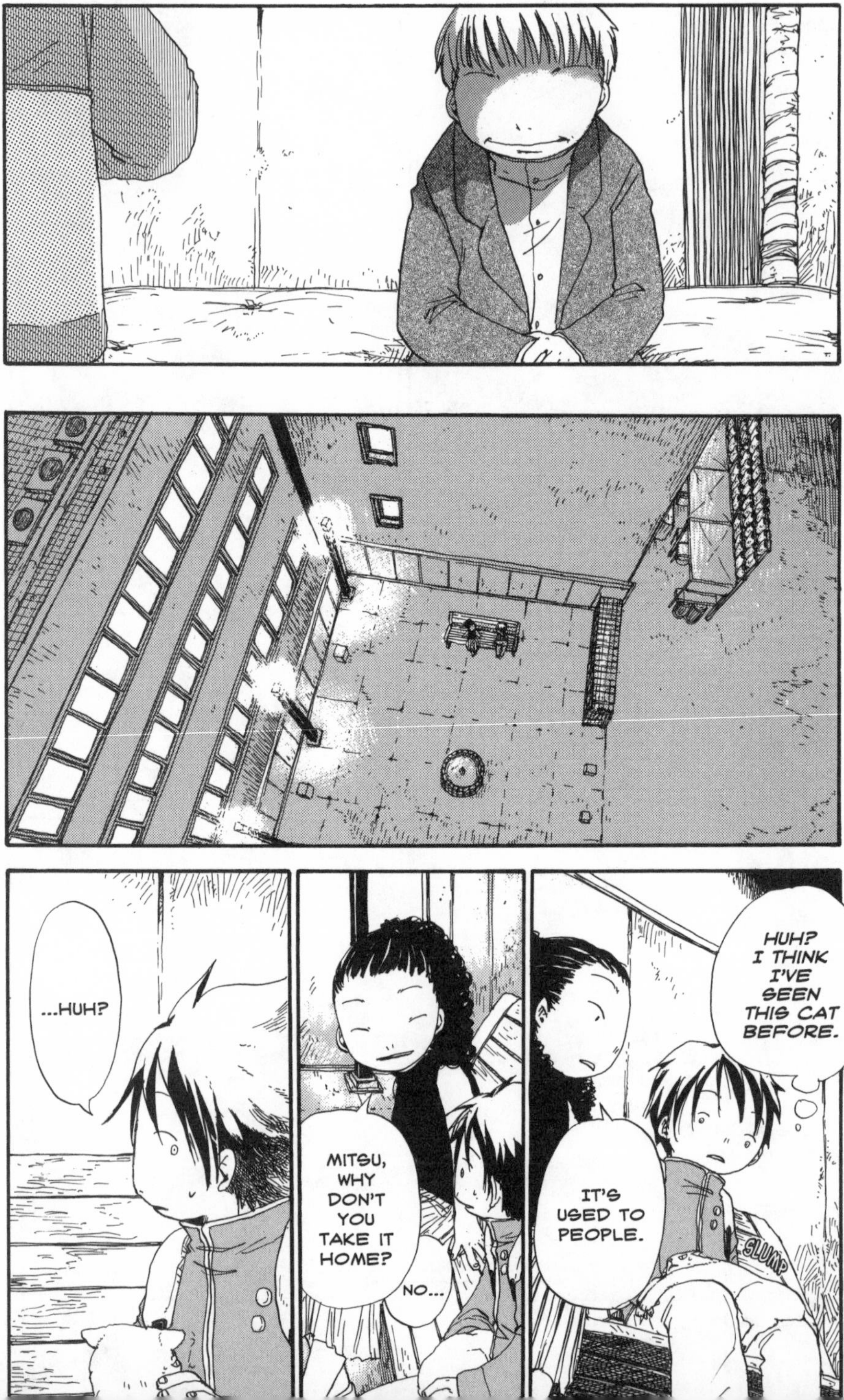
HUH? I THINK I'VE SEEN THIS CAT BEFORE.
IT'S USED TO PEOPLE.
SLUMP
MITSU, WHY DON'T YOU TAKE IT HOME?
NO...
...HUH?

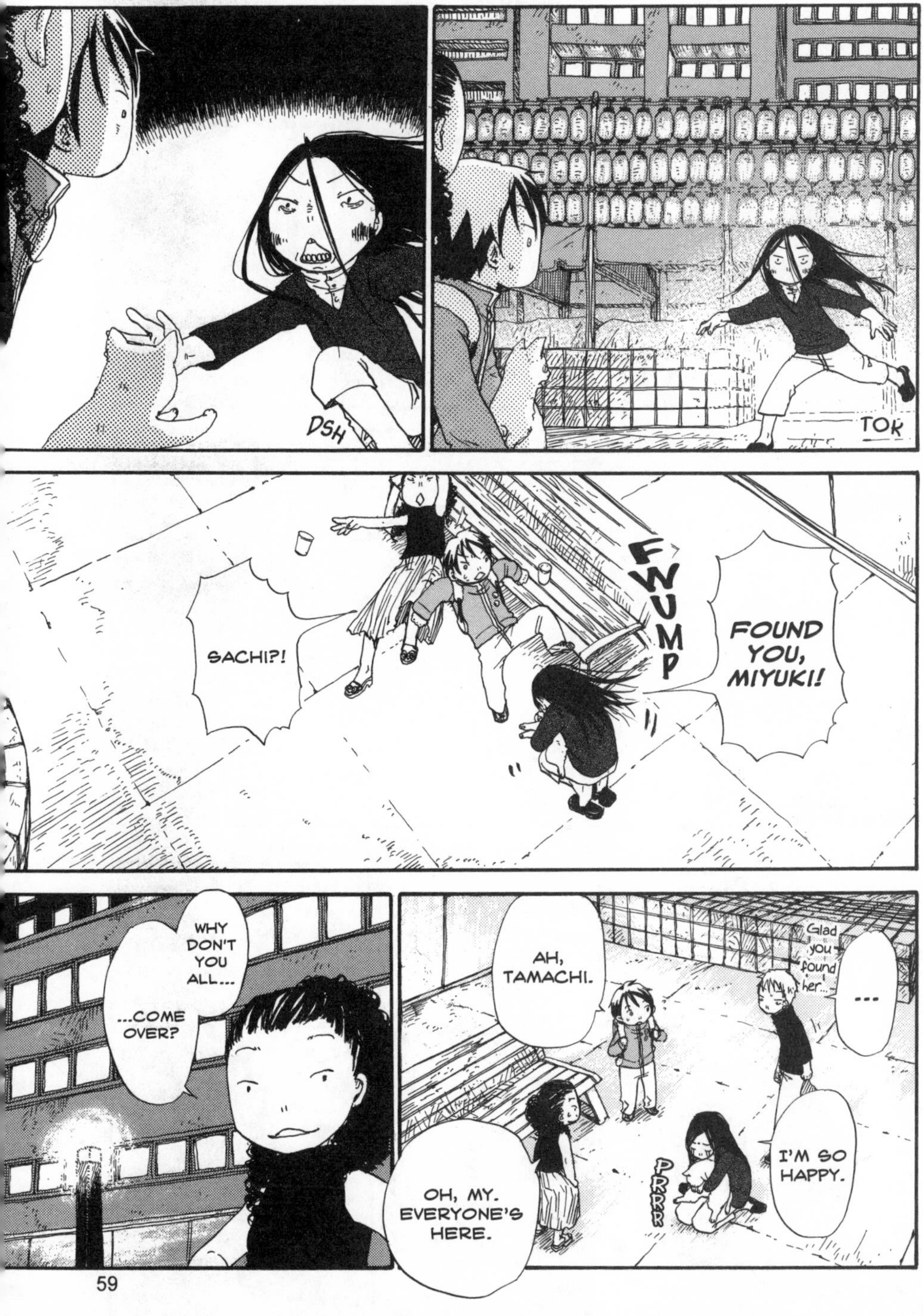
TOK
DSH
FOUND YOU, MIYUKI!
FWUMP
SACHI?!
Glad you found her...
...
AH, TAMACHI.
I'M SO HAPPY.
PRRRR
OH, MY. EVERYONE'S HERE.
WHY DON'T YOU ALL...
...COME OVER?

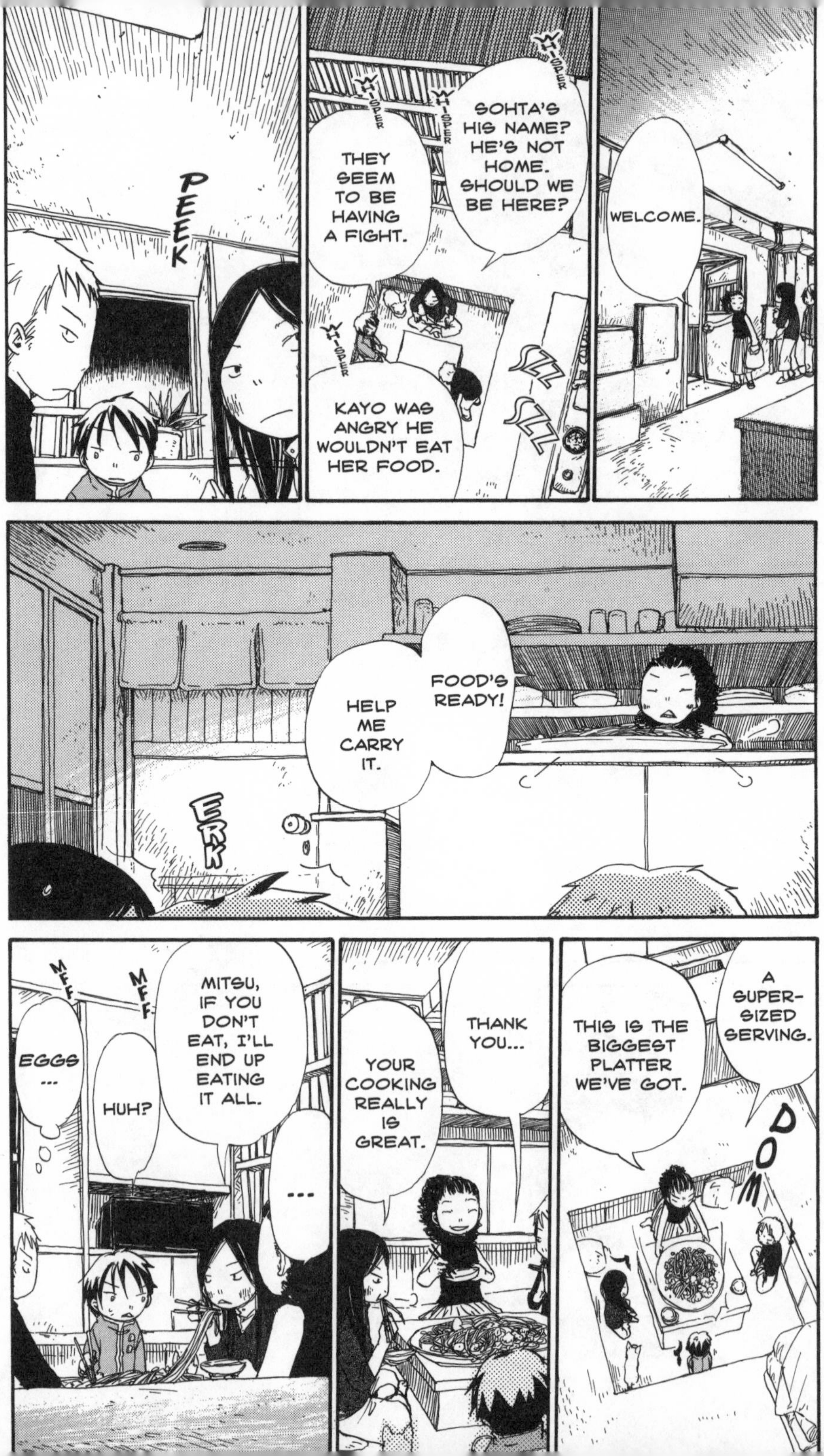
WELCOME.
WHISPER
SOHTA'S HIS NAME? HE'S NOT HOME. SHOULD WE BE HERE?
WHISPER
THEY SEEM TO BE HAVING A FIGHT.
WHISPER
KAYO WAS ANGRY HE WOULDN'T EAT HER FOOD.
ZZZ
ZZZ
PEEK
FOOD'S READY!
HELP ME CARRY IT.
ERK
A SUPER-SIZED SERVING.
THIS IS THE BIGGEST PLATTER WE'VE GOT.
DOM
THANK YOU...
YOUR COOKING REALLY IS GREAT.
...
MITSU, IF YOU DON'T EAT, I'LL END UP EATING IT ALL.
MFF
HUH?
MFF
EGGS...

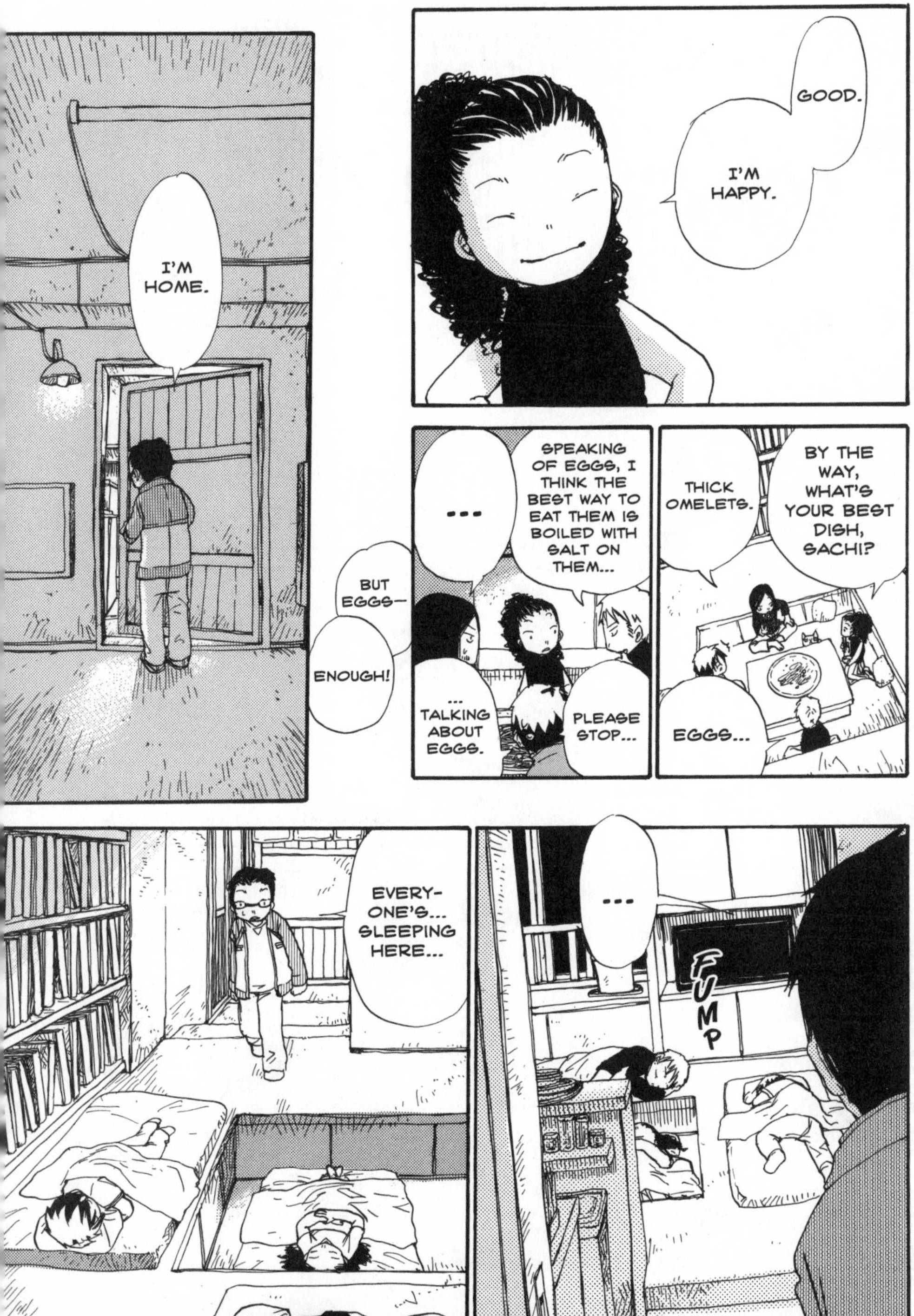
GOOD.
I'M HAPPY.
BY THE WAY, WHAT'S YOUR BEST DISH, SACHI?
THICK OMELETS.
EGGS...
SPEAKING OF EGGS, I THINK THE BEST WAY TO EAT THEM IS BOILED WITH SALT ON THEM...
...
PLEASE STOP...
... TALKING ABOUT EGGS.
BUT EGGS—
ENOUGH!
I'M HOME.
...
FUMP
EVERY-ONE'S... SLEEPING HERE...

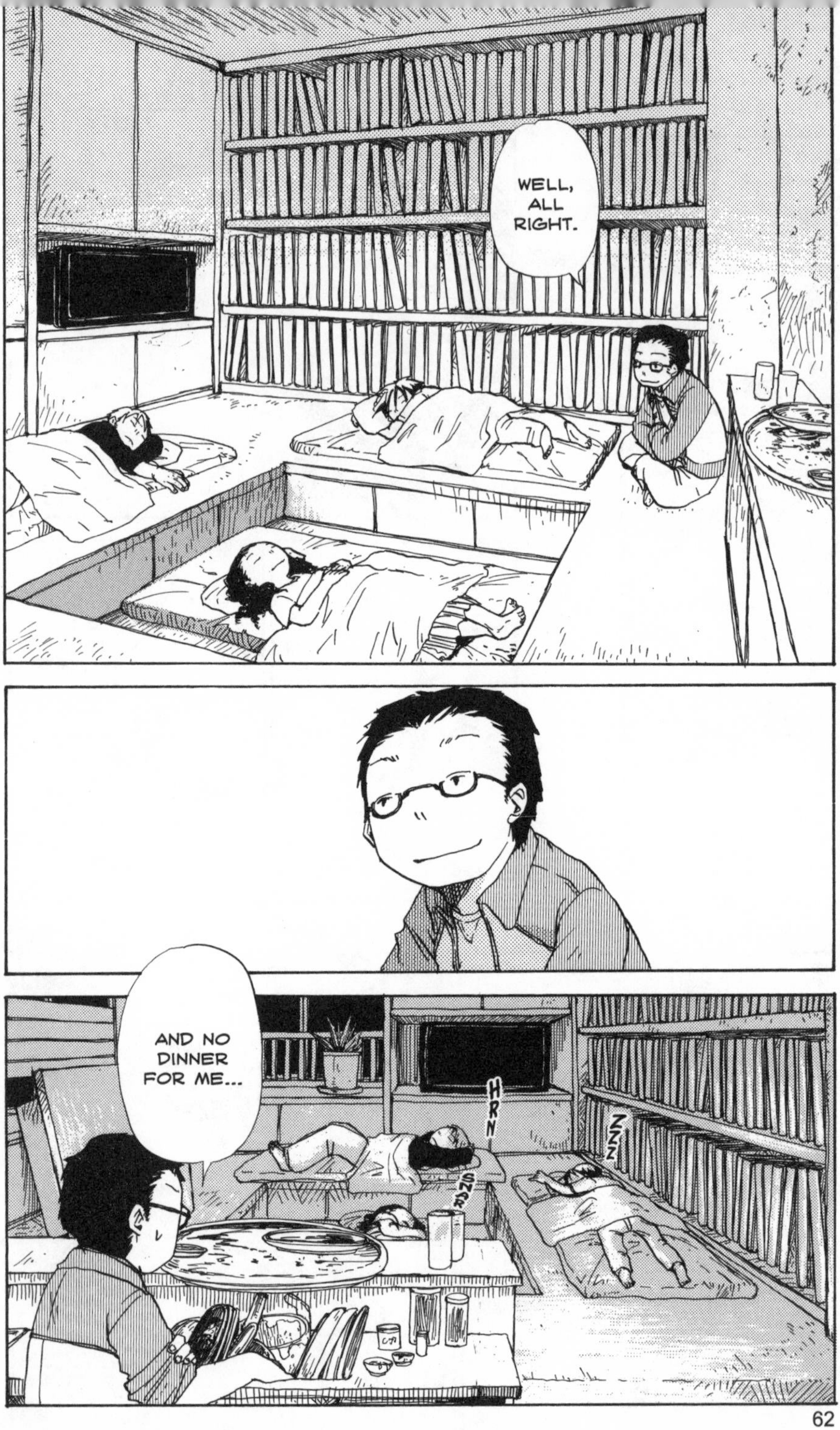
WELL, ALL RIGHT.
AND NO DINNER FOR ME...
HRN
ZZZ
SNAR

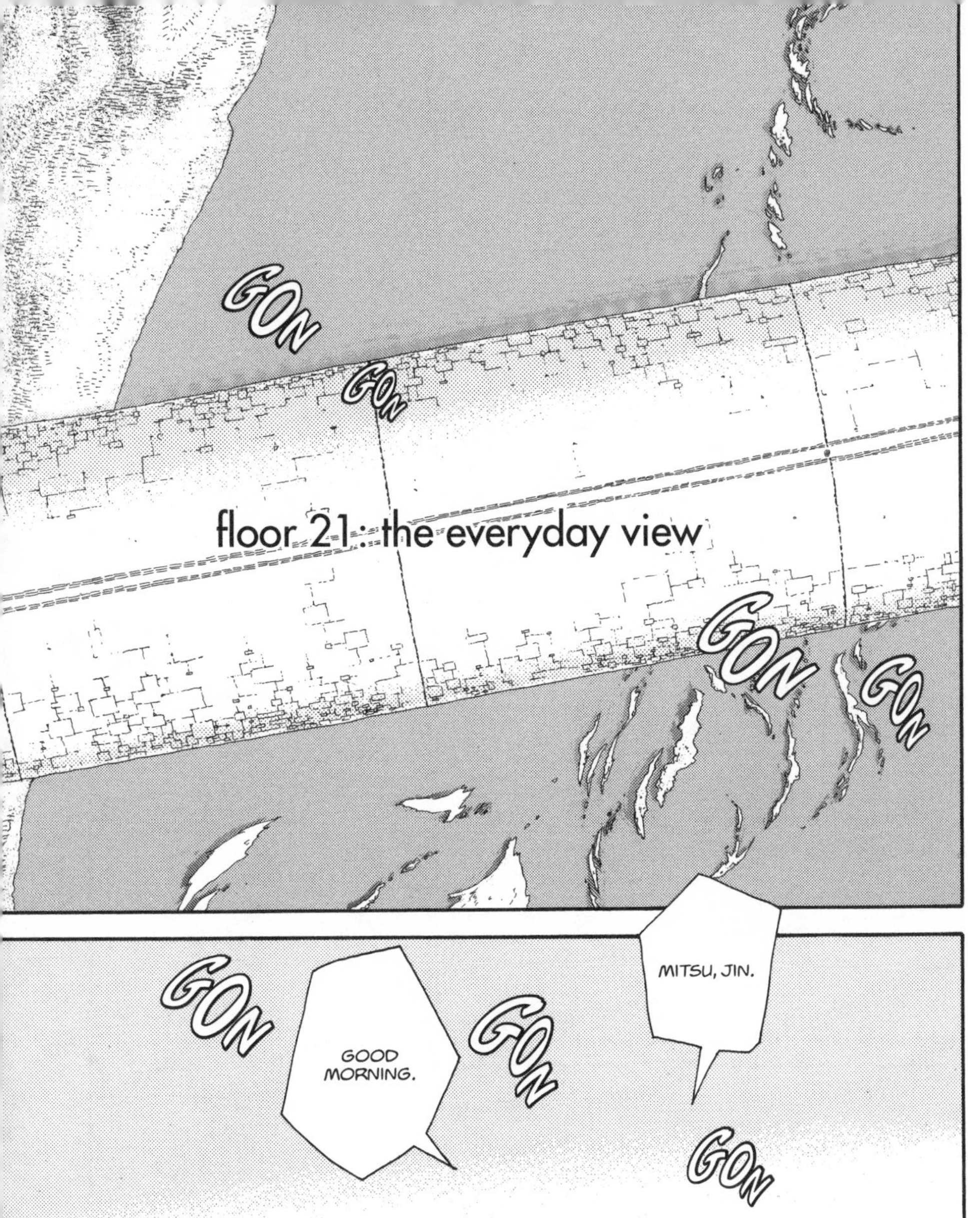

floor 21: the everyday view
GON GON
GON GON
MITSU, JIN.
GON
GON
GOOD MORNING.
GON
MORNING.

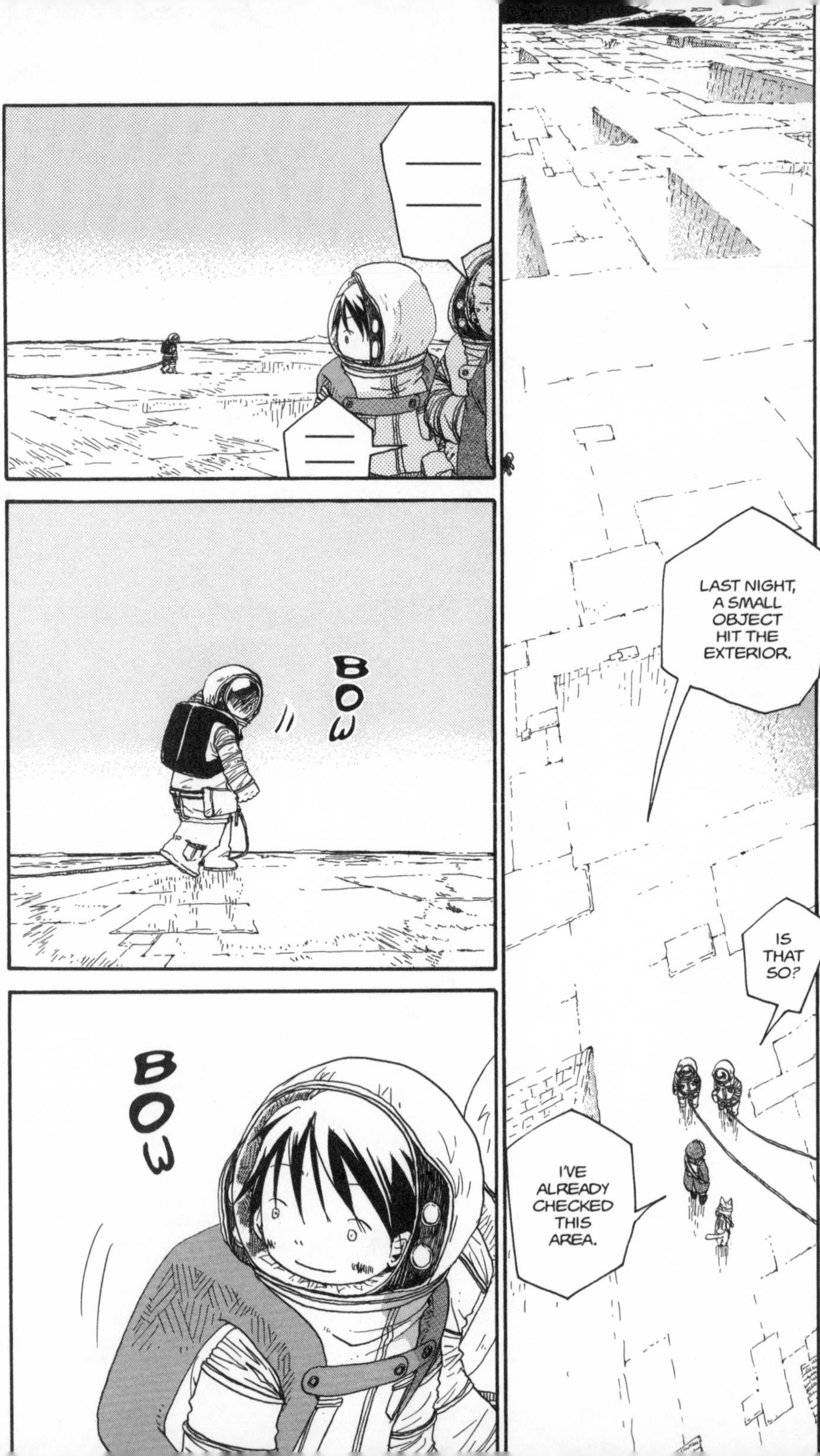
LAST NIGHT, A SMALL OBJECT HIT THE EXTERIOR.
IS THAT SO?
I'VE ALREADY CHECKED THIS AREA.
BOW
BOW

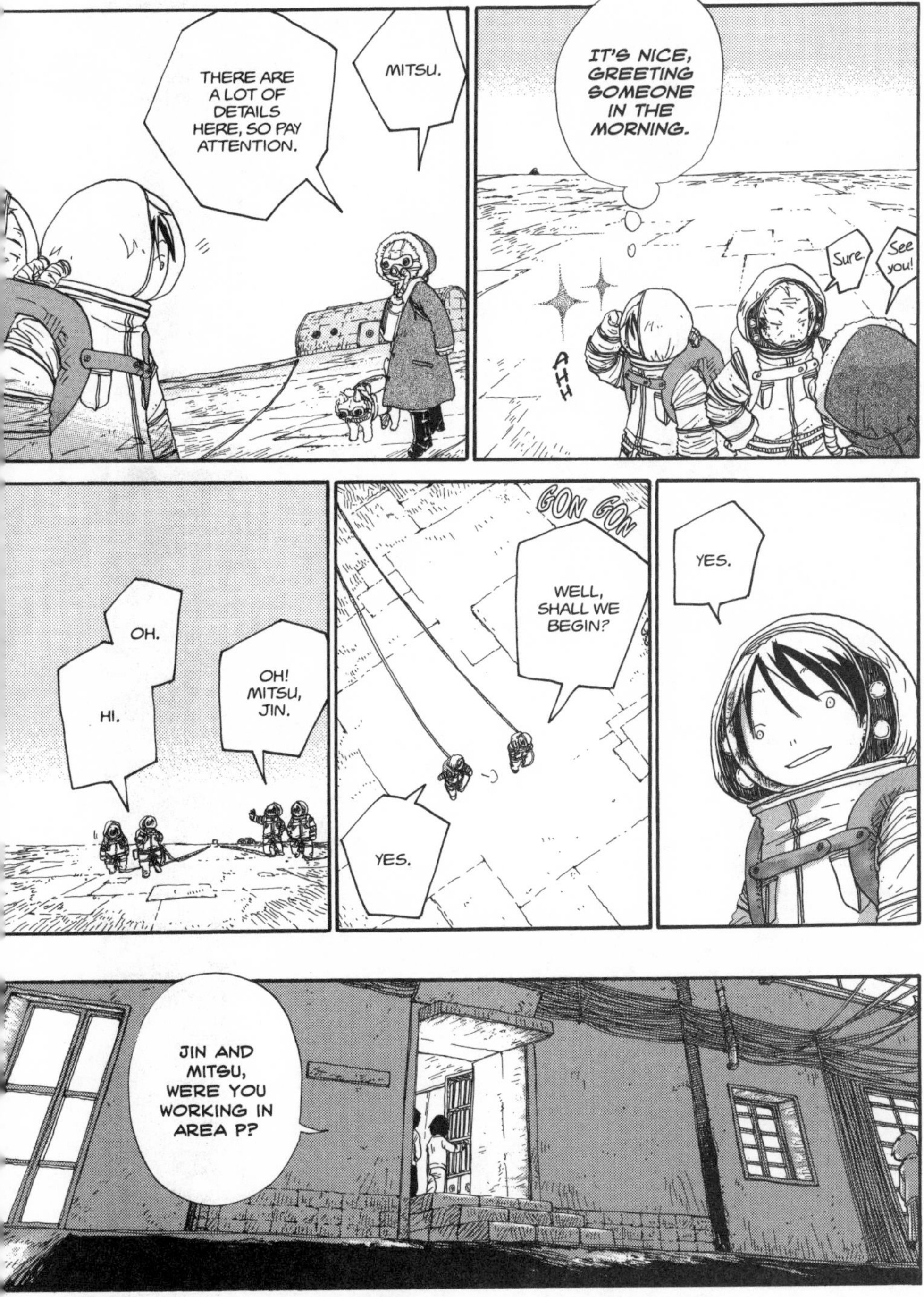
See you!
Sure.
IT'S NICE, GREETING SOMEONE IN THE MORNING.
AHH
MITSU.
THERE ARE A LOT OF DETAILS HERE, SO PAY ATTENTION.
YES.
GON GON
WELL, SHALL WE BEGIN?
YES.
OH! MITSU, JIN.
OH.
HI.
JIN AND MITSU, WERE YOU WORKING IN AREA P?

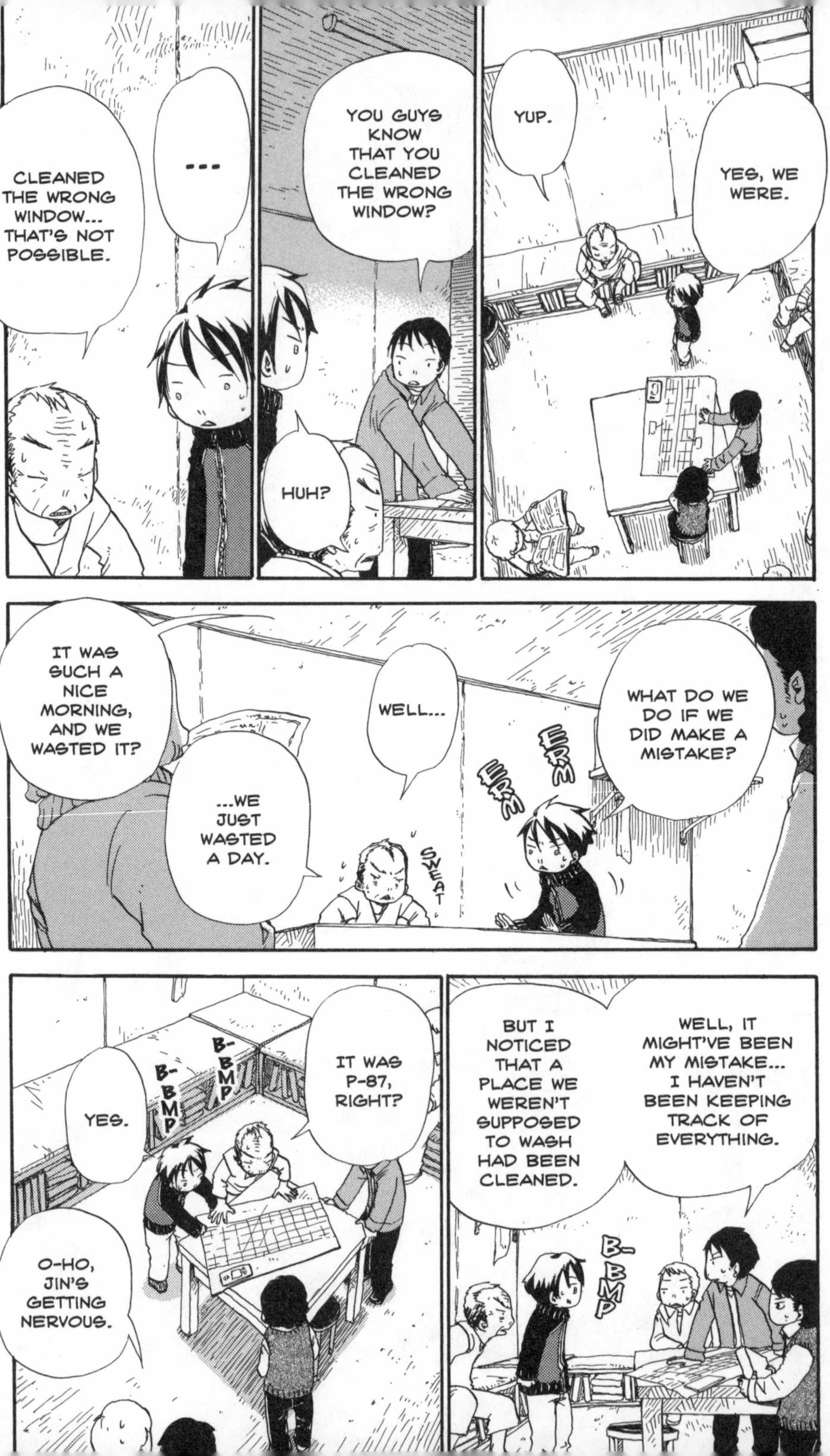
YES, WE WERE.
YUP.
YOU GUYS KNOW THAT YOU CLEANED THE WRONG WINDOW?
HUH?
...
CLEANED THE WRONG WINDOW... THAT'S NOT POSSIBLE.
WHAT DO WE DO IF WE DID MAKE A MISTAKE?
ERM
ERM
WELL...
SWEAT
IT WAS SUCH A NICE MORNING, AND WE WASTED IT?
...WE JUST WASTED A DAY.
WELL, IT MIGHT'VE BEEN MY MISTAKE... I HAVEN'T BEEN KEEPING TRACK OF EVERYTHING.
BUT I NOTICED THAT A PLACE WE WEREN'T SUPPOSED TO WASH HAD BEEN CLEANED.
B-BMP
IT WAS P-87, RIGHT?
B-BMP
B-BMP
YES.
O-HO, JIN'S GETTING NERVOUS.

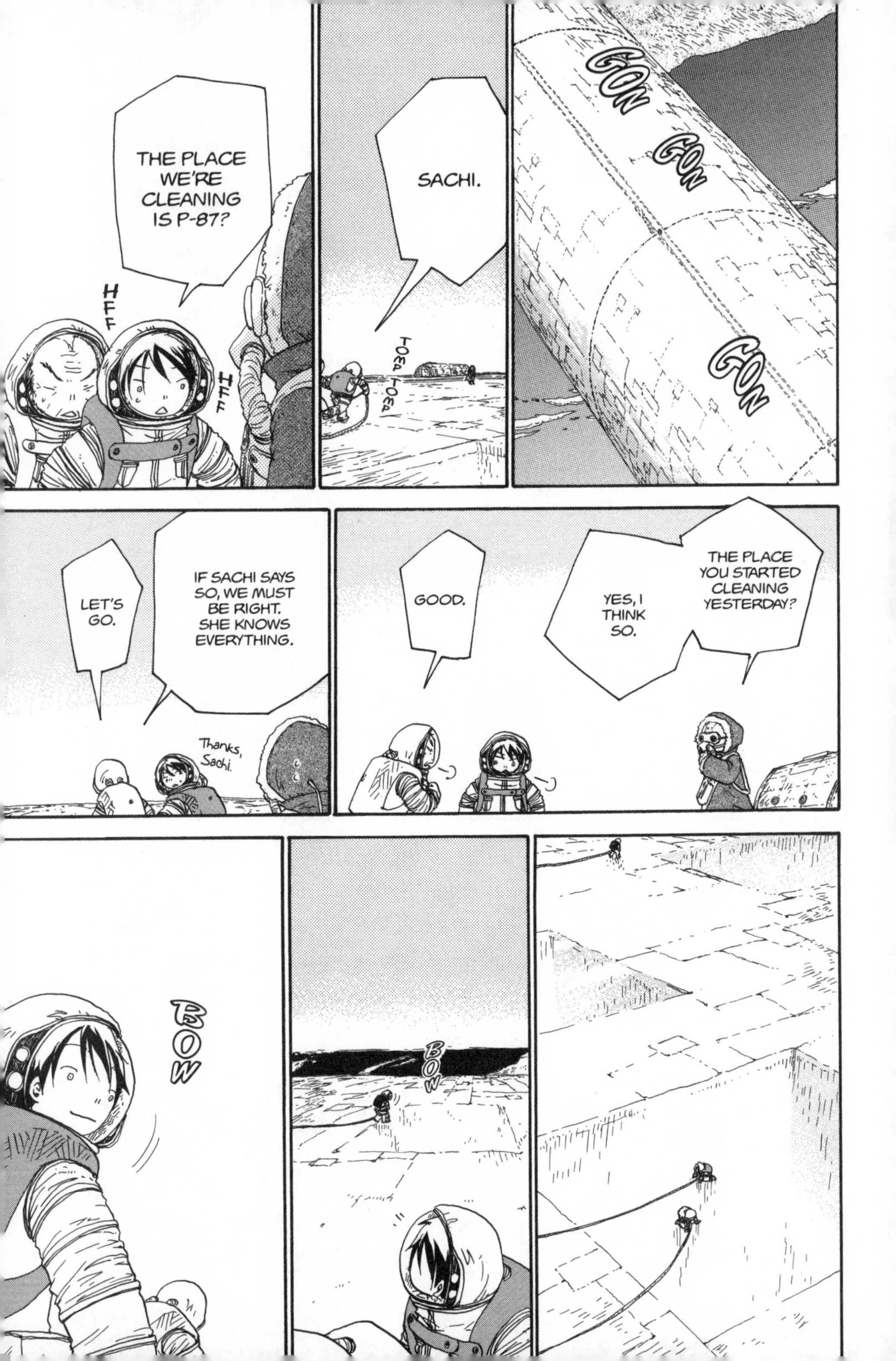
GON
GON
GON
SACHI.
TOMP TOMP
THE PLACE WE'RE CLEANING IS P-87?
HFF
HFF
THE PLACE YOU STARTED CLEANING YESTERDAY?
YES, I THINK SO.
GOOD.
IF SACHI SAYS SO, WE MUST BE RIGHT. SHE KNOWS EVERYTHING.
LET'S GO.
Thanks, Sachi.
BOW
BOW

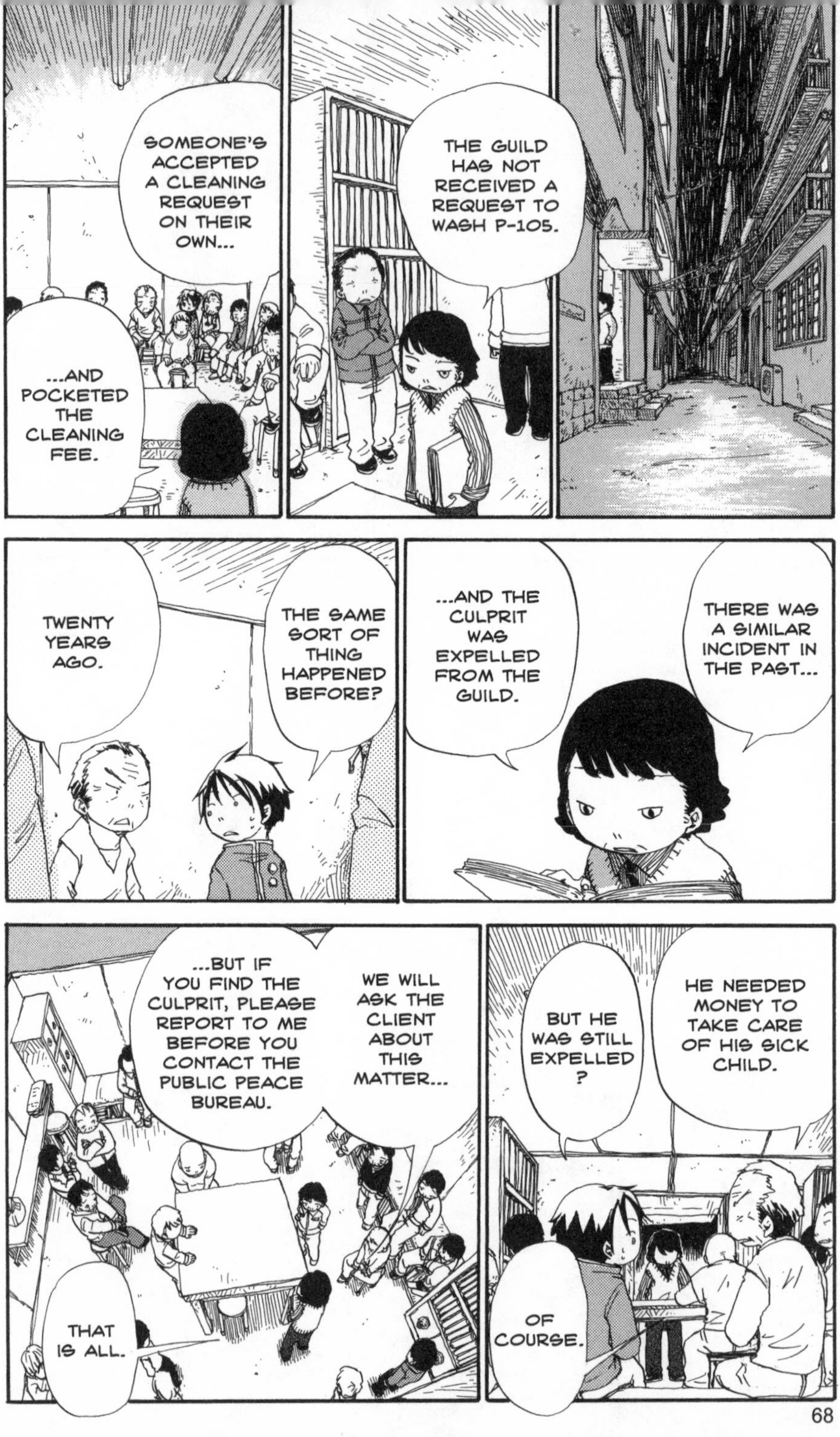
THE GUILD HAS NOT RECEIVED A REQUEST TO WASH P-105.
SOMEONE'S ACCEPTED A CLEANING REQUEST ON THEIR OWN...
...AND POCKETED THE CLEANING FEE.
THERE WAS A SIMILAR INCIDENT IN THE PAST...
...AND THE CULPRIT WAS EXPELLED FROM THE GUILD.
THE SAME SORT OF THING HAPPENED BEFORE?
TWENTY YEARS AGO.
HE NEEDED MONEY TO TAKE CARE OF HIS SICK CHILD.
BUT HE WAS STILL EXPELLED?
OF COURSE.
WE WILL ASK THE CLIENT ABOUT THIS MATTER...
...BUT IF YOU FIND THE CULPRIT, PLEASE REPORT TO ME BEFORE YOU CONTACT THE PUBLIC PEACE BUREAU.
THAT IS ALL.

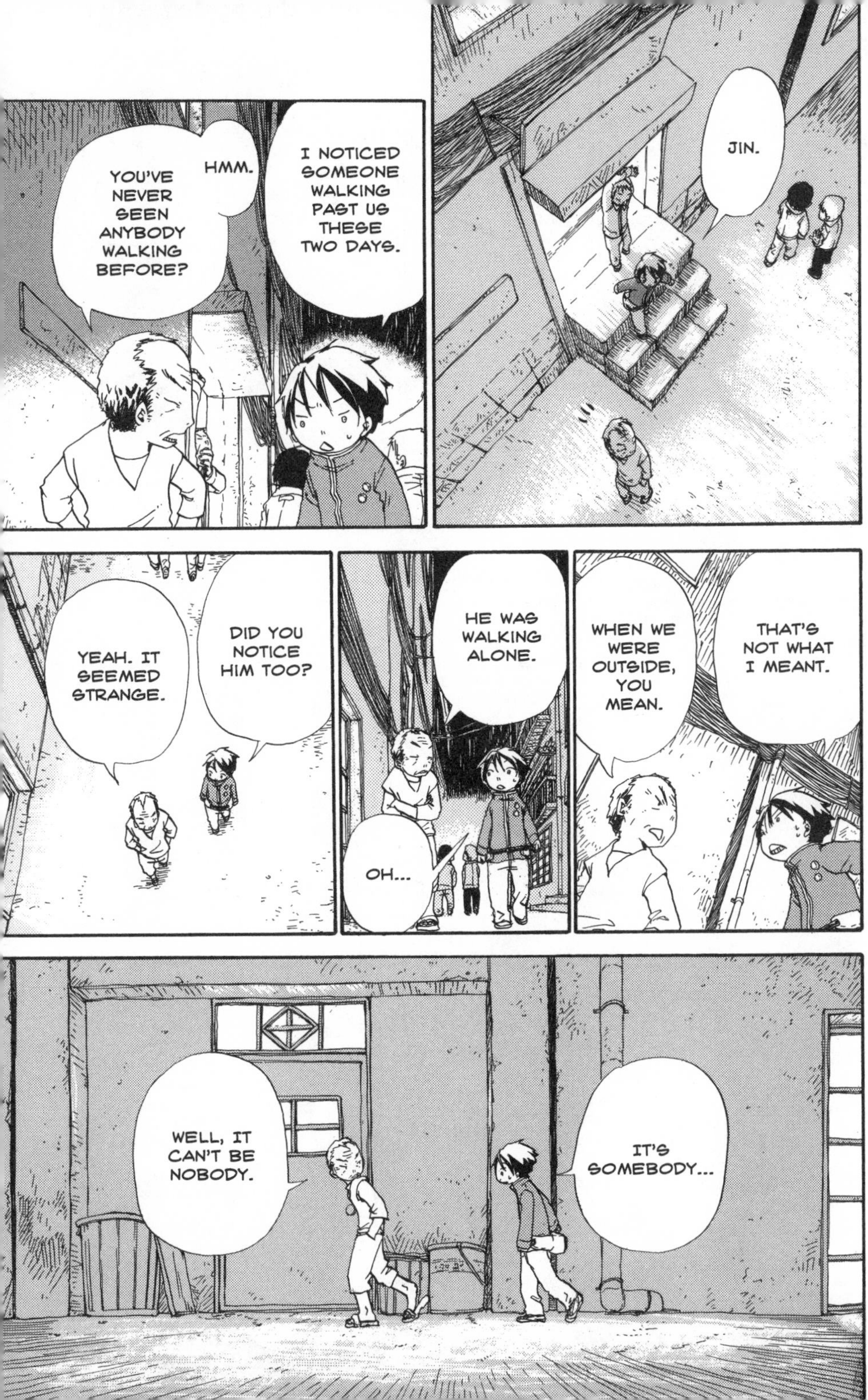
JIN.
I NOTICED SOMEONE WALKING PAST US THESE TWO DAYS.
HMM.
YOU'VE NEVER SEEN ANYBODY WALKING BEFORE?
THAT'S NOT WHAT I MEANT.
WHEN WE WERE OUTSIDE, YOU MEAN.
HE WAS WALKING ALONE.
OH...
DID YOU NOTICE HIM TOO?
YEAH. IT SEEMED STRANGE.
IT'S SOMEBODY...
WELL, IT CAN'T BE NOBODY.

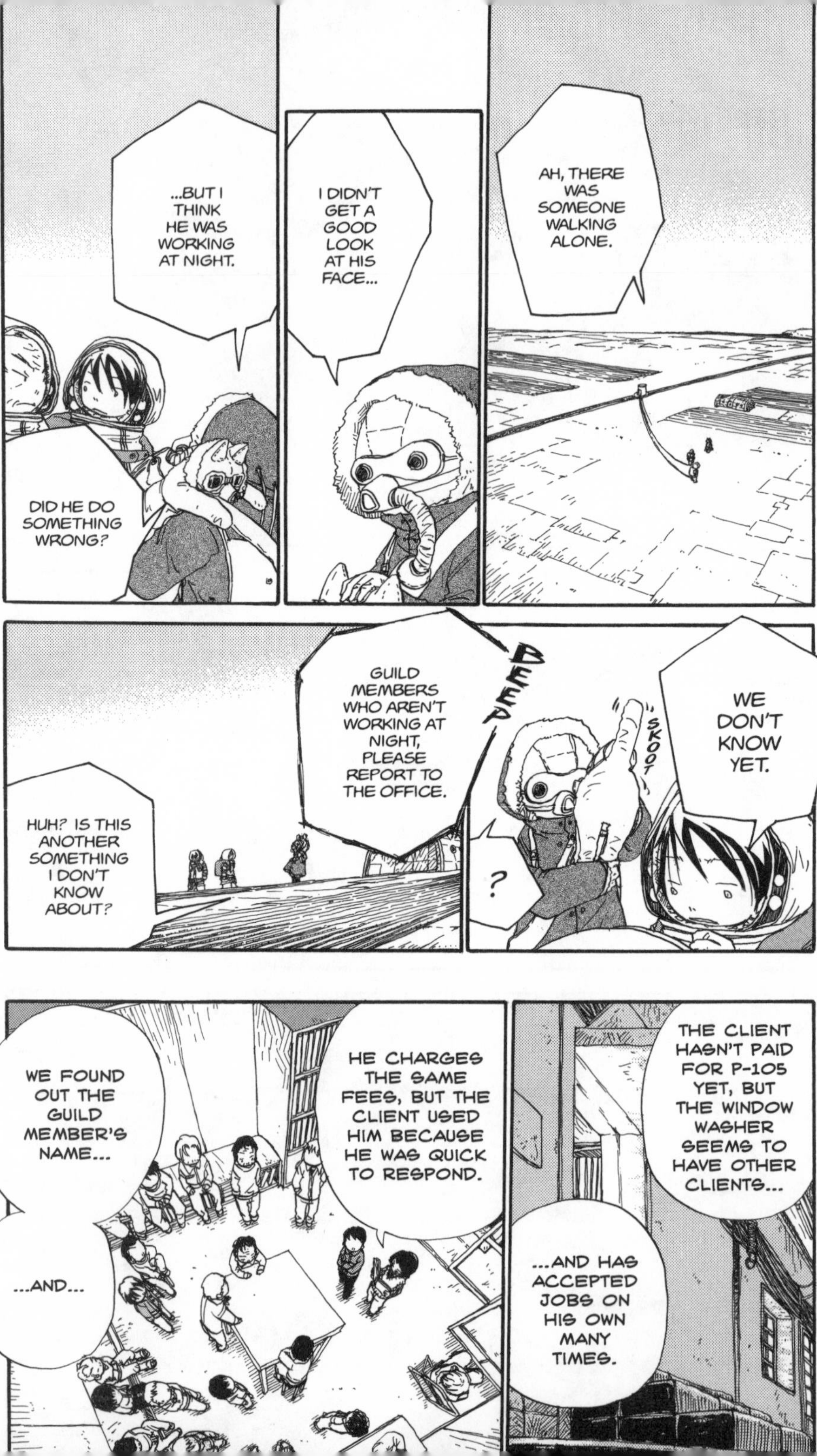
AH, THERE WAS SOMEONE WALKING ALONE.
I DIDN'T GET A GOOD LOOK AT HIS FACE...
...BUT I THINK HE WAS WORKING AT NIGHT.
DID HE DO SOMETHING WRONG?
WE DON'T KNOW YET.
SKOOT
?
BEEP
GUILD MEMBERS WHO AREN'T WORKING AT NIGHT, PLEASE REPORT TO THE OFFICE.
HUH? IS THIS ANOTHER SOMETHING I DON'T KNOW ABOUT?
THE CLIENT HASN'T PAID FOR P-105 YET, BUT THE WINDOW WASHER SEEMS TO HAVE OTHER CLIENTS...
...AND HAS ACCEPTED JOBS ON HIS OWN MANY TIMES.
HE CHARGES THE SAME FEES, BUT THE CLIENT USED HIM BECAUSE HE WAS QUICK TO RESPOND.
WE FOUND OUT THE GUILD MEMBER'S NAME...
...AND...

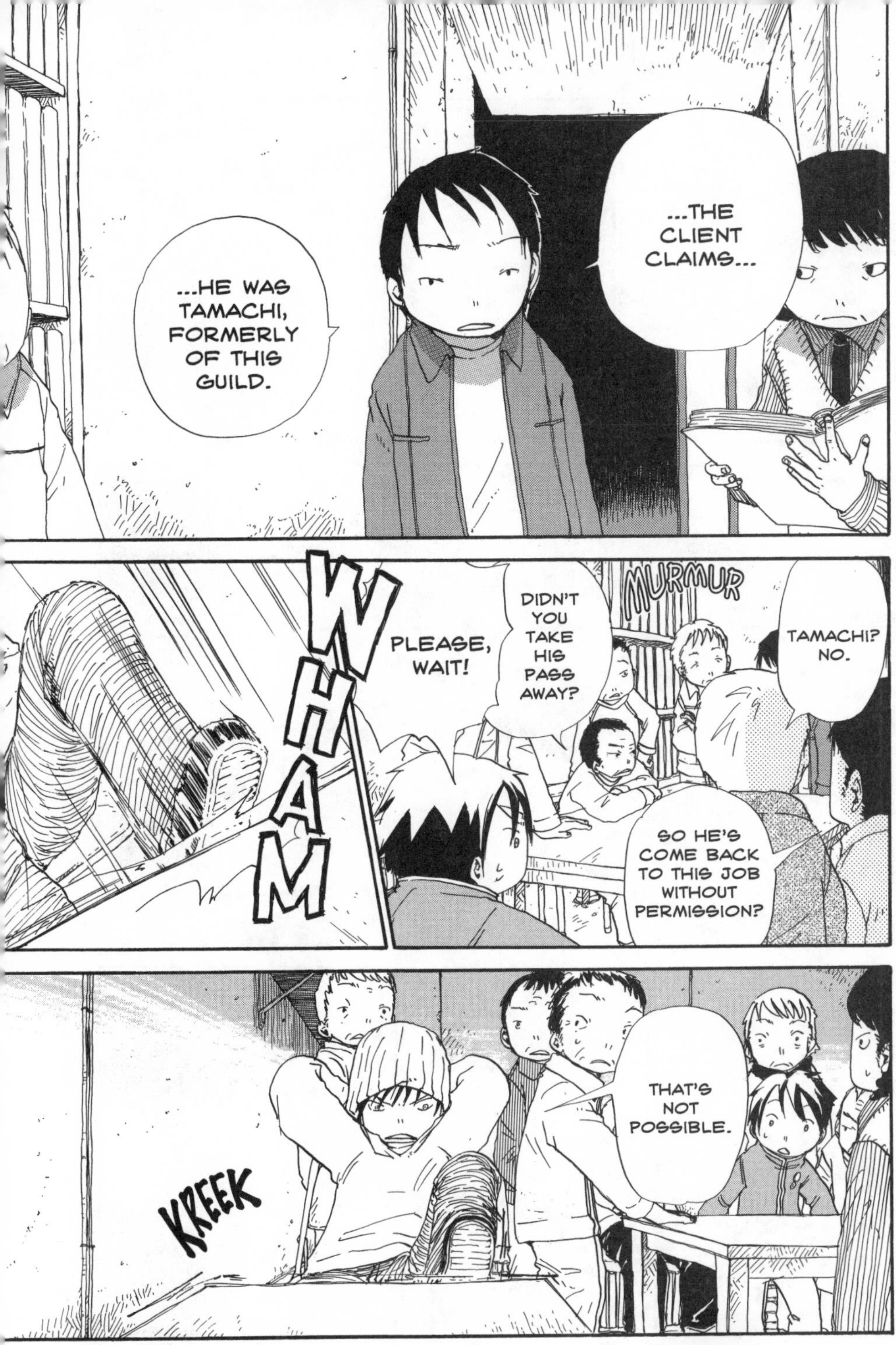
...THE CLIENT CLAIMS...
...HE WAS TAMACHI, FORMERLY OF THIS GUILD.
TAMACHI? NO.
MURMUR
DIDN'T YOU TAKE HIS PASS AWAY?
SO HE'S COME BACK TO THIS JOB WITHOUT PERMISSION?
PLEASE, WAIT!
WHAM
THAT'S NOT POSSIBLE.
KREEK

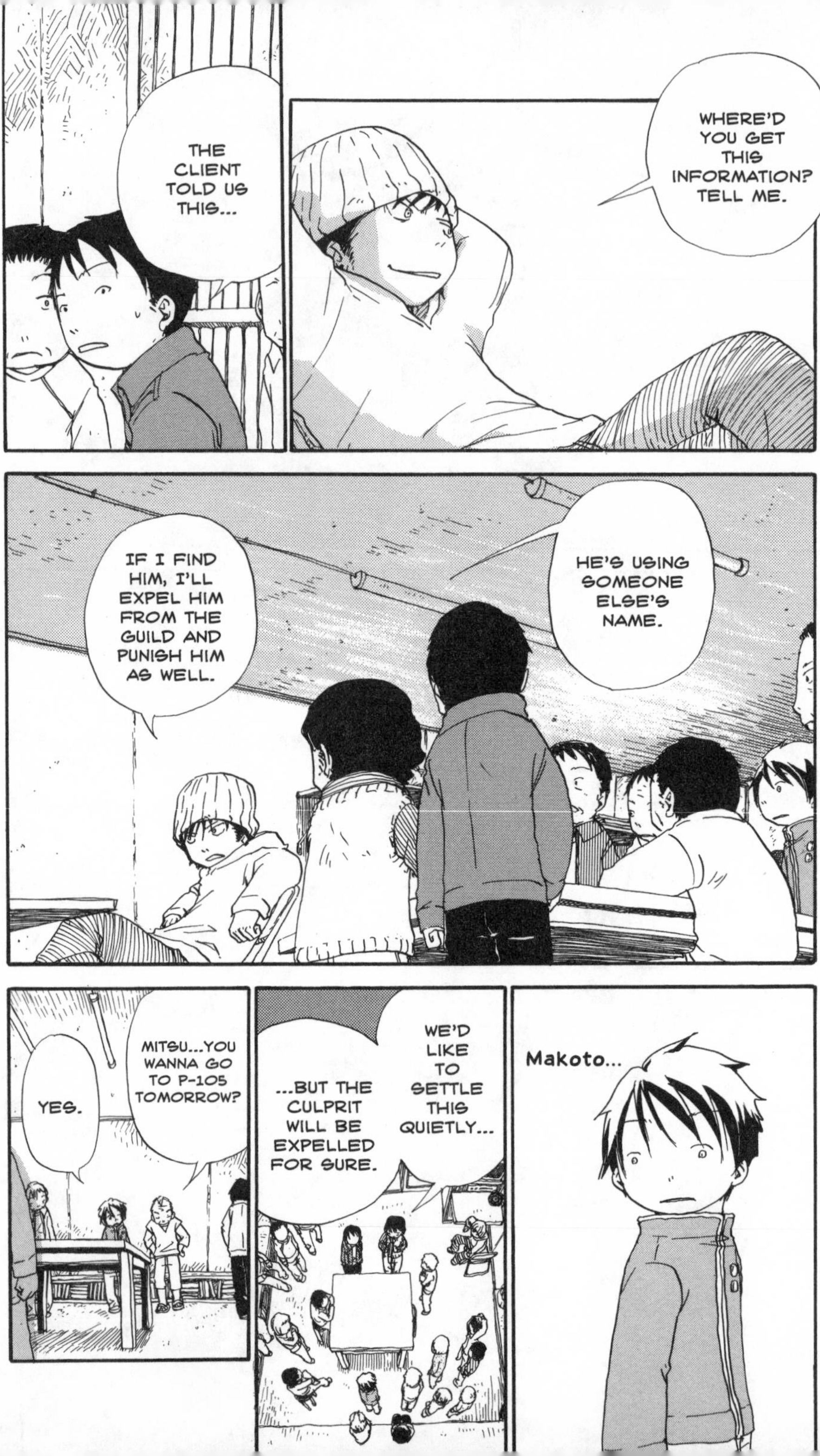
WHERE'D YOU GET THIS INFORMATION? TELL ME.
THE CLIENT TOLD US THIS...
HE'S USING SOMEONE ELSE'S NAME.
IF I FIND HIM, I'LL EXPEL HIM FROM THE GUILD AND PUNISH HIM AS WELL.
Makoto...
WE'D LIKE TO SETTLE THIS QUIETLY...
...BUT THE CULPRIT WILL BE EXPELLED FOR SURE.
MITSU...YOU WANNA GO TO P-105 TOMORROW?
YES.

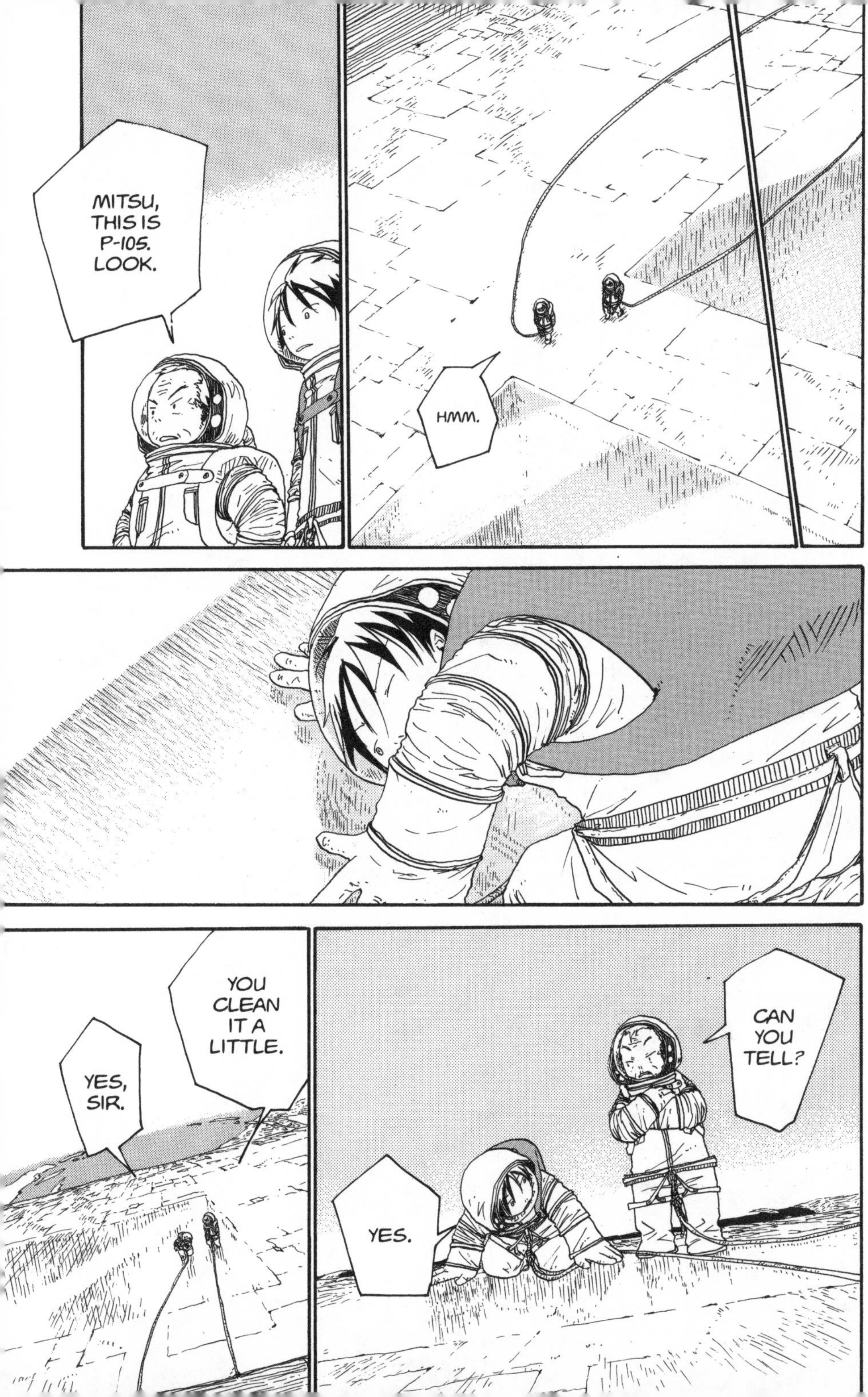
HMM.
MITSU, THIS IS P-105. LOOK.
CAN YOU TELL?
YES.
YOU CLEAN IT A LITTLE.
YES, SIR.

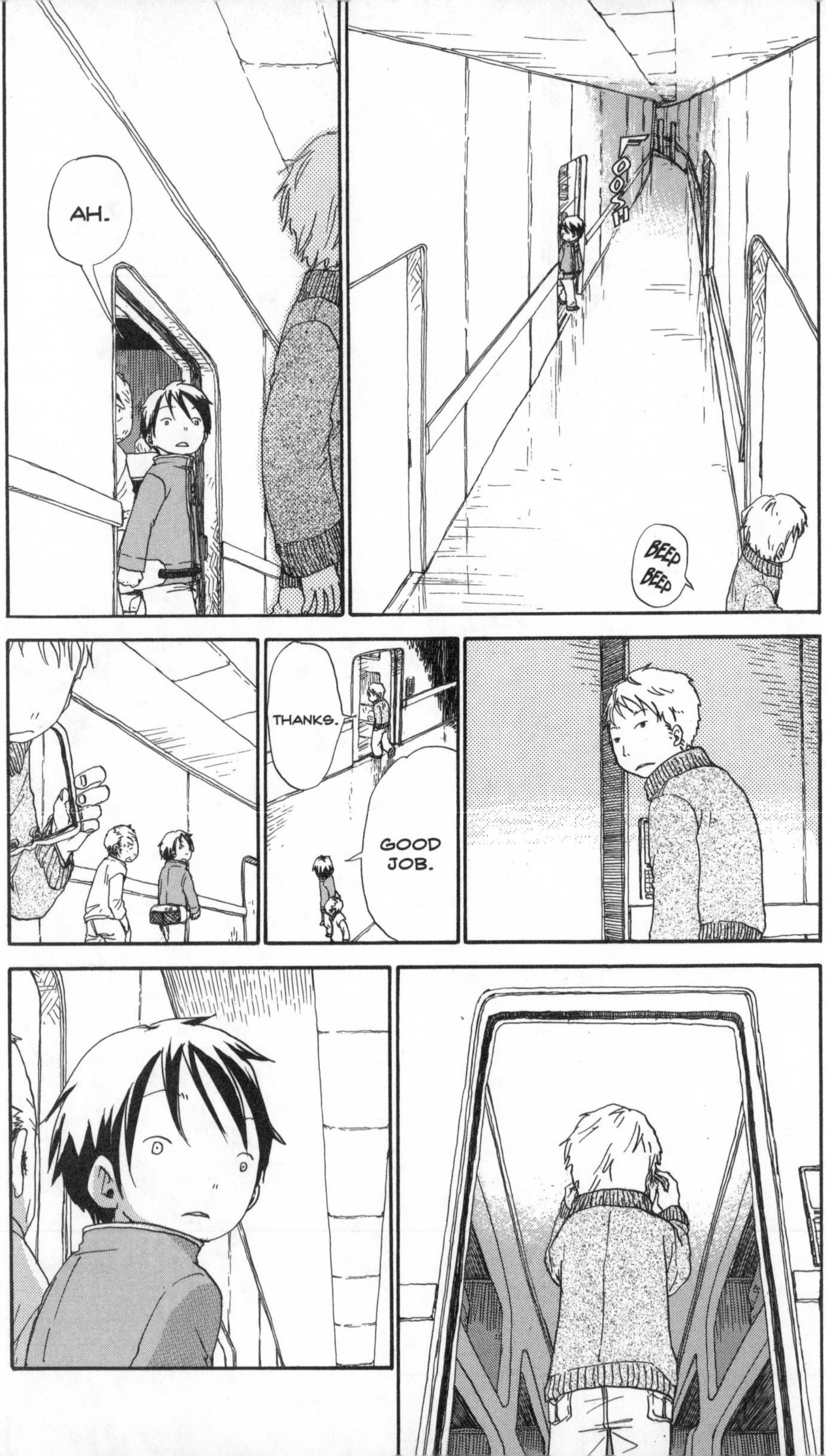
WOOSH
BEEP BEEP
AH.
THANKS.
GOOD JOB.

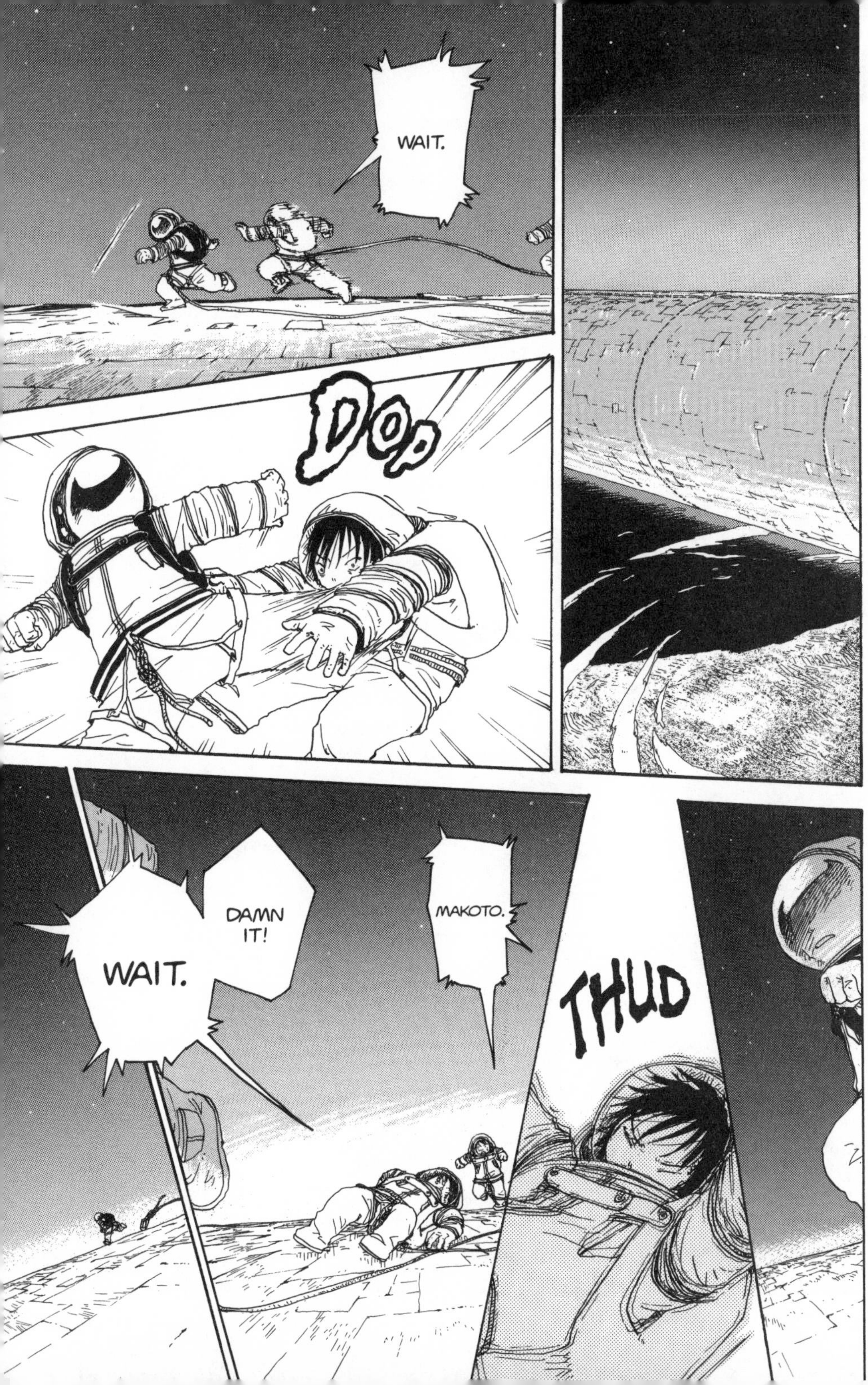
WAIT.
DOP
THUD
MAKOTO.
DAMN IT!
WAIT.

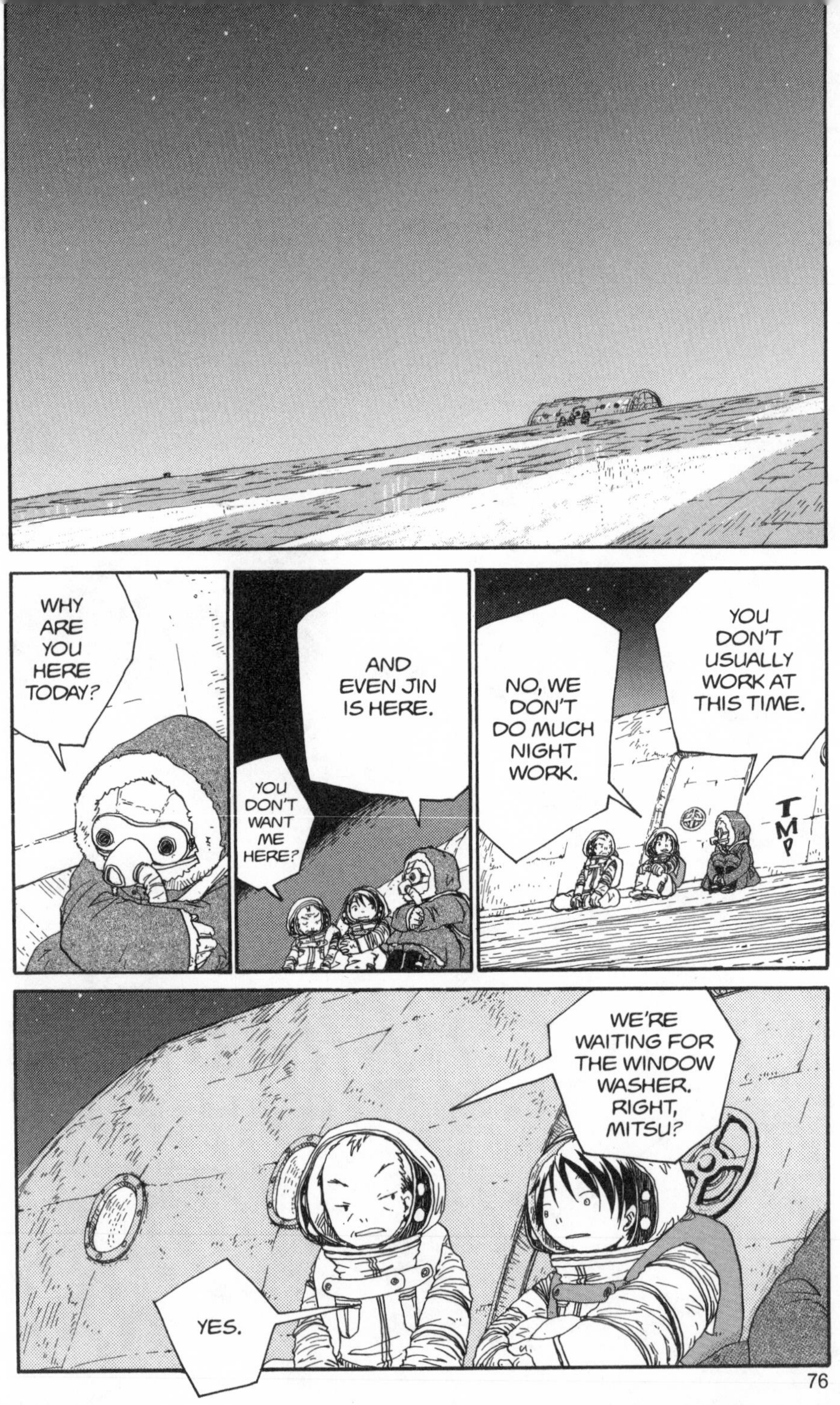
YOU DON'T USUALLY WORK AT THIS TIME.
TMP
NO, WE DON'T DO MUCH NIGHT WORK.
AND EVEN JIN IS HERE.
YOU DON'T WANT ME HERE?
WHY ARE YOU HERE TODAY?
WE'RE WAITING FOR THE WINDOW WASHER. RIGHT, MITSU?
YES.

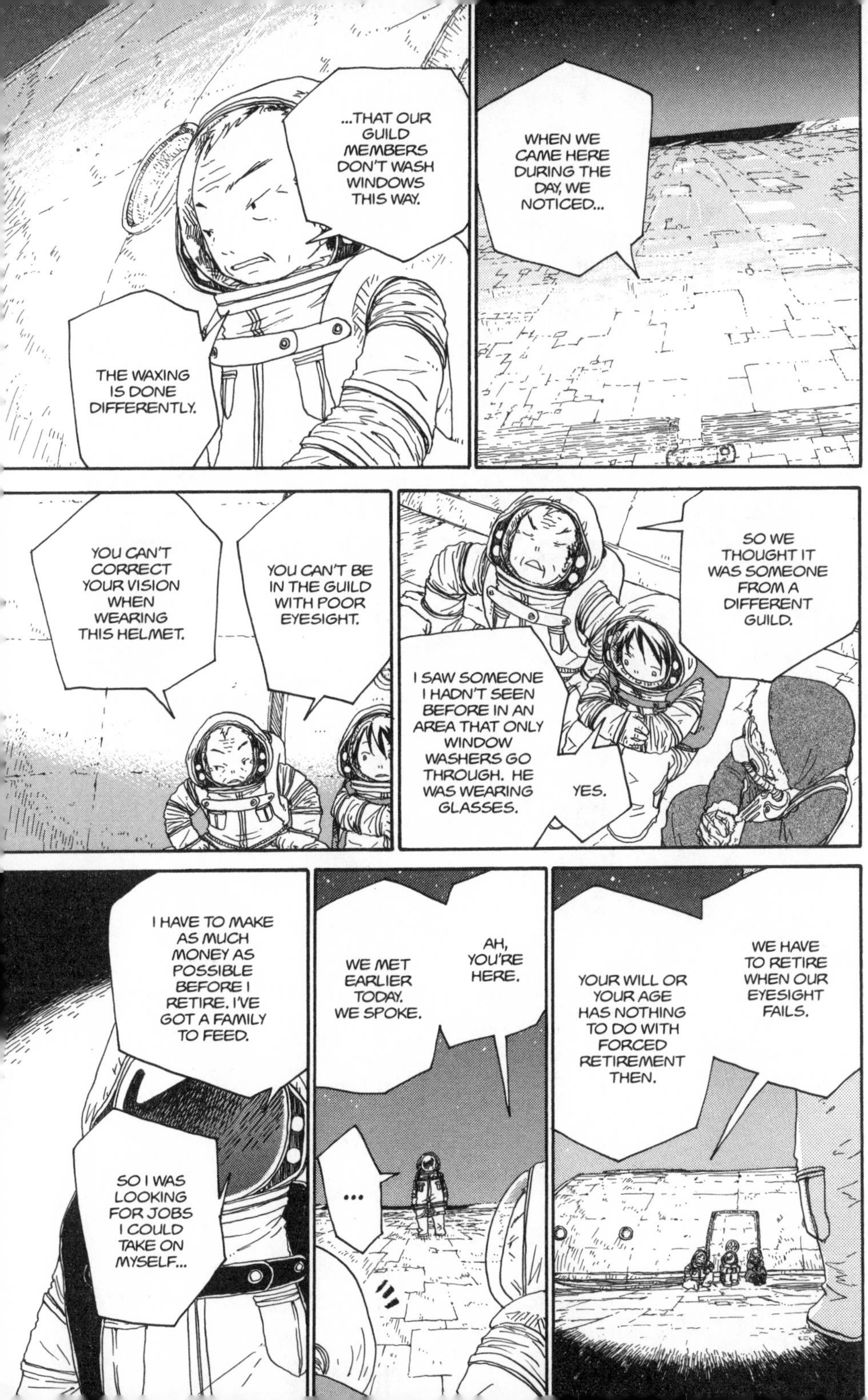
WHEN WE CAME HERE DURING THE DAY, WE NOTICED...
...THAT OUR GUILD MEMBERS DON'T WASH WINDOWS THIS WAY.
THE WAXING IS DONE DIFFERENTLY.
SO WE THOUGHT IT WAS SOMEONE FROM A DIFFERENT GUILD.
YES.
I SAW SOMEONE I HADN'T SEEN BEFORE IN AN AREA THAT ONLY WINDOW WASHERS GO THROUGH. HE WAS WEARING GLASSES.
YOU CAN'T BE IN THE GUILD WITH POOR EYESIGHT.
YOU CAN'T CORRECT YOUR VISION WHEN WEARING THIS HELMET.
WE HAVE TO RETIRE WHEN OUR EYESIGHT FAILS.
YOUR WILL OR YOUR AGE HAS NOTHING TO DO WITH FORCED RETIREMENT THEN.
AH, YOU'RE HERE.
WE MET EARLIER TODAY. WE SPOKE.
...
I HAVE TO MAKE AS MUCH MONEY AS POSSIBLE BEFORE I RETIRE. I'VE GOT A FAMILY TO FEED.
SO I WAS LOOKING FOR JOBS I COULD TAKE ON MYSELF...

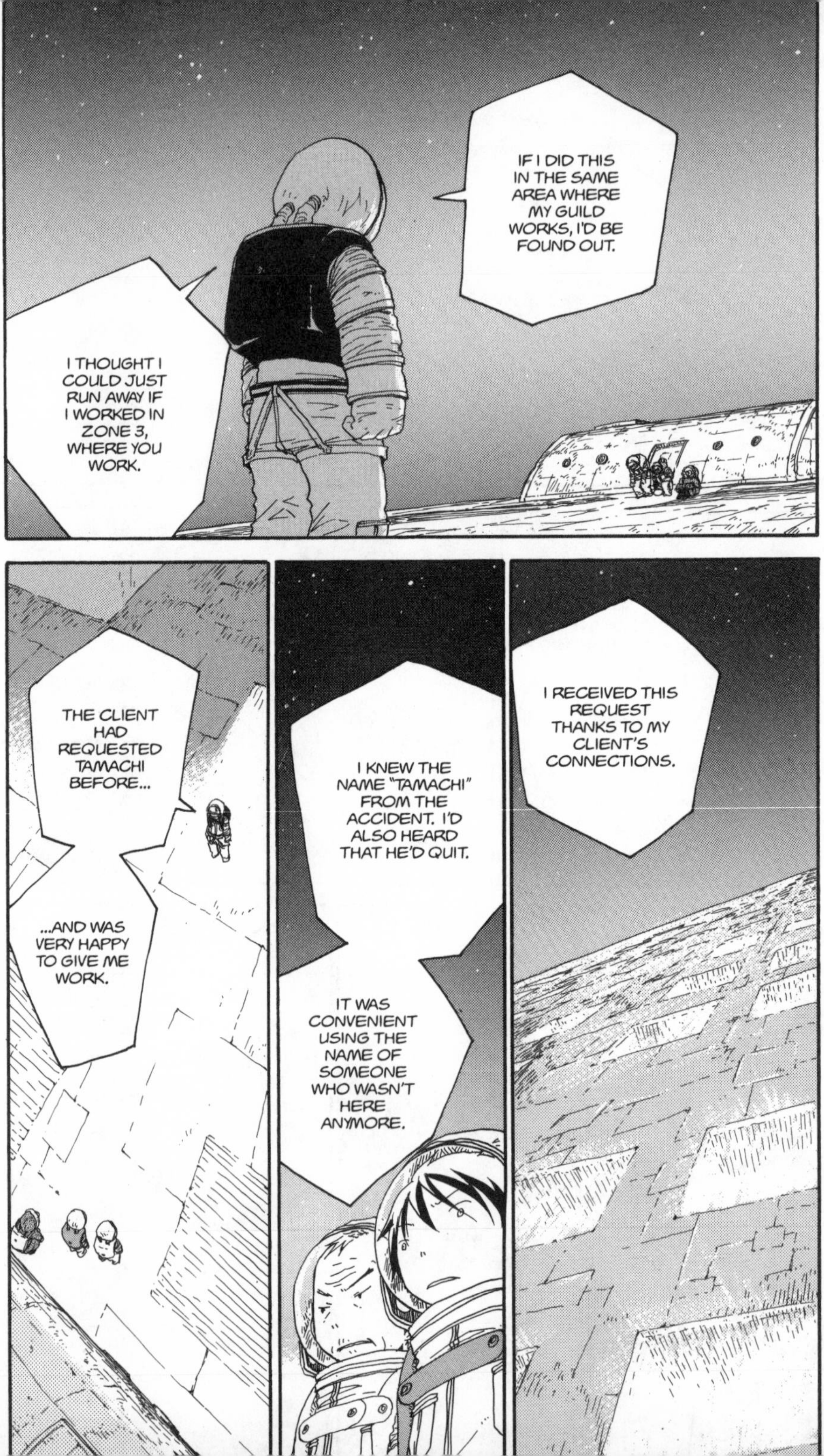
IF I DID THIS IN THE SAME AREA WHERE MY GUILD WORKS, I'D BE FOUND OUT.
I THOUGHT I COULD JUST RUN AWAY IF I WORKED IN ZONE 3, WHERE YOU WORK.
I RECEIVED THIS REQUEST THANKS TO MY CLIENT'S CONNECTIONS.
I KNEW THE NAME "TAMACHI" FROM THE ACCIDENT. I'D ALSO HEARD THAT HE'D QUIT.
IT WAS CONVENIENT USING THE NAME OF SOMEONE WHO WASN'T HERE ANYMORE.
THE CLIENT HAD REQUESTED TAMACHI BEFORE...
...AND WAS VERY HAPPY TO GIVE ME WORK.

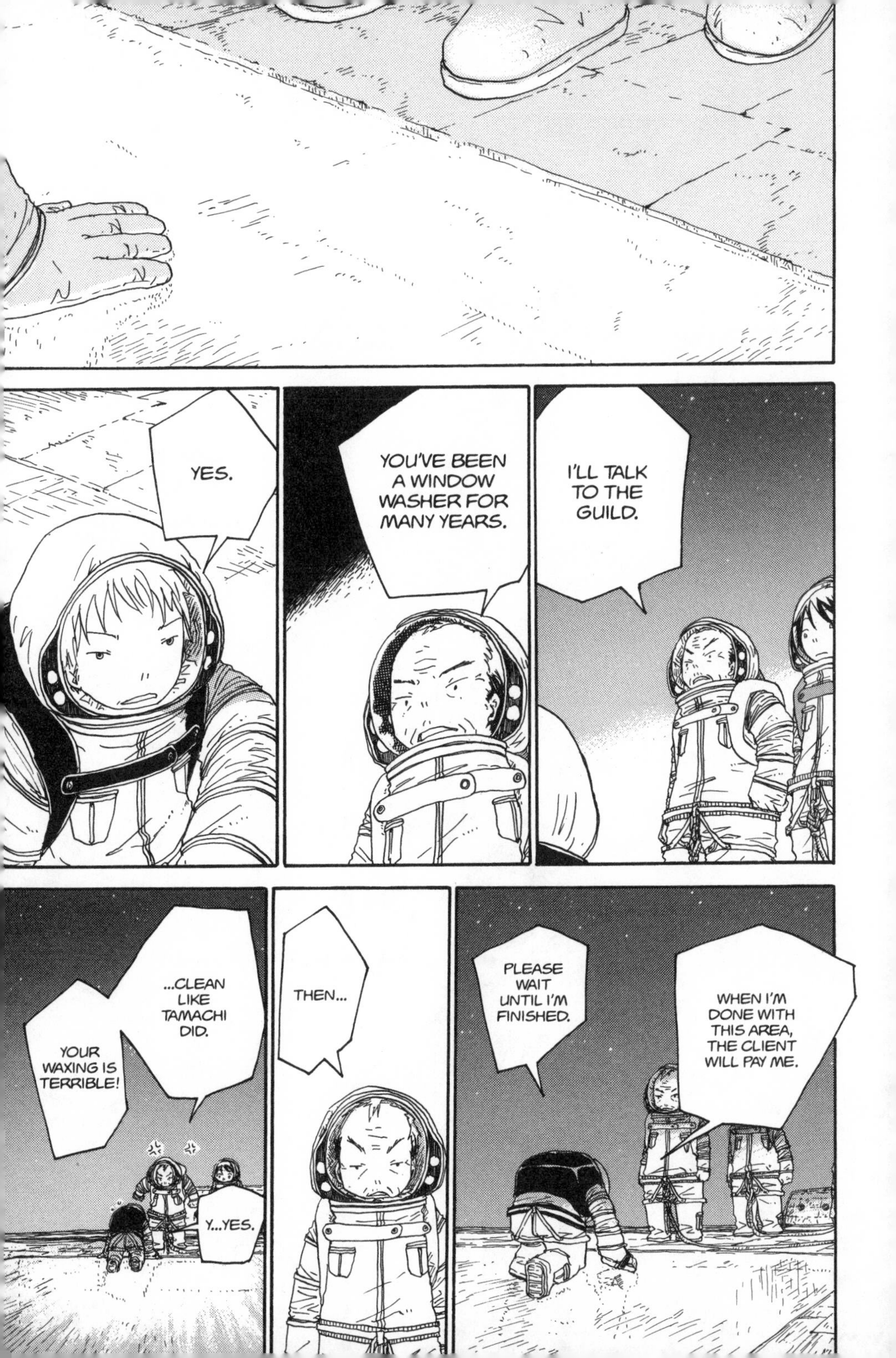
I'LL TALK TO THE GUILD.
YOU'VE BEEN A WINDOW WASHER FOR MANY YEARS.
YES.
WHEN I'M DONE WITH THIS AREA, THE CLIENT WILL PAY ME.
PLEASE WAIT UNTIL I'M FINISHED.
THEN...
...CLEAN LIKE TAMACHI DID.
YOUR WAXING IS TERRIBLE!
Y...YES.

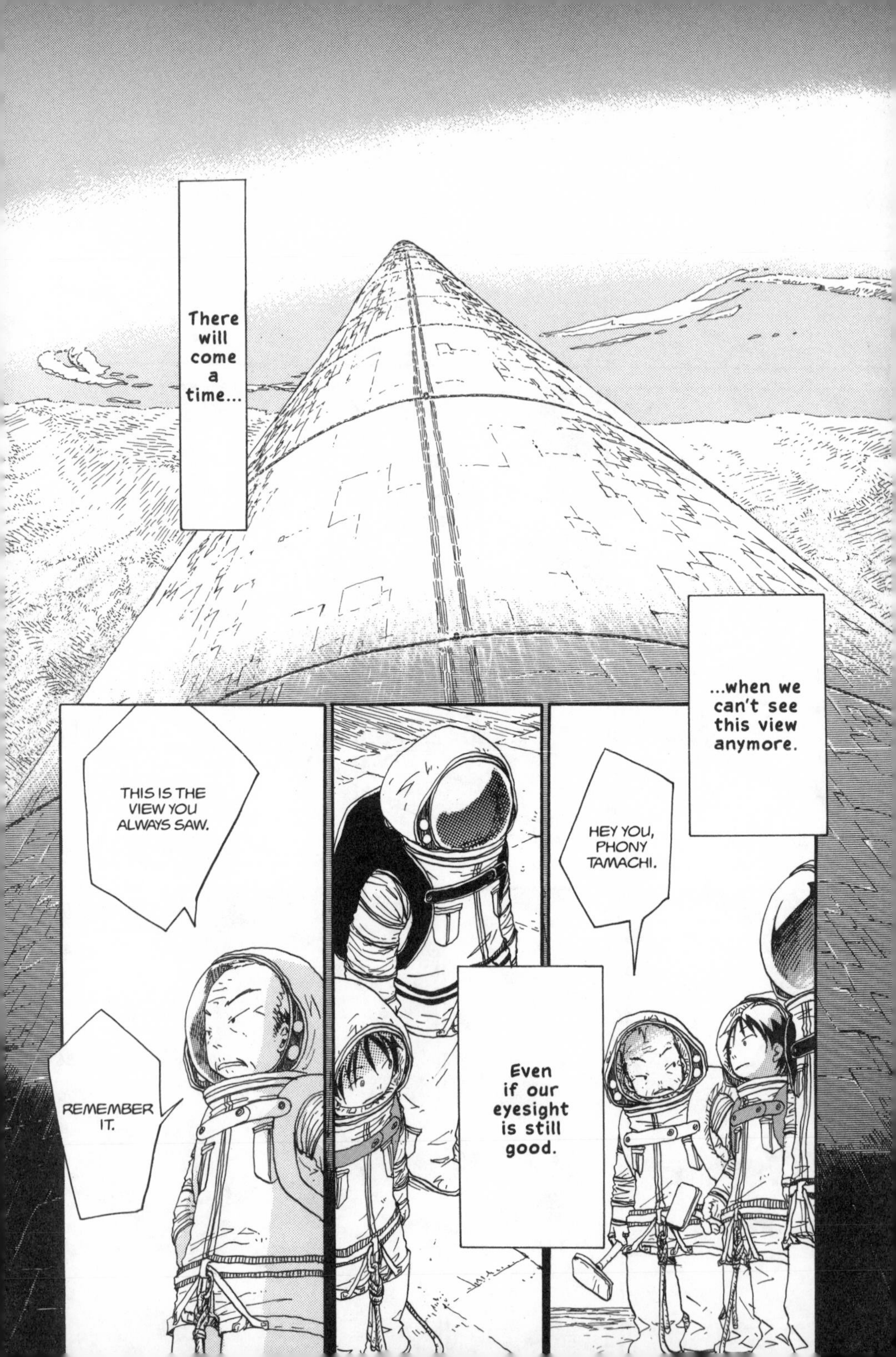
There will come a time...
...when we can't see this view anymore.
HEY YOU, PHONY TAMACHI.
Even if our eyesight is still good.
THIS IS THE VIEW YOU ALWAYS SAW.
REMEMBER IT.

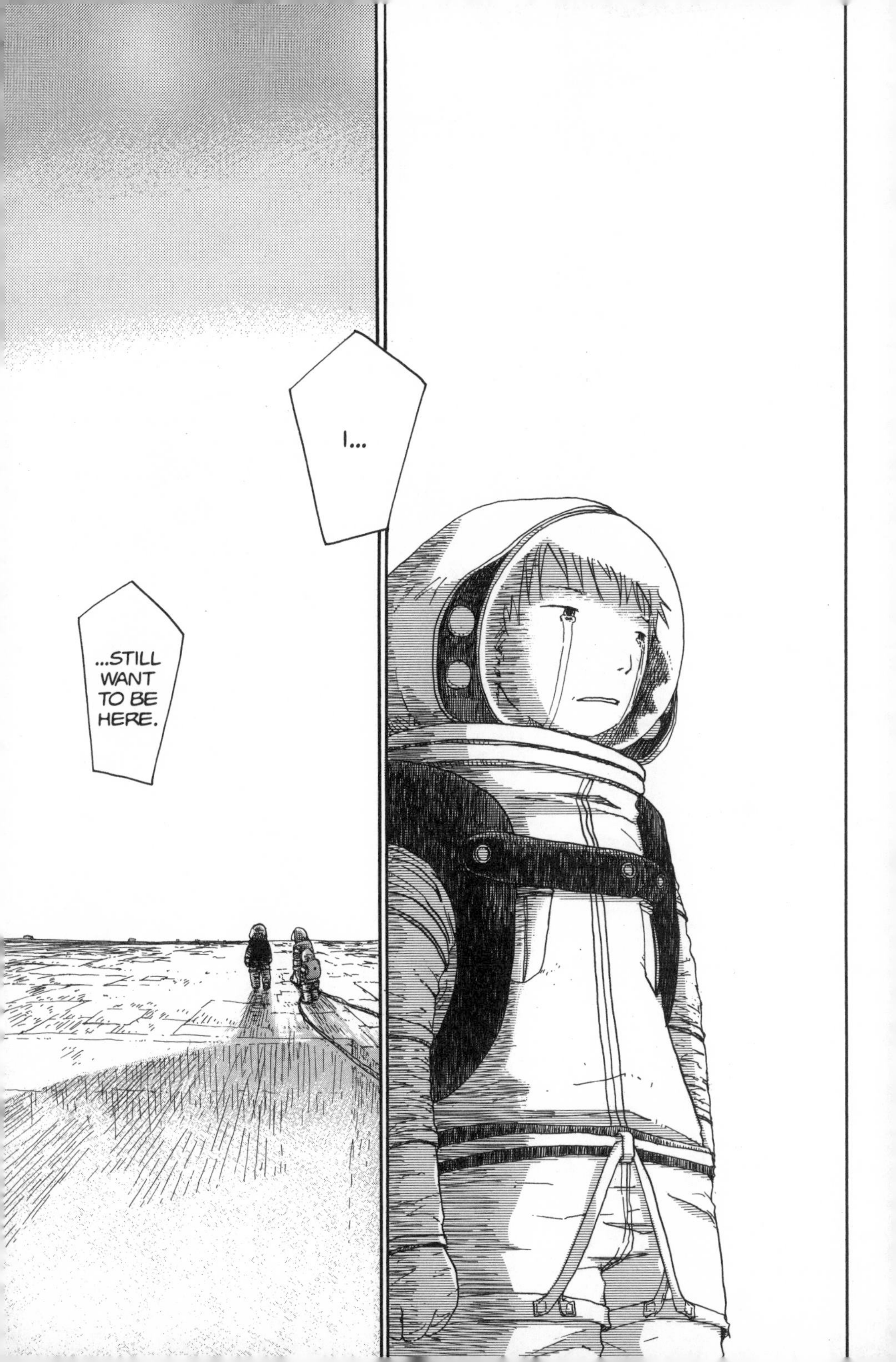
I...
...STILL WANT TO BE HERE.

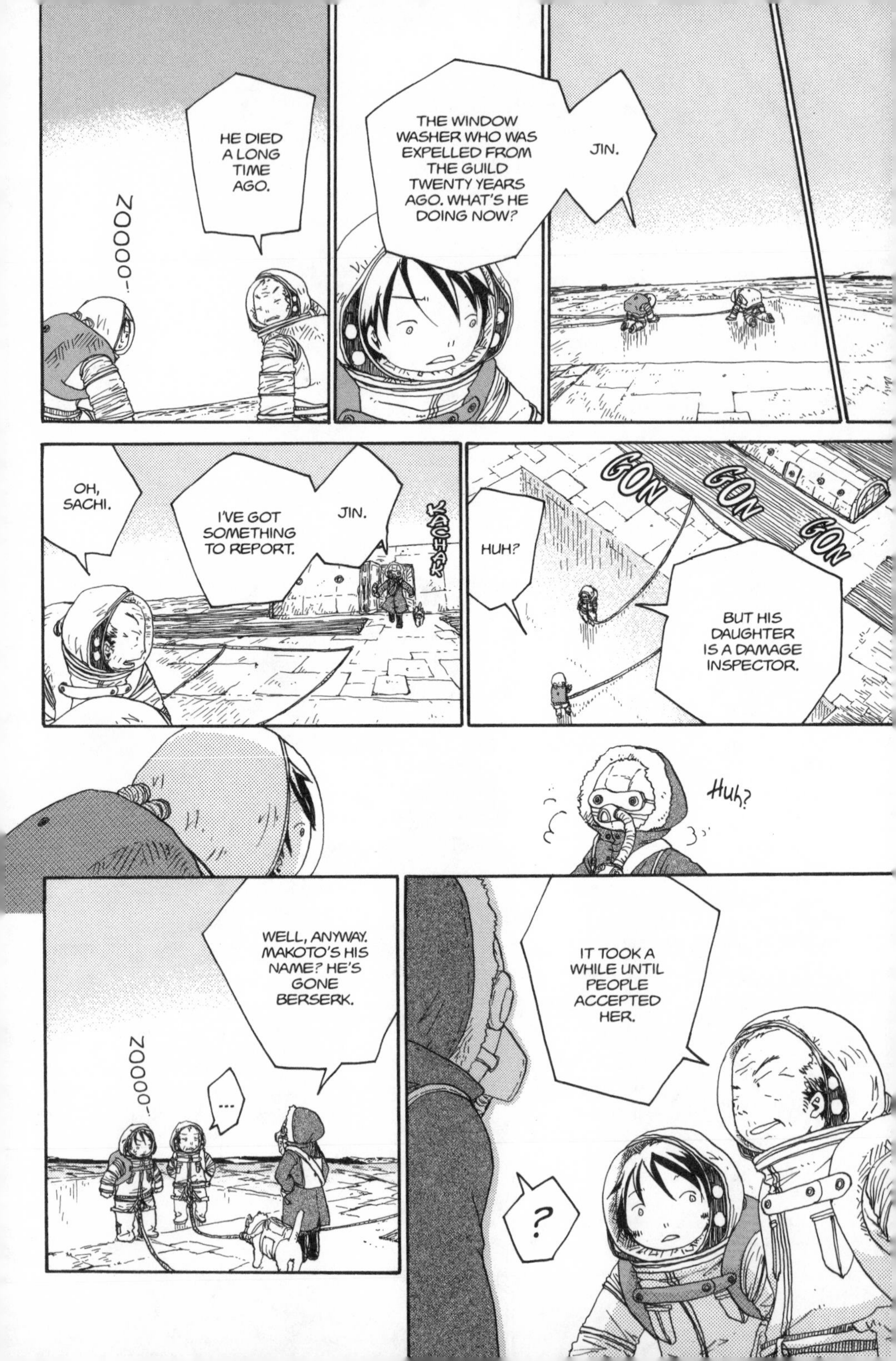
JIN.
THE WINDOW WASHER WHO WAS EXPELLED FROM THE GUILD TWENTY YEARS AGO. WHAT'S HE DOING NOW?
HE DIED A LONG TIME AGO.
NOOOO-!
GON GON GON
HUH?
BUT HIS DAUGHTER IS A DAMAGE INSPECTOR.
KACHAK
JIN.
I'VE GOT SOMETHING TO REPORT.
OH, SACHI.
Huh?
IT TOOK A WHILE UNTIL PEOPLE ACCEPTED HER.
?
WELL, ANYWAY. MAKOTO'S HIS NAME? HE'S GONE BERSERK.
...
NOOOO-!

floor 22: a room with a roof

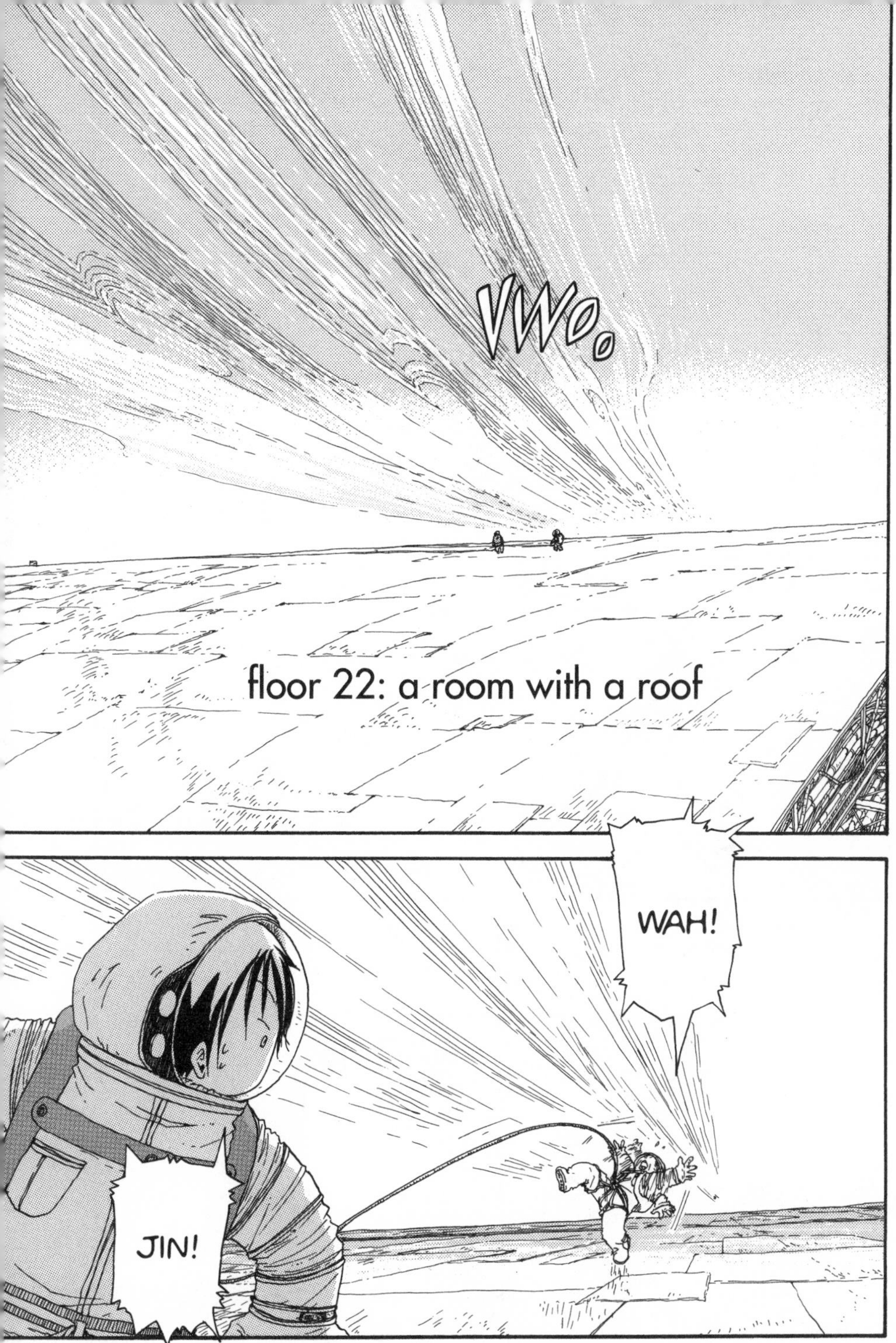
VWOO
WAH!
JIN!

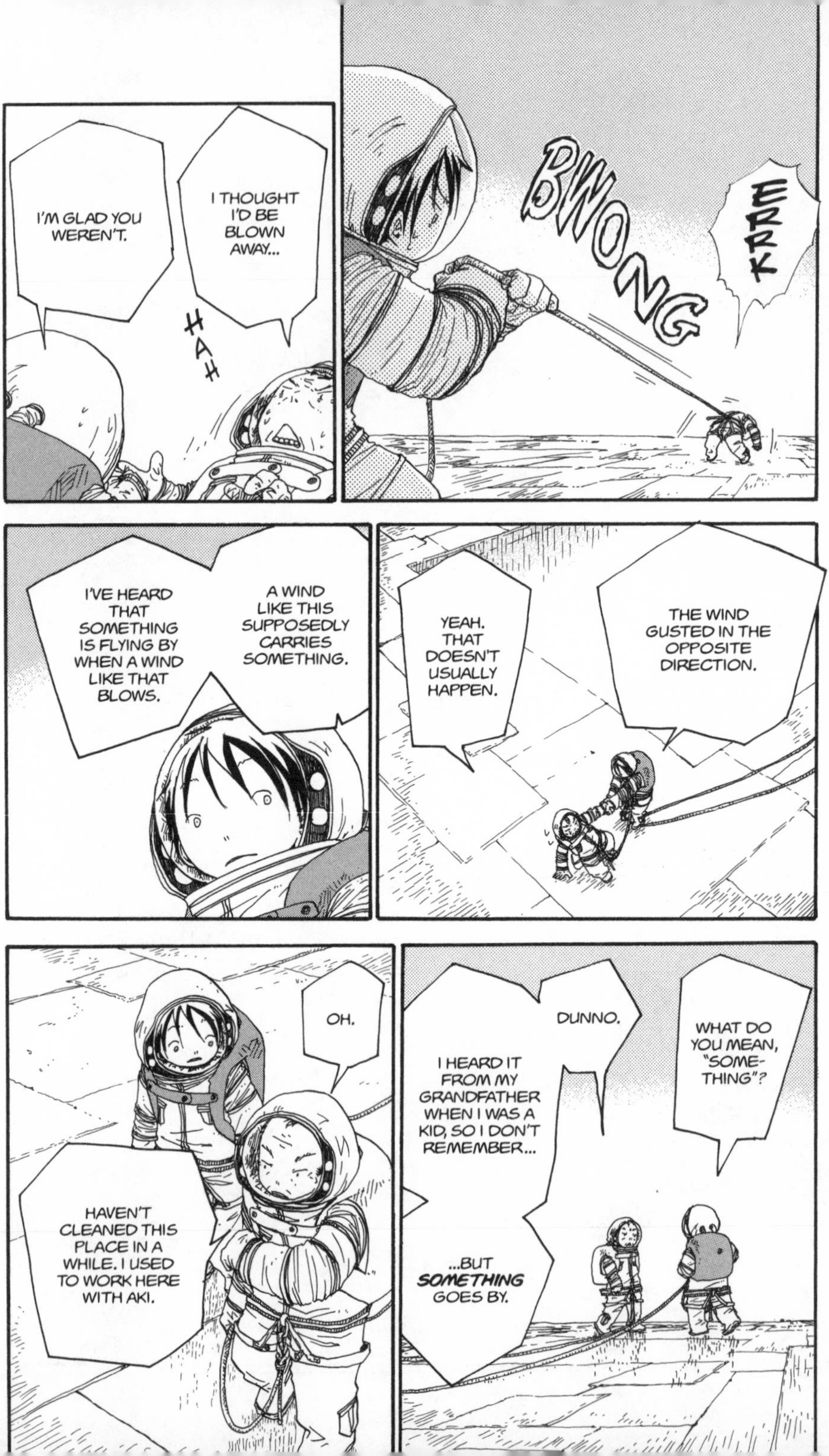
BWONG
ERRK
I THOUGHT I'D BE BLOWN AWAY...
HAH
I'M GLAD YOU WEREN'T.
THE WIND GUSTED IN THE OPPOSITE DIRECTION.
YEAH. THAT DOESN'T USUALLY HAPPEN.
A WIND LIKE THIS SUPPOSEDLY CARRIES SOMETHING.
I'VE HEARD THAT SOMETHING IS FLYING BY WHEN A WIND LIKE THAT BLOWS.
WHAT DO YOU MEAN, "SOME-THING"?
DUNNO.
I HEARD IT FROM MY GRANDFATHER WHEN I WAS A KID, SO I DON'T REMEMBER...
...BUT *SOMETHING* GOES BY.
OH.
HAVEN'T CLEANED THIS PLACE IN A WHILE. I USED TO WORK HERE WITH AKI.

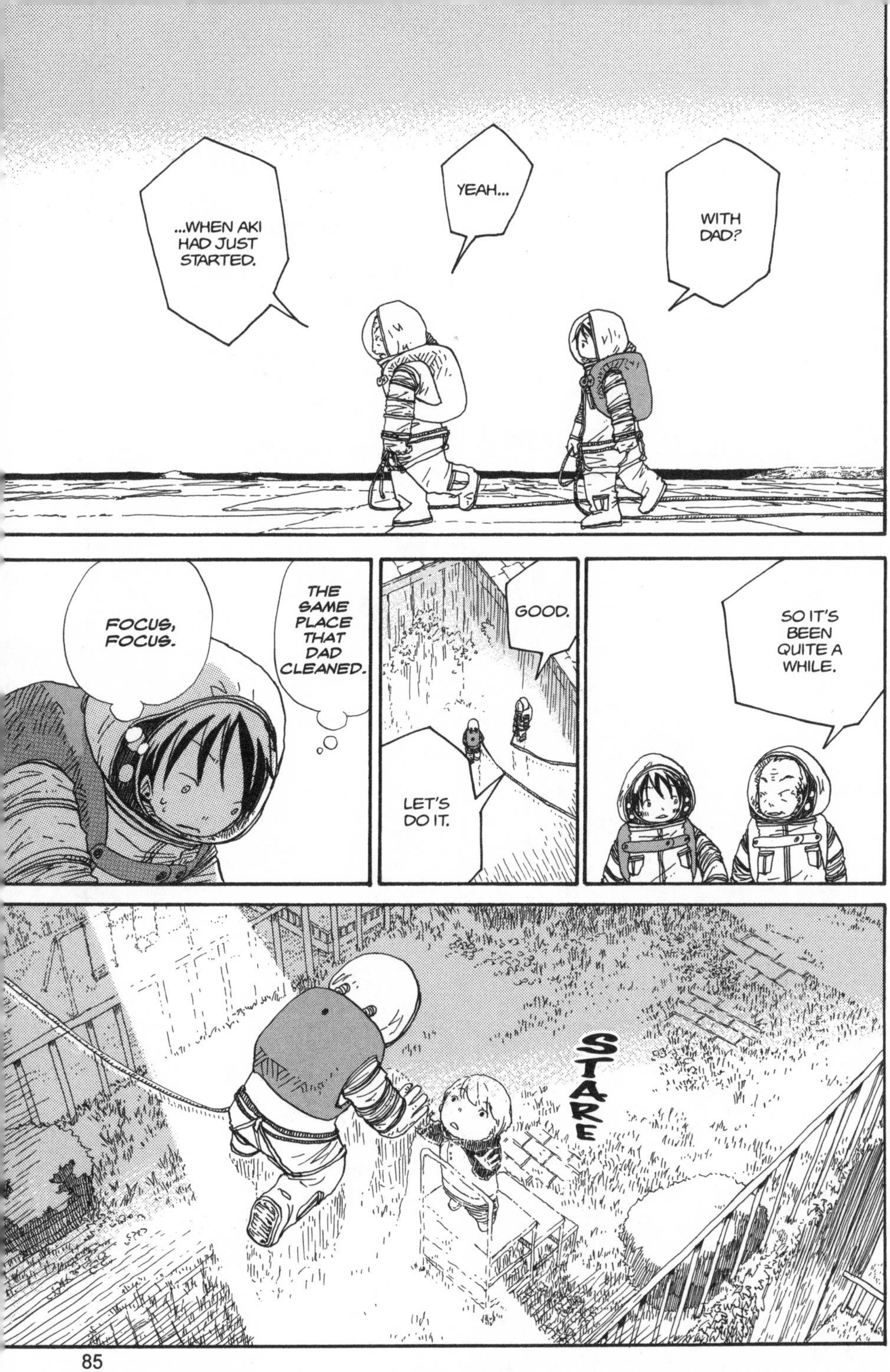
WITH DAD?
YEAH...
...WHEN AKI HAD JUST STARTED.
SO IT'S BEEN QUITE A WHILE.
GOOD.
LET'S DO IT.
THE SAME PLACE THAT DAD CLEANED.
FOCUS, FOCUS.
STARE

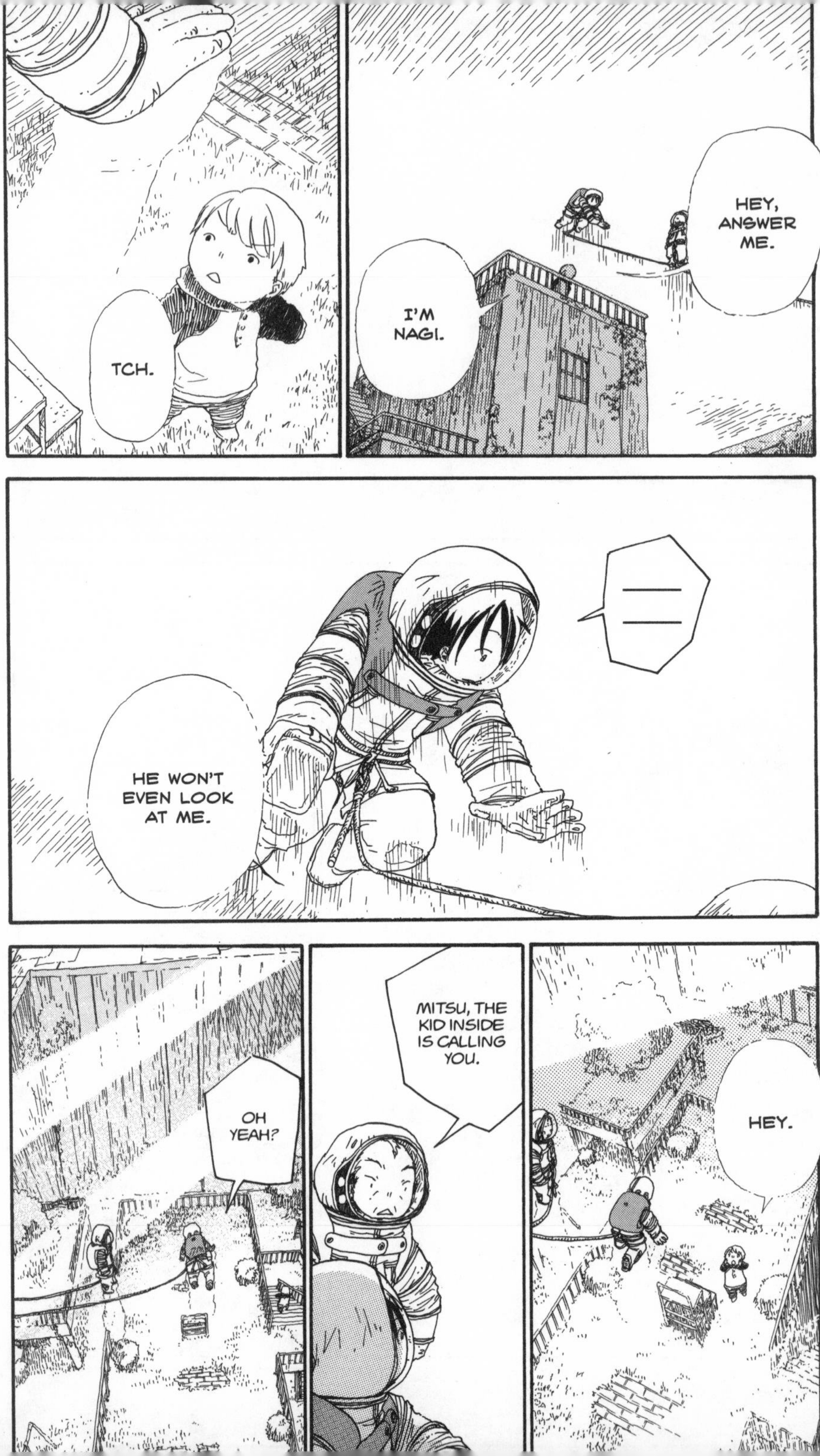
HEY, ANSWER ME.
I'M NAGI.
TCH.
——
HE WON'T EVEN LOOK AT ME.
HEY.
MITSU, THE KID INSIDE IS CALLING YOU.
OH YEAH?

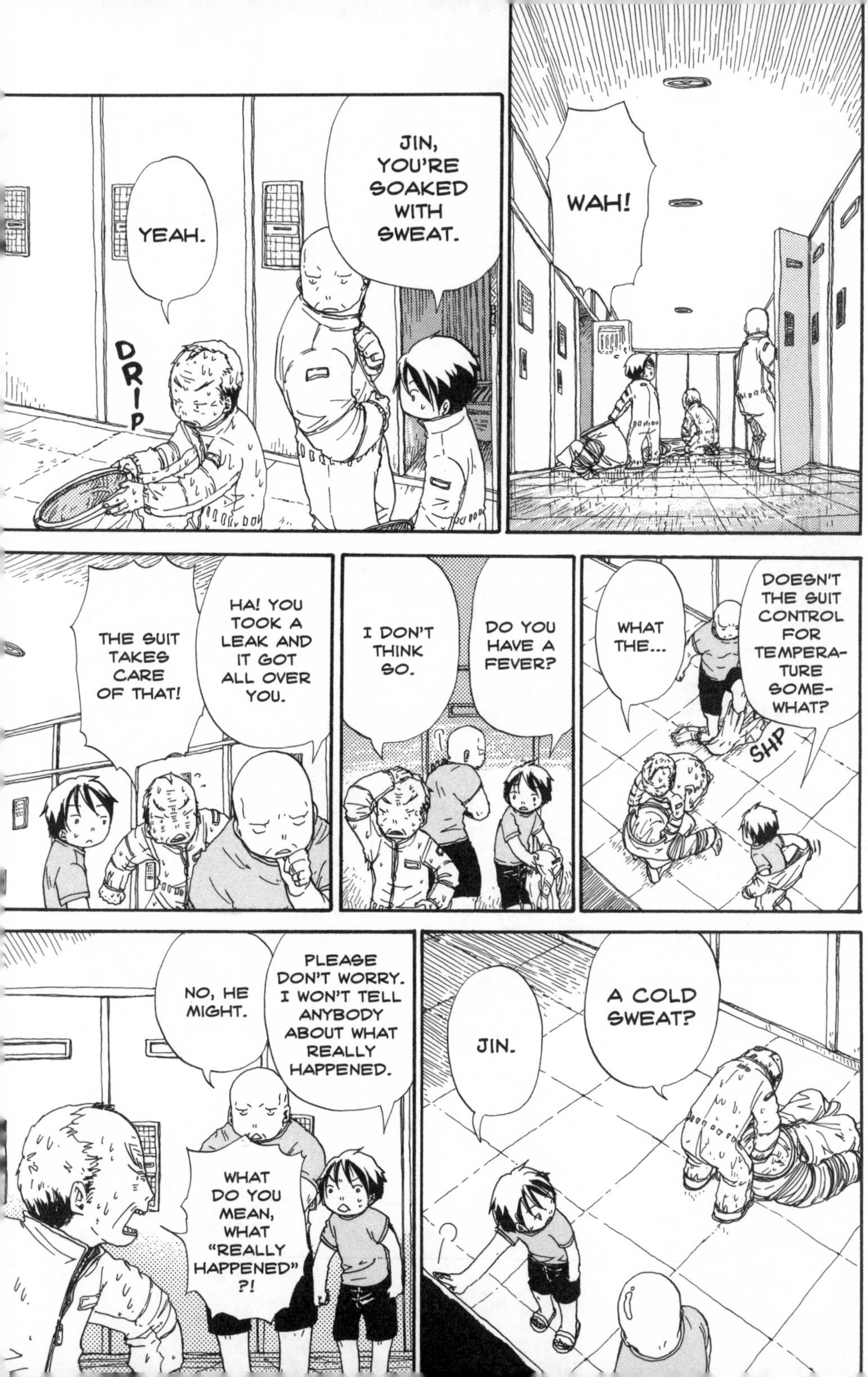
WAH!
JIN, YOU'RE SOAKED WITH SWEAT.
YEAH.
DRIP
DOESN'T THE SUIT CONTROL FOR TEMPERA-TURE SOME-WHAT?
WHAT THE...
SHP
DO YOU HAVE A FEVER?
I DON'T THINK SO.
HA! YOU TOOK A LEAK AND IT GOT ALL OVER YOU.
THE SUIT TAKES CARE OF THAT!
A COLD SWEAT?
JIN.
PLEASE DON'T WORRY. I WON'T TELL ANYBODY ABOUT WHAT REALLY HAPPENED.
NO, HE MIGHT.
WHAT DO YOU MEAN, WHAT "REALLY HAPPENED"?!

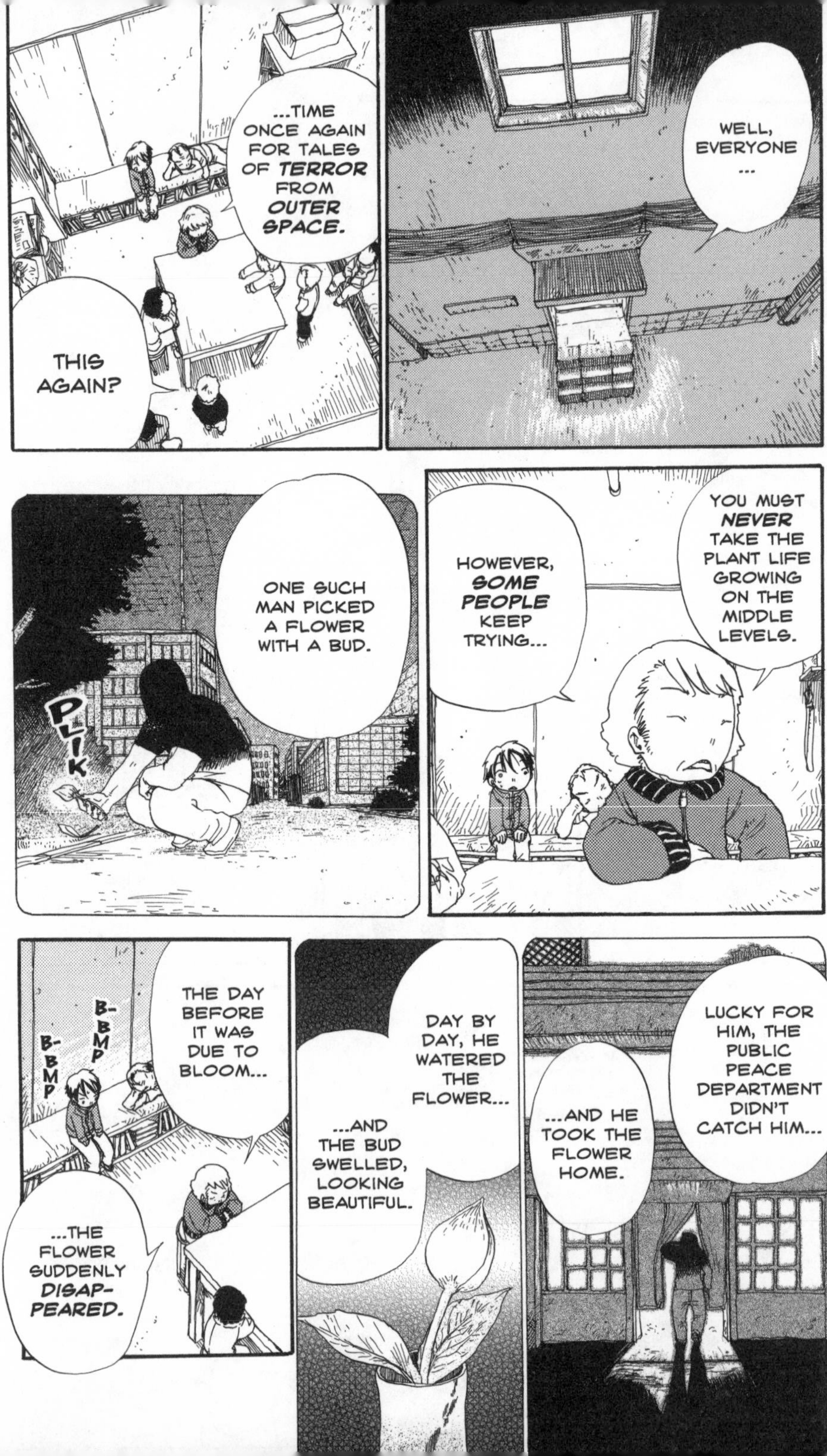
WELL, EVERYONE ...
...TIME ONCE AGAIN FOR TALES OF *TERROR* FROM *OUTER SPACE.*
THIS AGAIN?
YOU MUST *NEVER* TAKE THE PLANT LIFE GROWING ON THE MIDDLE LEVELS.
HOWEVER, *SOME PEOPLE* KEEP TRYING...
ONE SUCH MAN PICKED A FLOWER WITH A BUD.
PLIK
LUCKY FOR HIM, THE PUBLIC PEACE DEPARTMENT DIDN'T CATCH HIM...
...AND HE TOOK THE FLOWER HOME.
DAY BY DAY, HE WATERED THE FLOWER...
...AND THE BUD SWELLED, LOOKING BEAUTIFUL.
THE DAY BEFORE IT WAS DUE TO BLOOM...
B-BMP
B-BMP
...THE FLOWER SUDDENLY *DISAP-PEARED.*

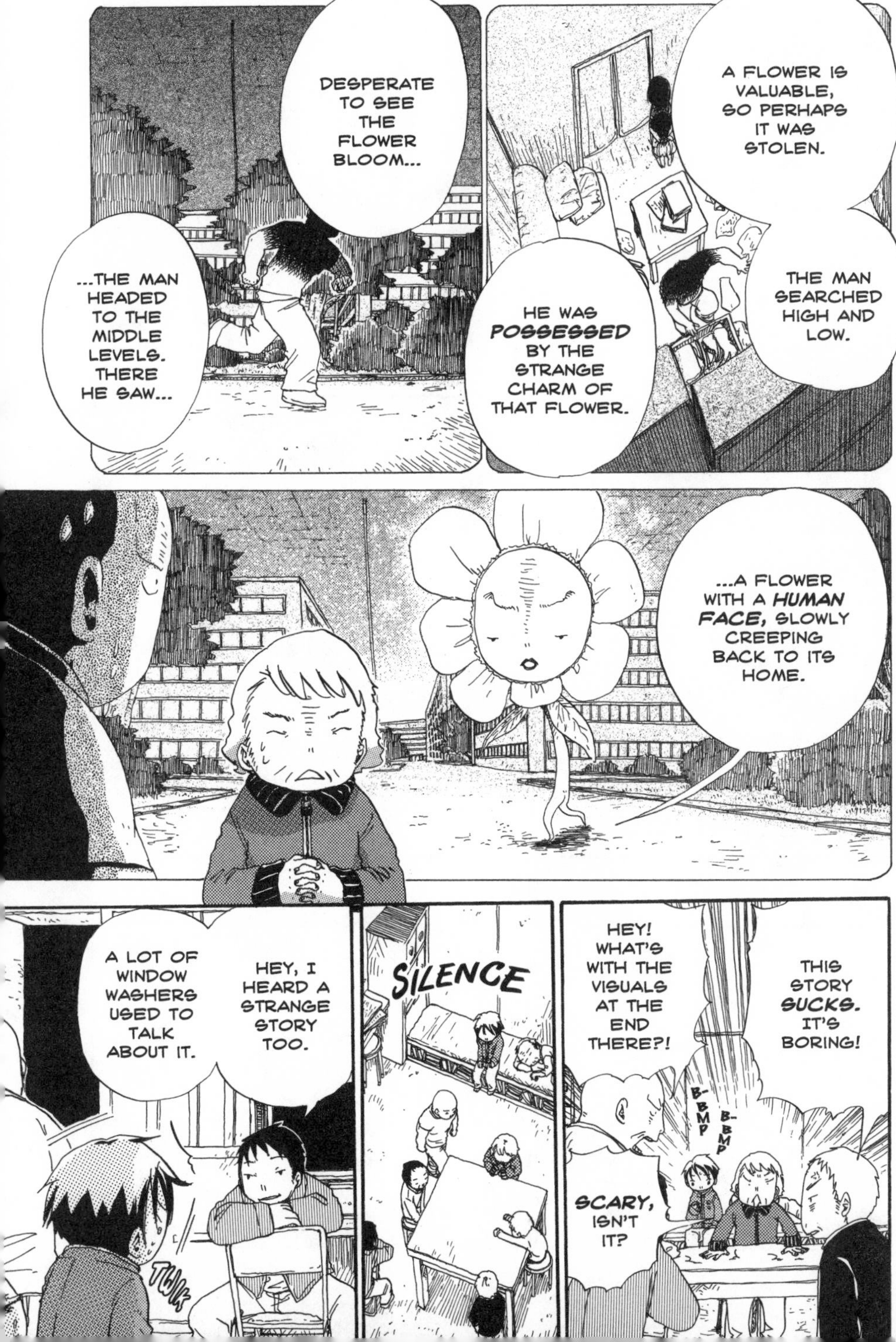
A FLOWER IS VALUABLE, SO PERHAPS IT WAS STOLEN.
THE MAN SEARCHED HIGH AND LOW.
HE WAS POSSESSED BY THE STRANGE CHARM OF THAT FLOWER.
DESPERATE TO SEE THE FLOWER BLOOM...
...THE MAN HEADED TO THE MIDDLE LEVELS. THERE HE SAW...
...A FLOWER WITH A HUMAN FACE, SLOWLY CREEPING BACK TO ITS HOME.
THIS STORY SUCKS. IT'S BORING!
HEY! WHAT'S WITH THE VISUALS AT THE END THERE?!
B-BMP
B-BMP
SCARY, ISN'T IT?
SILENCE
HEY, I HEARD A STRANGE STORY TOO.
A LOT OF WINDOW WASHERS USED TO TALK ABOUT IT.
TWK

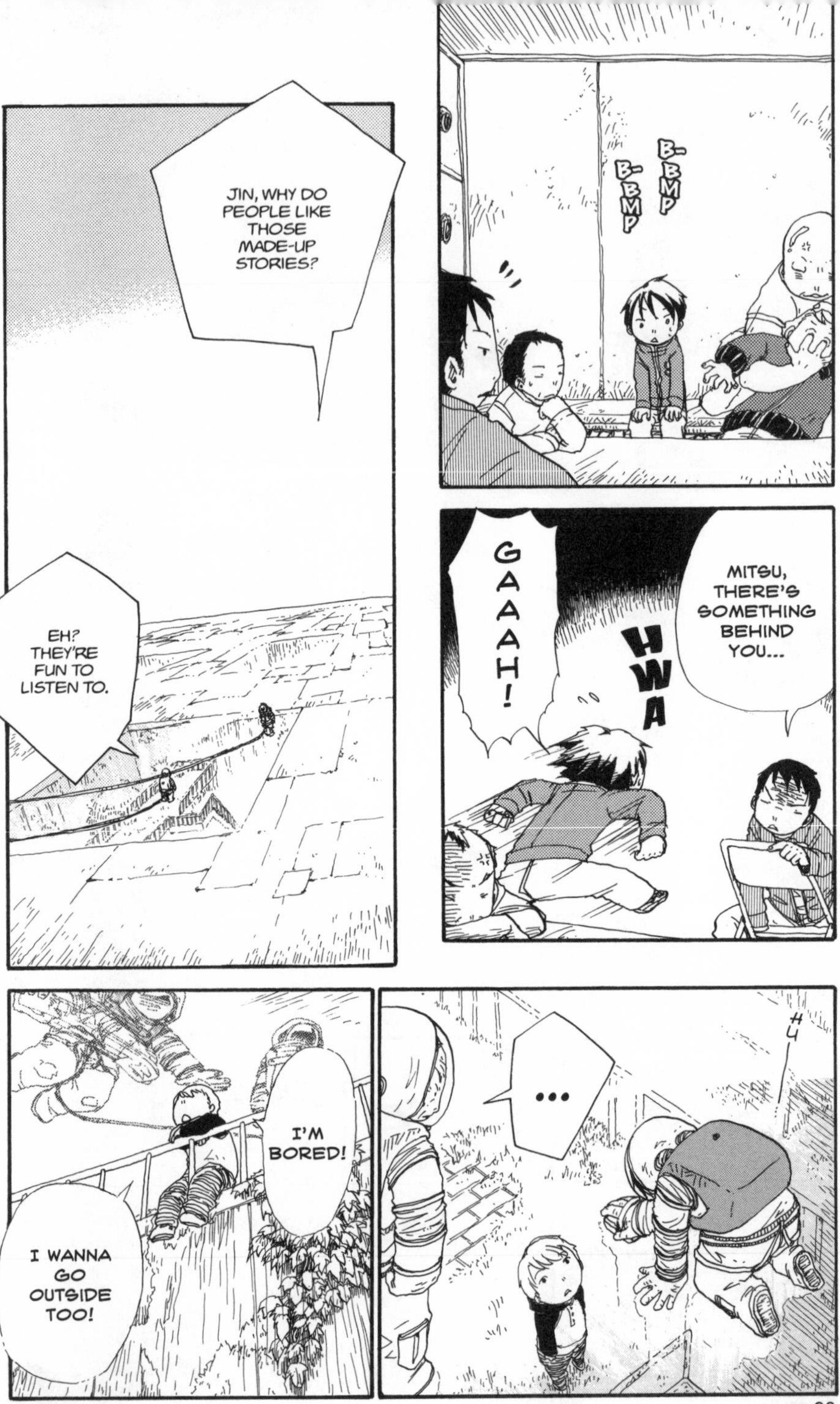
B-BMP
B-BMP
MITSU, THERE'S SOMETHING BEHIND YOU...
HWA
GAAAH!
JIN, WHY DO PEOPLE LIKE THOSE MADE-UP STORIES?
EH? THEY'RE FUN TO LISTEN TO.
...
I'M BORED!
I WANNA GO OUTSIDE TOO!

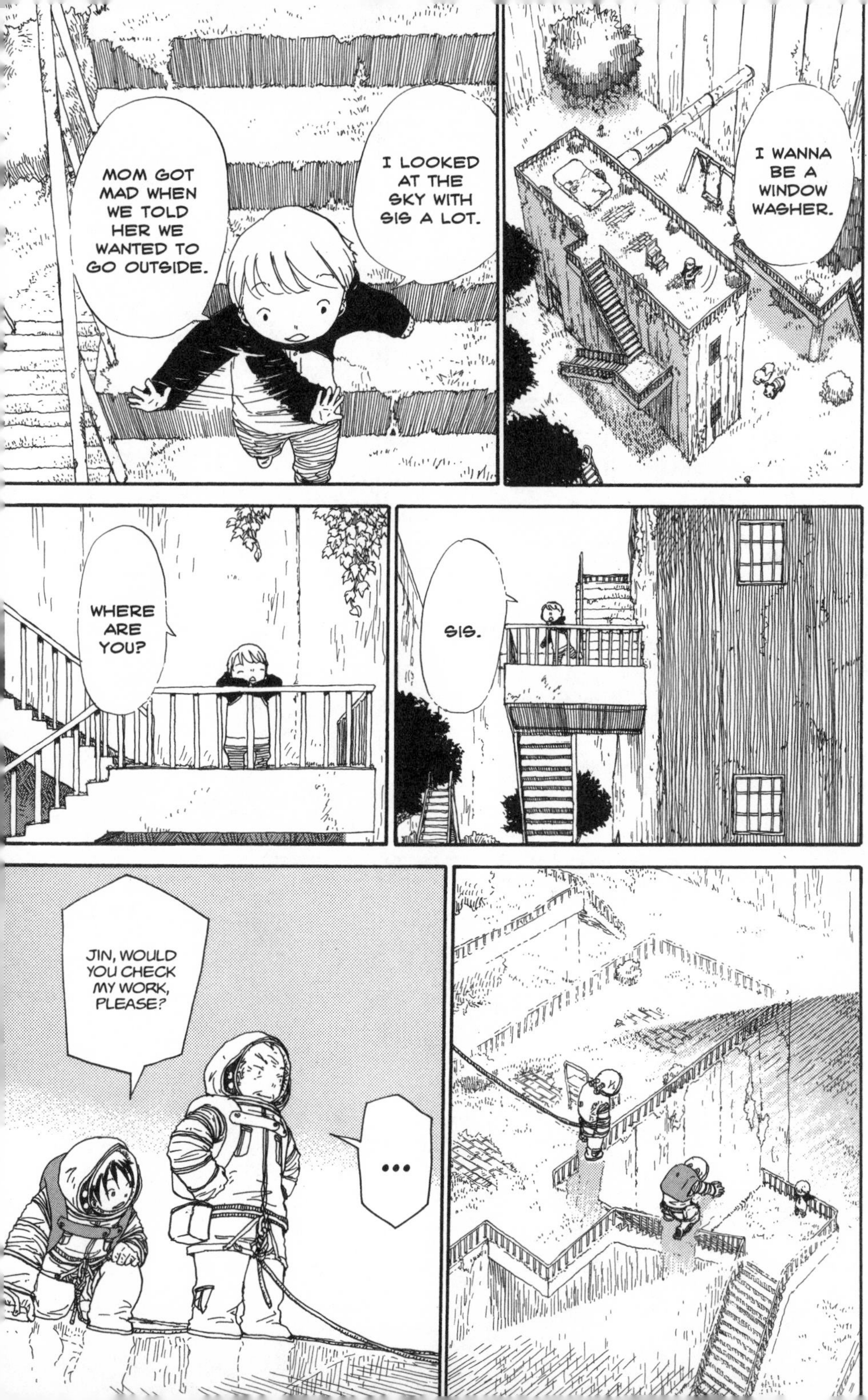
I WANNA BE A WINDOW WASHER.
I LOOKED AT THE SKY WITH SIS A LOT.
MOM GOT MAD WHEN WE TOLD HER WE WANTED TO GO OUTSIDE.
SIS.
WHERE ARE YOU?
JIN, WOULD YOU CHECK MY WORK, PLEASE?
...

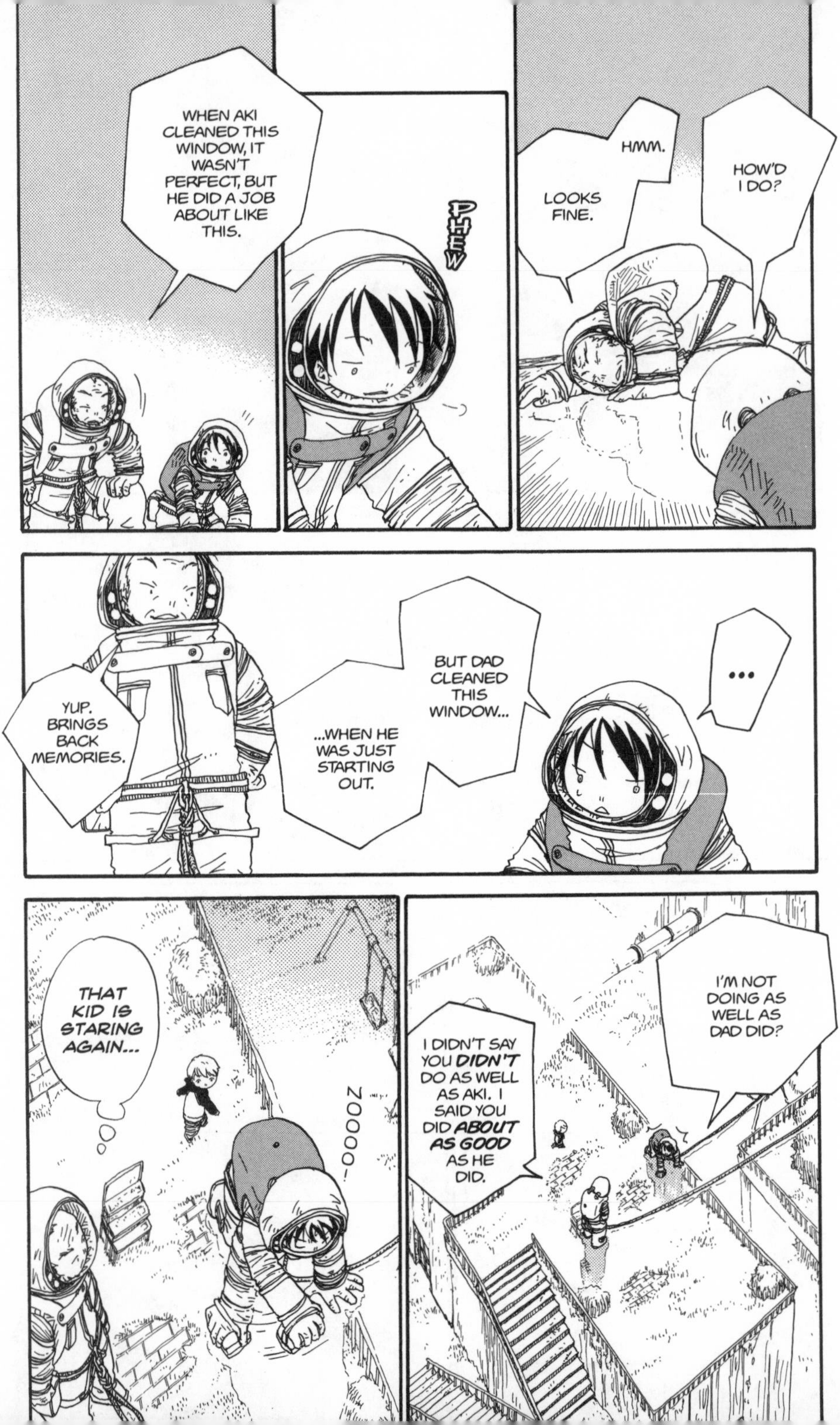
HOW'D I DO?
HMM.
LOOKS FINE.
PHEW
WHEN AKI CLEANED THIS WINDOW, IT WASN'T PERFECT, BUT HE DID A JOB ABOUT LIKE THIS.
...
BUT DAD CLEANED THIS WINDOW...
...WHEN HE WAS JUST STARTING OUT.
YUP. BRINGS BACK MEMORIES.
I'M NOT DOING AS WELL AS DAD DID?
I DIDN'T SAY YOU *DIDN'T* DO AS WELL AS AKI. I SAID YOU DID *ABOUT AS GOOD* AS HE DID.
NOOOO!
THAT KID IS STARING AGAIN...

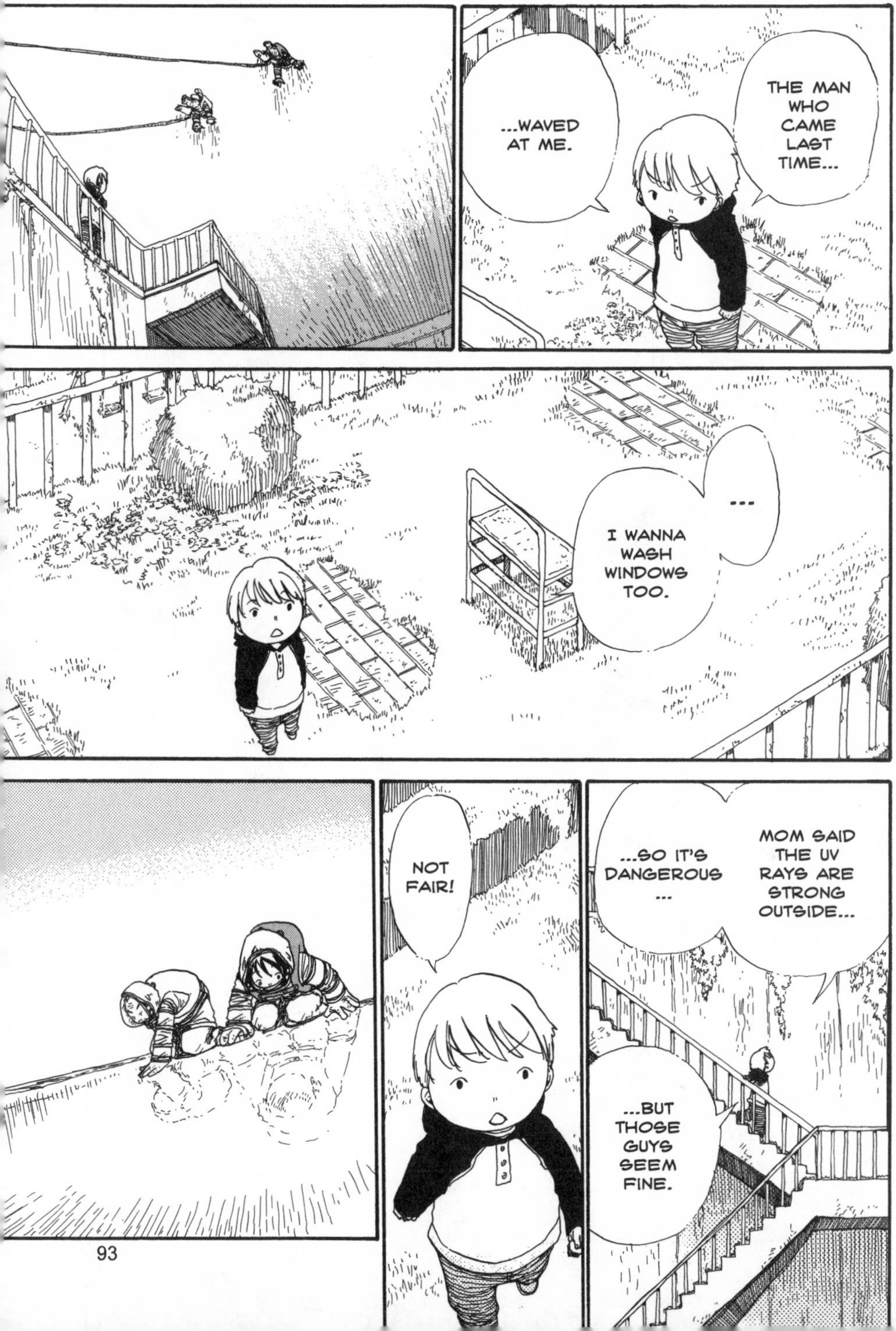
THE MAN WHO CAME LAST TIME...
...WAVED AT ME.
...
I WANNA WASH WINDOWS TOO.
MOM SAID THE UV RAYS ARE STRONG OUTSIDE...
...SO IT'S DANGEROUS...
...BUT THOSE GUYS SEEM FINE.
NOT FAIR!

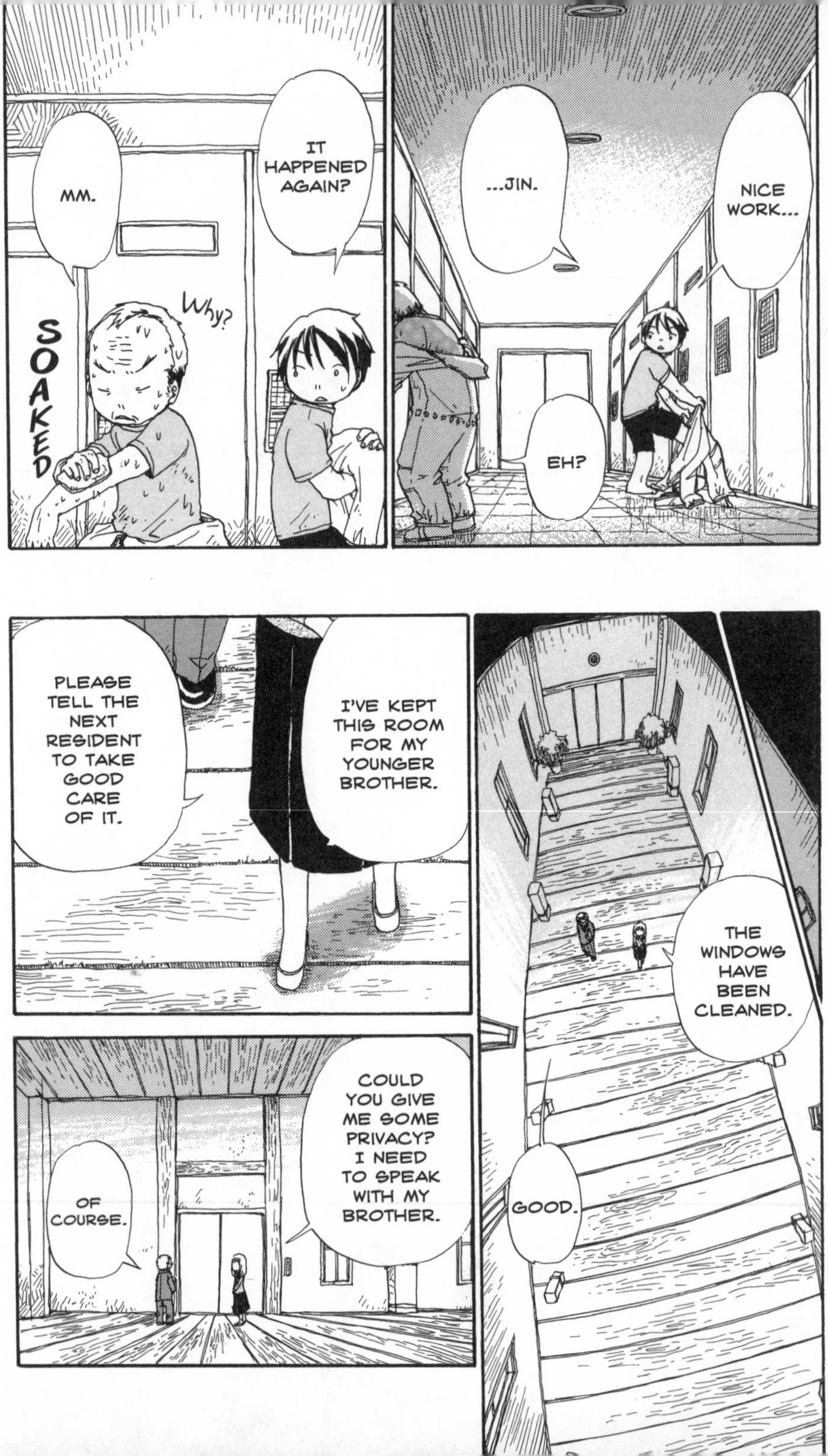
NICE WORK...
...JIN.
EH?
IT HAPPENED AGAIN?
MM.
Why?
SOAKED
THE WINDOWS HAVE BEEN CLEANED.
GOOD.
I'VE KEPT THIS ROOM FOR MY YOUNGER BROTHER.
PLEASE TELL THE NEXT RESIDENT TO TAKE GOOD CARE OF IT.
COULD YOU GIVE ME SOME PRIVACY? I NEED TO SPEAK WITH MY BROTHER.
OF COURSE.

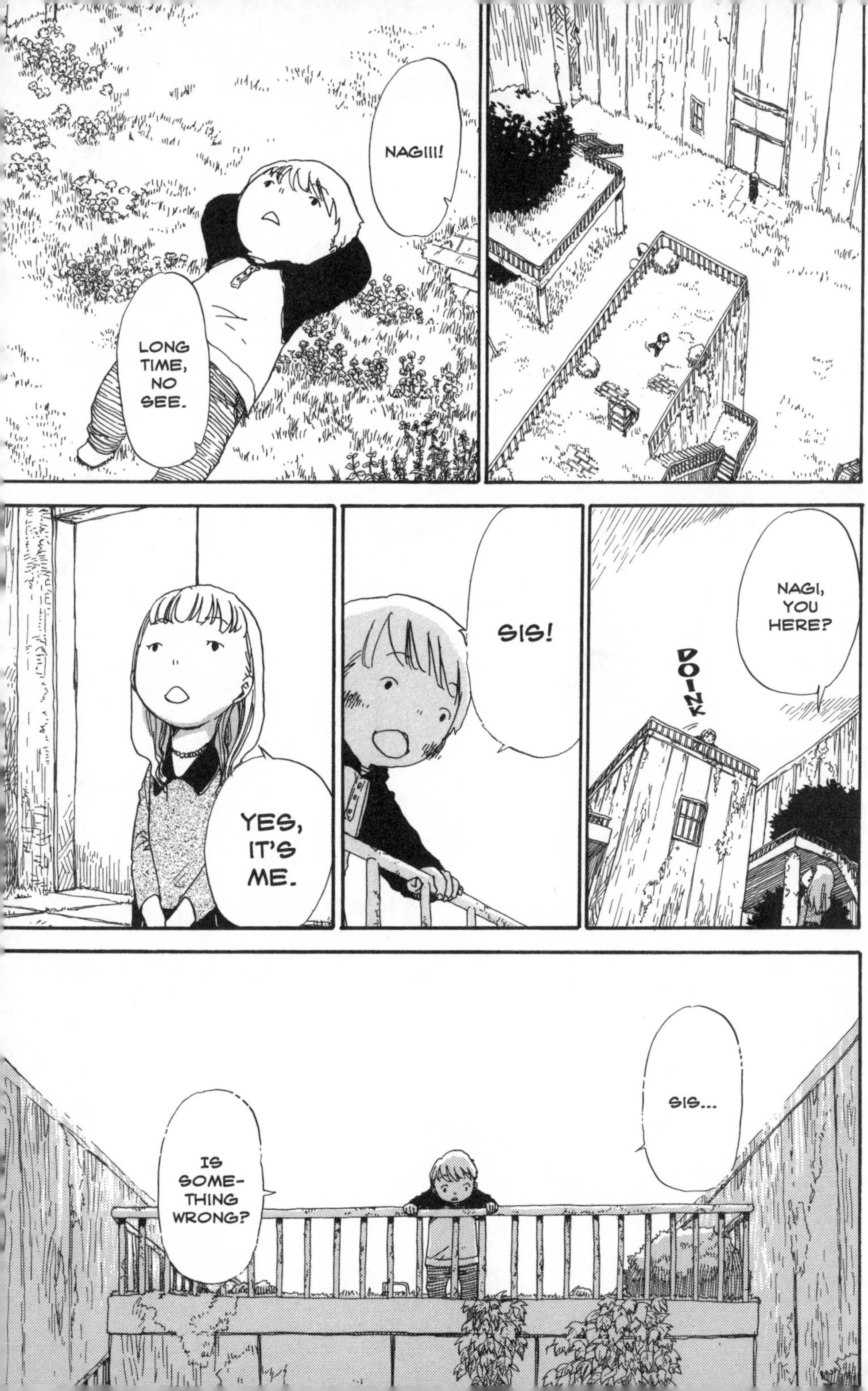
NAGIII!
LONG TIME, NO SEE.
NAGI, YOU HERE?
DOINK
SIS!
YES, IT'S ME.
SIS...
IS SOME-THING WRONG?

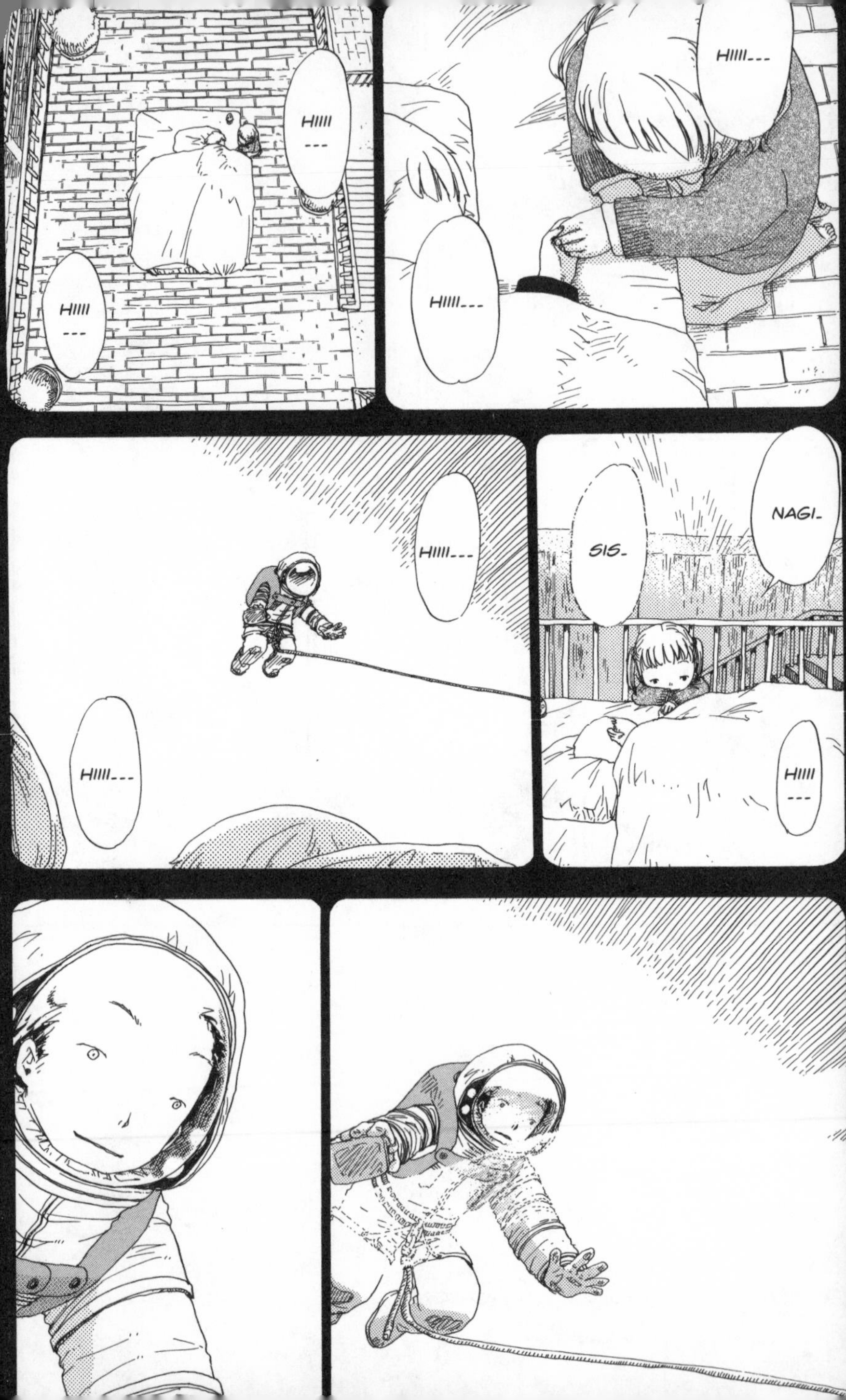
HIIII---
HIIII---
HIIII---
HIIII---
NAGI-
SIS-
HIIII---
HIIII---
HIIII---

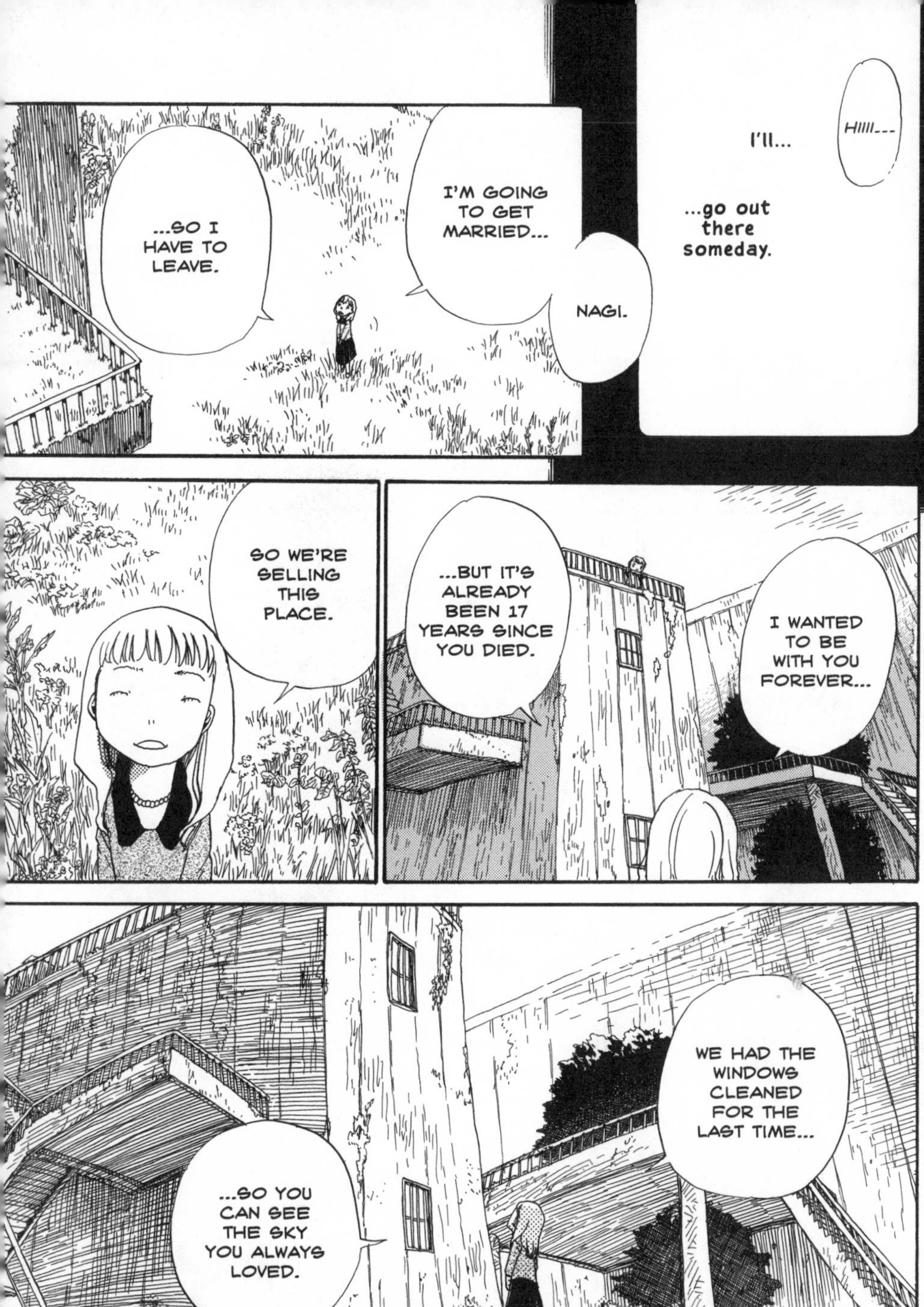
HIIII---
I'll...
...go out there someday.
NAGI.
I'M GOING TO GET MARRIED...
...SO I HAVE TO LEAVE.
I WANTED TO BE WITH YOU FOREVER...
...BUT IT'S ALREADY BEEN 17 YEARS SINCE YOU DIED.
SO WE'RE SELLING THIS PLACE.
WE HAD THE WINDOWS CLEANED FOR THE LAST TIME...
...SO YOU CAN SEE THE SKY YOU ALWAYS LOVED.

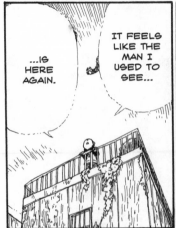

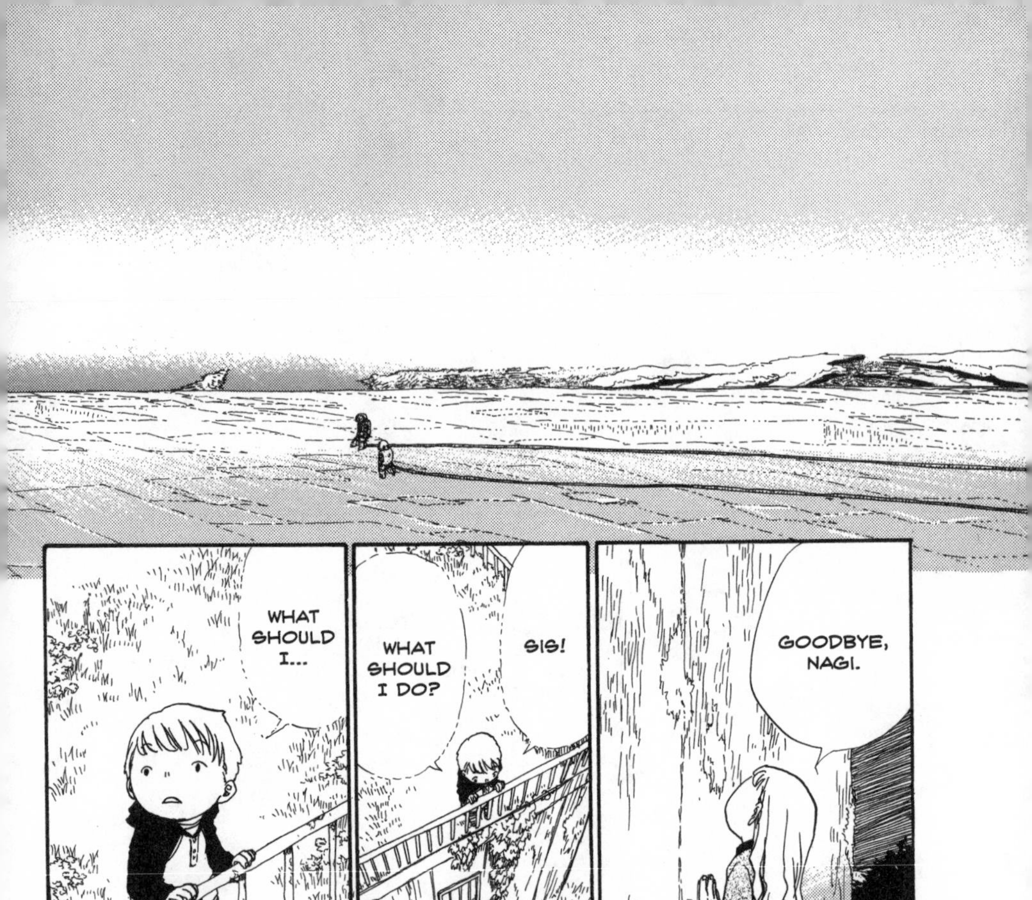
GOODBYE, NAGI.
SIS!
WHAT SHOULD I DO?
WHAT SHOULD I...
IT FEELS LIKE THE MAN I USED TO SEE...
...IS HERE AGAIN.

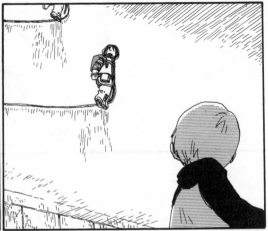

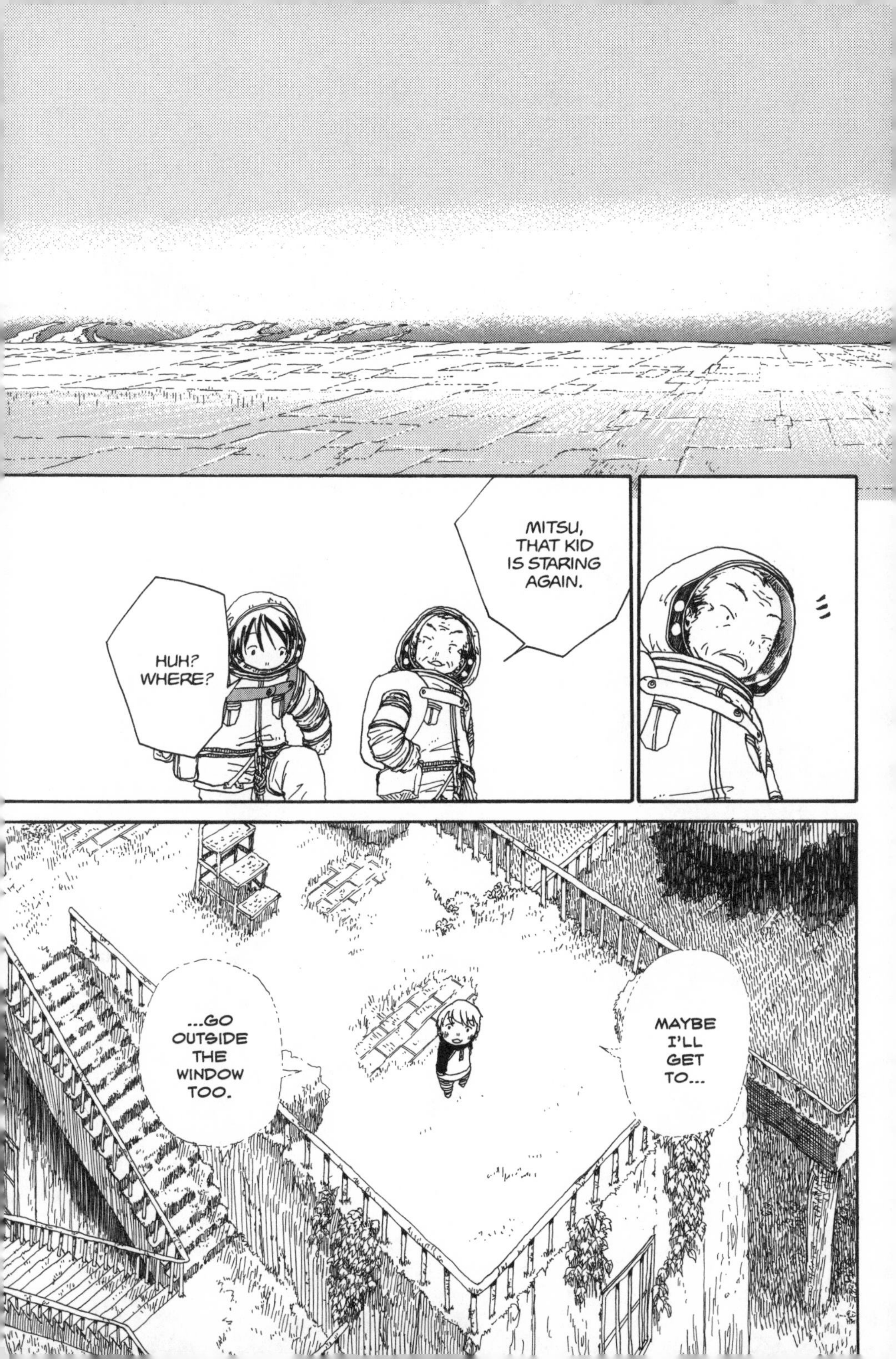
MITSU, THAT KID IS STARING AGAIN.
HUH? WHERE?
MAYBE I'LL GET TO...
...GO OUTSIDE THE WINDOW TOO.

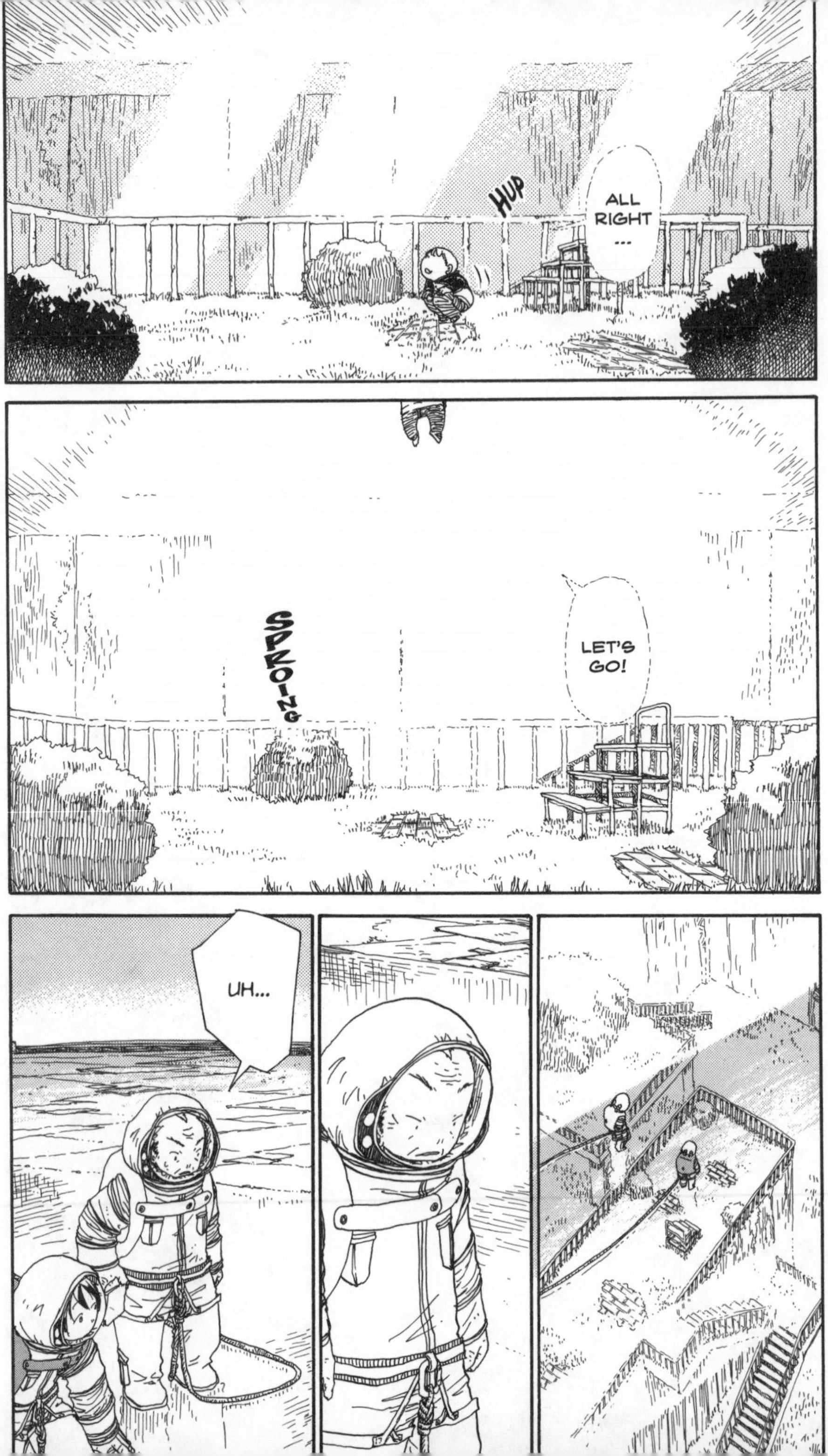
ALL RIGHT ...
HUP
LET'S GO!
SPROING
UH...

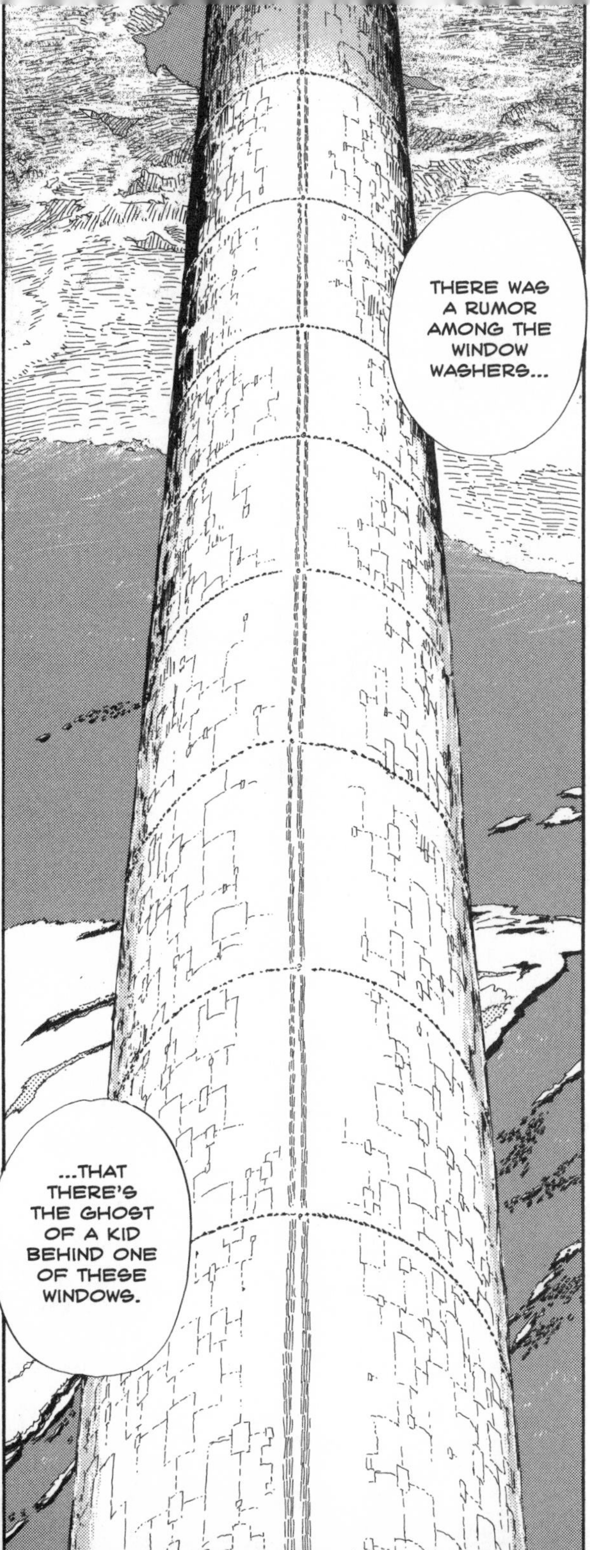
THERE WAS A RUMOR AMONG THE WINDOW WASHERS...
...THAT THERE'S THE GHOST OF A KID BEHIND ONE OF THESE WINDOWS.
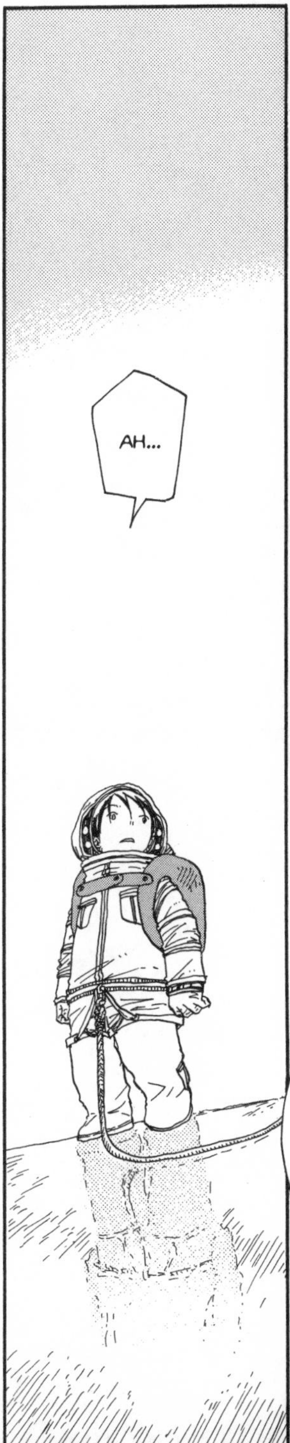
AH...

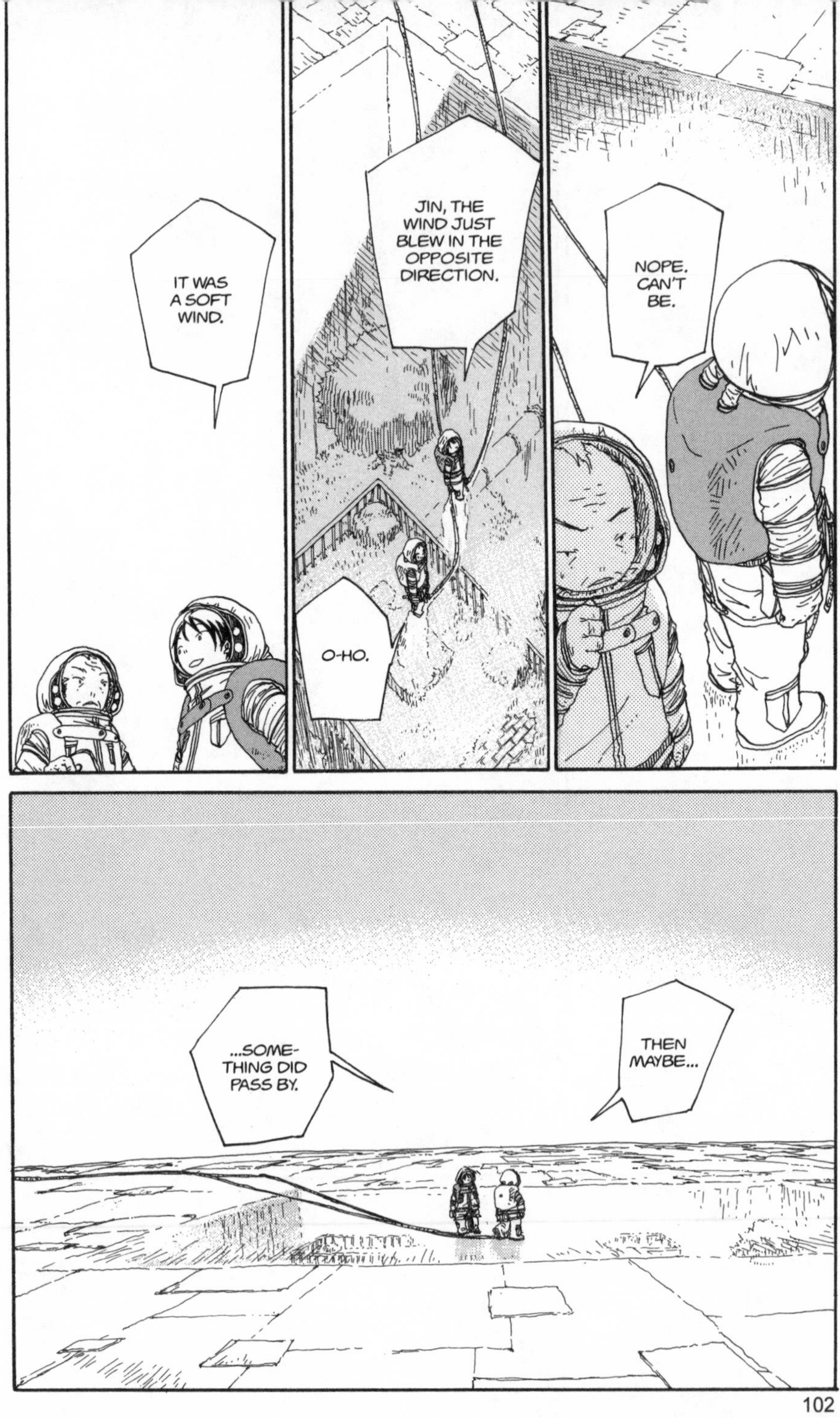
NOPE. CAN'T BE.
JIN, THE WIND JUST BLEW IN THE OPPOSITE DIRECTION.
O-HO.
IT WAS A SOFT WIND.
THEN MAYBE...
...SOME-THING DID PASS BY.

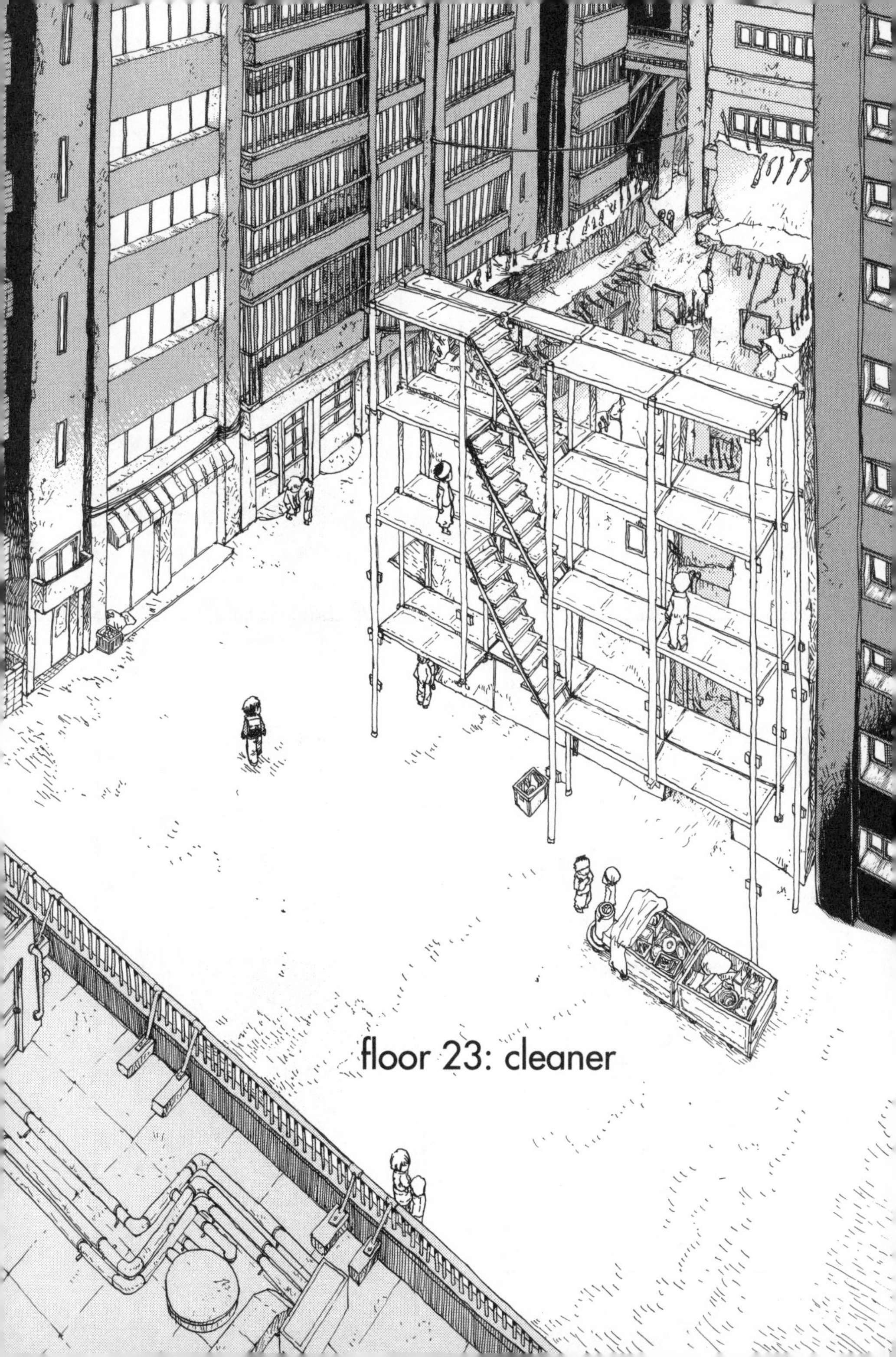

floor 23: cleaner

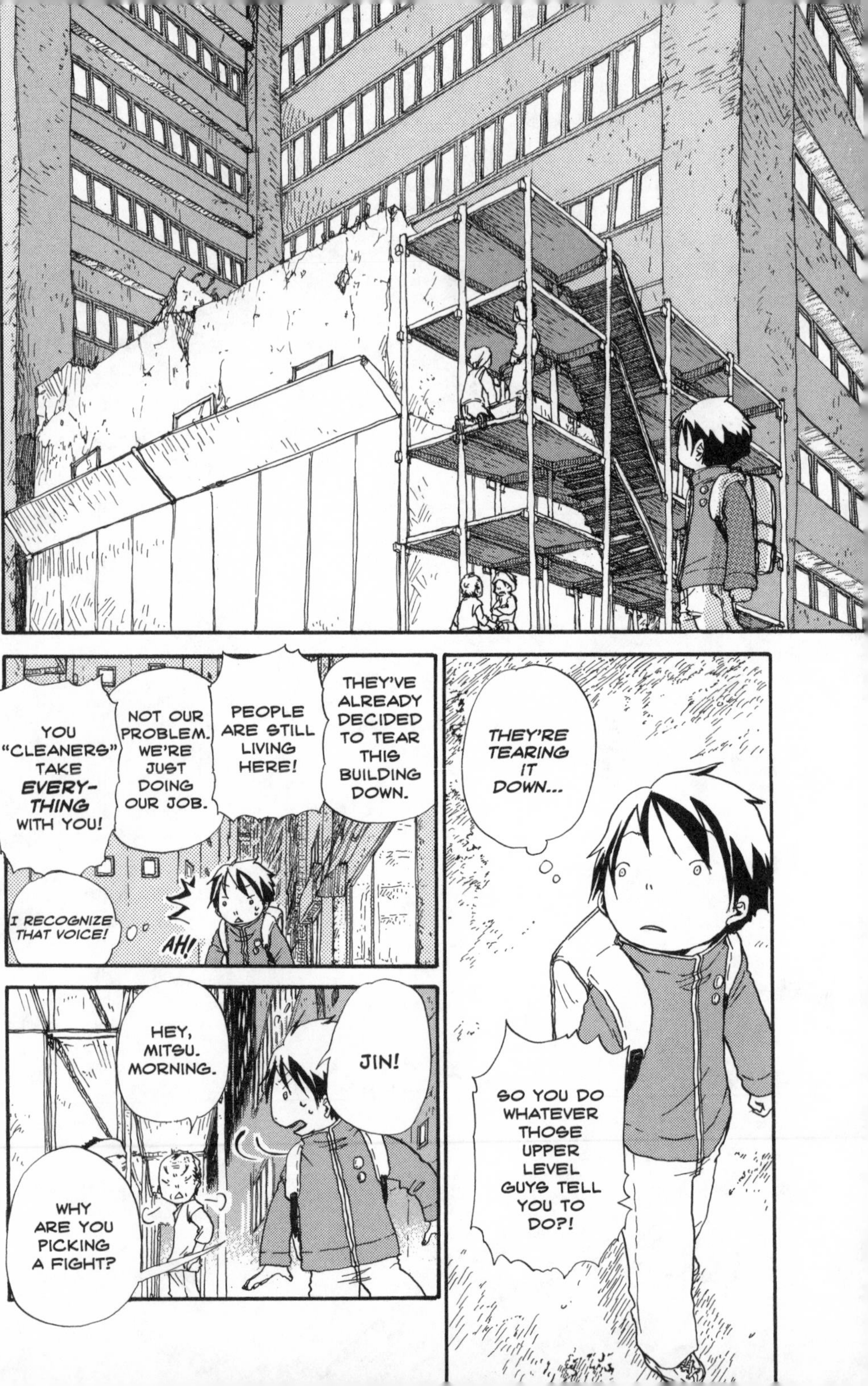
THEY'RE TEARING IT DOWN...
SO YOU DO WHATEVER THOSE UPPER LEVEL GUYS TELL YOU TO DO?!
THEY'VE ALREADY DECIDED TO TEAR THIS BUILDING DOWN.
PEOPLE ARE STILL LIVING HERE!
NOT OUR PROBLEM. WE'RE JUST DOING OUR JOB.
YOU "CLEANERS" TAKE EVERYTHING WITH YOU!
I RECOGNIZE THAT VOICE!
AH!
JIN!
HEY, MITSU. MORNING.
WHY ARE YOU PICKING A FIGHT?

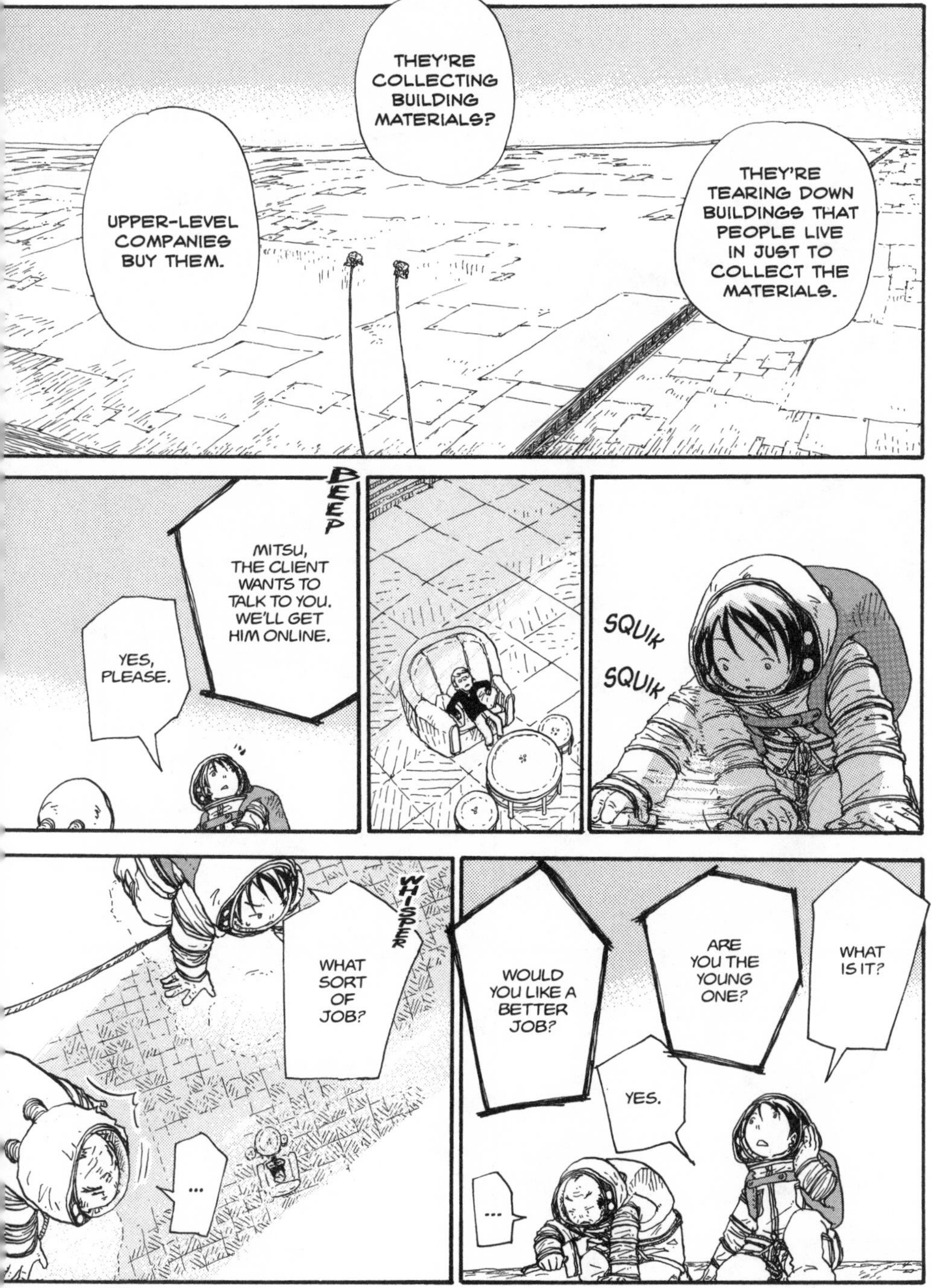

THEY'RE TEARING DOWN BUILDINGS THAT PEOPLE LIVE IN JUST TO COLLECT THE MATERIALS.
THEY'RE COLLECTING BUILDING MATERIALS?
UPPER-LEVEL COMPANIES BUY THEM.
SQUIK
SQUIK
BEEP
MITSU, THE CLIENT WANTS TO TALK TO YOU. WE'LL GET HIM ONLINE.
YES, PLEASE.
WHAT IS IT?
ARE YOU THE YOUNG ONE?
YES.
WOULD YOU LIKE A BETTER JOB?
...
WHISPER
WHAT SORT OF JOB?
...

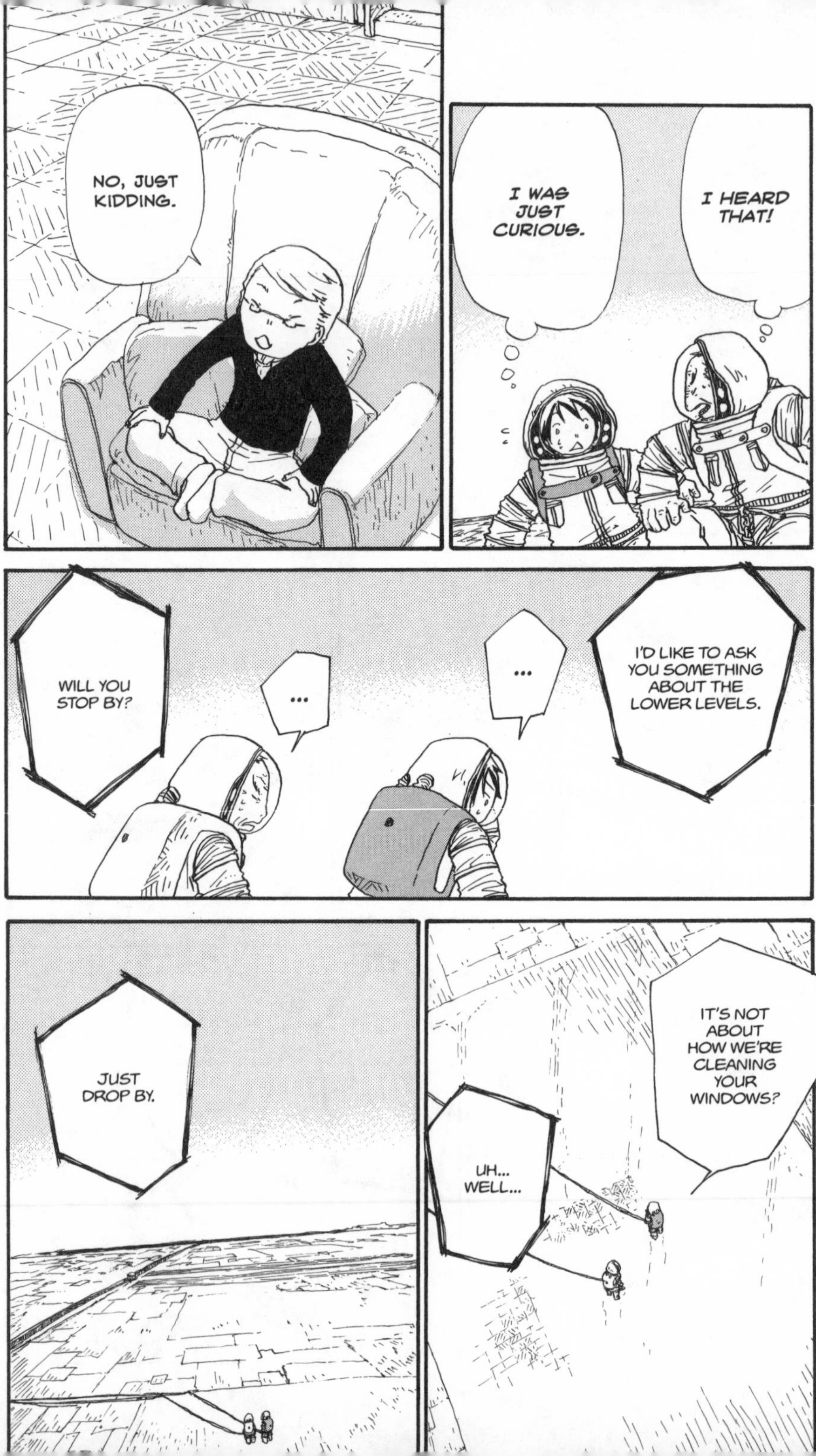
I HEARD THAT!
I WAS JUST CURIOUS.
NO, JUST KIDDING.
I'D LIKE TO ASK YOU SOMETHING ABOUT THE LOWER LEVELS.
...
...
WILL YOU STOP BY?
IT'S NOT ABOUT HOW WE'RE CLEANING YOUR WINDOWS?
UH... WELL...
JUST DROP BY.

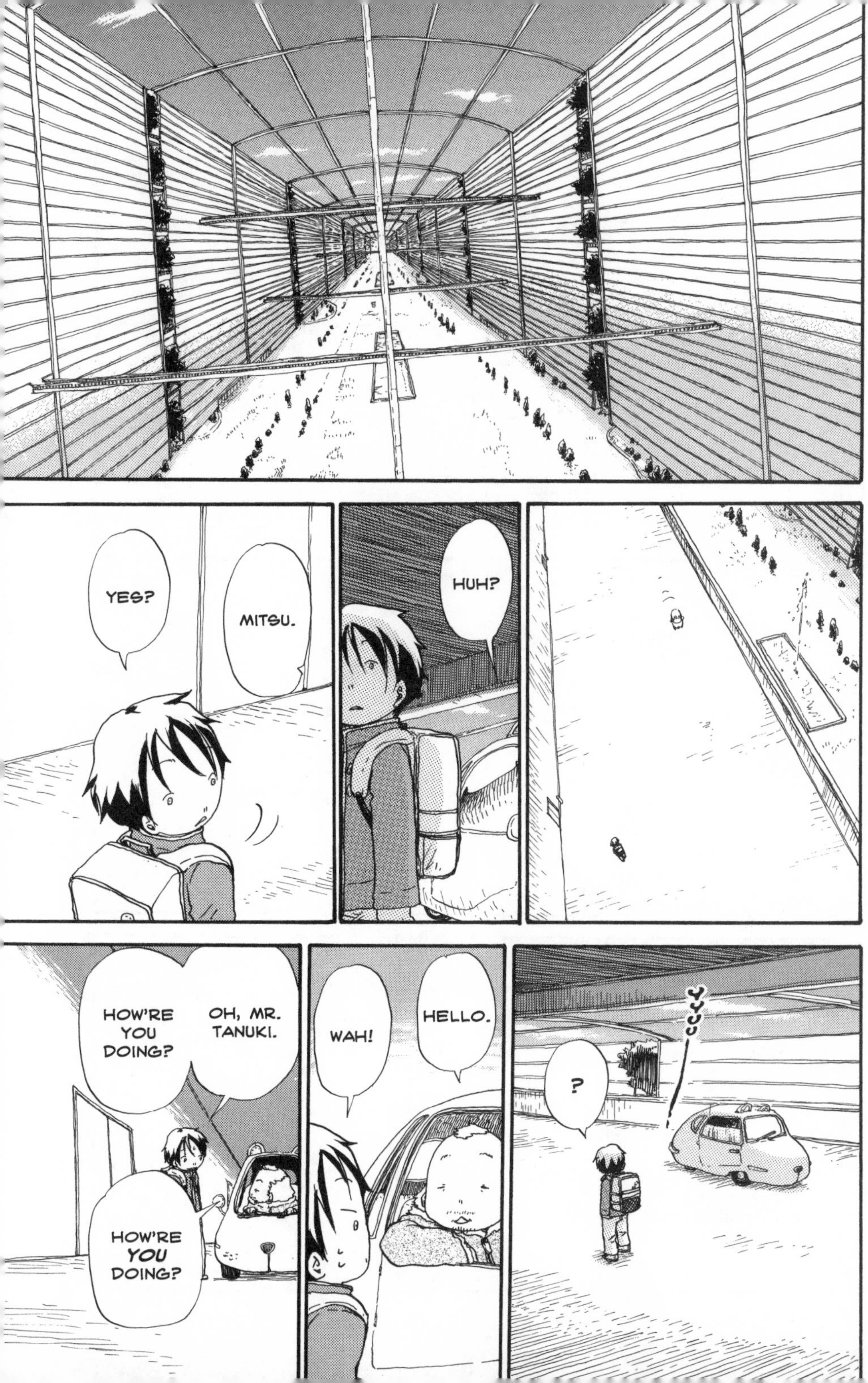
HUH?
MITSU.
YES?
YYUU
?
HELLO.
WAH!
OH, MR. TANUKI.
HOW'RE YOU DOING?
HOW'RE *YOU* DOING?

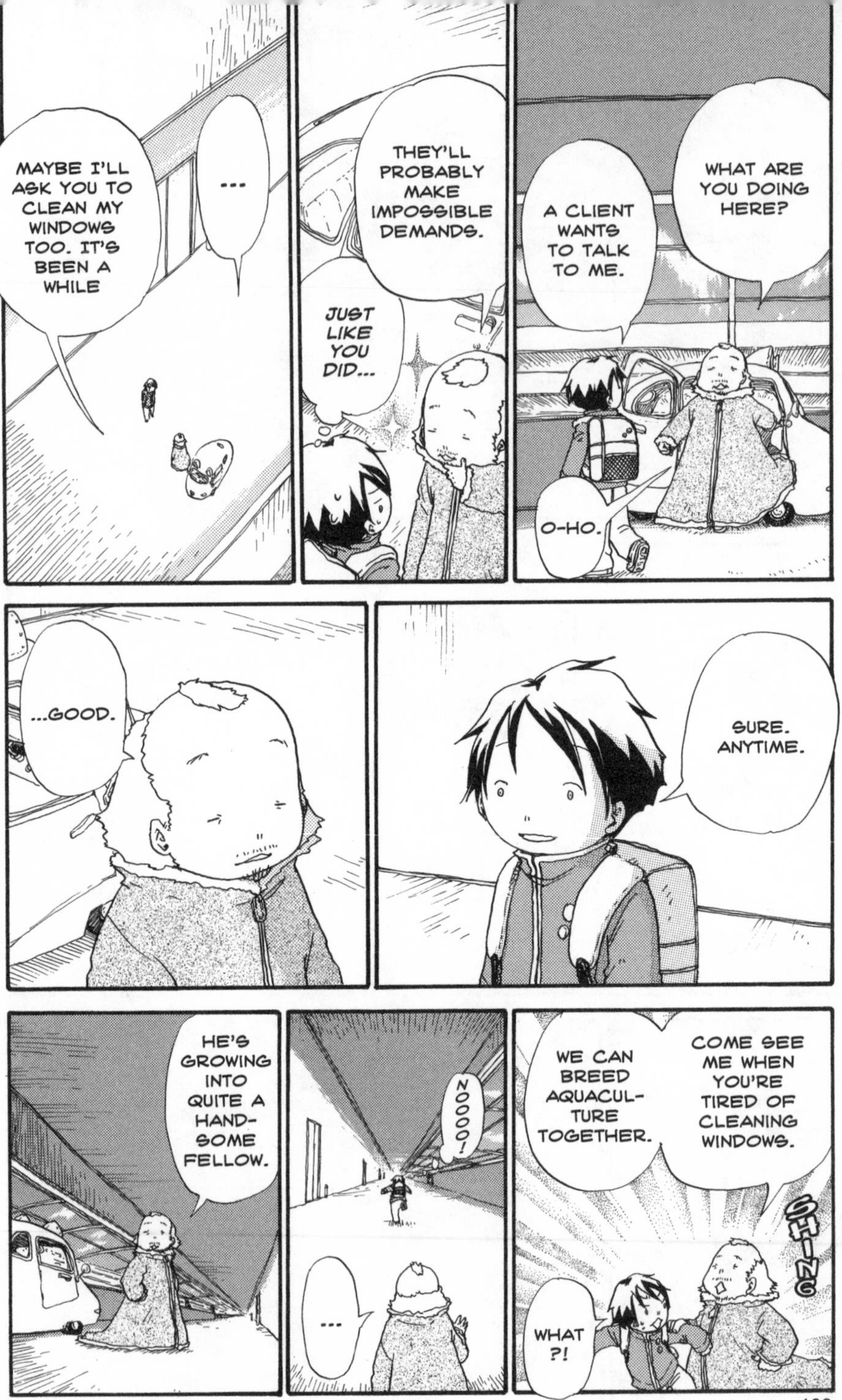
WHAT ARE YOU DOING HERE?
A CLIENT WANTS TO TALK TO ME.
O-HO.
THEY'LL PROBABLY MAKE IMPOSSIBLE DEMANDS.
JUST LIKE YOU DID...
...
MAYBE I'LL ASK YOU TO CLEAN MY WINDOWS TOO. IT'S BEEN A WHILE
SURE. ANYTIME.
...GOOD.
COME SEE ME WHEN YOU'RE TIRED OF CLEANING WINDOWS.
WE CAN BREED AQUACUL-TURE TOGETHER.
SHING
WHAT?!
NOOOO!
...
HE'S GROWING INTO QUITE A HAND-SOME FELLOW.

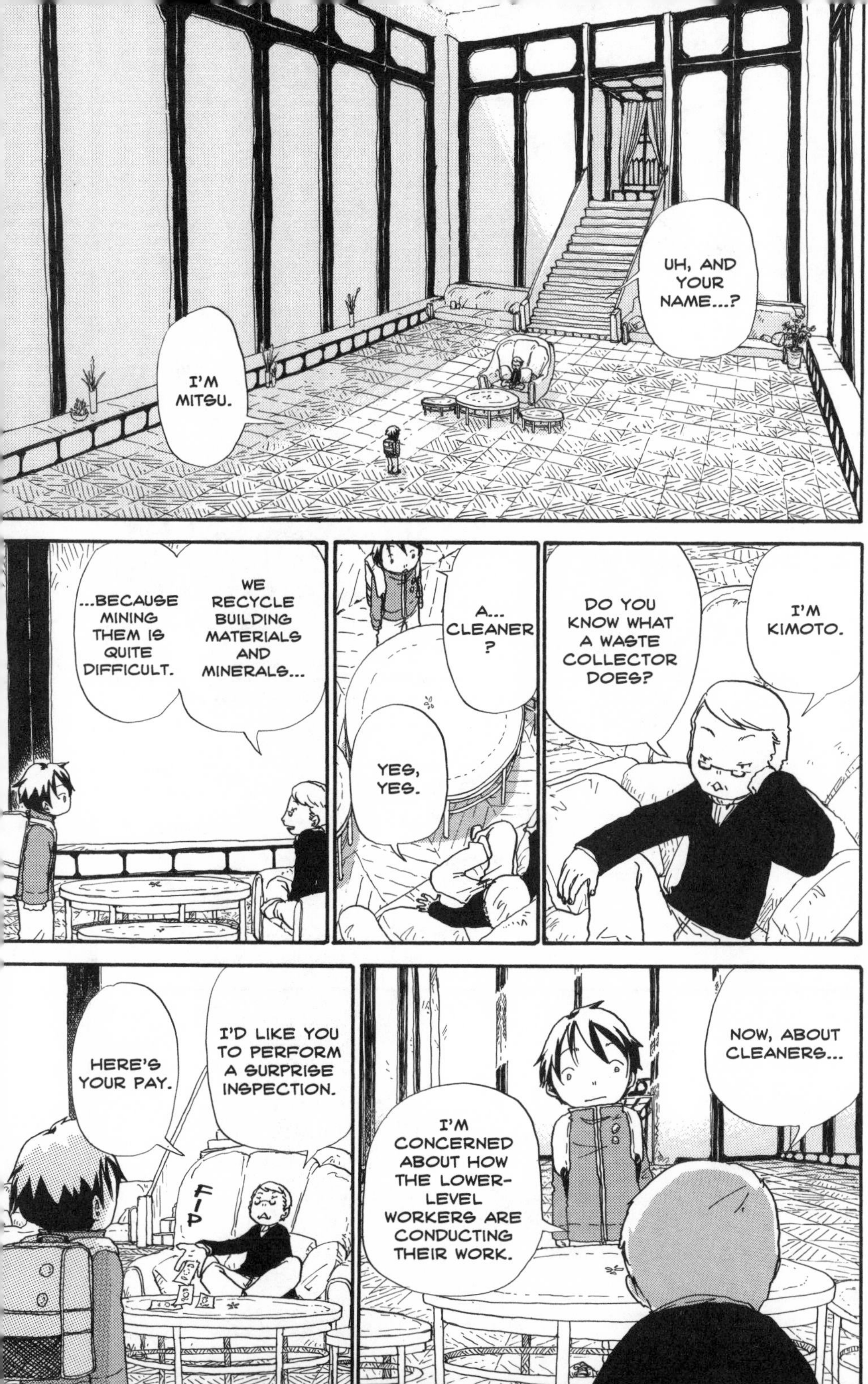
UH, AND YOUR NAME...?
I'M MITSU.
I'M KIMOTO.
DO YOU KNOW WHAT A WASTE COLLECTOR DOES?
A... CLEANER?
YES, YES.
WE RECYCLE BUILDING MATERIALS AND MINERALS...
...BECAUSE MINING THEM IS QUITE DIFFICULT.
NOW, ABOUT CLEANERS...
I'M CONCERNED ABOUT HOW THE LOWER-LEVEL WORKERS ARE CONDUCTING THEIR WORK.
I'D LIKE YOU TO PERFORM A SURPRISE INSPECTION.
FIP
HERE'S YOUR PAY.

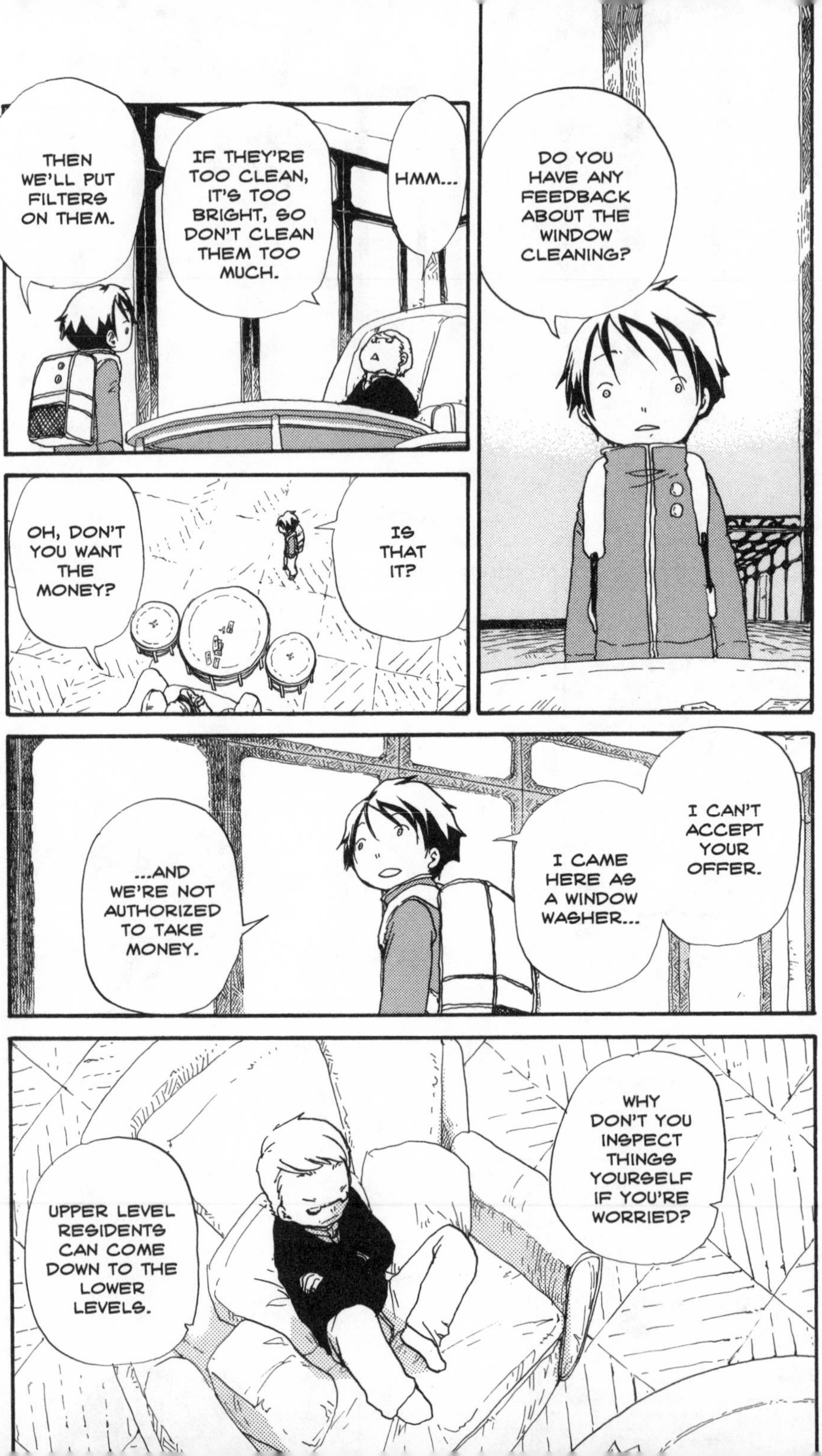
DO YOU HAVE ANY FEEDBACK ABOUT THE WINDOW CLEANING?
HMM...
IF THEY'RE TOO CLEAN, IT'S TOO BRIGHT, SO DON'T CLEAN THEM TOO MUCH.
THEN WE'LL PUT FILTERS ON THEM.
IS THAT IT?
OH, DON'T YOU WANT THE MONEY?
I CAN'T ACCEPT YOUR OFFER.
I CAME HERE AS A WINDOW WASHER...
...AND WE'RE NOT AUTHORIZED TO TAKE MONEY.
WHY DON'T YOU INSPECT THINGS YOURSELF IF YOU'RE WORRIED?
UPPER LEVEL RESIDENTS CAN COME DOWN TO THE LOWER LEVELS.

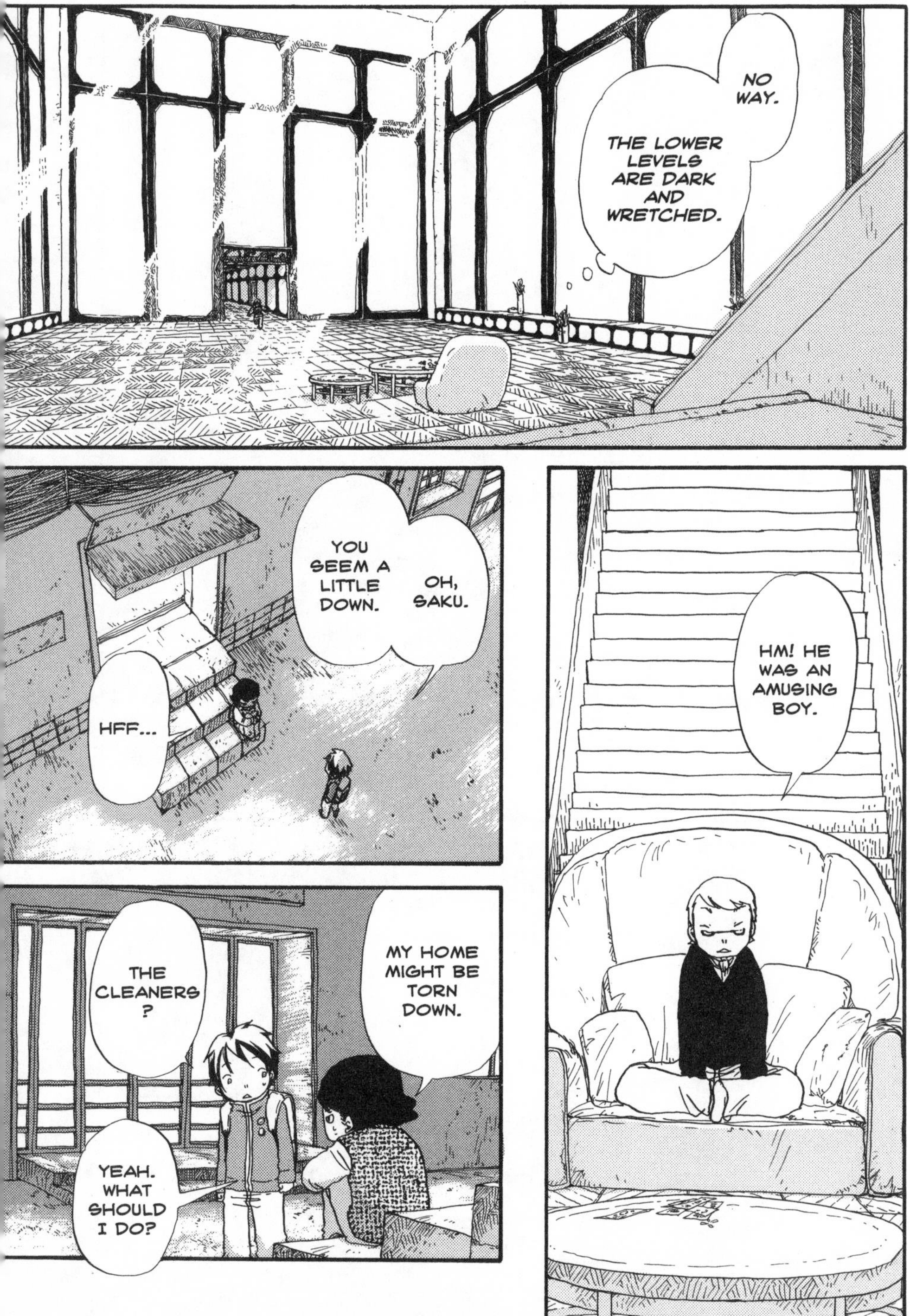
NO WAY.
THE LOWER LEVELS ARE DARK AND WRETCHED.
HM! HE WAS AN AMUSING BOY.
OH, SAKU.
YOU SEEM A LITTLE DOWN.
HFF...
MY HOME MIGHT BE TORN DOWN.
THE CLEANERS?
YEAH. WHAT SHOULD I DO?

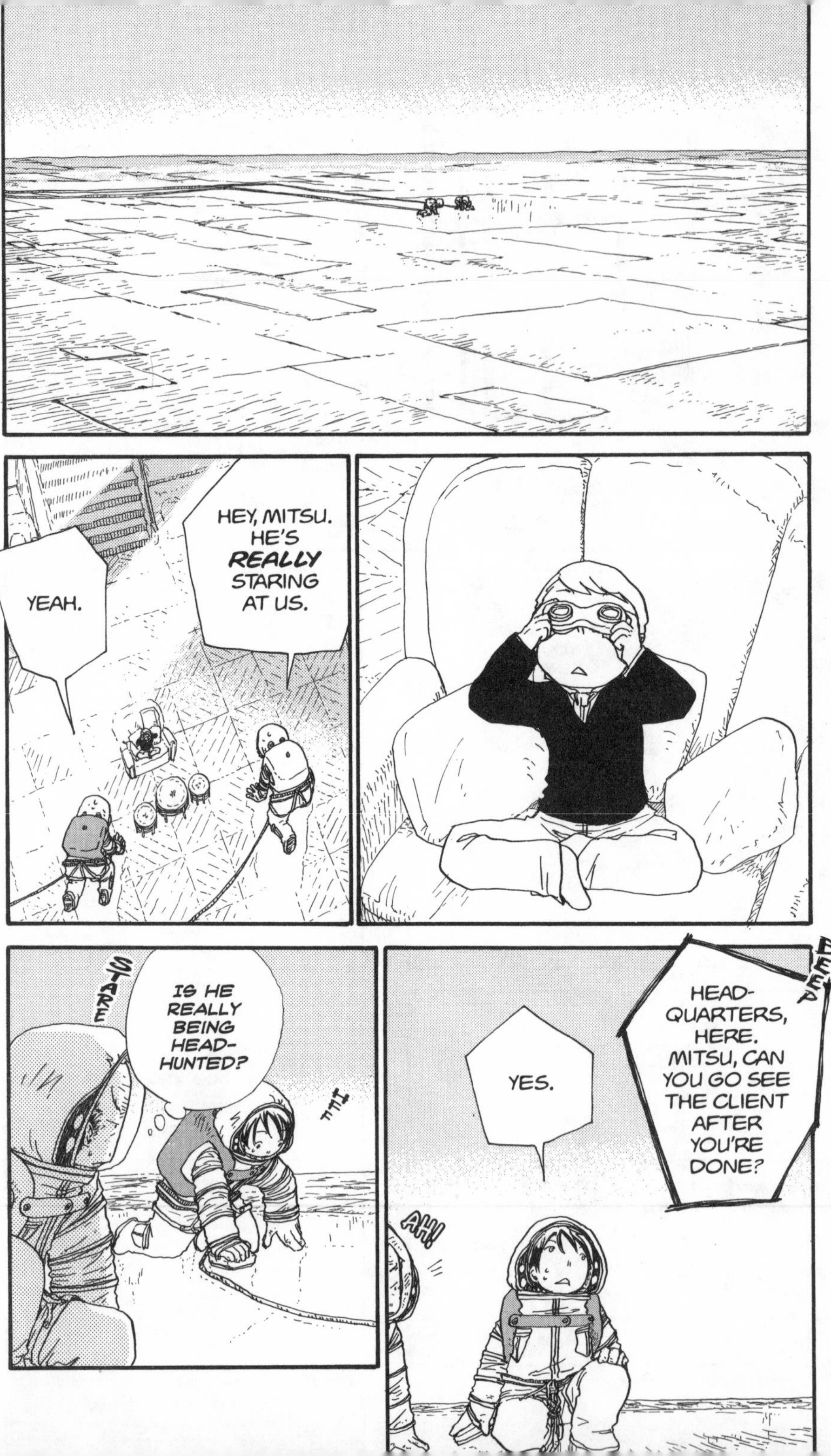
HEY, MITSU. HE'S ***REALLY*** STARING AT US.
YEAH.
BEEP
HEAD-QUARTERS, HERE. MITSU, CAN YOU GO SEE THE CLIENT AFTER YOU'RE DONE?
YES.
AH!
STARE
IS HE REALLY BEING HEAD-HUNTED?

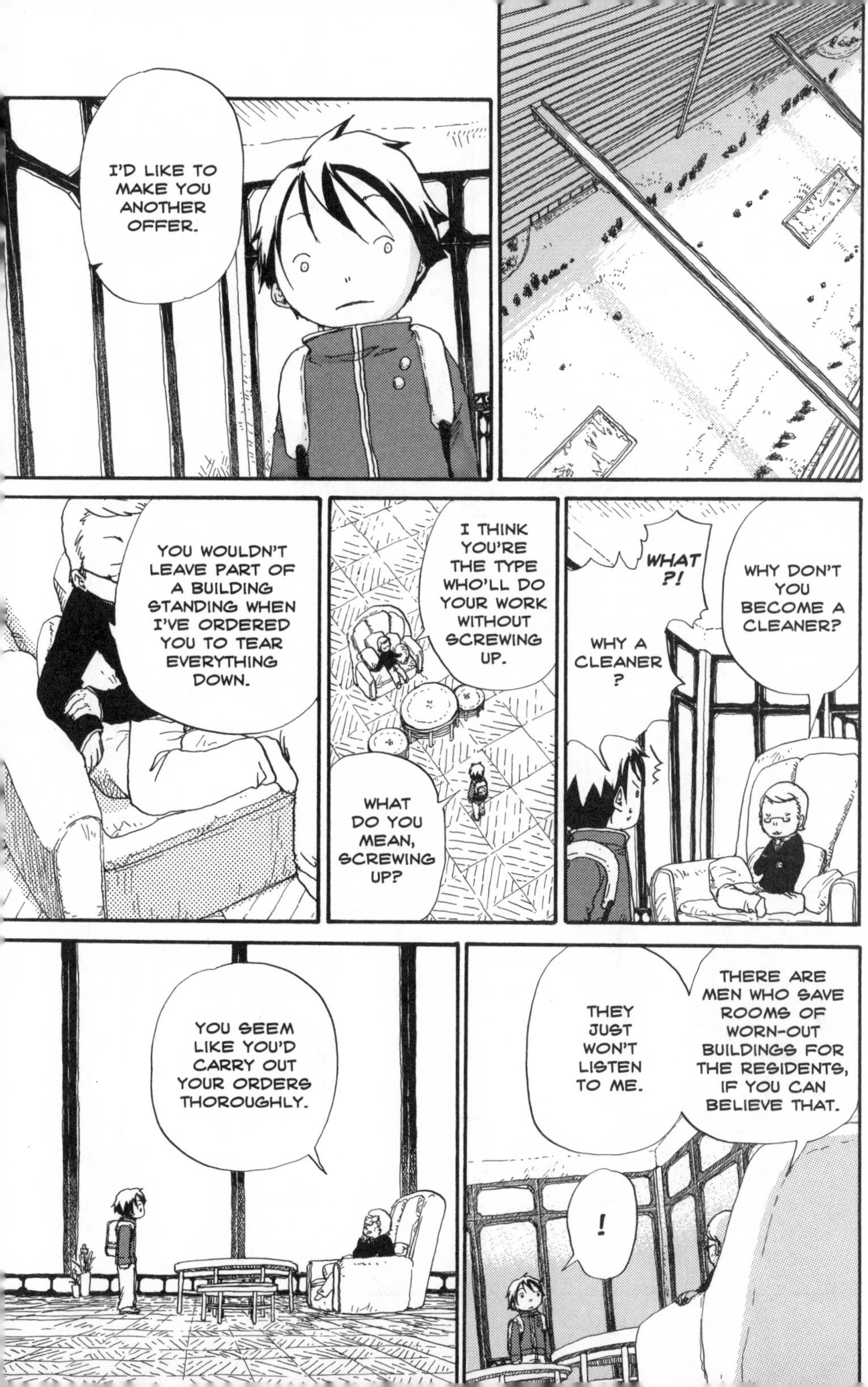
I'D LIKE TO MAKE YOU ANOTHER OFFER.
WHY DON'T YOU BECOME A CLEANER?
WHAT?!
WHY A CLEANER?
I THINK YOU'RE THE TYPE WHO'LL DO YOUR WORK WITHOUT SCREWING UP.
WHAT DO YOU MEAN, SCREWING UP?
YOU WOULDN'T LEAVE PART OF A BUILDING STANDING WHEN I'VE ORDERED YOU TO TEAR EVERYTHING DOWN.
THERE ARE MEN WHO SAVE ROOMS OF WORN-OUT BUILDINGS FOR THE RESIDENTS, IF YOU CAN BELIEVE THAT.
THEY JUST WON'T LISTEN TO ME.
!
YOU SEEM LIKE YOU'D CARRY OUT YOUR ORDERS THOROUGHLY.

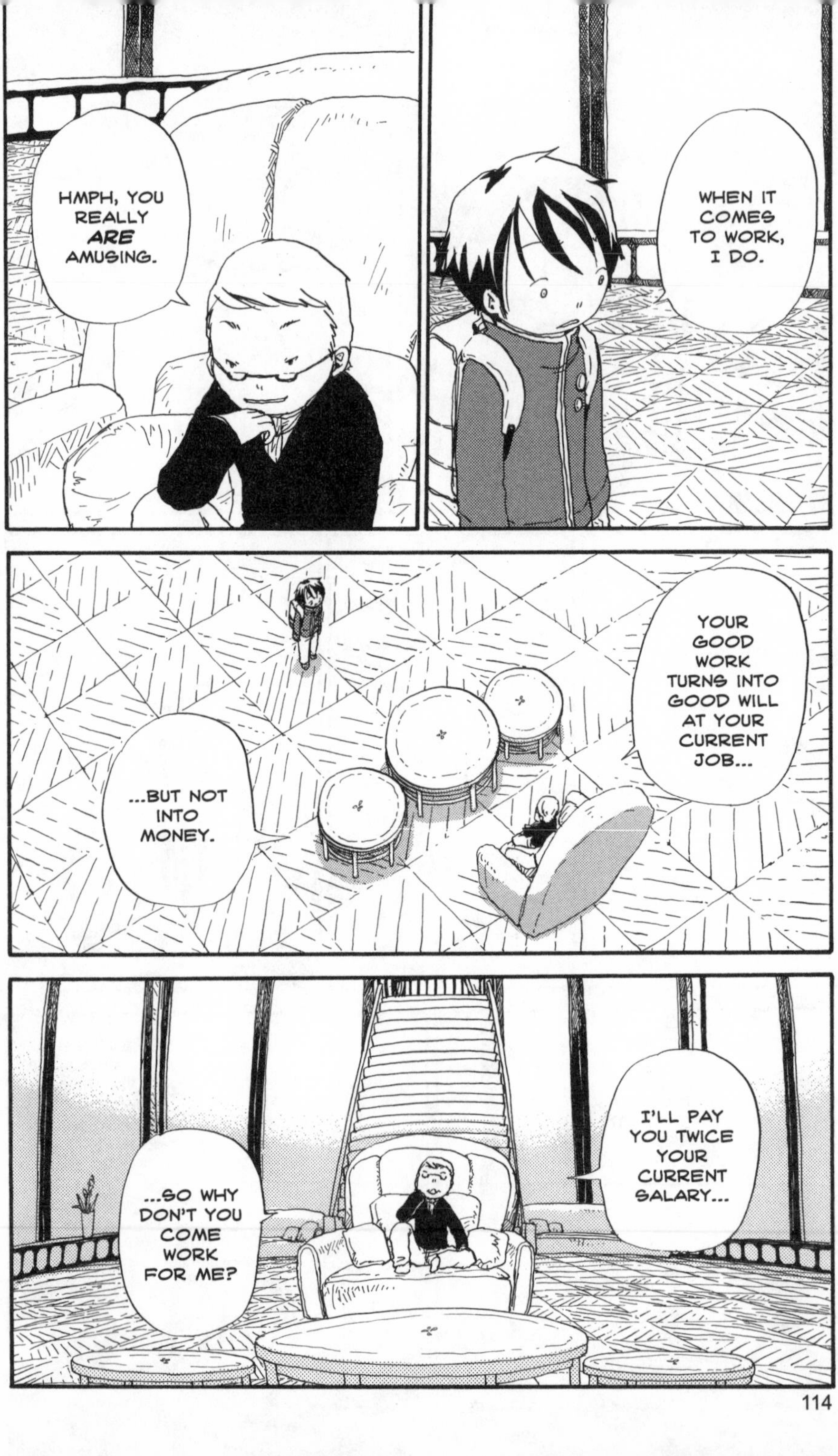
WHEN IT COMES TO WORK, I DO.
HMPH, YOU REALLY **ARE** AMUSING.
YOUR GOOD WORK TURNS INTO GOOD WILL AT YOUR CURRENT JOB...
...BUT NOT INTO MONEY.
I'LL PAY YOU TWICE YOUR CURRENT SALARY...
...SO WHY DON'T YOU COME WORK FOR ME?

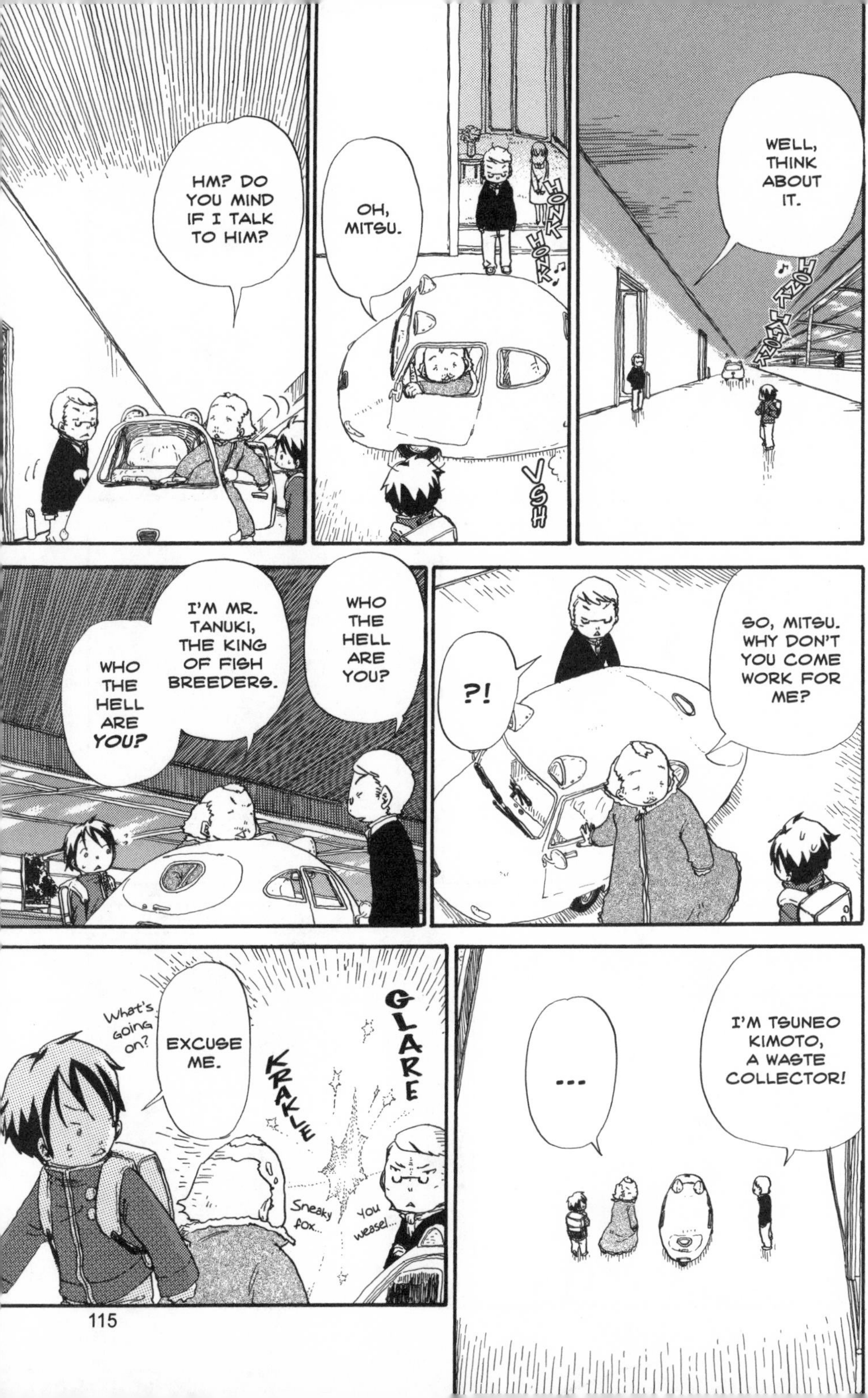
WELL, THINK ABOUT IT.
HONK HONK
OH, MITSU.
HONK HONK
VSH
HM? DO YOU MIND IF I TALK TO HIM?
SO, MITSU. WHY DON'T YOU COME WORK FOR ME?
?!
WHO THE HELL ARE YOU?
I'M MR. TANUKI, THE KING OF FISH BREEDERS.
WHO THE HELL ARE *YOU?*
I'M TSUNEO KIMOTO, A WASTE COLLECTOR!
...
GLARE
EXCUSE ME.
What's going on?
KRAKLE
You weasel...
Sneaky fox..

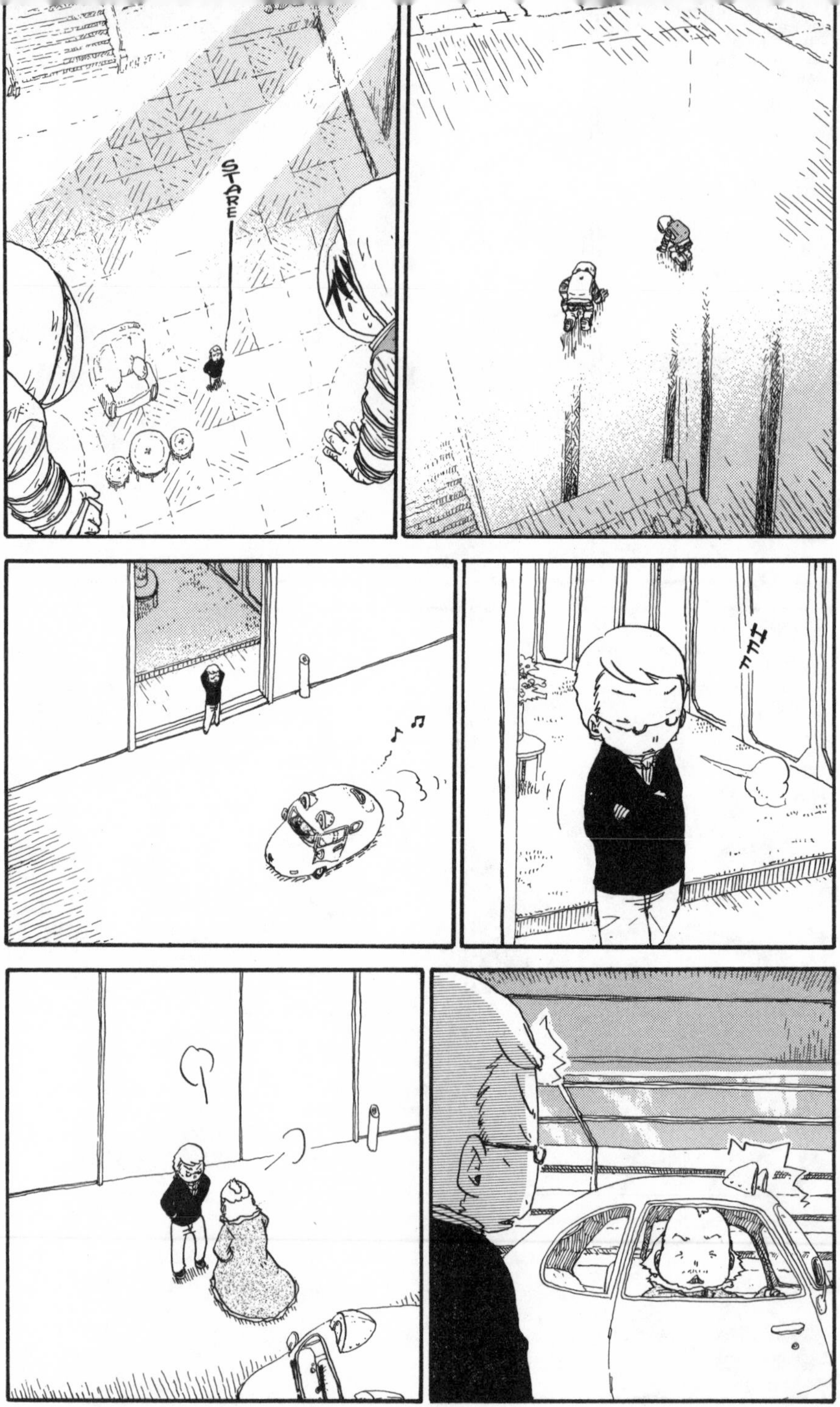
STARE
HFF

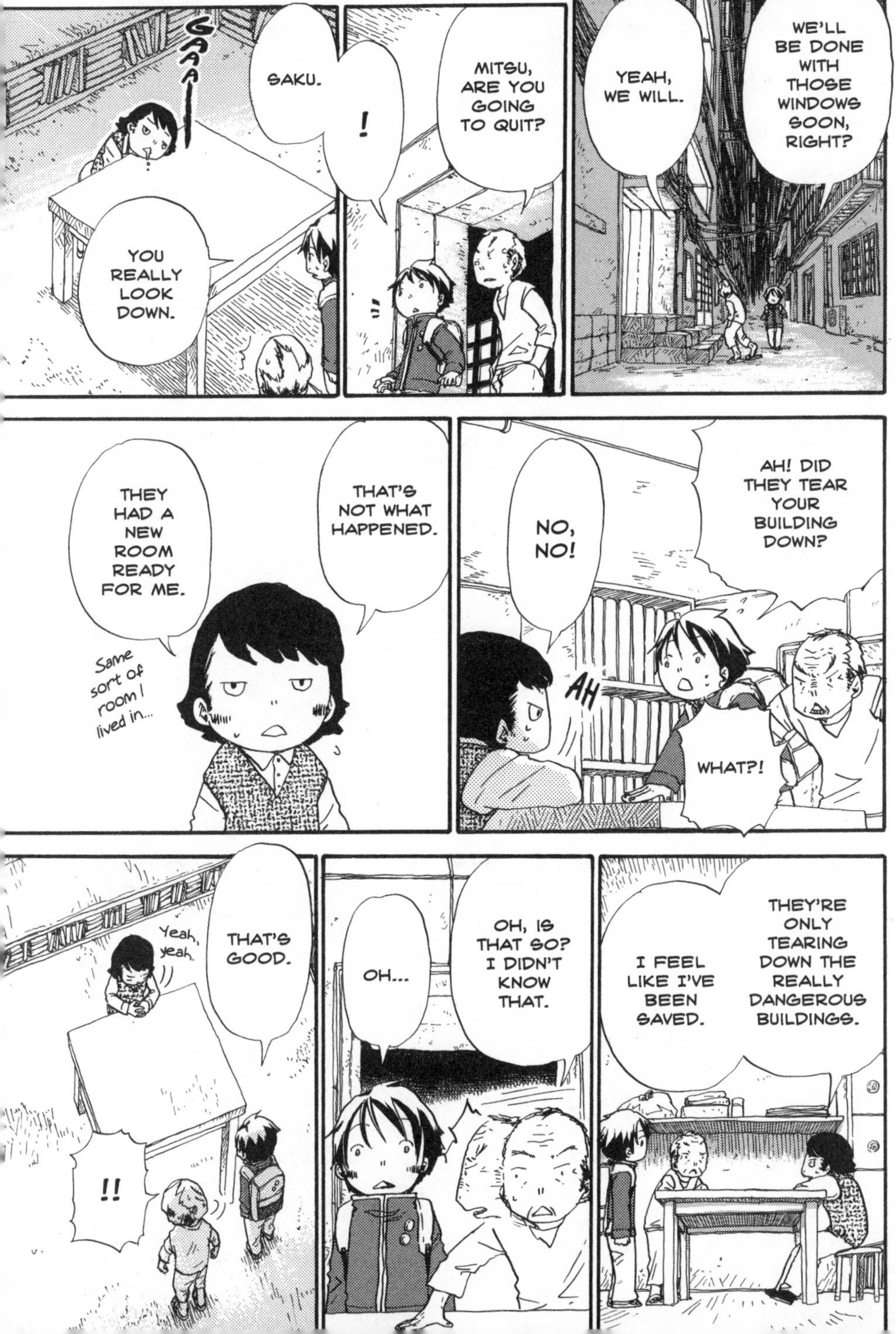
WE'LL BE DONE WITH THOSE WINDOWS SOON, RIGHT?
YEAH, WE WILL.
MITSU, ARE YOU GOING TO QUIT?
!
SAKU.
GAAA
YOU REALLY LOOK DOWN.
AH! DID THEY TEAR YOUR BUILDING DOWN?
NO, NO!
AH
WHAT?!
THAT'S NOT WHAT HAPPENED.
THEY HAD A NEW ROOM READY FOR ME.
Same sort of room I lived in...
THEY'RE ONLY TEARING DOWN THE REALLY DANGEROUS BUILDINGS.
I FEEL LIKE I'VE BEEN SAVED.
OH, IS THAT SO? I DIDN'T KNOW THAT.
OH...
THAT'S GOOD.
Yeah, yeah.
!!

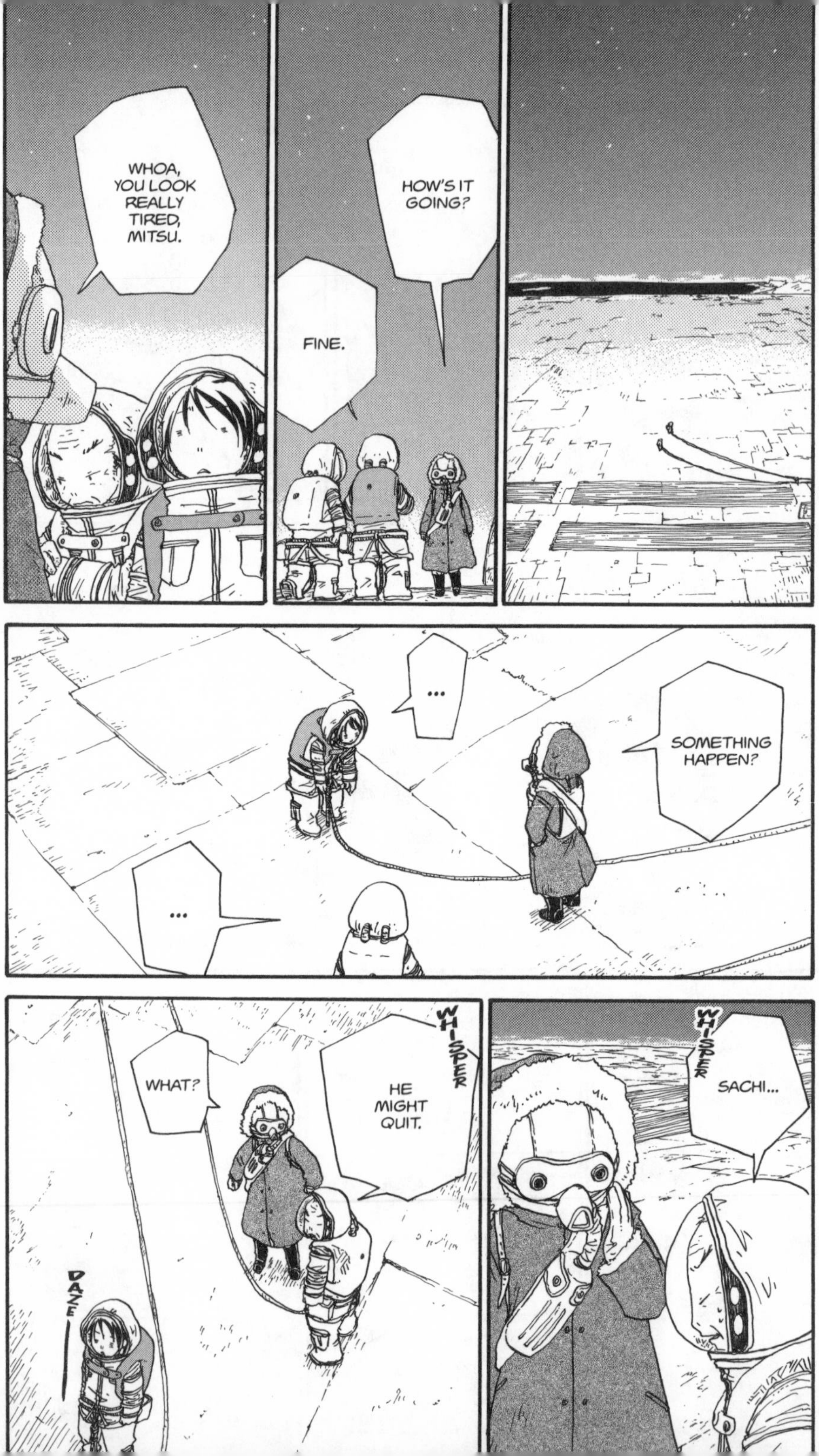
HOW'S IT GOING?
FINE.
WHOA, YOU LOOK REALLY TIRED, MITSU.
SOMETHING HAPPEN?
...
...
WHISPER
SACHI...
WHISPER
HE MIGHT QUIT.
WHAT?
DAZE

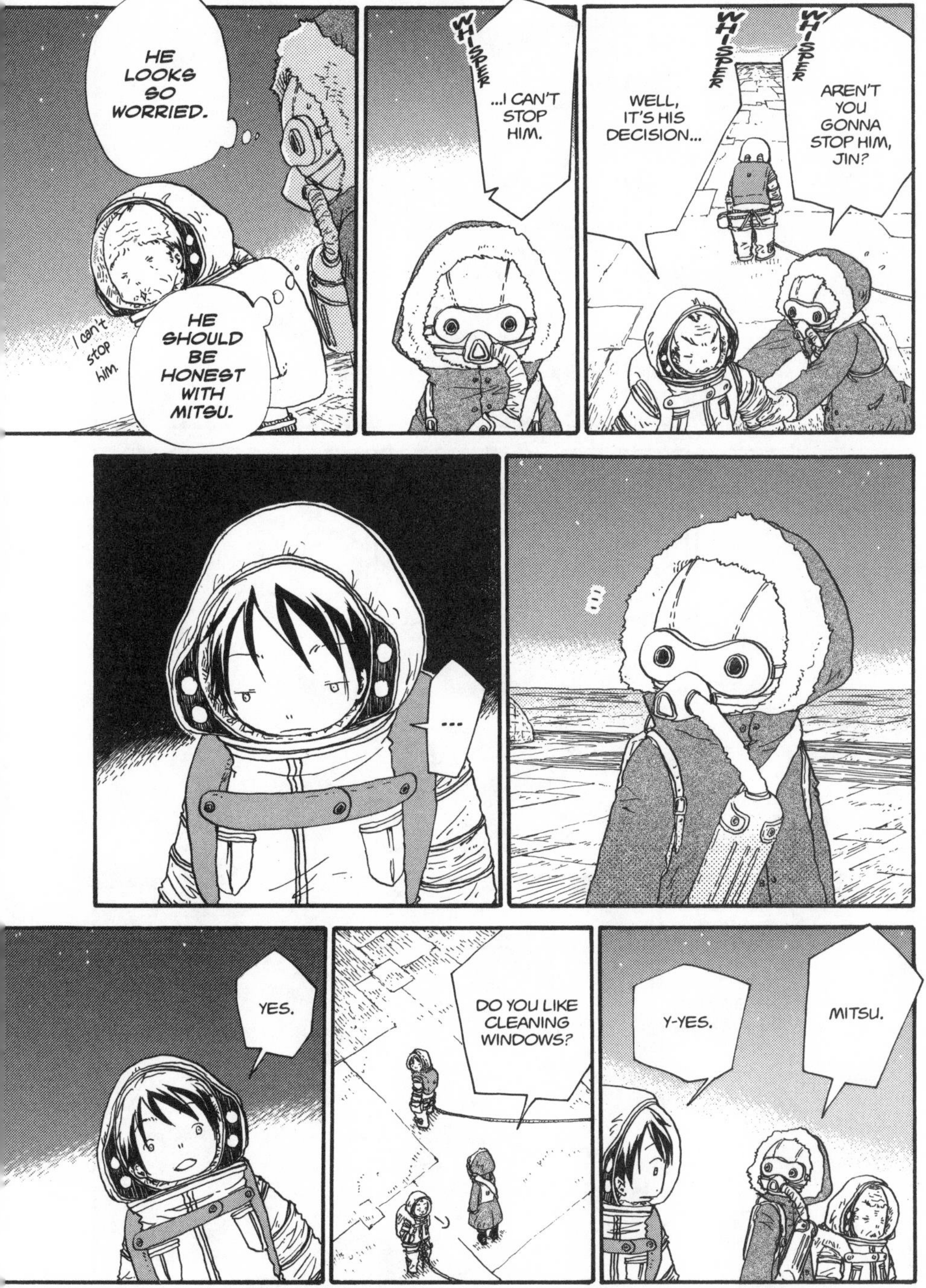
WHISPER
AREN'T YOU GONNA STOP HIM, JIN?
WHISPER
WELL, IT'S HIS DECISION...
WHISPER
...I CAN'T STOP HIM.
HE LOOKS SO WORRIED.
HE SHOULD BE HONEST WITH MITSU.
I can't stop him.
...
...
MITSU.
Y-YES.
DO YOU LIKE CLEANING WINDOWS?
YES.

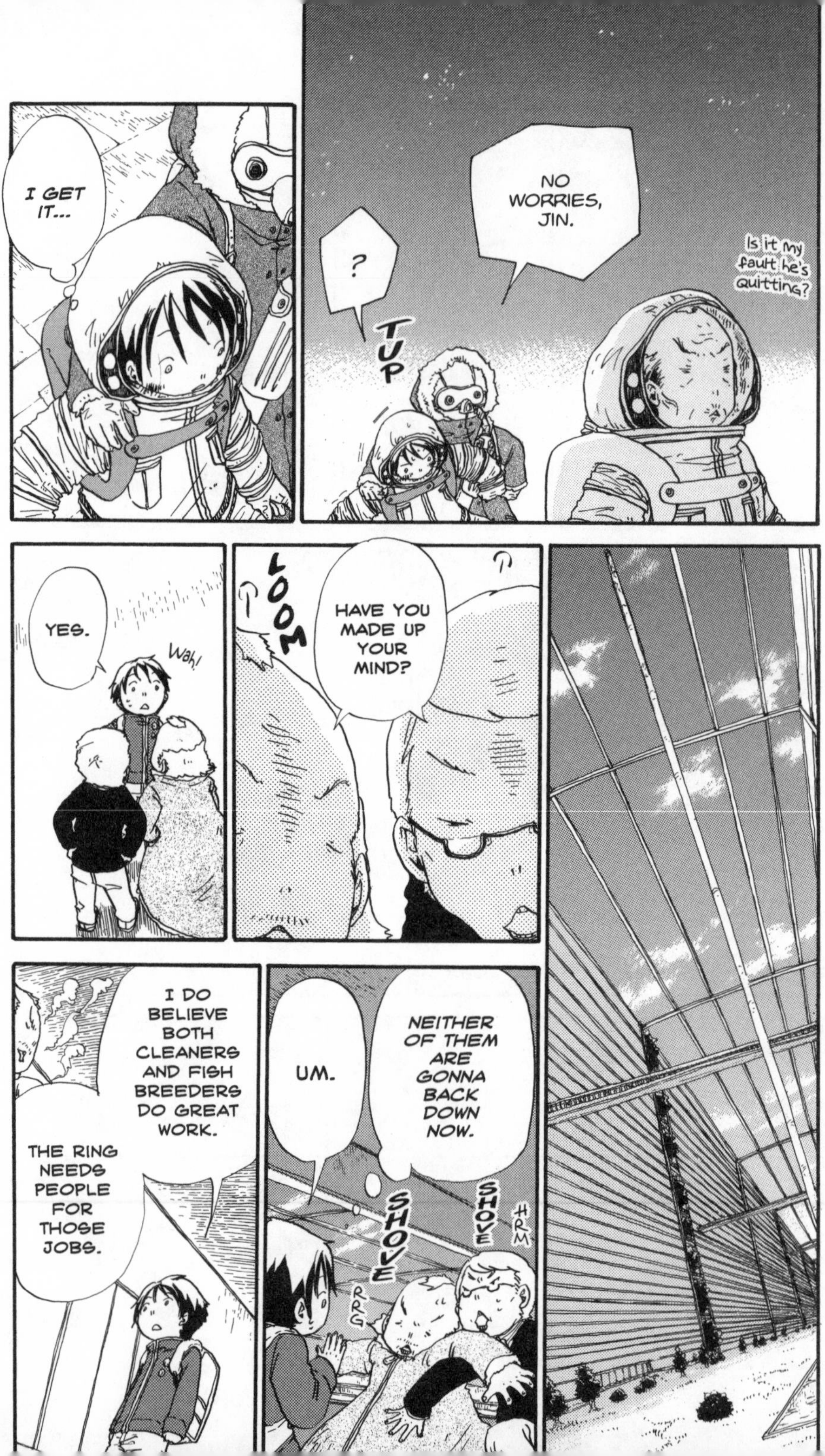
NO WORRIES, JIN.
Is it my fault he's quitting?
?
TUP
I GET IT...
HAVE YOU MADE UP YOUR MIND?
LOOM
YES.
Wah!
NEITHER OF THEM ARE GONNA BACK DOWN NOW.
SHOVE
HRM
UM.
SHOVE
RRG
I DO BELIEVE BOTH CLEANERS AND FISH BREEDERS DO GREAT WORK.
THE RING NEEDS PEOPLE FOR THOSE JOBS.

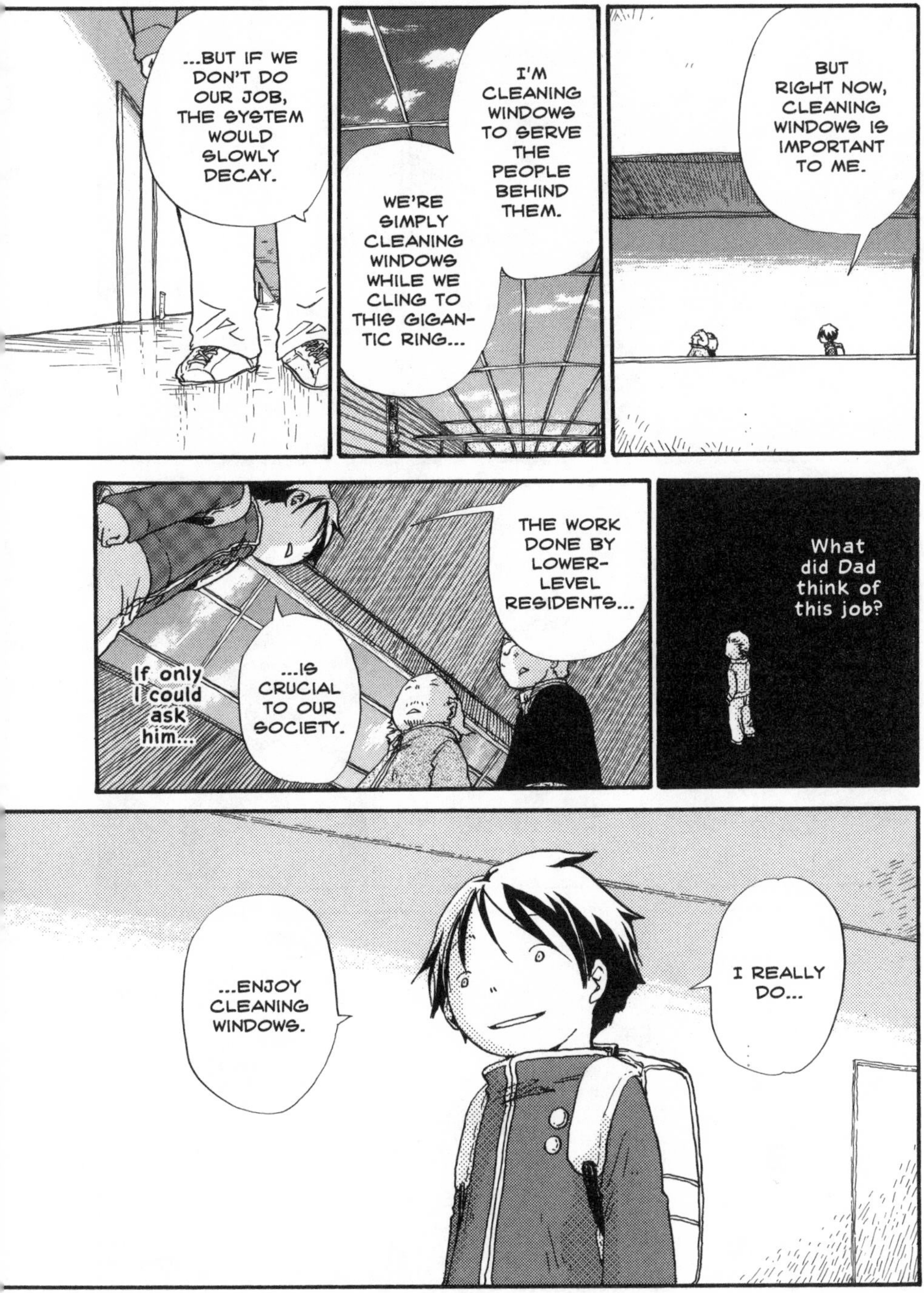
BUT RIGHT NOW, CLEANING WINDOWS IS IMPORTANT TO ME.
I'M CLEANING WINDOWS TO SERVE THE PEOPLE BEHIND THEM.
WE'RE SIMPLY CLEANING WINDOWS WHILE WE CLING TO THIS GIGANTIC RING...
...BUT IF WE DON'T DO OUR JOB, THE SYSTEM WOULD SLOWLY DECAY.
What did Dad think of this job?
THE WORK DONE BY LOWER-LEVEL RESIDENTS...
...IS CRUCIAL TO OUR SOCIETY.
If only I could ask him...
I REALLY DO...
...ENJOY CLEANING WINDOWS.

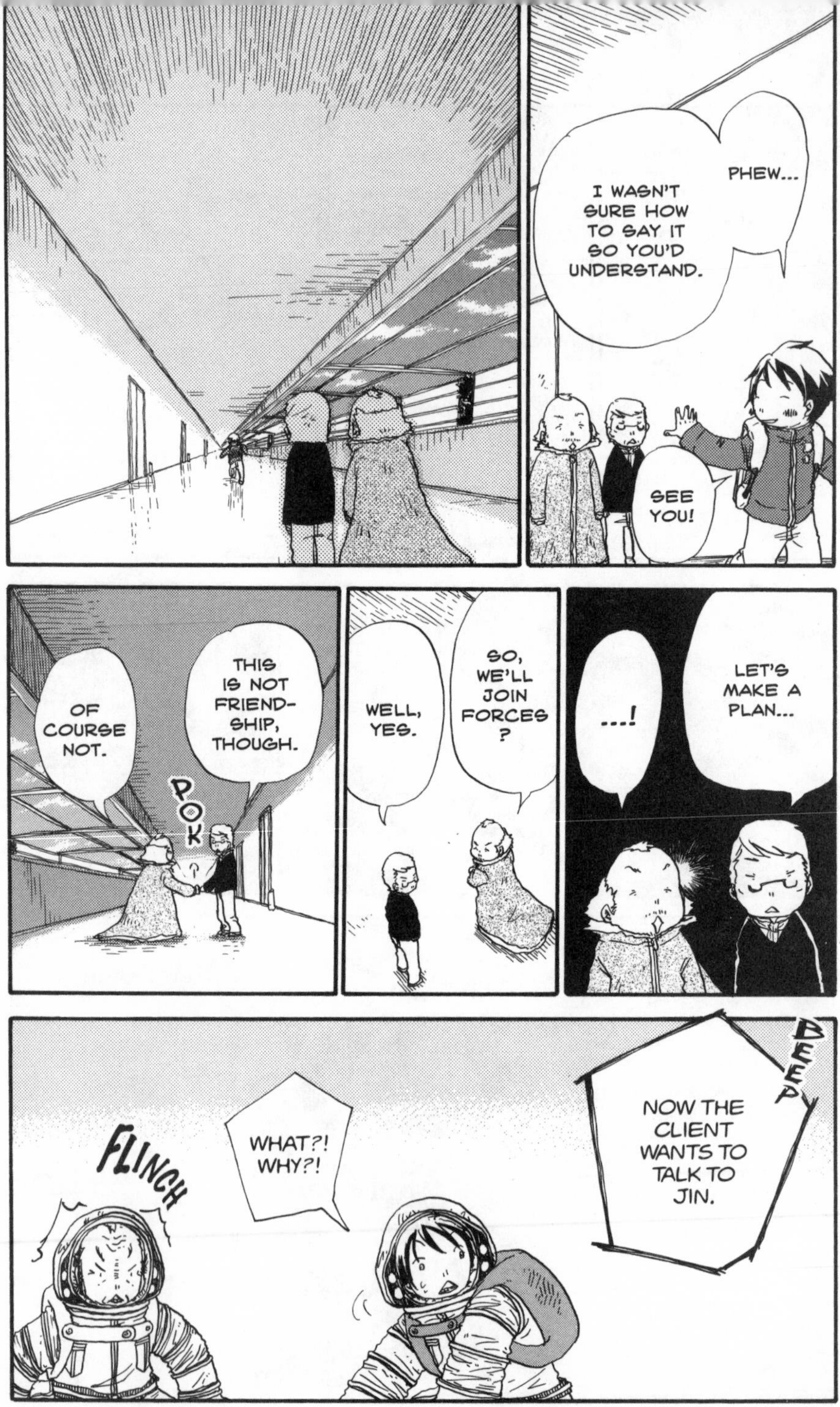
PHEW...
I WASN'T SURE HOW TO SAY IT SO YOU'D UNDERSTAND.
SEE YOU!
LET'S MAKE A PLAN...
...!
SO, WE'LL JOIN FORCES?
WELL, YES.
THIS IS NOT FRIEND-SHIP, THOUGH.
OF COURSE NOT.
POK
BEEP
NOW THE CLIENT WANTS TO TALK TO JIN.
WHAT?! WHY?!
FLINCH

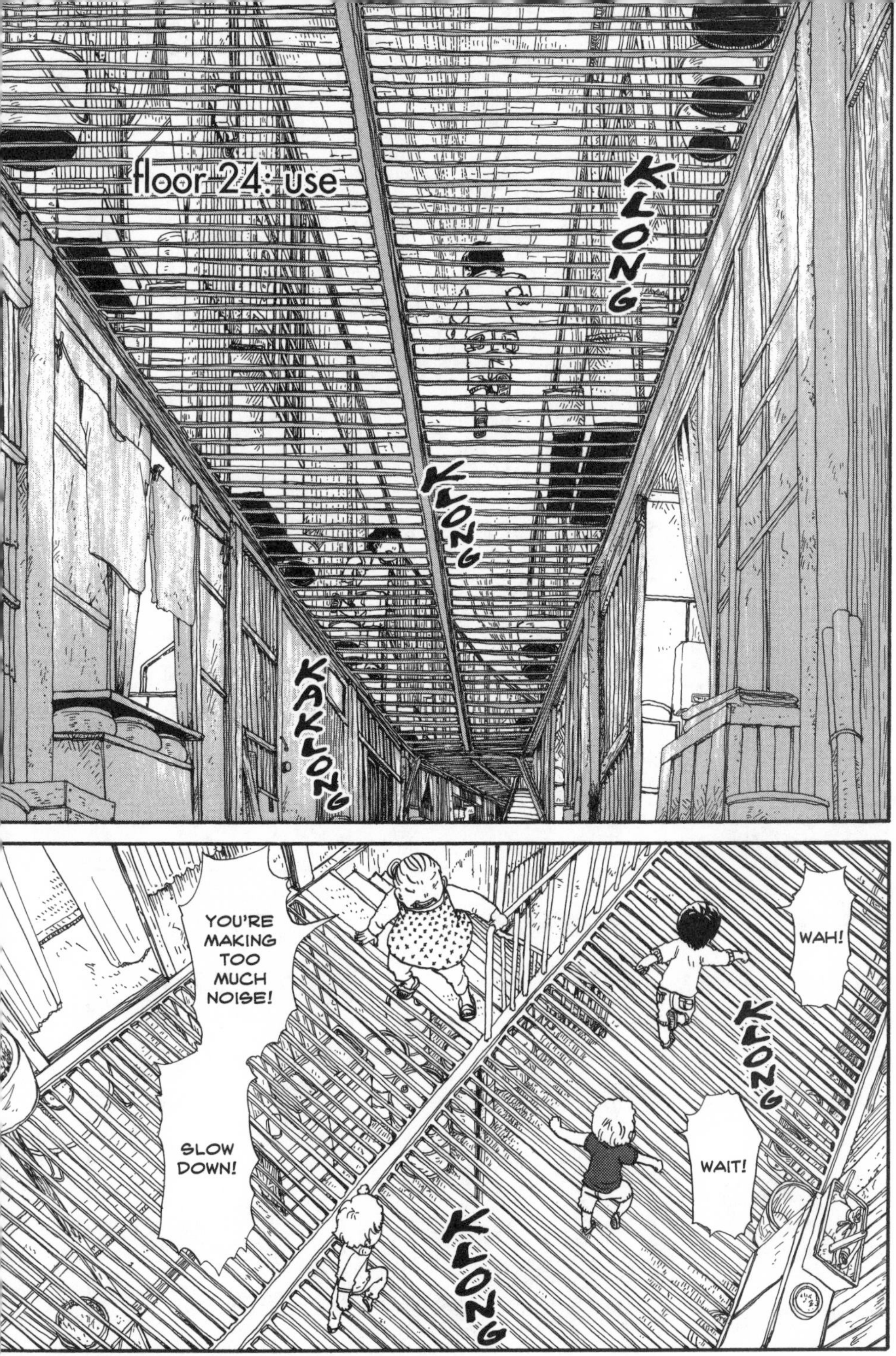
floor 24: use
KLONG
KLONG
KAKLONG
WAH!
KLONG
WAIT!
YOU'RE MAKING TOO MUCH NOISE!
SLOW DOWN!
KLONG

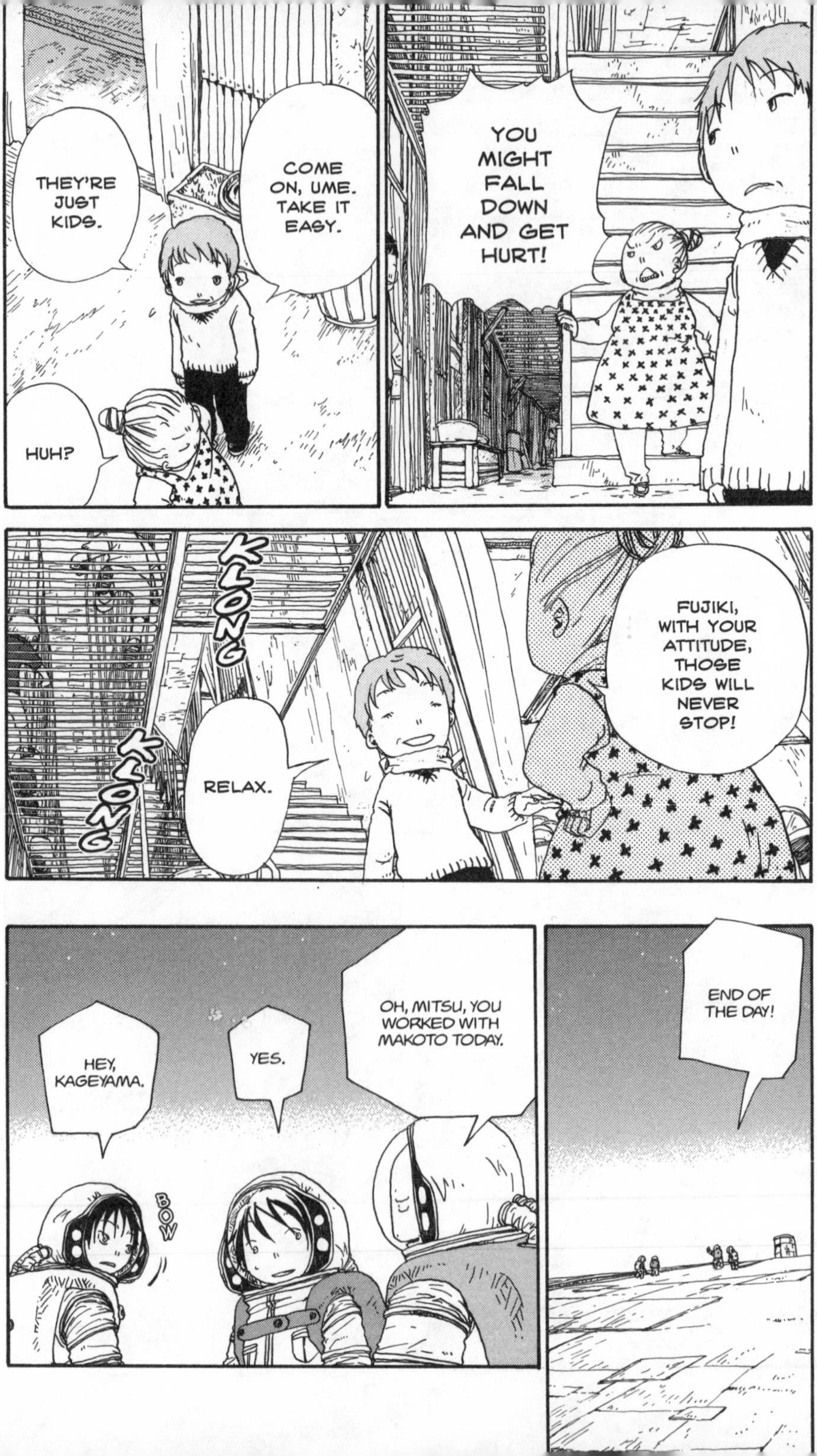
YOU MIGHT FALL DOWN AND GET HURT!
COME ON, UME. TAKE IT EASY.
THEY'RE JUST KIDS.
HUH?
FUJIKI, WITH YOUR ATTITUDE, THOSE KIDS WILL NEVER STOP!
KLONG
RELAX.
KLONG
END OF THE DAY!
OH, MITSU, YOU WORKED WITH MAKOTO TODAY.
YES.
HEY, KAGEYAMA.
BOW

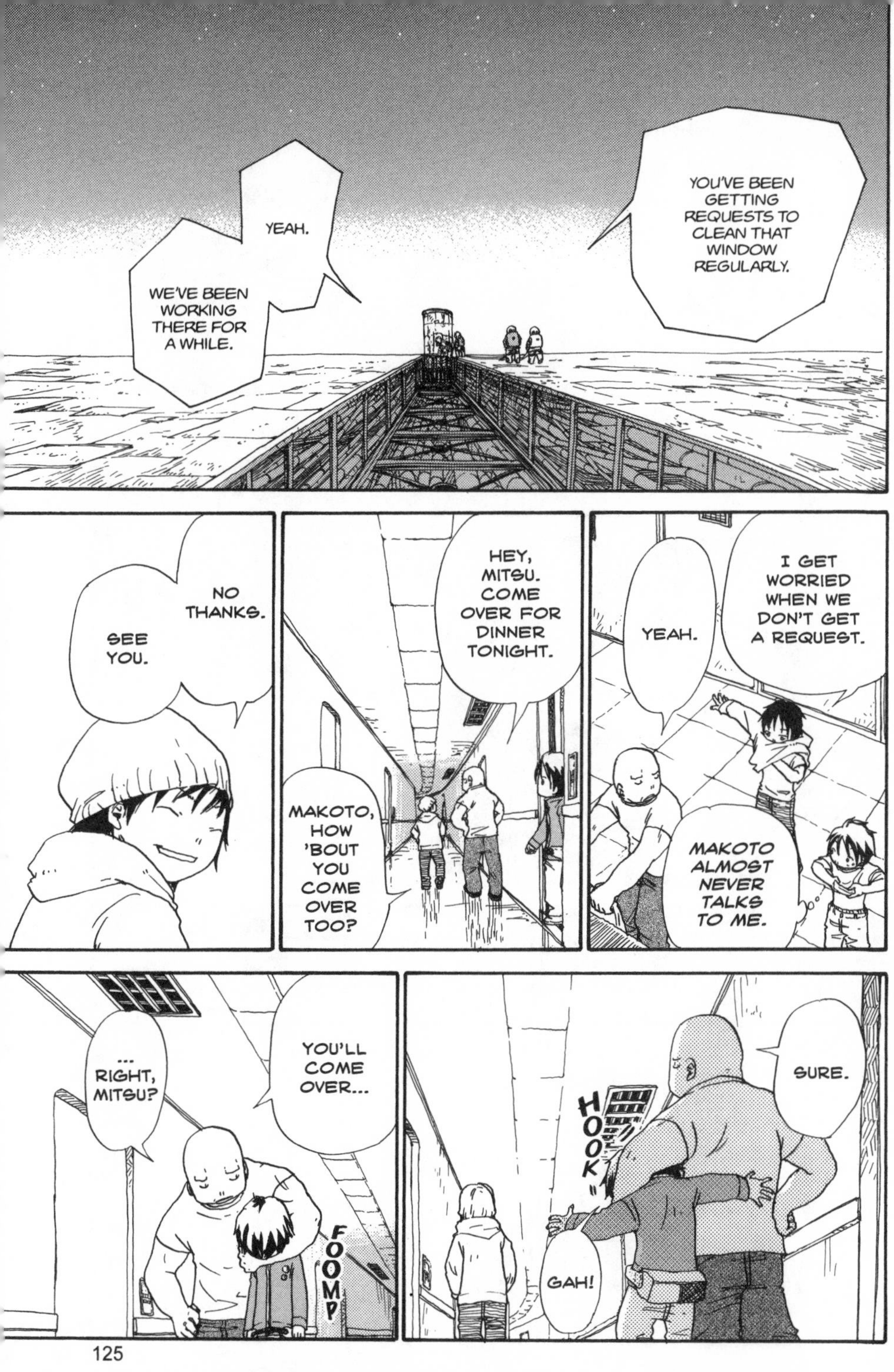

YOU'VE BEEN GETTING REQUESTS TO CLEAN THAT WINDOW REGULARLY.
YEAH.
WE'VE BEEN WORKING THERE FOR A WHILE.
I GET WORRIED WHEN WE DON'T GET A REQUEST.
YEAH.
MAKOTO ALMOST NEVER TALKS TO ME.
HEY, MITSU. COME OVER FOR DINNER TONIGHT.
MAKOTO, HOW 'BOUT YOU COME OVER TOO?
NO THANKS.
SEE YOU.
SURE.
HOOK
GAH!
YOU'LL COME OVER...
... RIGHT, MITSU?
FOOMP

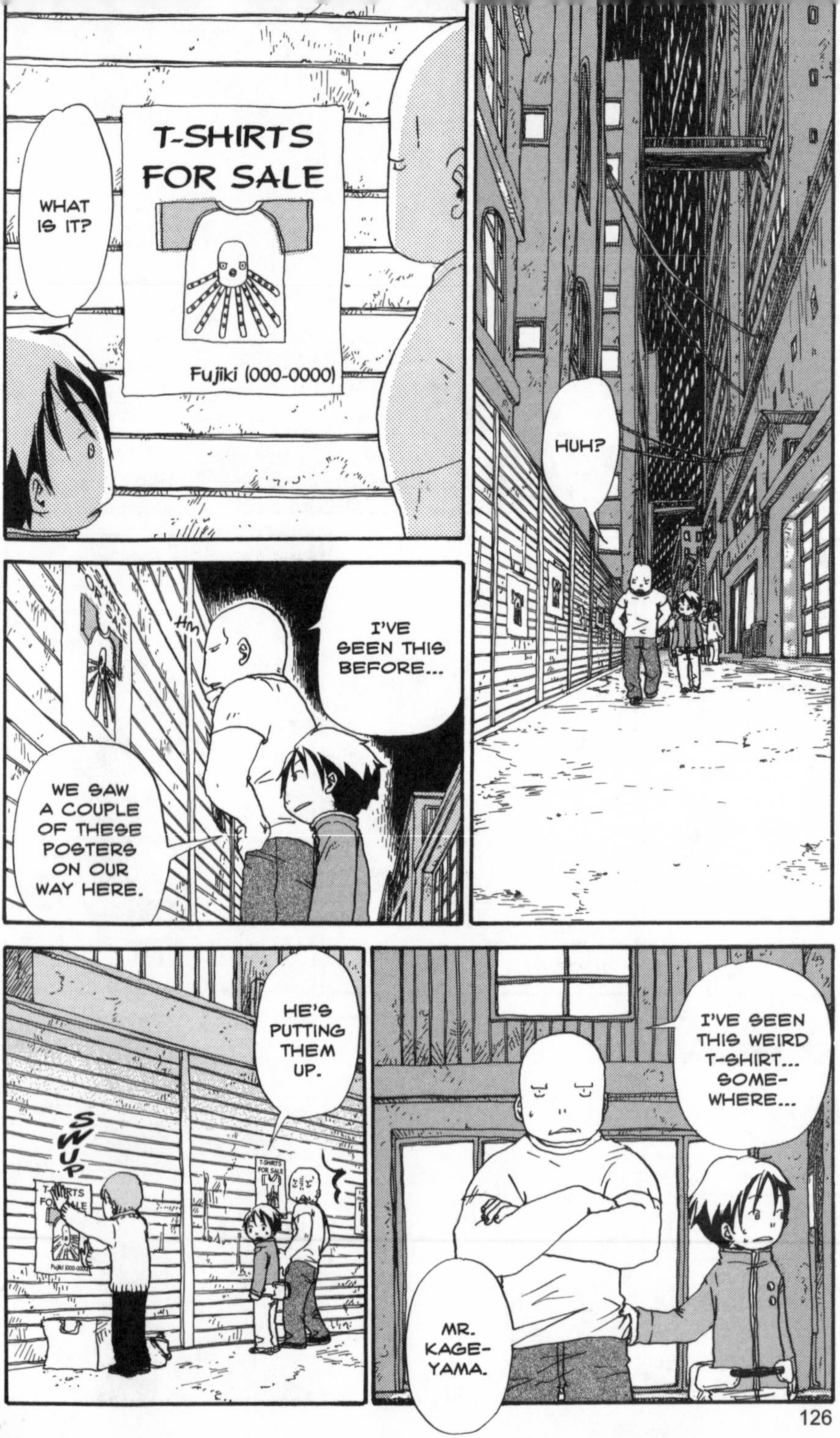
HUH?
T-SHIRTS
FOR SALE
Fujiki (000-0000)
WHAT IS IT?
Hm
I'VE SEEN THIS BEFORE...
WE SAW A COUPLE OF THESE POSTERS ON OUR WAY HERE.
I'VE SEEN THIS WEIRD T-SHIRT... SOME-WHERE...
MR. KAGE-YAMA.
HE'S PUTTING THEM UP.
SWUP

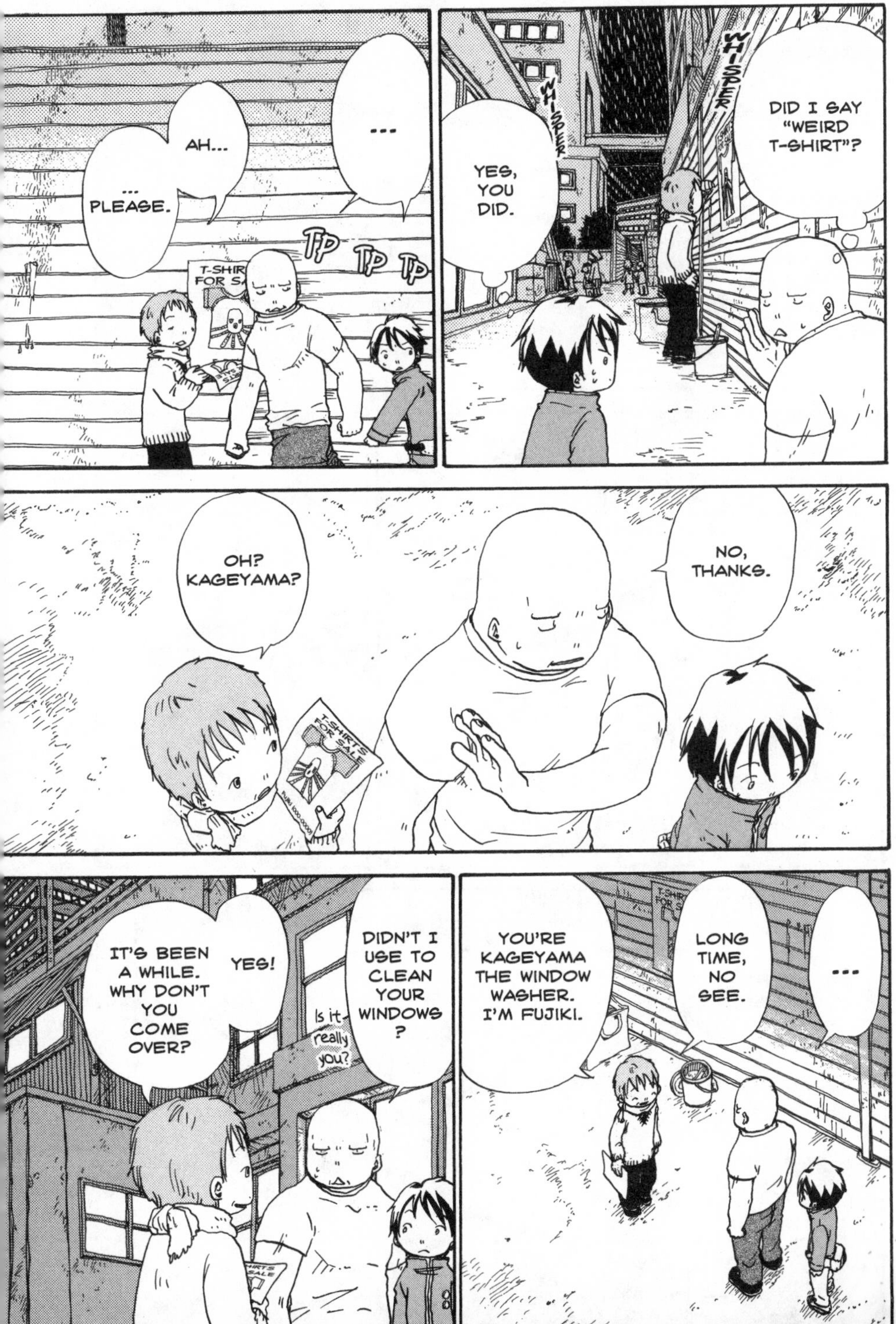
WHISPER
DID I SAY "WEIRD T-SHIRT"?
WHISPER
YES, YOU DID.
...
AH... ...PLEASE.
TP TP TP
NO, THANKS.
OH? KAGEYAMA?
T-SHIRTS FOR SALE
...
LONG TIME, NO SEE.
YOU'RE KAGEYAMA THE WINDOW WASHER. I'M FUJIKI.
DIDN'T I USE TO CLEAN YOUR WINDOWS?
Is it really you?
YES!
IT'S BEEN A WHILE. WHY DON'T YOU COME OVER?

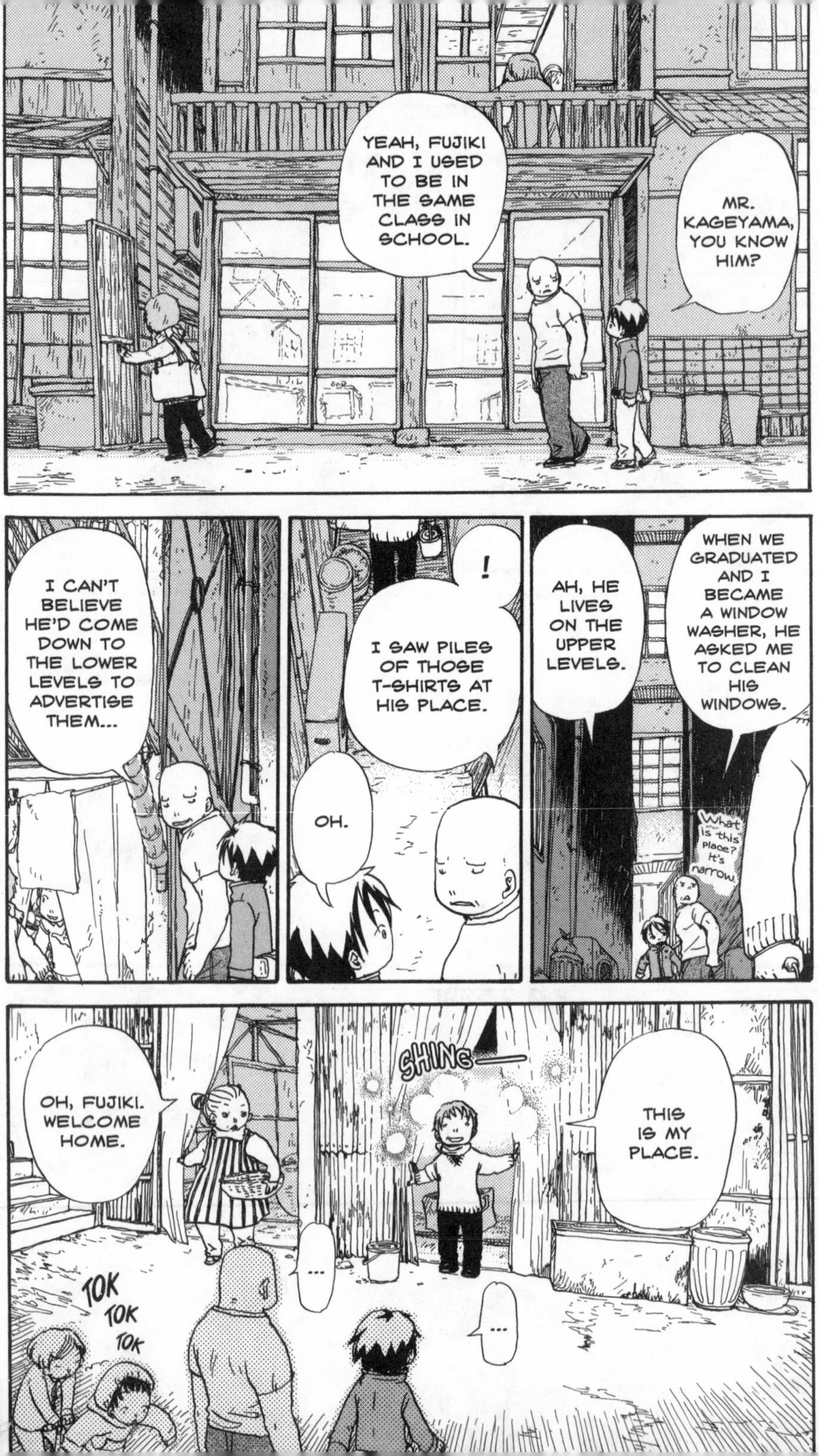
MR. KAGEYAMA, YOU KNOW HIM?
YEAH, FUJIKI AND I USED TO BE IN THE SAME CLASS IN SCHOOL.
WHEN WE GRADUATED AND I BECAME A WINDOW WASHER, HE ASKED ME TO CLEAN HIS WINDOWS.
AH, HE LIVES ON THE UPPER LEVELS.
What is this place? It's narrow.
!
I SAW PILES OF THOSE T-SHIRTS AT HIS PLACE.
OH.
I CAN'T BELIEVE HE'D COME DOWN TO THE LOWER LEVELS TO ADVERTISE THEM...
SHINE——
THIS IS MY PLACE.
...
...
OH, FUJIKI. WELCOME HOME.
TOK TOK TOK

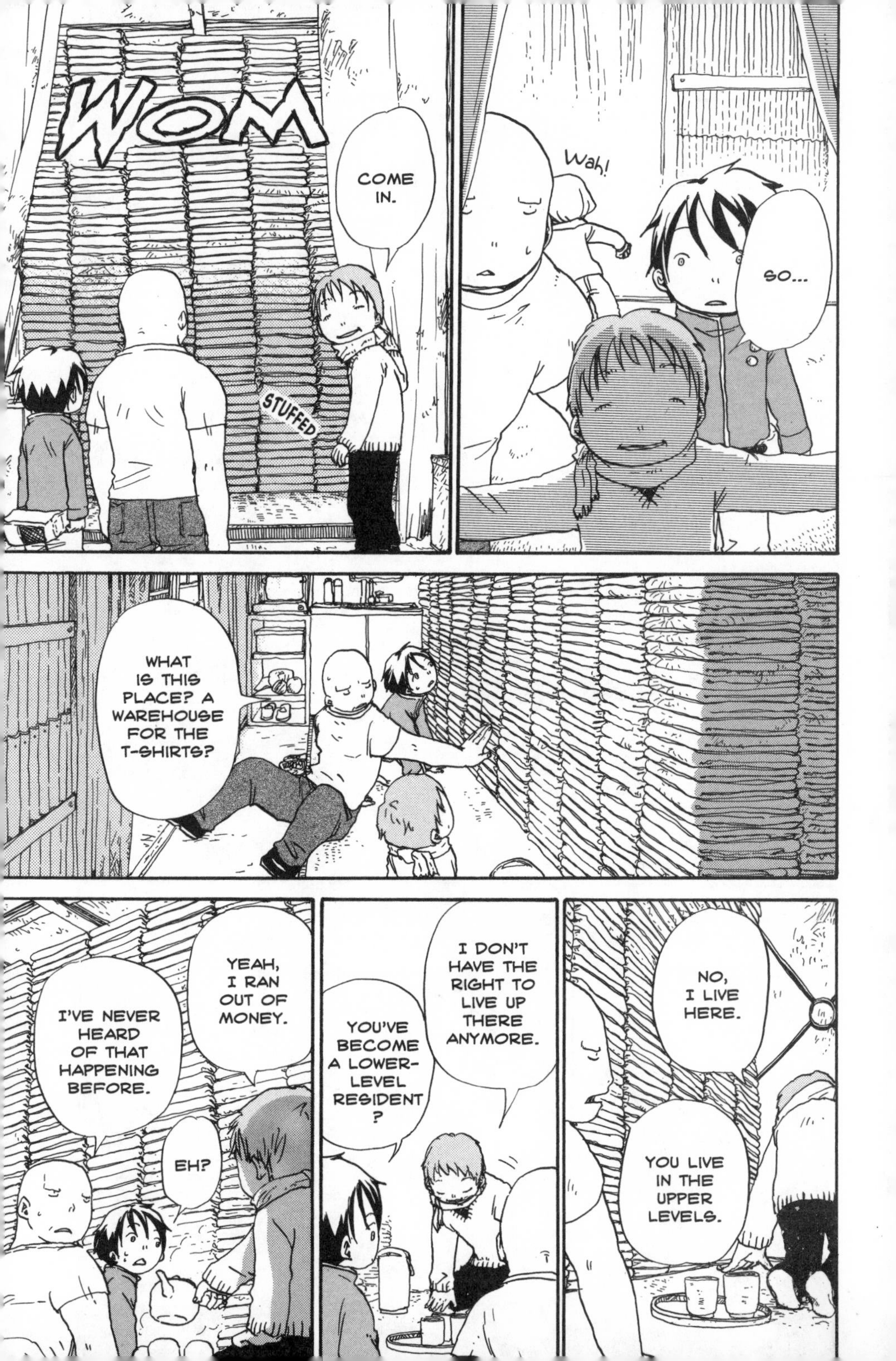
Wah!
SO...
WOM
COME IN.
STUFFED
WHAT IS THIS PLACE? A WAREHOUSE FOR THE T-SHIRTS?
NO, I LIVE HERE.
YOU LIVE IN THE UPPER LEVELS.
I DON'T HAVE THE RIGHT TO LIVE UP THERE ANYMORE.
YOU'VE BECOME A LOWER-LEVEL RESIDENT?
YEAH, I RAN OUT OF MONEY.
I'VE NEVER HEARD OF THAT HAPPENING BEFORE.
EH?

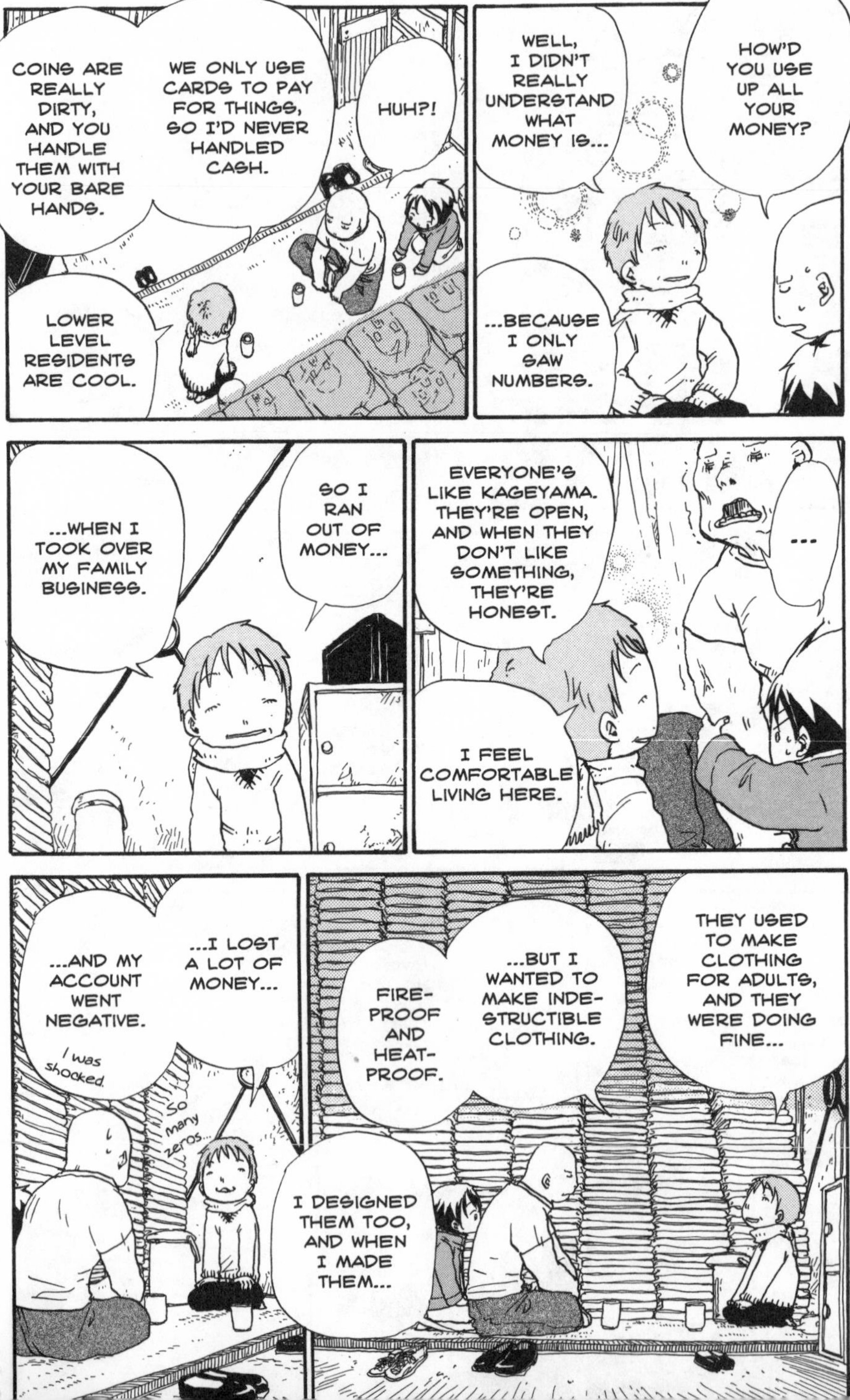
HOW'D YOU USE UP ALL YOUR MONEY?
WELL, I DIDN'T REALLY UNDERSTAND WHAT MONEY IS...
...BECAUSE I ONLY SAW NUMBERS.
HUH?!
WE ONLY USE CARDS TO PAY FOR THINGS, SO I'D NEVER HANDLED CASH.
COINS ARE REALLY DIRTY, AND YOU HANDLE THEM WITH YOUR BARE HANDS.
LOWER LEVEL RESIDENTS ARE COOL.
...
EVERYONE'S LIKE KAGEYAMA. THEY'RE OPEN, AND WHEN THEY DON'T LIKE SOMETHING, THEY'RE HONEST.
I FEEL COMFORTABLE LIVING HERE.
SO I RAN OUT OF MONEY...
...WHEN I TOOK OVER MY FAMILY BUSINESS.
THEY USED TO MAKE CLOTHING FOR ADULTS, AND THEY WERE DOING FINE...
...BUT I WANTED TO MAKE INDE-STRUCTIBLE CLOTHING.
FIRE-PROOF AND HEAT-PROOF.
I DESIGNED THEM TOO, AND WHEN I MADE THEM...
...I LOST A LOT OF MONEY...
...AND MY ACCOUNT WENT NEGATIVE.
I was shocked.
So many zeros...

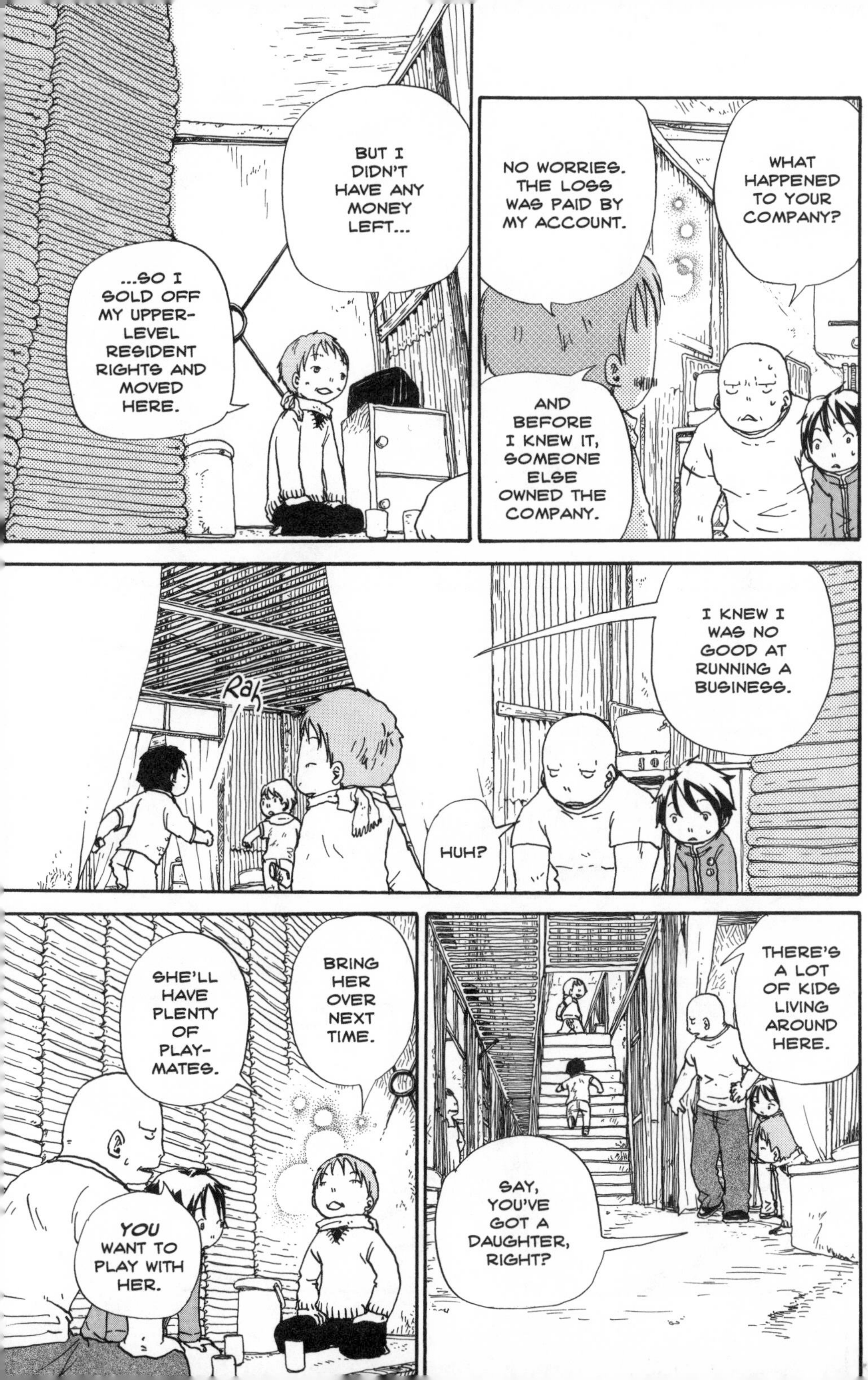
WHAT HAPPENED TO YOUR COMPANY?
NO WORRIES. THE LOSS WAS PAID BY MY ACCOUNT.
AND BEFORE I KNEW IT, SOMEONE ELSE OWNED THE COMPANY.
BUT I DIDN'T HAVE ANY MONEY LEFT...
...SO I SOLD OFF MY UPPER-LEVEL RESIDENT RIGHTS AND MOVED HERE.
I KNEW I WAS NO GOOD AT RUNNING A BUSINESS.
HUH?
Rah
THERE'S A LOT OF KIDS LIVING AROUND HERE.
SAY, YOU'VE GOT A DAUGHTER, RIGHT?
BRING HER OVER NEXT TIME.
SHE'LL HAVE PLENTY OF PLAY-MATES.
YOU WANT TO PLAY WITH HER.

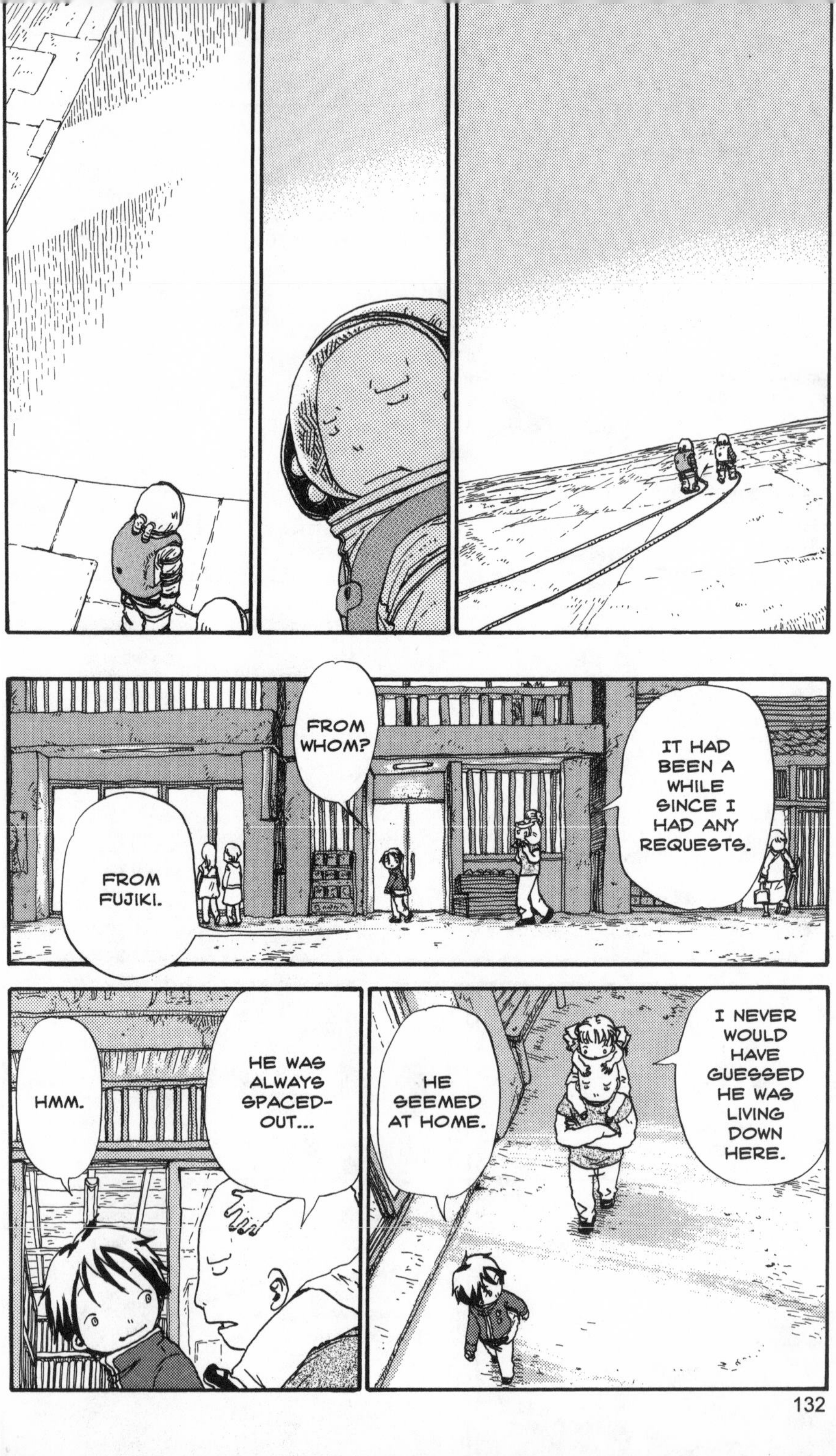
IT HAD BEEN A WHILE SINCE I HAD ANY REQUESTS.
FROM WHOM?
FROM FUJIKI.
I NEVER WOULD HAVE GUESSED HE WAS LIVING DOWN HERE.
HE SEEMED AT HOME.
HE WAS ALWAYS SPACED-OUT...
HMM.

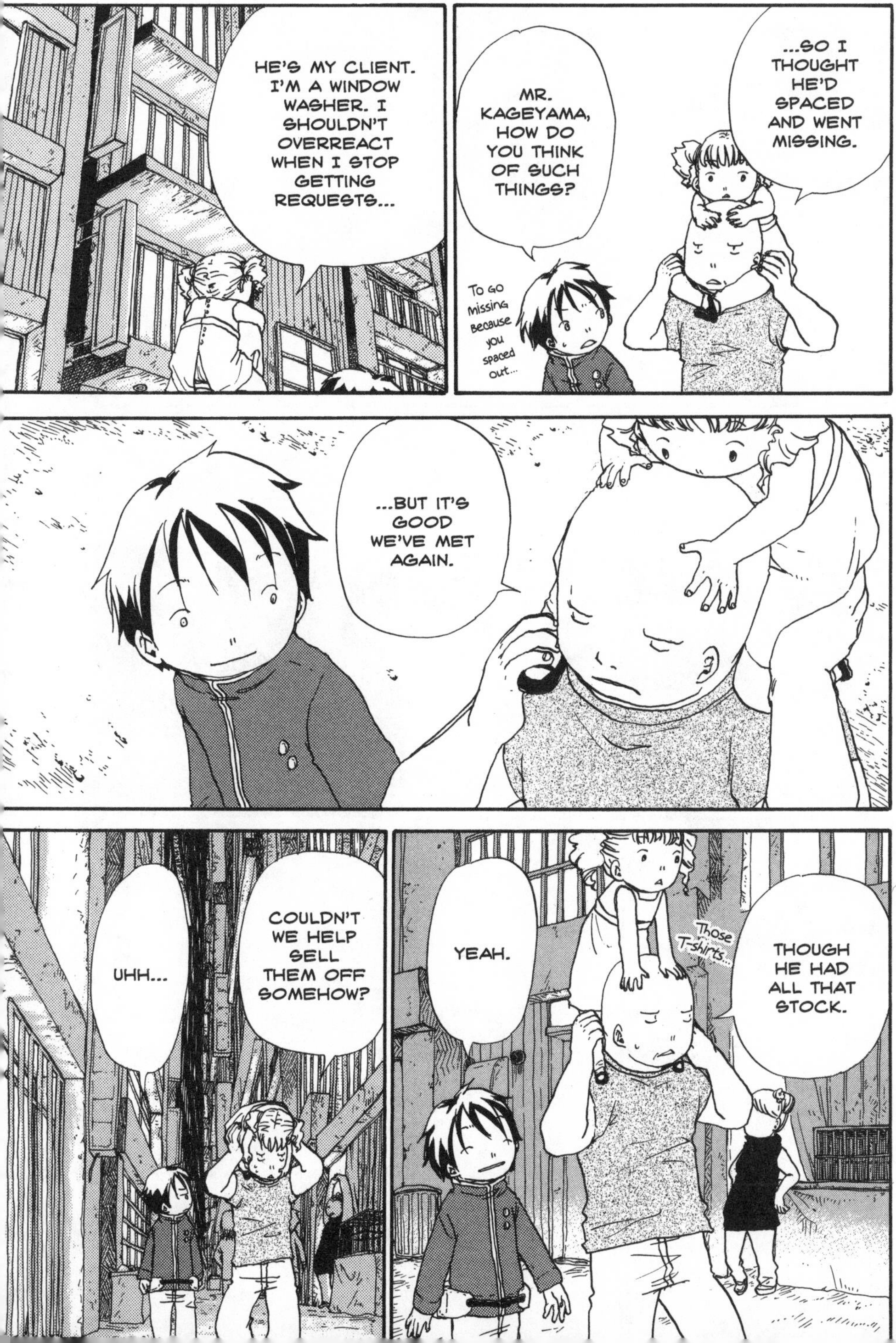
...SO I THOUGHT HE'D SPACED AND WENT MISSING.
MR. KAGEYAMA, HOW DO YOU THINK OF SUCH THINGS?
To go missing because you spaced out...
HE'S MY CLIENT. I'M A WINDOW WASHER. I SHOULDN'T OVERREACT WHEN I STOP GETTING REQUESTS...
...BUT IT'S GOOD WE'VE MET AGAIN.
THOUGH HE HAD ALL THAT STOCK.
Those T-shirts...
YEAH.
COULDN'T WE HELP SELL THEM OFF SOMEHOW?
UHH...

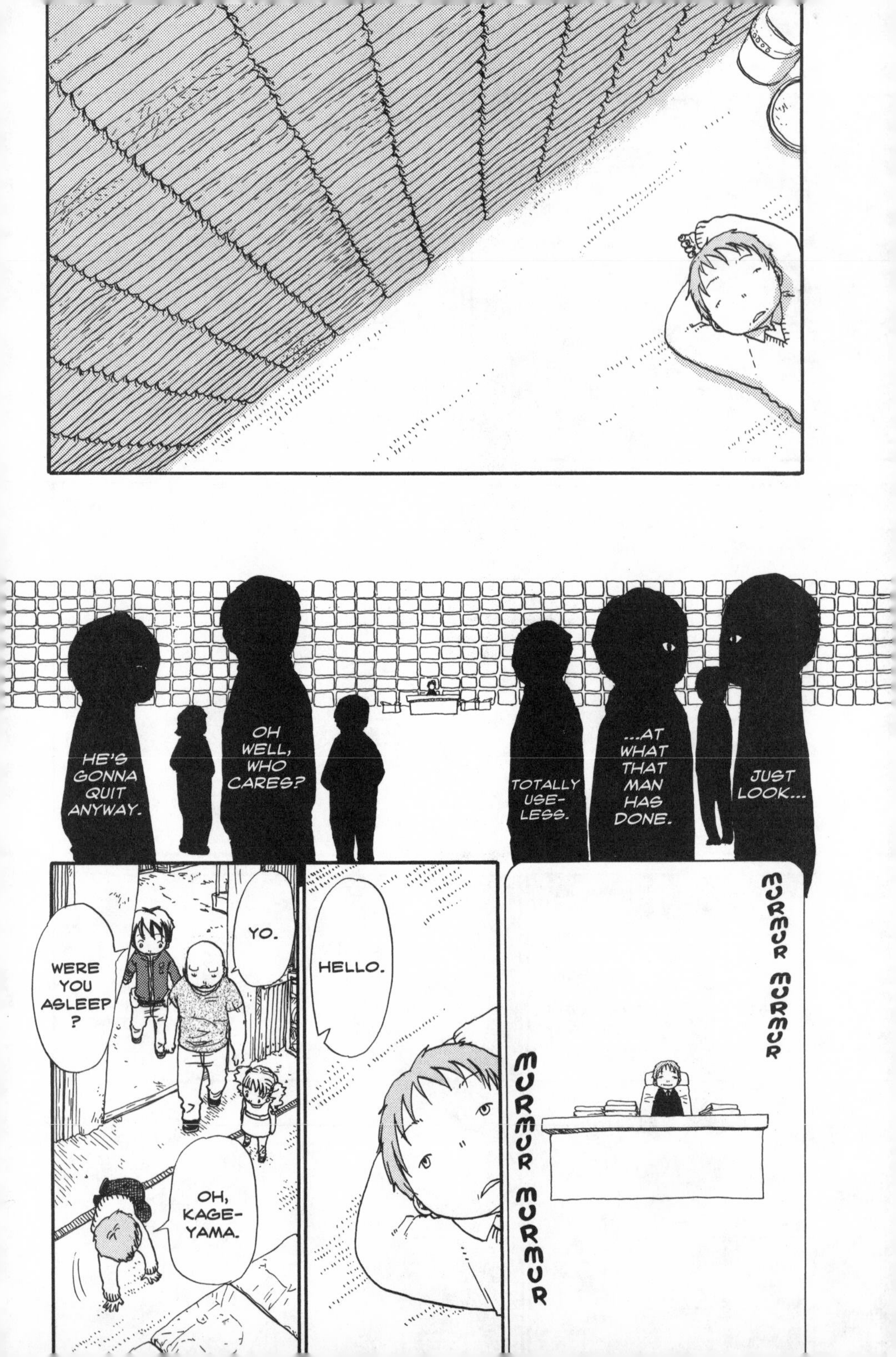
JUST LOOK...
...AT WHAT THAT MAN HAS DONE.
TOTALLY USELESS.
OH WELL, WHO CARES?
HE'S GONNA QUIT ANYWAY.
MURMUR MURMUR
MURMUR MURMUR
HELLO.
YO.
WERE YOU ASLEEP?
OH, KAGEYAMA.

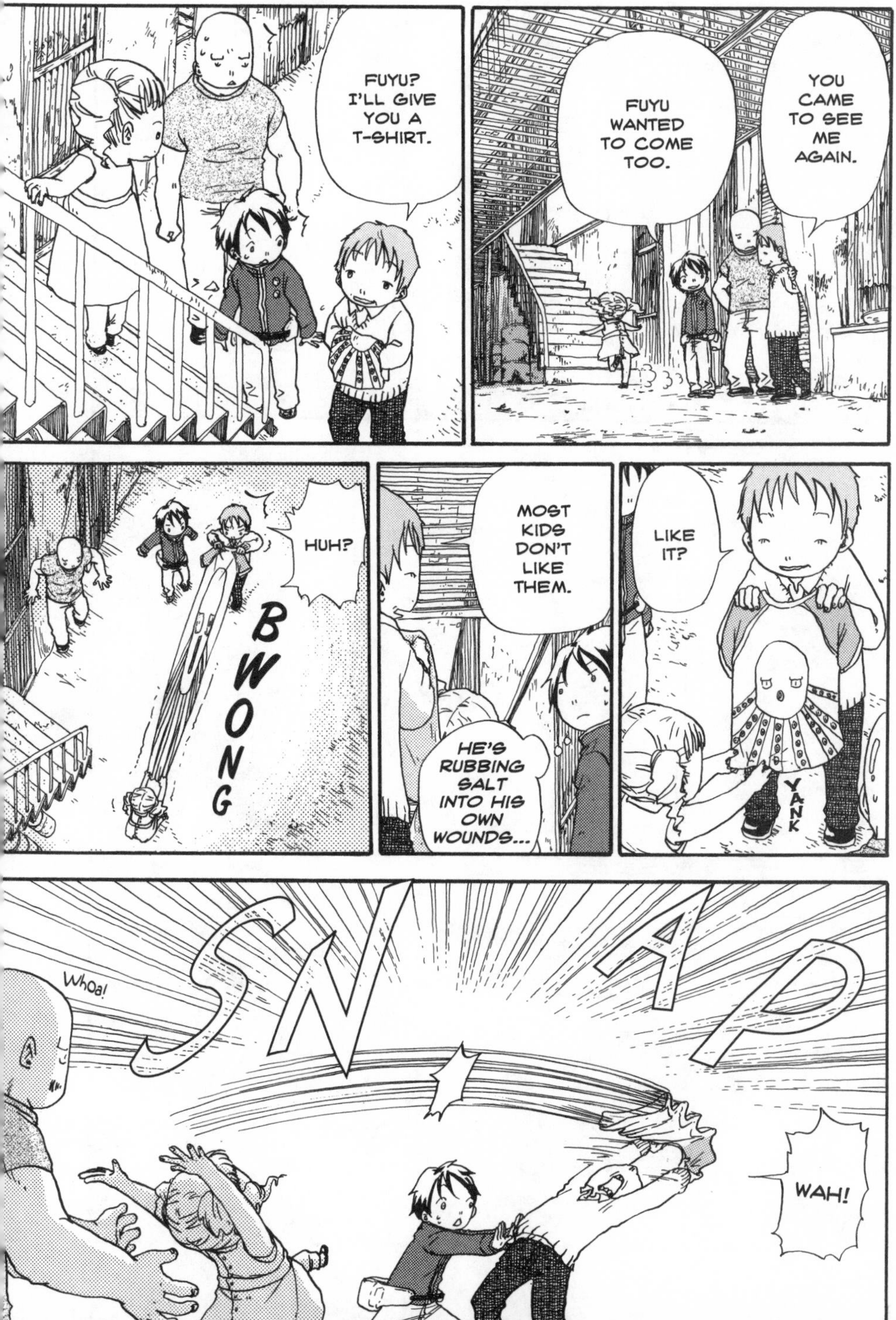
YOU CAME TO SEE ME AGAIN.
FUYU WANTED TO COME TOO.
FUYU? I'LL GIVE YOU A T-SHIRT.
LIKE IT?
YANK
MOST KIDS DON'T LIKE THEM.
HE'S RUBBING SALT INTO HIS OWN WOUNDS...
HUH?
BWONG
SNAP
WAH!
Whoa!

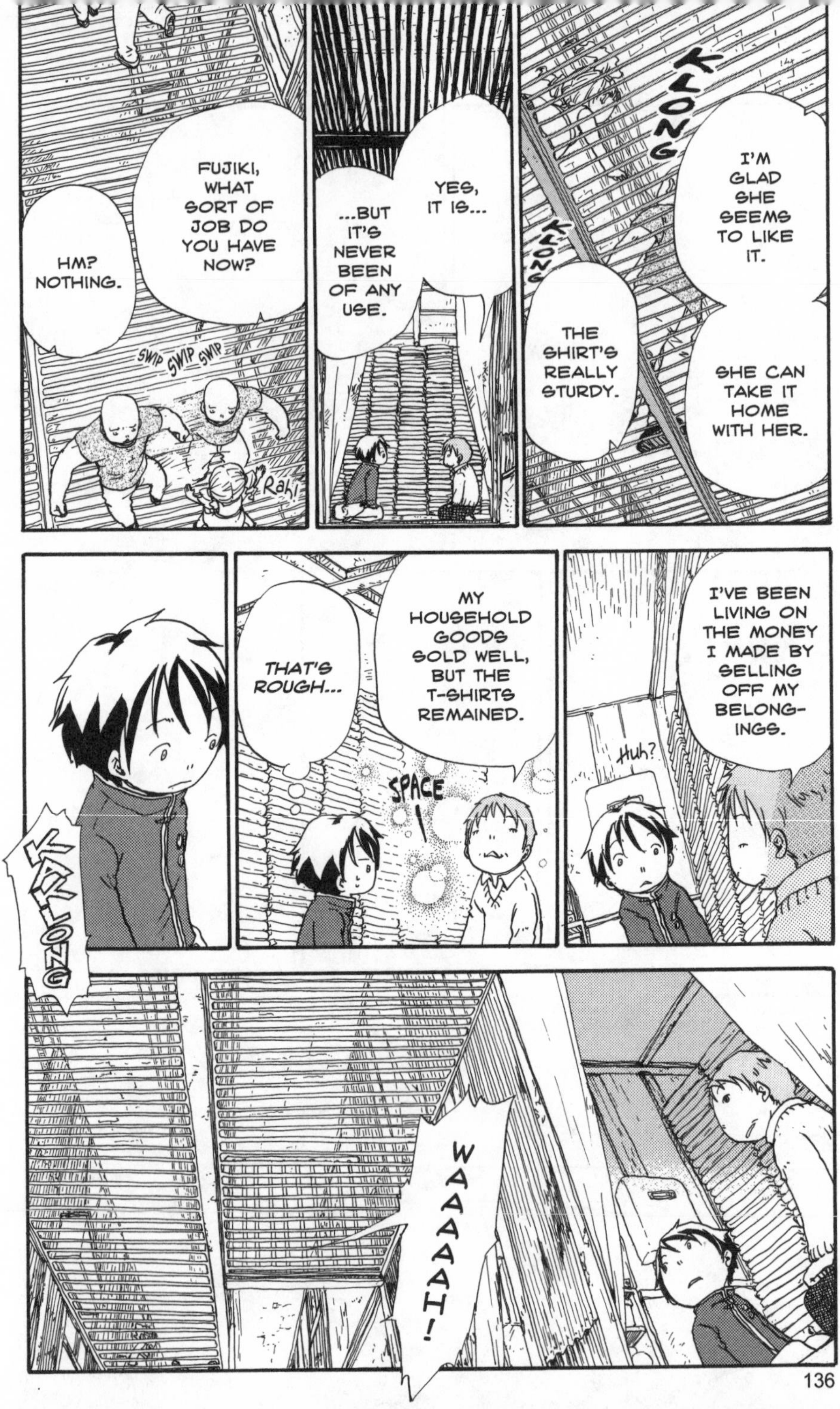
KLONG
I'M GLAD SHE SEEMS TO LIKE IT.
KLONG
SHE CAN TAKE IT HOME WITH HER.
THE SHIRT'S REALLY STURDY.
YES, IT IS...
...BUT IT'S NEVER BEEN OF ANY USE.
FUJIKI, WHAT SORT OF JOB DO YOU HAVE NOW?
HM? NOTHING.
SWIP SWIP SWIP
Rah!
I'VE BEEN LIVING ON THE MONEY I MADE BY SELLING OFF MY BELONG-INGS.
Huh?
MY HOUSEHOLD GOODS SOLD WELL, BUT THE T-SHIRTS REMAINED.
THAT'S ROUGH...
SPACE
KALONG
WAAAAAH!

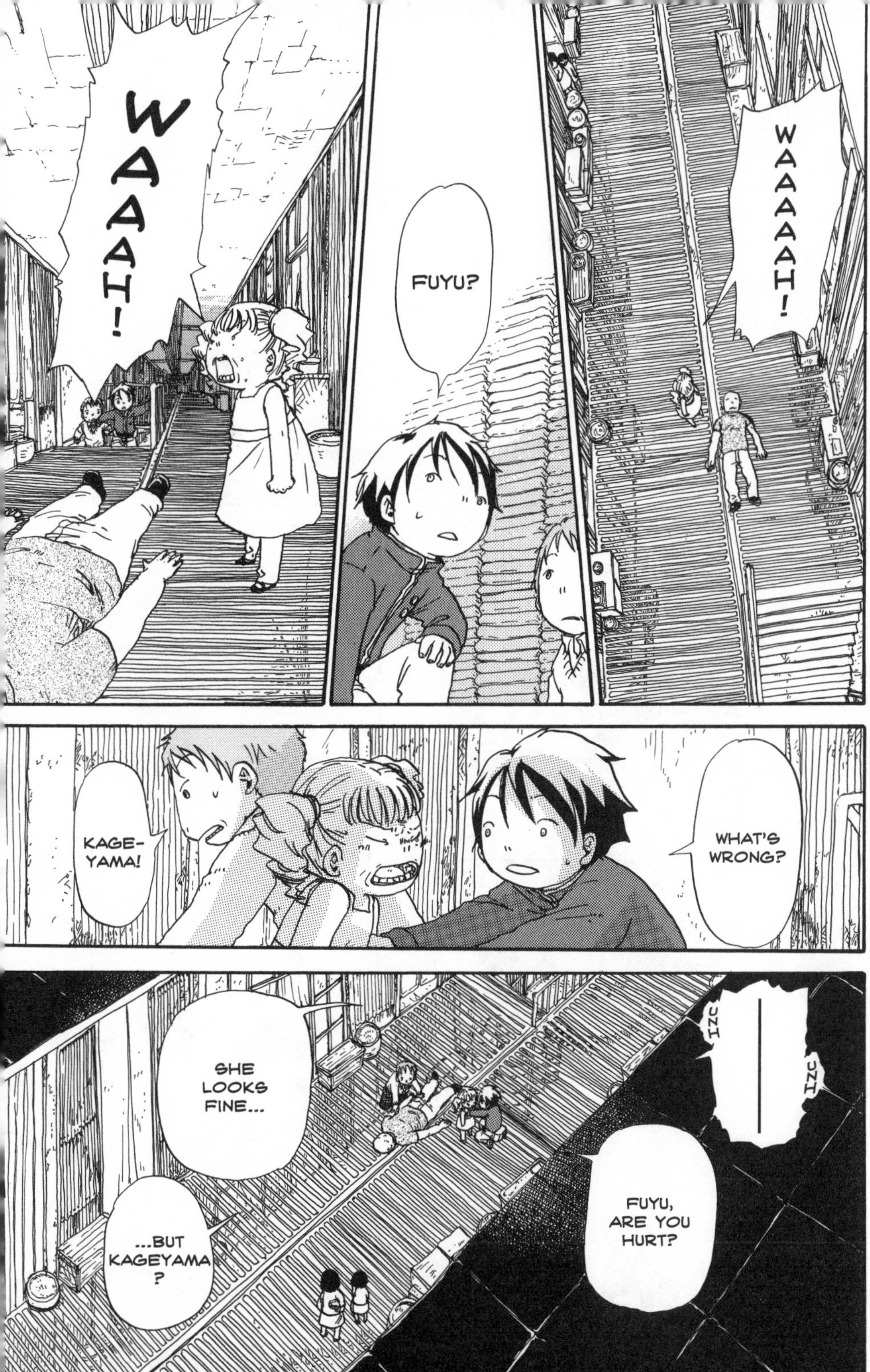
WAAAAAAH!
FUYU?
WAAAH!
WHAT'S WRONG?
KAGE-YAMA!
UNH
UNH
FUYU, ARE YOU HURT?
SHE LOOKS FINE...
...BUT KAGEYAMA?

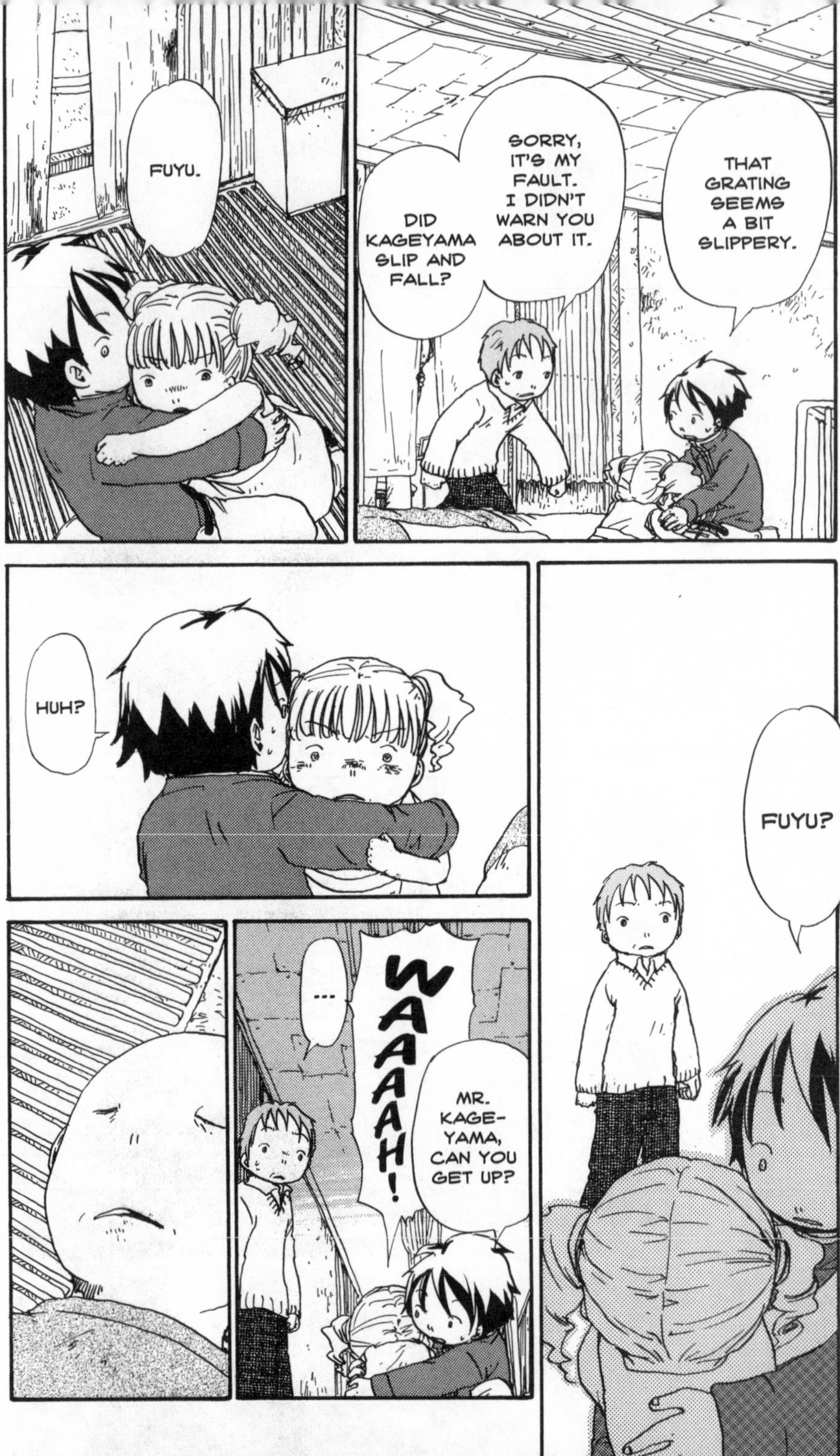
THAT GRATING SEEMS A BIT SLIPPERY.
SORRY, IT'S MY FAULT. I DIDN'T WARN YOU ABOUT IT.
DID KAGEYAMA SLIP AND FALL?
FUYU.
FUYU?
HUH?
WAAAAH!
...
MR. KAGE-YAMA, CAN YOU GET UP?

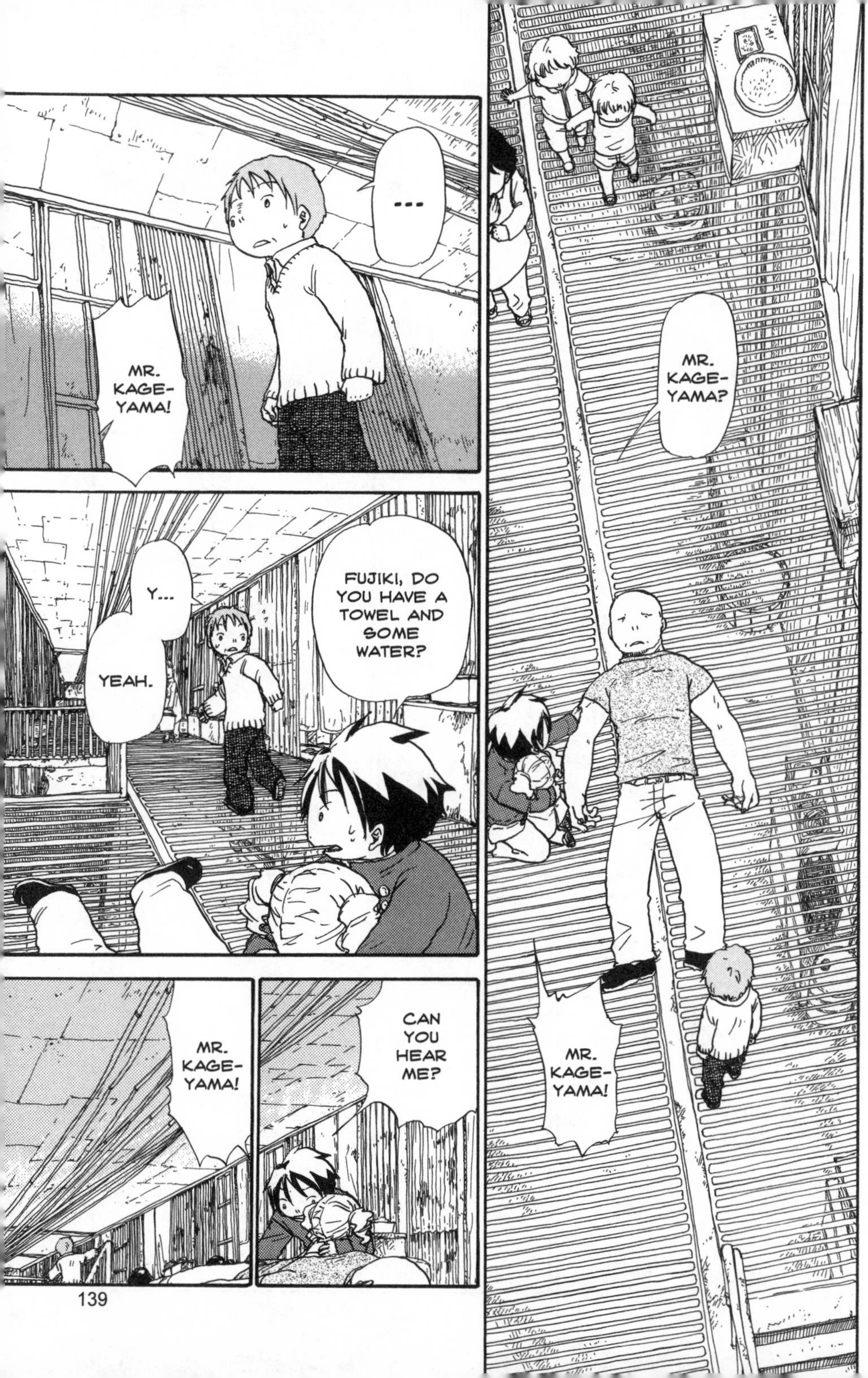
MR. KAGE-YAMA?
MR. KAGE-YAMA!
...
MR. KAGE-YAMA!
FUJIKI, DO YOU HAVE A TOWEL AND SOME WATER?
Y...
YEAH.
CAN YOU HEAR ME?
MR. KAGE-YAMA!

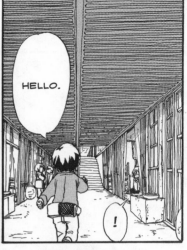

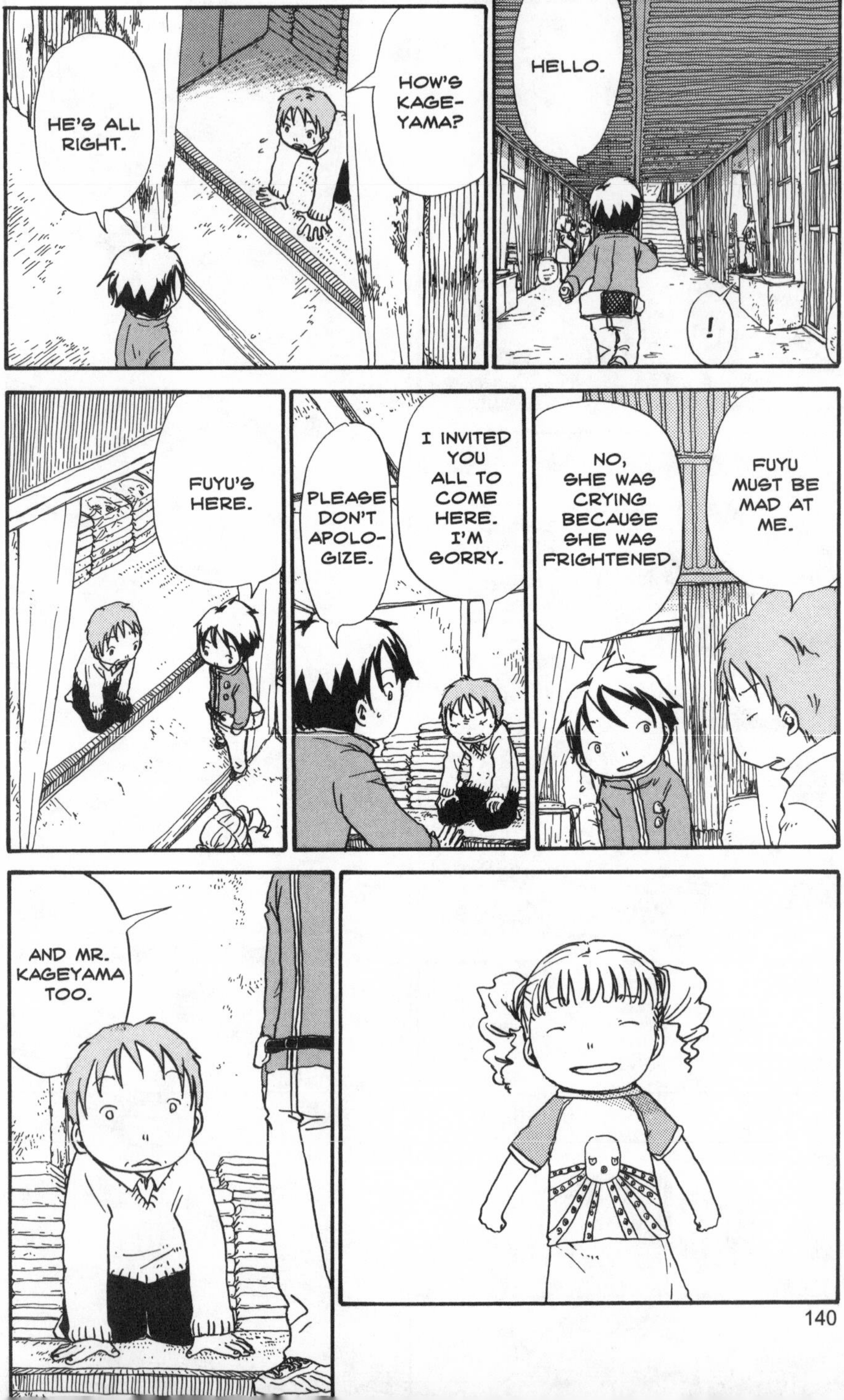
HELLO.
!
HOW'S KAGE-YAMA?
HE'S ALL RIGHT.
FUYU MUST BE MAD AT ME.
NO, SHE WAS CRYING BECAUSE SHE WAS FRIGHTENED.
I INVITED YOU ALL TO COME HERE. I'M SORRY.
PLEASE DON'T APOLO-GIZE.
FUYU'S HERE.
AND MR. KAGEYAMA TOO.

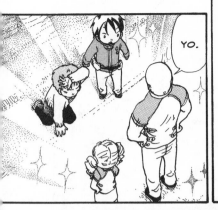

YO.
THIS T-SHIRT IS NO GOOD...
SORRY I MADE YOU WORRY.
I THINK I'M ALL RIGHT.
BY THE WAY...
...FUYU REALLY LOVES THIS SHIRT...
TUMP
TUMP
...SO I'M WEARING IT TOO.
LOOKS GOOD ON YOU.
ONLY FUYU LIKES IT THOUGH.
I KNEW THE PASSAGE-WAY UPSTAIRS WAS SLIPPERY ...
...BUT I HADN'T DONE ANYTHING ABOUT IT...

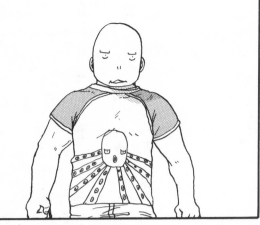

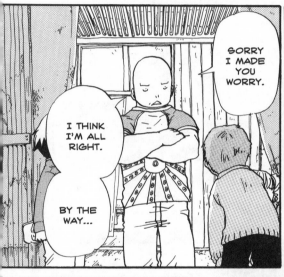

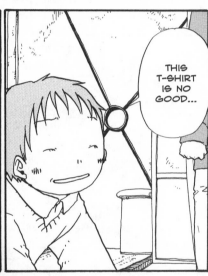

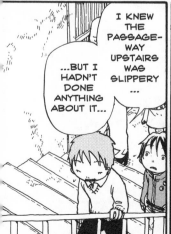

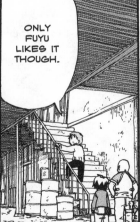

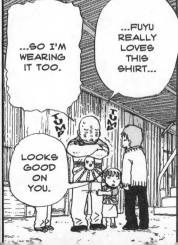

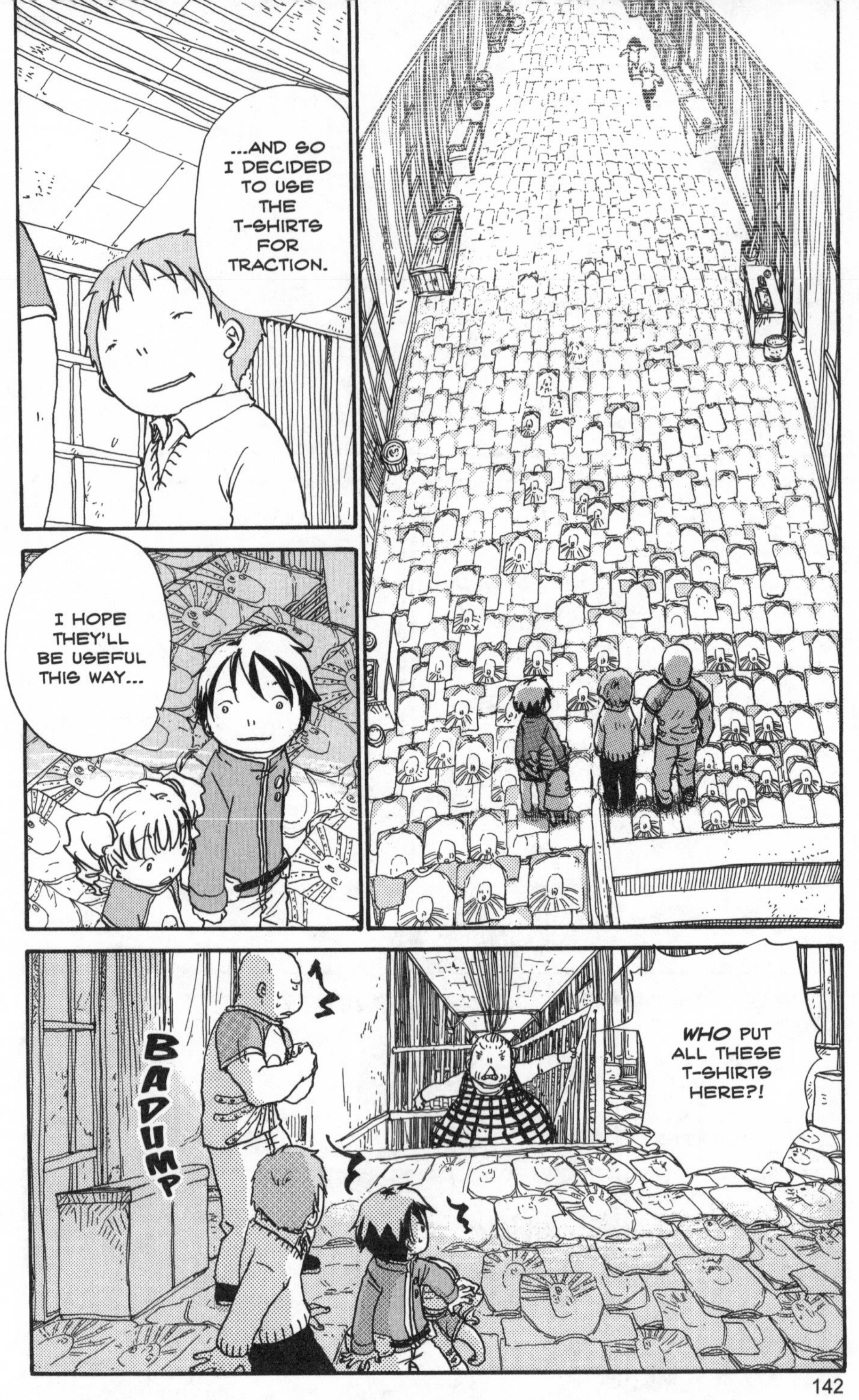
...AND SO I DECIDED TO USE THE T-SHIRTS FOR TRACTION.
I HOPE THEY'LL BE USEFUL THIS WAY...
WHO PUT ALL THESE T-SHIRTS HERE?!
BADUMP

floor 25: the long way around

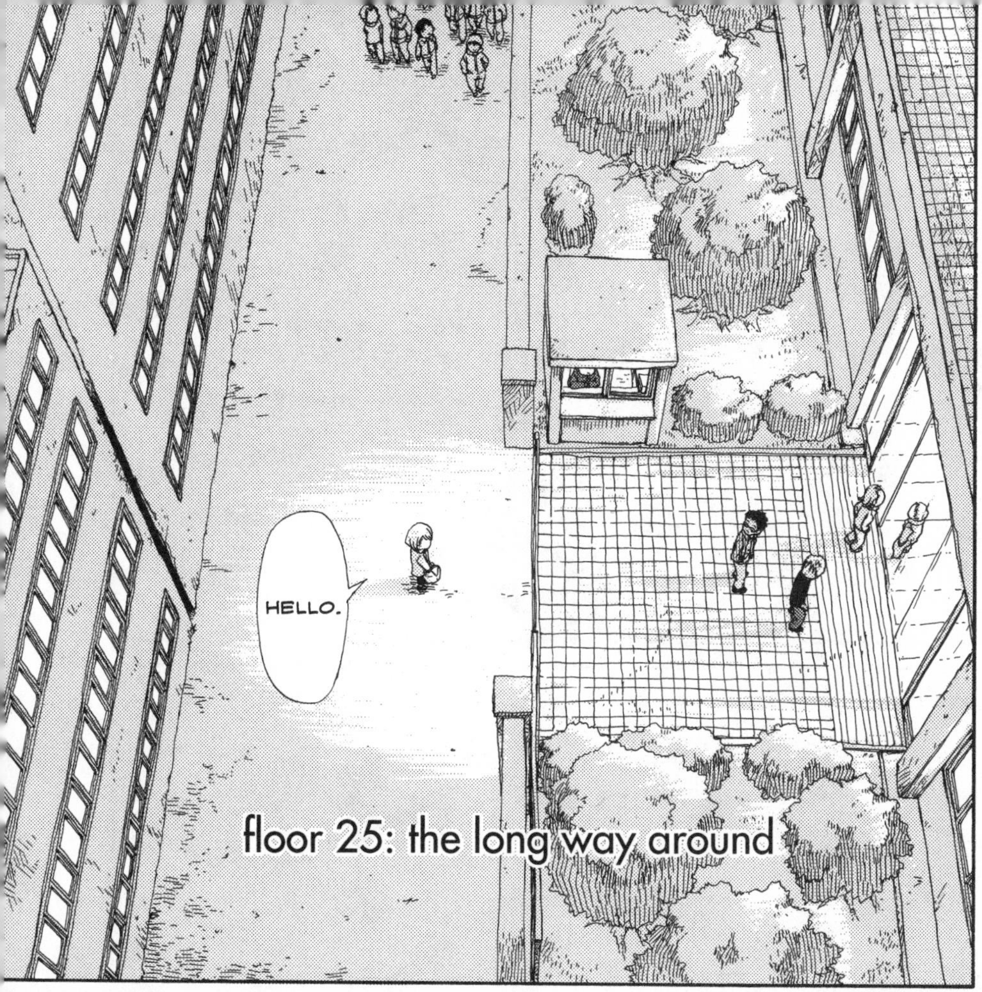
HELLO.

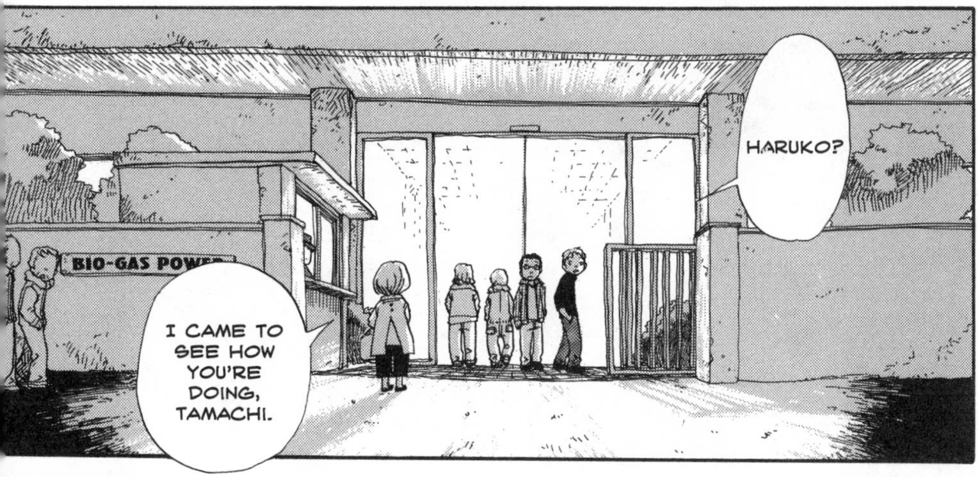
HARUKO?
I CAME TO SEE HOW YOU'RE DOING, TAMACHI.

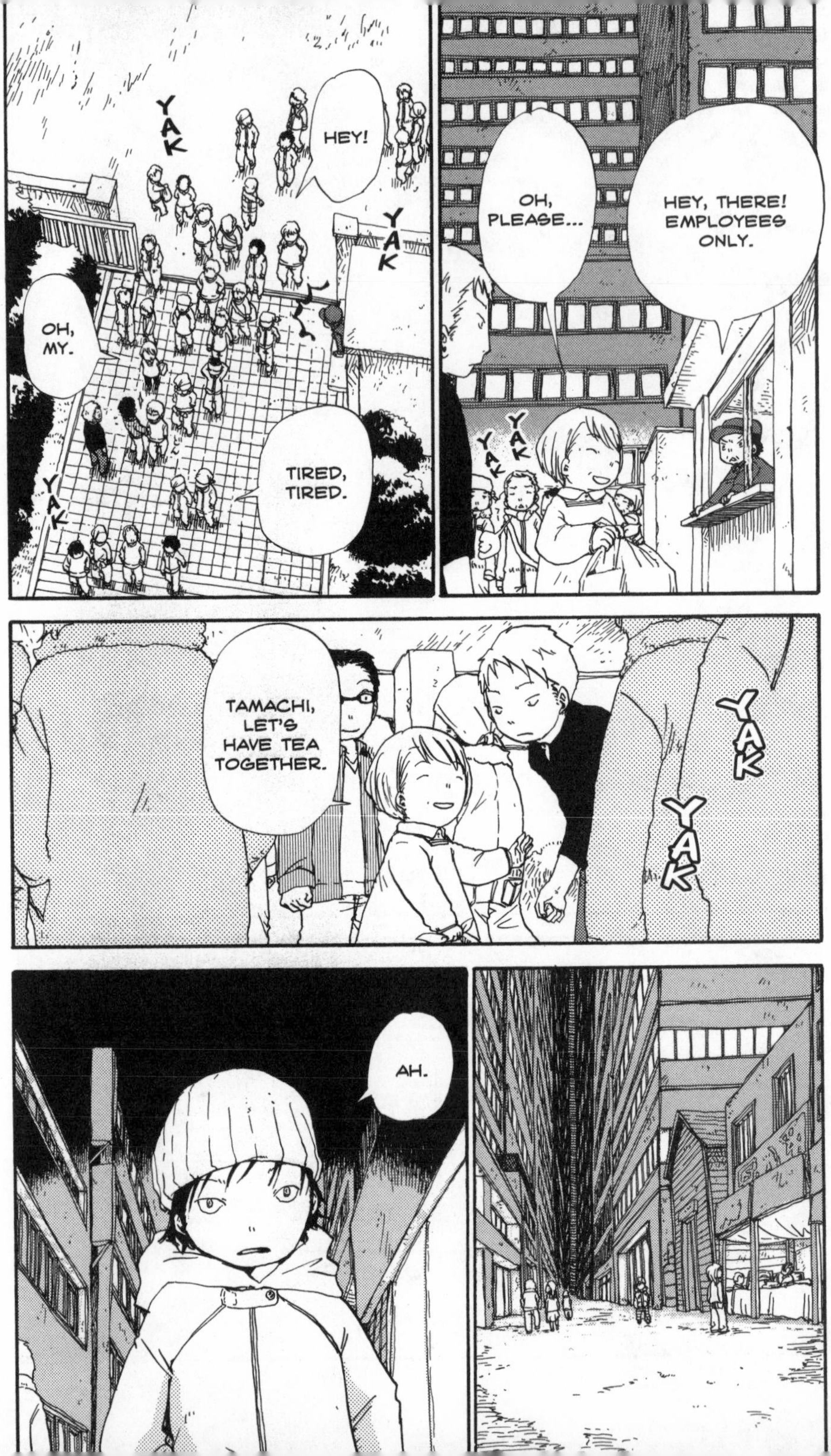
HEY, THERE! EMPLOYEES ONLY.
OH, PLEASE...
YAK
YAK
HEY!
YAK
YAK
OH, MY.
TIRED, TIRED.
YAK
YAK
YAK
TAMACHI, LET'S HAVE TEA TOGETHER.
AH.

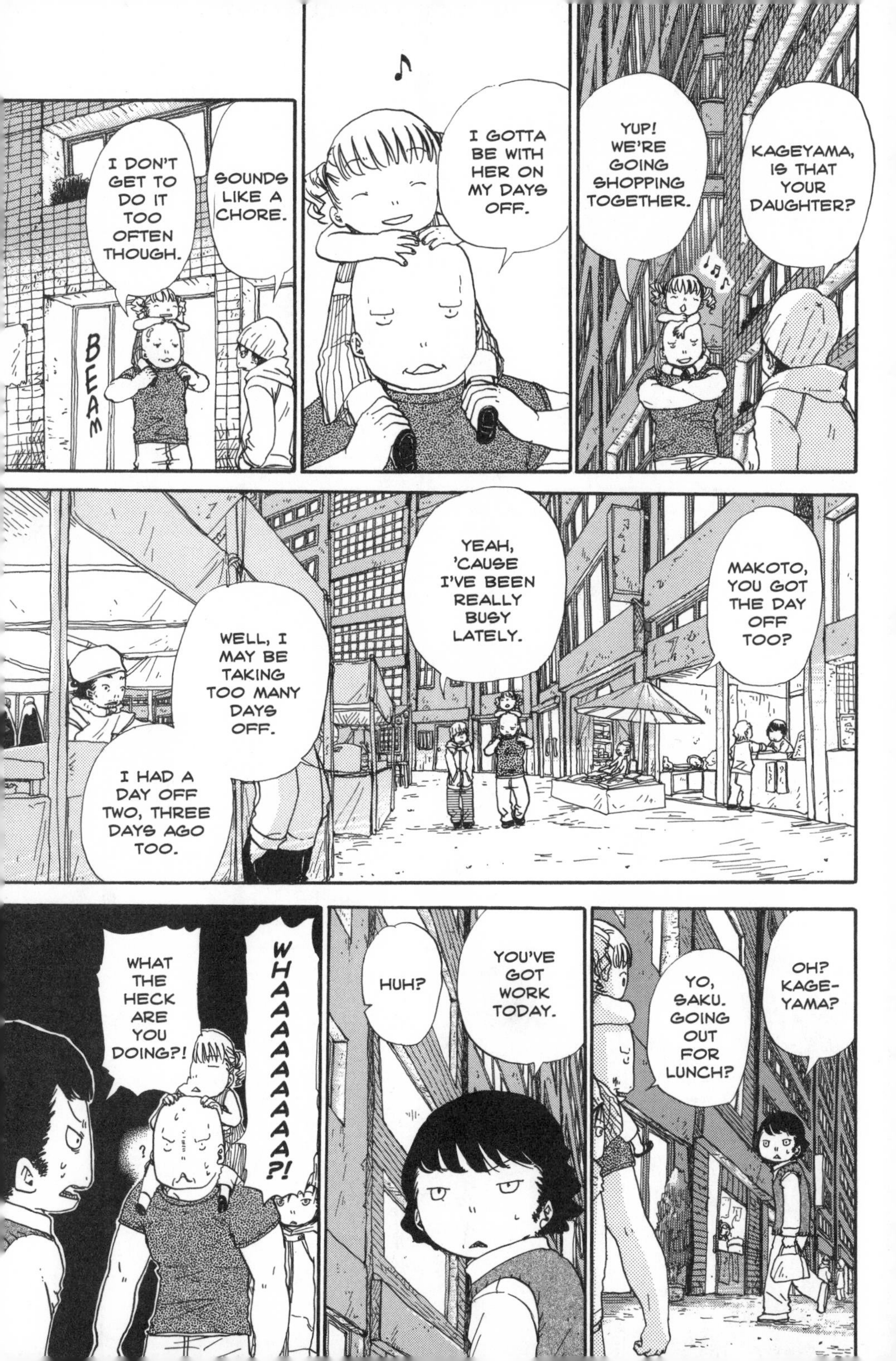
KAGEYAMA, IS THAT YOUR DAUGHTER?
YUP! WE'RE GOING SHOPPING TOGETHER.
♪
I GOTTA BE WITH HER ON MY DAYS OFF.
SOUNDS LIKE A CHORE.
I DON'T GET TO DO IT TOO OFTEN THOUGH.
BEAM
MAKOTO, YOU GOT THE DAY OFF TOO?
YEAH, 'CAUSE I'VE BEEN REALLY BUSY LATELY.
WELL, I MAY BE TAKING TOO MANY DAYS OFF.
I HAD A DAY OFF TWO, THREE DAYS AGO TOO.
OH? KAGE-YAMA?
YO, SAKU. GOING OUT FOR LUNCH?
YOU'VE GOT WORK TODAY.
HUH?
WHAAAAAAAAAA?!
WHAT THE HECK ARE YOU DOING?!

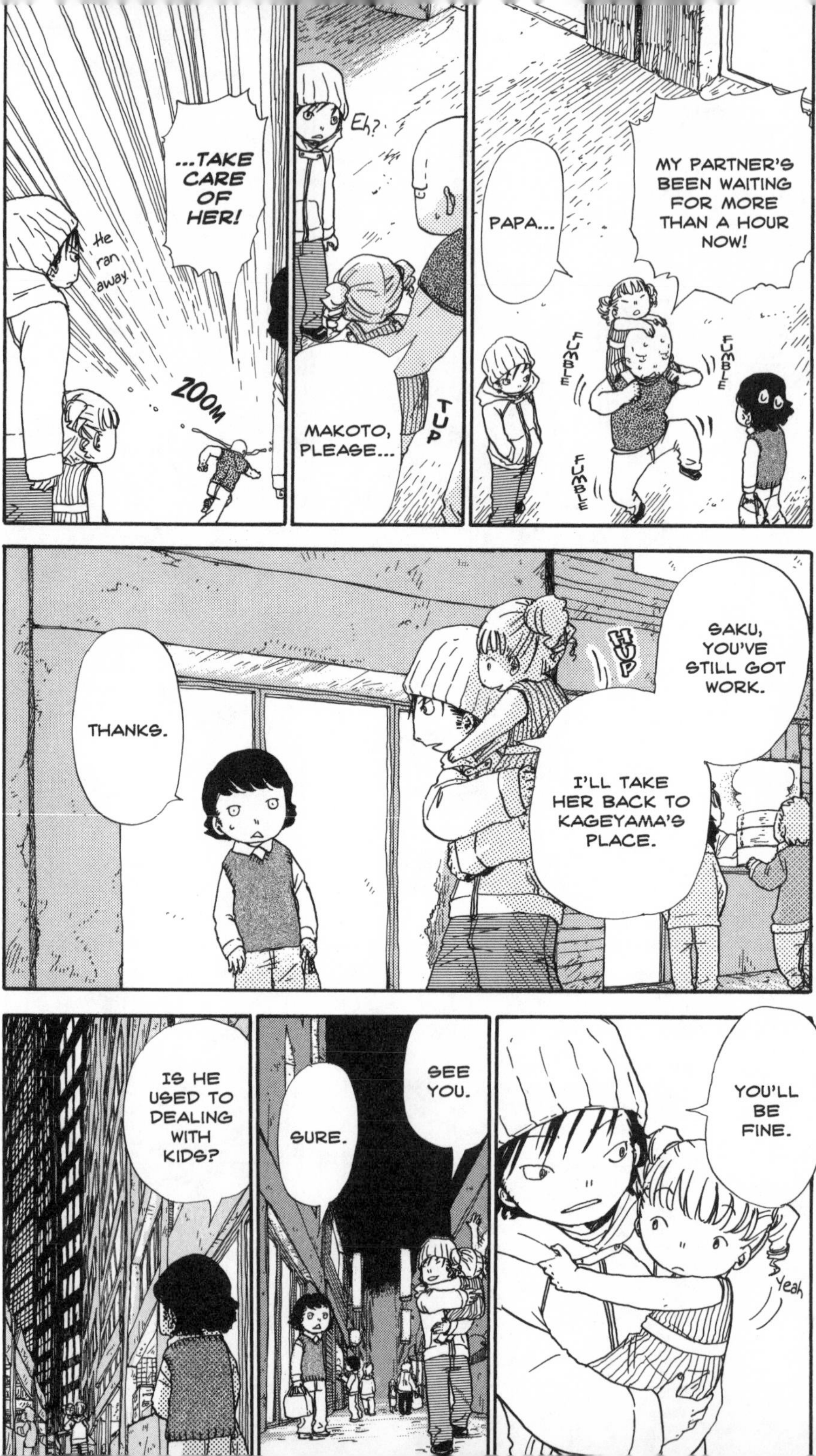
MY PARTNER'S BEEN WAITING FOR MORE THAN A HOUR NOW!
PAPA...
FUMBLE
FUMBLE
FUMBLE
Eh?
MAKOTO, PLEASE...
TUP
...TAKE CARE OF HER!
He ran away.
ZOOM
SAKU, YOU'VE STILL GOT WORK.
HUP
I'LL TAKE HER BACK TO KAGEYAMA'S PLACE.
THANKS.
YOU'LL BE FINE.
Yeah
SEE YOU.
SURE.
IS HE USED TO DEALING WITH KIDS?

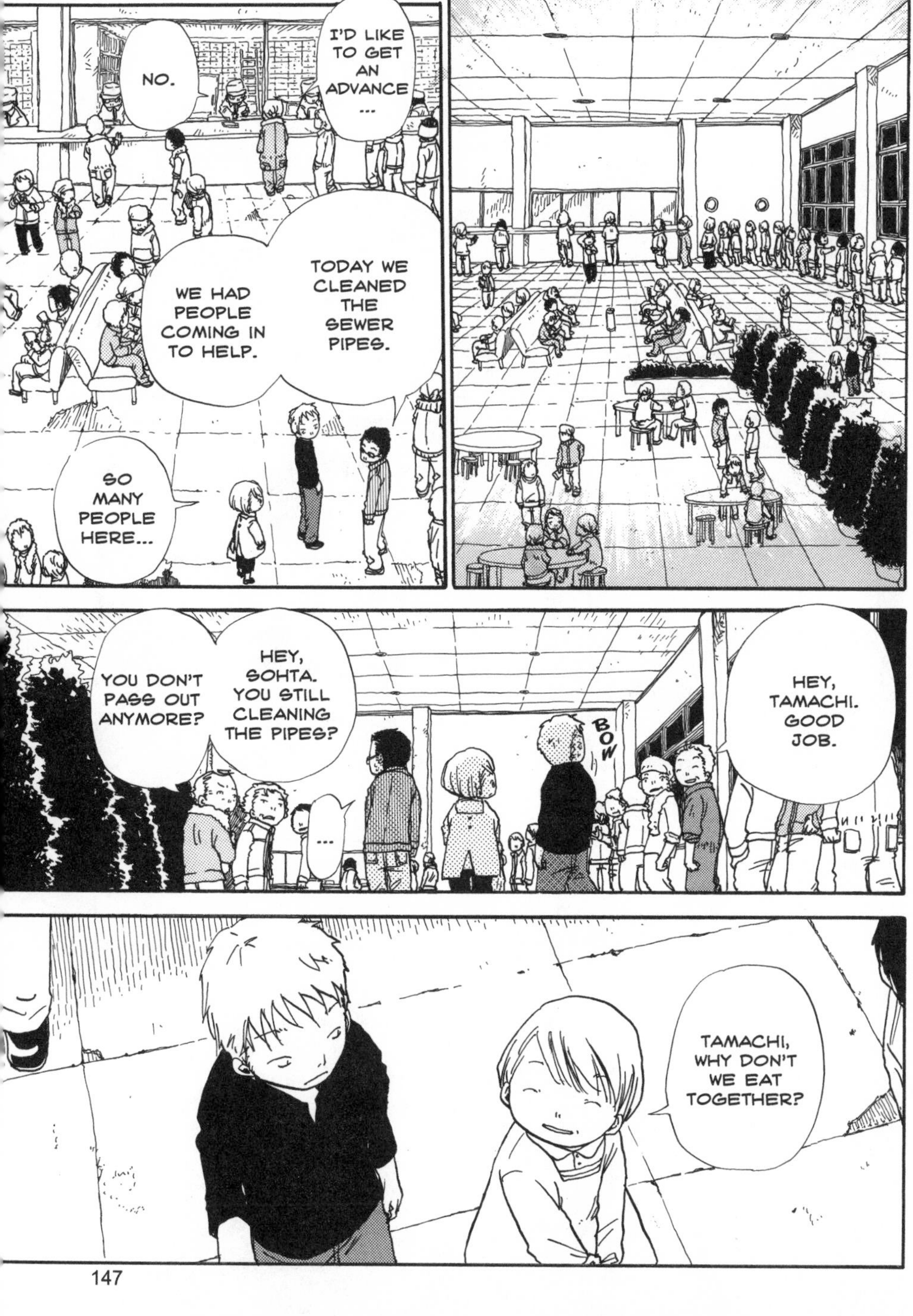
I'D LIKE TO GET AN ADVANCE ...
NO.
TODAY WE CLEANED THE SEWER PIPES.
WE HAD PEOPLE COMING IN TO HELP.
SO MANY PEOPLE HERE...
HEY, TAMACHI. GOOD JOB.
BOW
HEY, SOHTA. YOU STILL CLEANING THE PIPES?
YOU DON'T PASS OUT ANYMORE?
...
TAMACHI, WHY DON'T WE EAT TOGETHER?

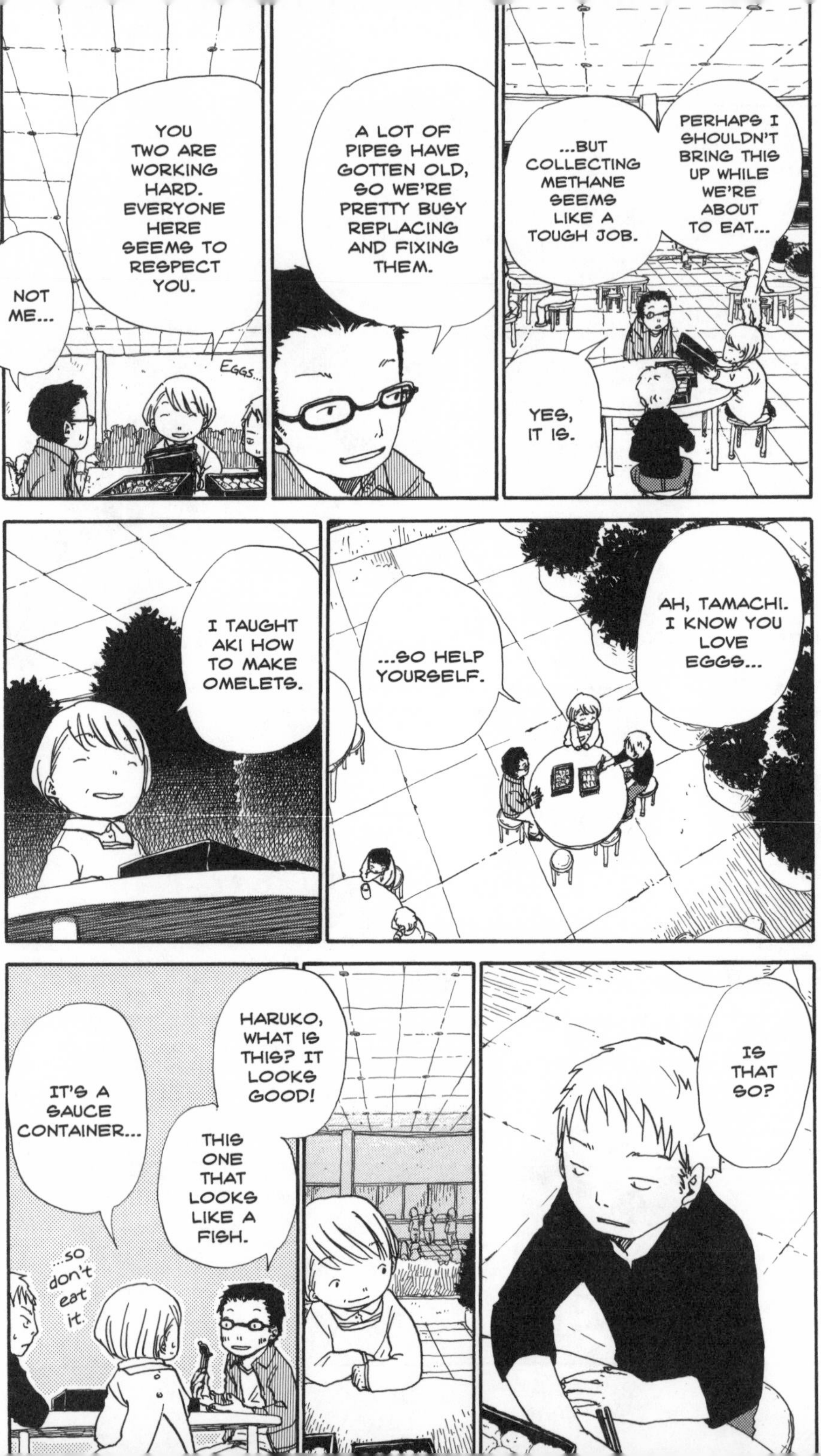
PERHAPS I SHOULDN'T BRING THIS UP WHILE WE'RE ABOUT TO EAT...
...BUT COLLECTING METHANE SEEMS LIKE A TOUGH JOB.
YES, IT IS.
A LOT OF PIPES HAVE GOTTEN OLD, SO WE'RE PRETTY BUSY REPLACING AND FIXING THEM.
YOU TWO ARE WORKING HARD. EVERYONE HERE SEEMS TO RESPECT YOU.
NOT ME...
EGGS...
AH, TAMACHI. I KNOW YOU LOVE EGGS...
...SO HELP YOURSELF.
I TAUGHT AKI HOW TO MAKE OMELETS.
IS THAT SO?
HARUKO, WHAT IS THIS? IT LOOKS GOOD!
THIS ONE THAT LOOKS LIKE A FISH.
IT'S A SAUCE CONTAINER...
...so don't eat it.

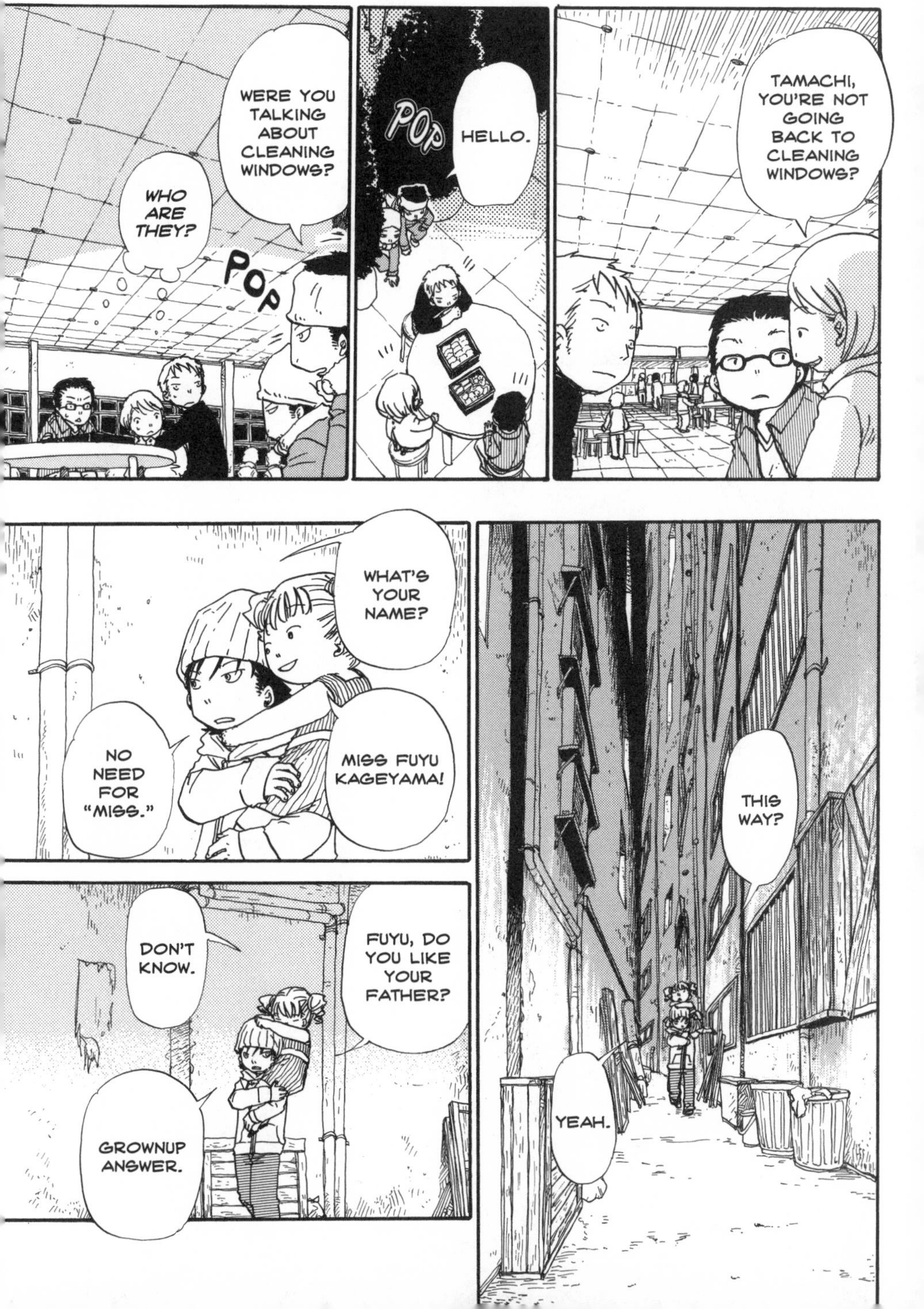
TAMACHI, YOU'RE NOT GOING BACK TO CLEANING WINDOWS?
POP
HELLO.
WERE YOU TALKING ABOUT CLEANING WINDOWS?
WHO ARE THEY?
POP
THIS WAY?
YEAH.
WHAT'S YOUR NAME?
MISS FUYU KAGEYAMA!
NO NEED FOR "MISS."
FUYU, DO YOU LIKE YOUR FATHER?
DON'T KNOW.
GROWNUP ANSWER.

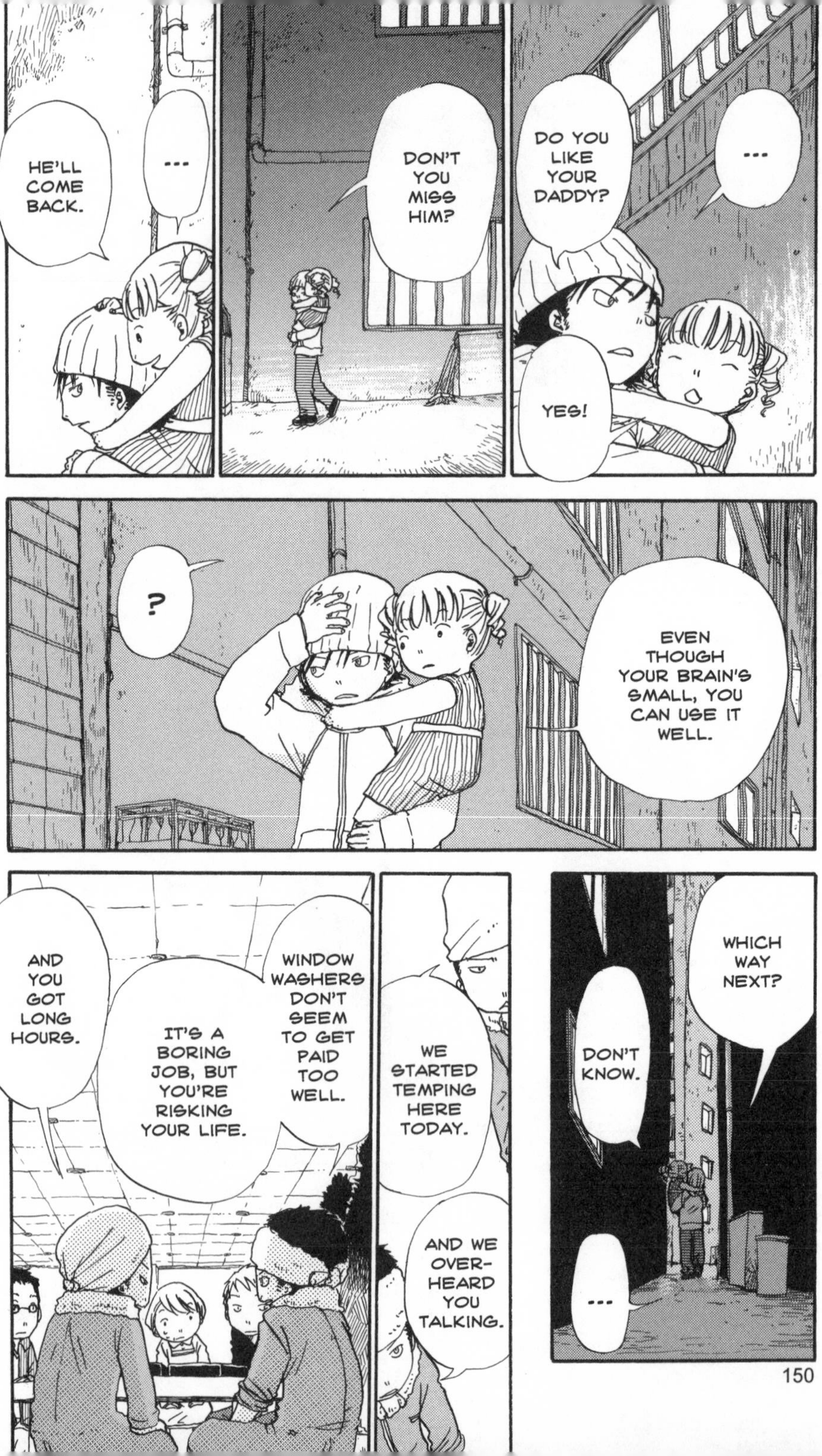

DO YOU LIKE YOUR DADDY?
YES!
DON'T YOU MISS HIM?

HE'LL COME BACK.
EVEN THOUGH YOUR BRAIN'S SMALL, YOU CAN USE IT WELL.
?
WHICH WAY NEXT?
DON'T KNOW.

WE STARTED TEMPING HERE TODAY.
AND WE OVER-HEARD YOU TALKING.
WINDOW WASHERS DON'T SEEM TO GET PAID TOO WELL.
IT'S A BORING JOB, BUT YOU'RE RISKING YOUR LIFE.
AND YOU GOT LONG HOURS.

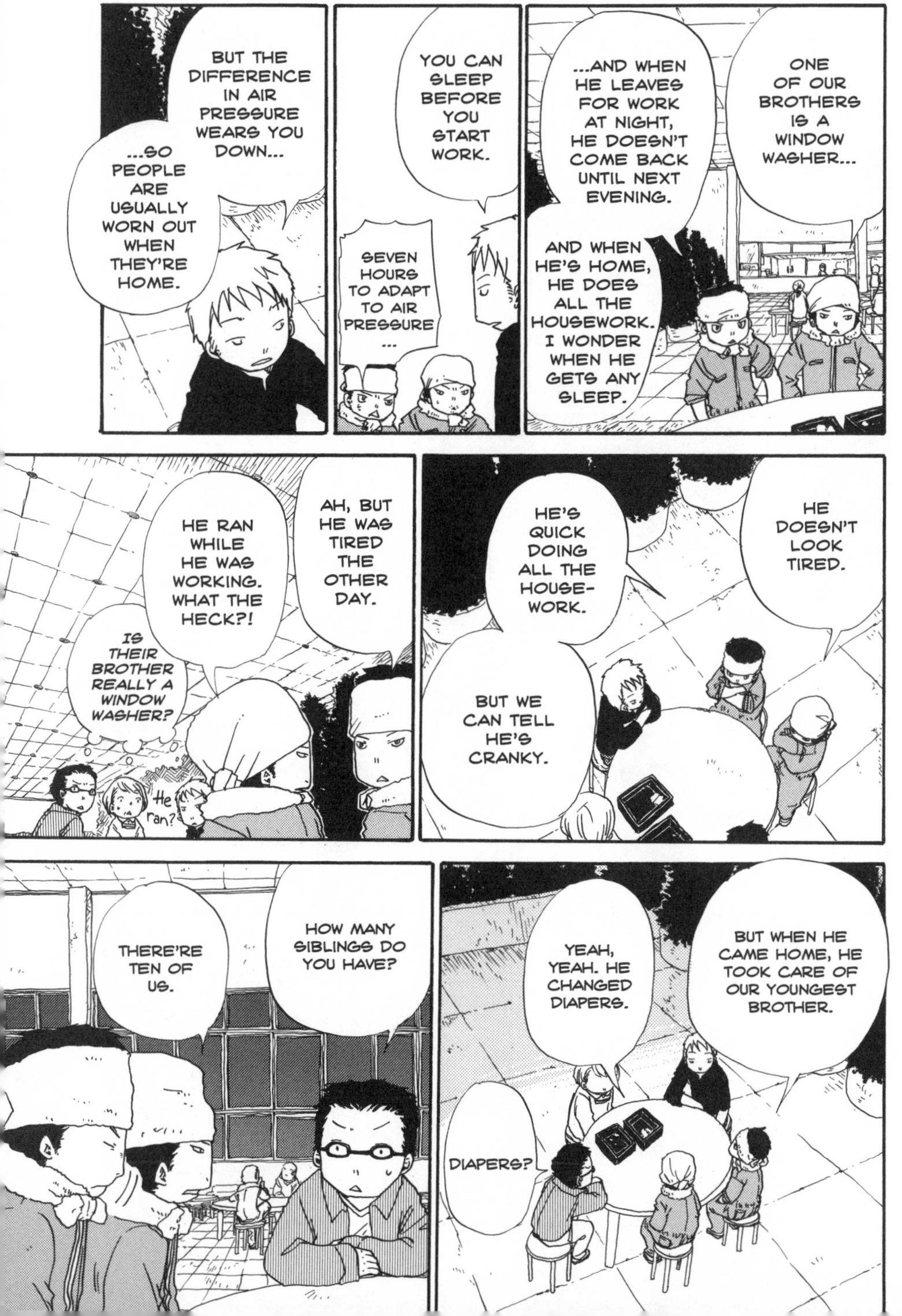
ONE OF OUR BROTHERS IS A WINDOW WASHER...
...AND WHEN HE LEAVES FOR WORK AT NIGHT, HE DOESN'T COME BACK UNTIL NEXT EVENING.
AND WHEN HE'S HOME, HE DOES ALL THE HOUSEWORK. I WONDER WHEN HE GETS ANY SLEEP.
YOU CAN SLEEP BEFORE YOU START WORK.
SEVEN HOURS TO ADAPT TO AIR PRESSURE ...
BUT THE DIFFERENCE IN AIR PRESSURE WEARS YOU DOWN...
...SO PEOPLE ARE USUALLY WORN OUT WHEN THEY'RE HOME.
HE DOESN'T LOOK TIRED.
HE'S QUICK DOING ALL THE HOUSE-WORK.
BUT WE CAN TELL HE'S CRANKY.
AH, BUT HE WAS TIRED THE OTHER DAY.
HE RAN WHILE HE WAS WORKING. WHAT THE HECK?!
IS THEIR BROTHER REALLY A WINDOW WASHER?
He ran?
BUT WHEN HE CAME HOME, HE TOOK CARE OF OUR YOUNGEST BROTHER.
YEAH, YEAH. HE CHANGED DIAPERS.
DIAPERS?
HOW MANY SIBLINGS DO YOU HAVE?
THERE'RE TEN OF US.

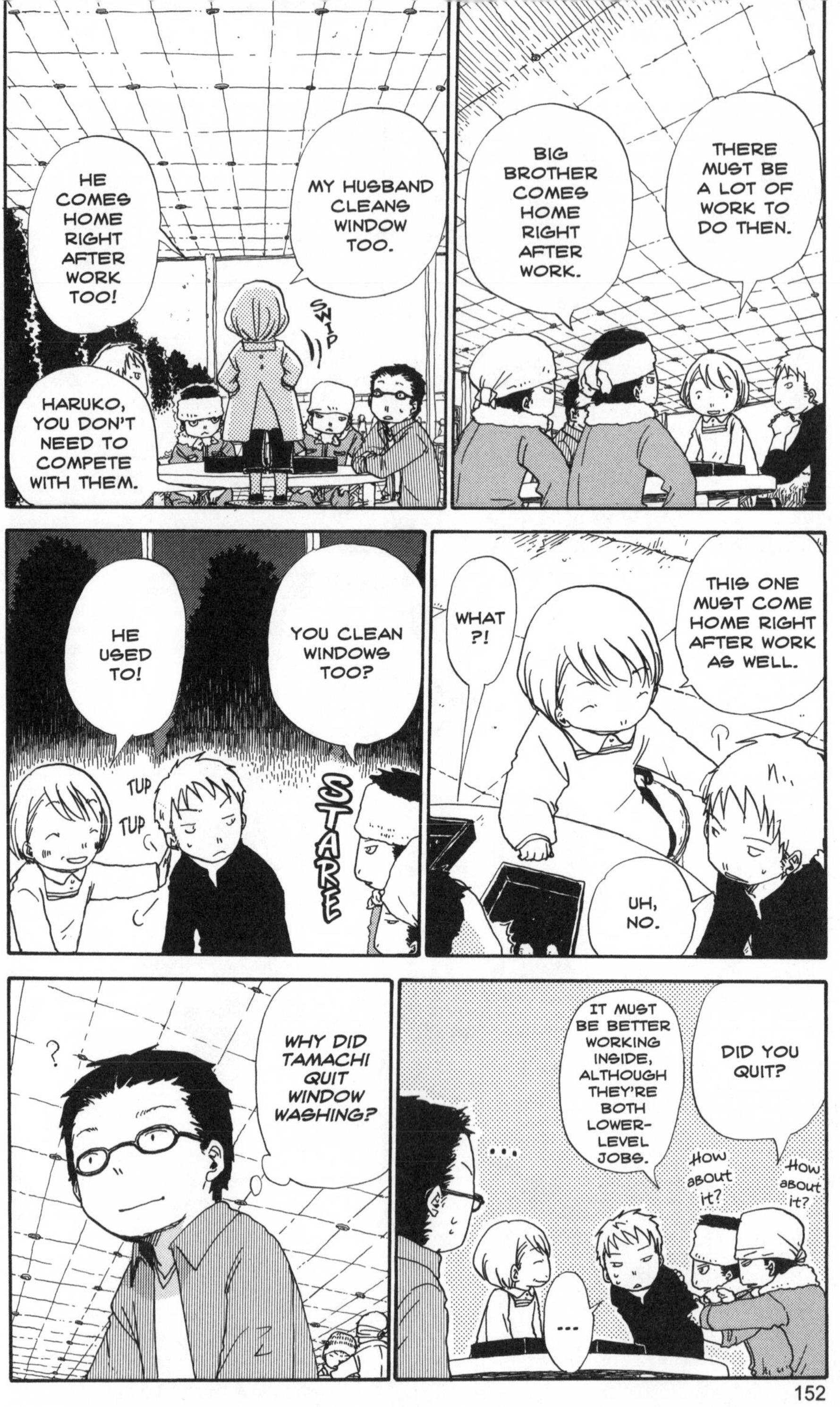
THERE MUST BE A LOT OF WORK TO DO THEN.
BIG BROTHER COMES HOME RIGHT AFTER WORK.
MY HUSBAND CLEANS WINDOW TOO.
SWIP
HE COMES HOME RIGHT AFTER WORK TOO!
HARUKO, YOU DON'T NEED TO COMPETE WITH THEM.
THIS ONE MUST COME HOME RIGHT AFTER WORK AS WELL.
WHAT ?!
UH, NO.
YOU CLEAN WINDOWS TOO?
STARE
HE USED TO!
TUP
TUP
DID YOU QUIT?
How about it?
IT MUST BE BETTER WORKING INSIDE, ALTHOUGH THEY'RE BOTH LOWER-LEVEL JOBS.
How about it?
...
...
WHY DID TAMACHI QUIT WINDOW WASHING?
?

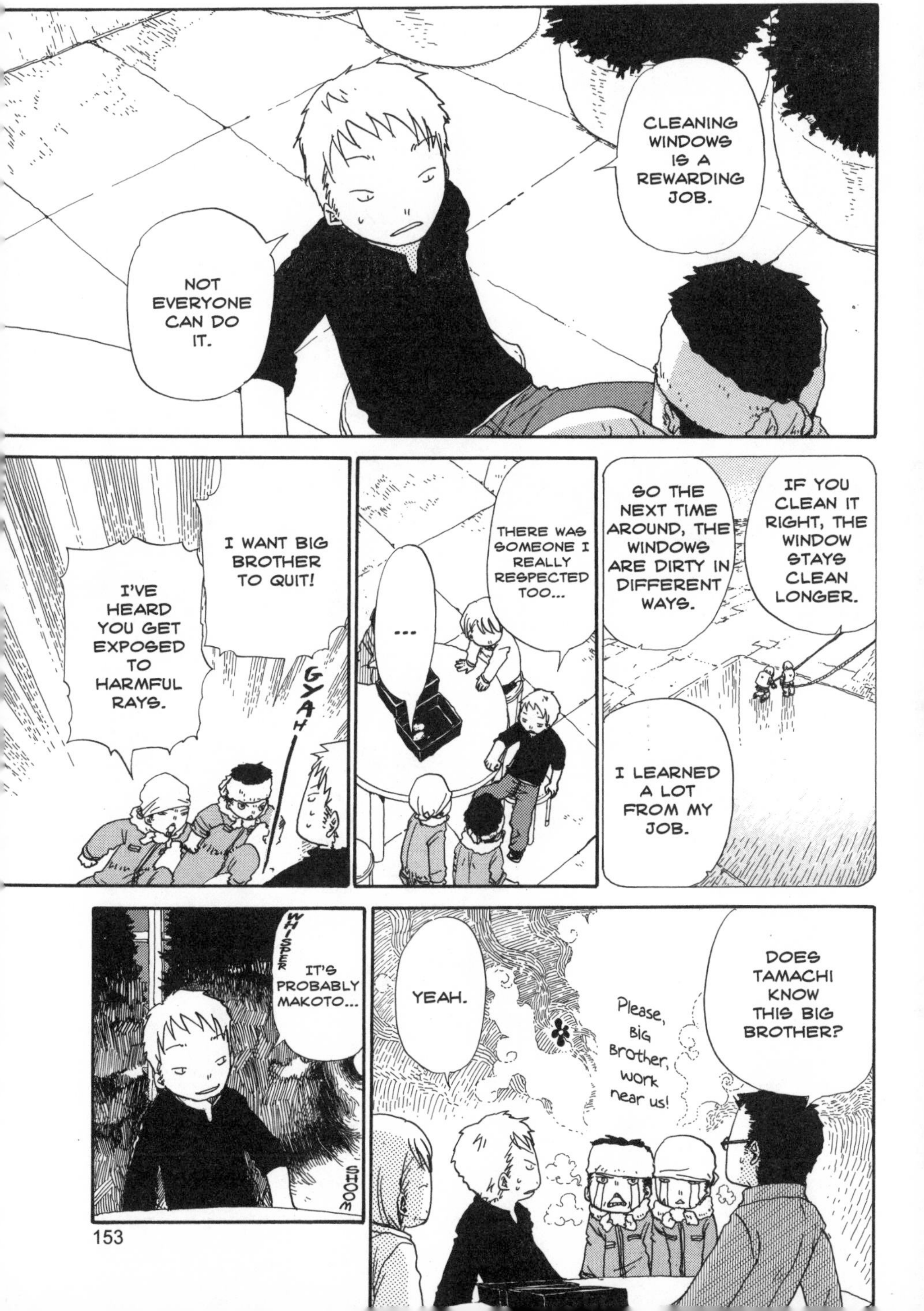
CLEANING WINDOWS IS A REWARDING JOB.
NOT EVERYONE CAN DO IT.
IF YOU CLEAN IT RIGHT, THE WINDOW STAYS CLEAN LONGER.
SO THE NEXT TIME AROUND, THE WINDOWS ARE DIRTY IN DIFFERENT WAYS.
I LEARNED A LOT FROM MY JOB.
THERE WAS SOMEONE I REALLY RESPECTED TOO...
...
I WANT BIG BROTHER TO QUIT!
I'VE HEARD YOU GET EXPOSED TO HARMFUL RAYS.
GYAH!
DOES TAMACHI KNOW THIS BIG BROTHER?
Please, Big Brother, work near us!
YEAH.
WHISPER
IT'S PROBABLY MAKOTO...
SHOOM

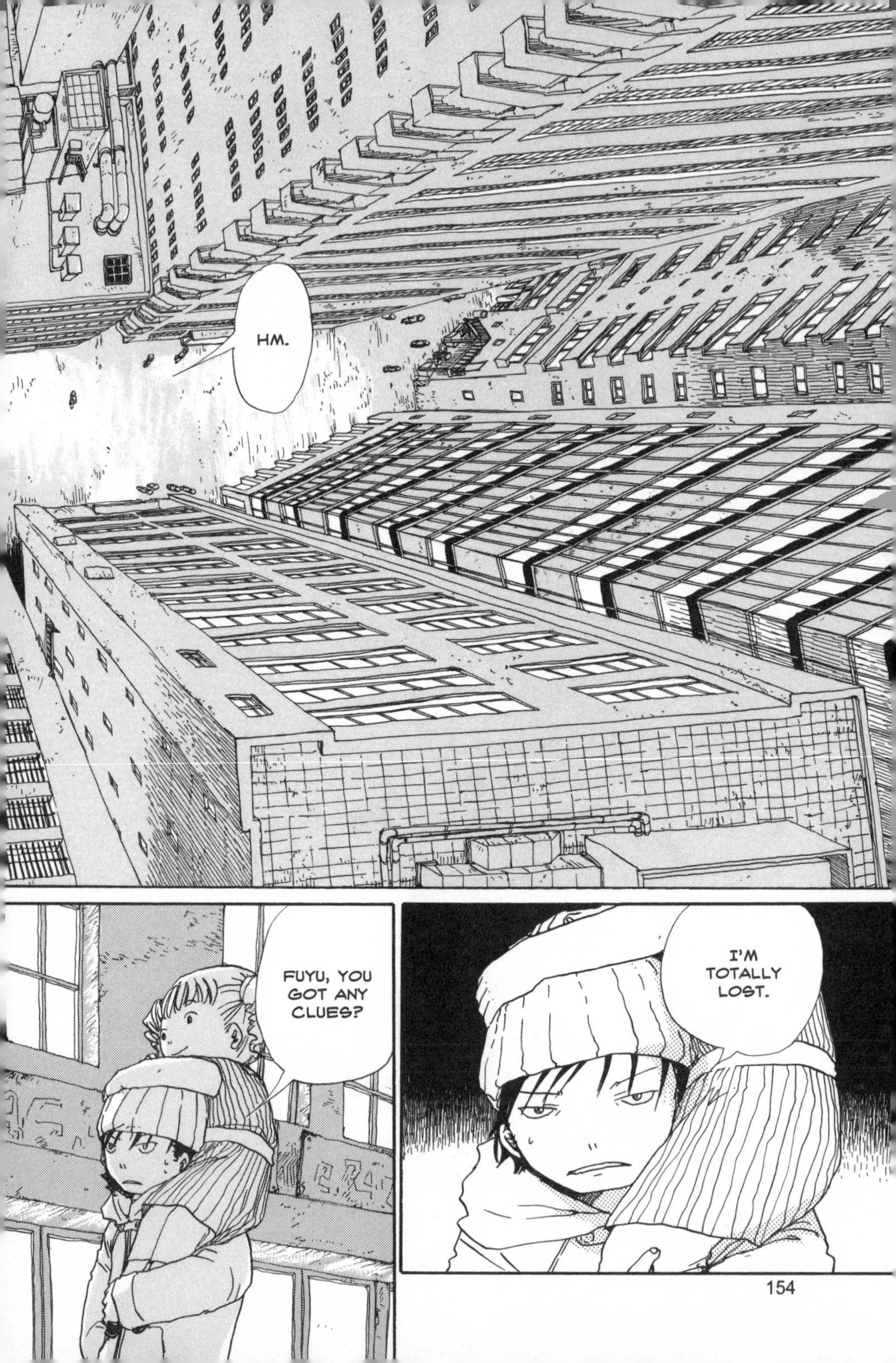
HM.
I'M TOTALLY LOST.
FUYU, YOU GOT ANY CLUES?

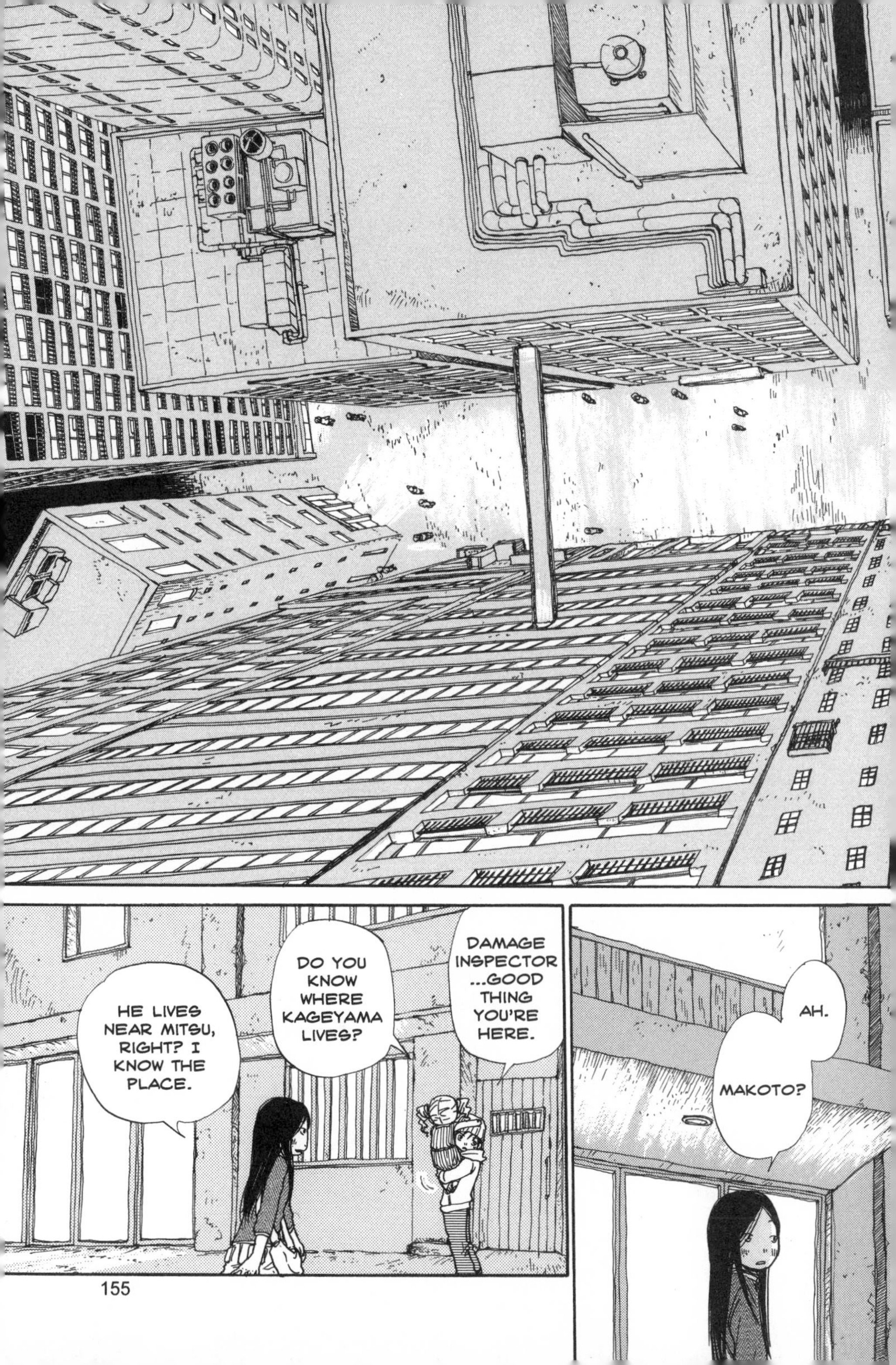
AH.
MAKOTO?
DAMAGE INSPECTOR ...GOOD THING YOU'RE HERE.
DO YOU KNOW WHERE KAGEYAMA LIVES?
HE LIVES NEAR MITSU, RIGHT? I KNOW THE PLACE.

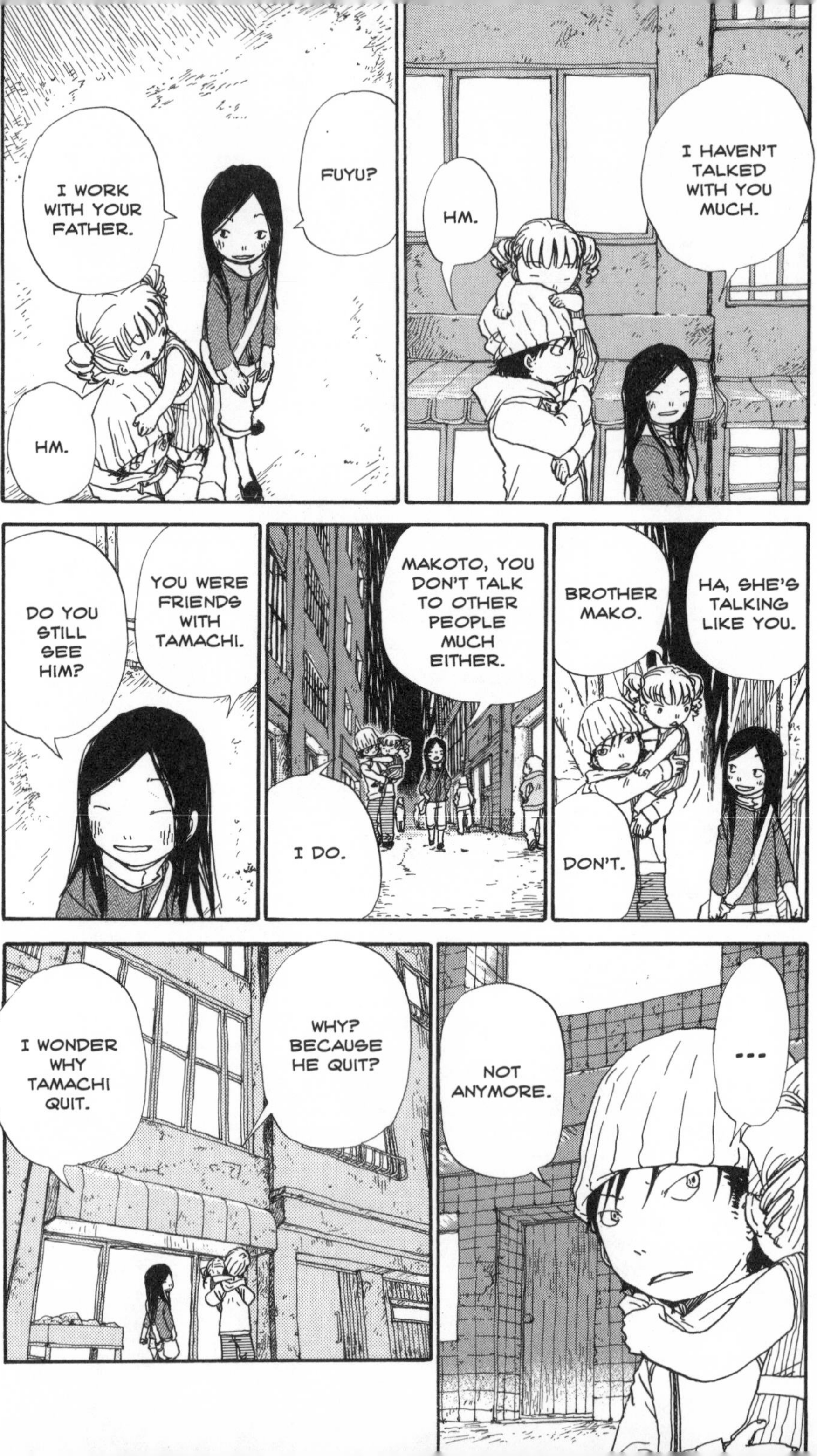
I HAVEN'T TALKED WITH YOU MUCH.
HM.
FUYU?
I WORK WITH YOUR FATHER.
HM.
HA, SHE'S TALKING LIKE YOU.
BROTHER MAKO.
DON'T.
MAKOTO, YOU DON'T TALK TO OTHER PEOPLE MUCH EITHER.
I DO.
YOU WERE FRIENDS WITH TAMACHI.
DO YOU STILL SEE HIM?
...
NOT ANYMORE.
WHY? BECAUSE HE QUIT?
I WONDER WHY TAMACHI QUIT.

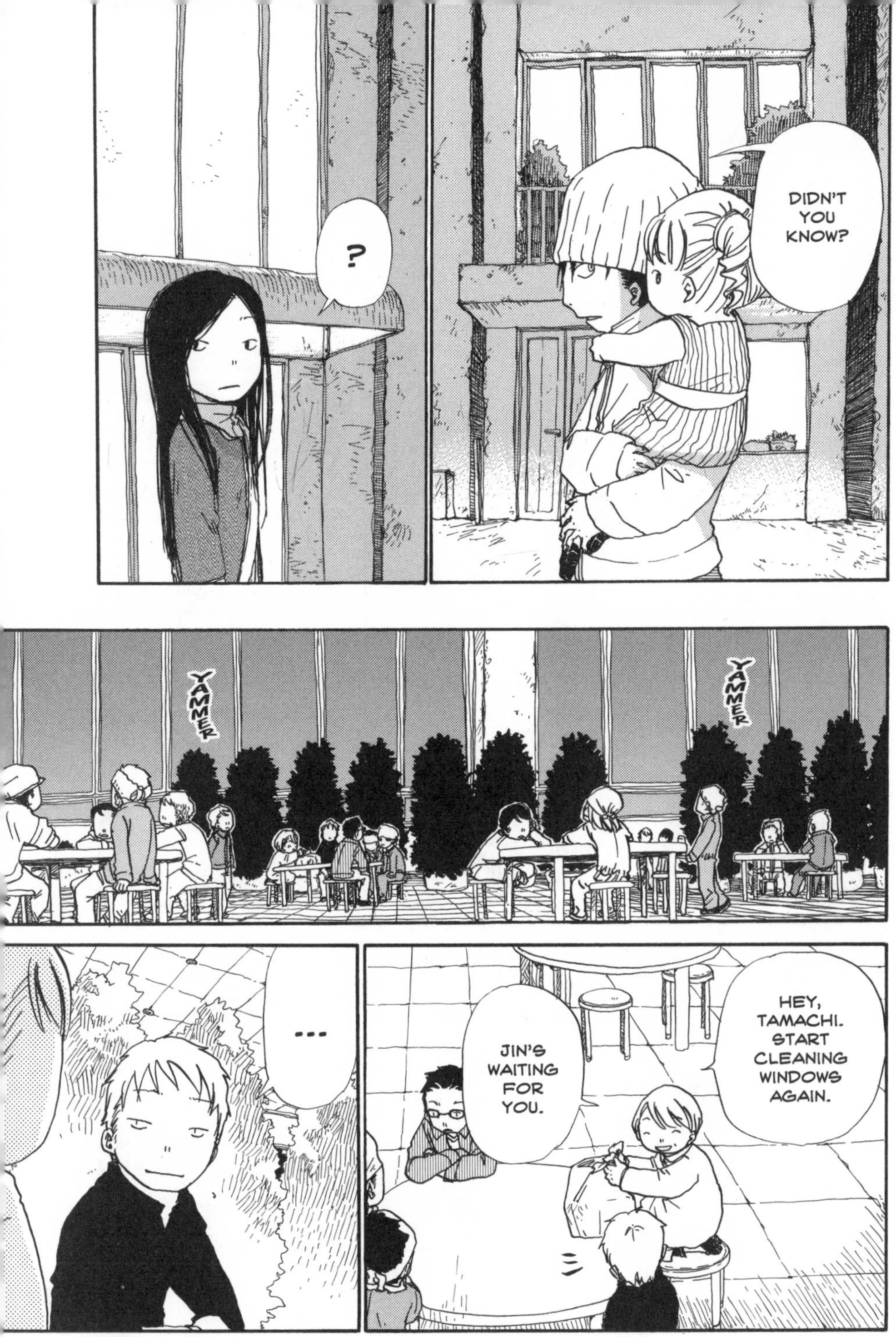
DIDN'T YOU KNOW?
?
YAMMER
YAMMER
HEY, TAMACHI. START CLEANING WINDOWS AGAIN.
JIN'S WAITING FOR YOU.
...

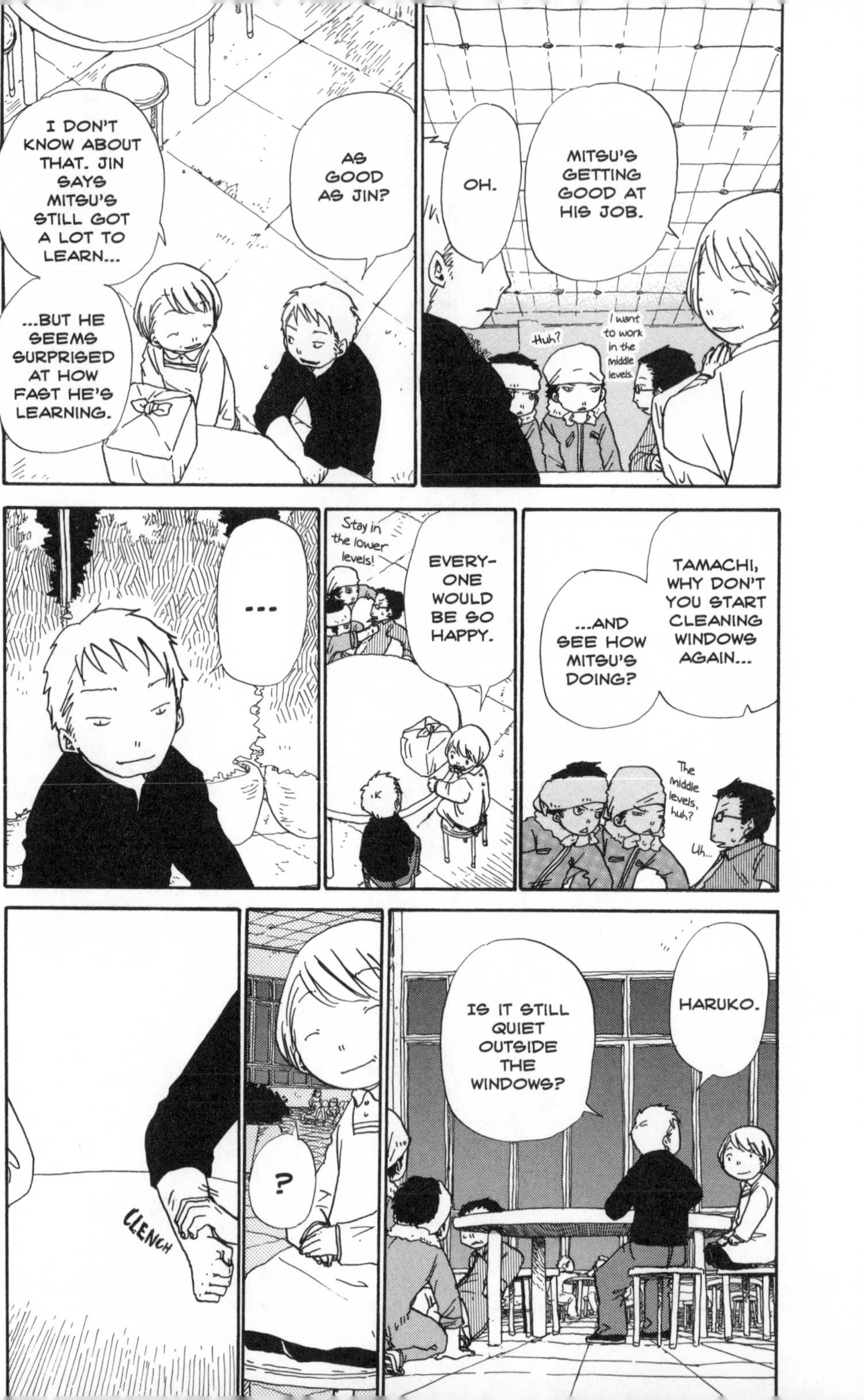
MITSU'S GETTING GOOD AT HIS JOB.
OH.
I want to work in the middle levels.
Huh?
AS GOOD AS JIN?
I DON'T KNOW ABOUT THAT. JIN SAYS MITSU'S STILL GOT A LOT TO LEARN...
...BUT HE SEEMS SURPRISED AT HOW FAST HE'S LEARNING.
TAMACHI, WHY DON'T YOU START CLEANING WINDOWS AGAIN...
...AND SEE HOW MITSU'S DOING?
The middle levels, huh?
Uh...
Stay in the lower levels!
EVERYONE WOULD BE SO HAPPY.
...
HARUKO.
IS IT STILL QUIET OUTSIDE THE WINDOWS?
?
CLENCH

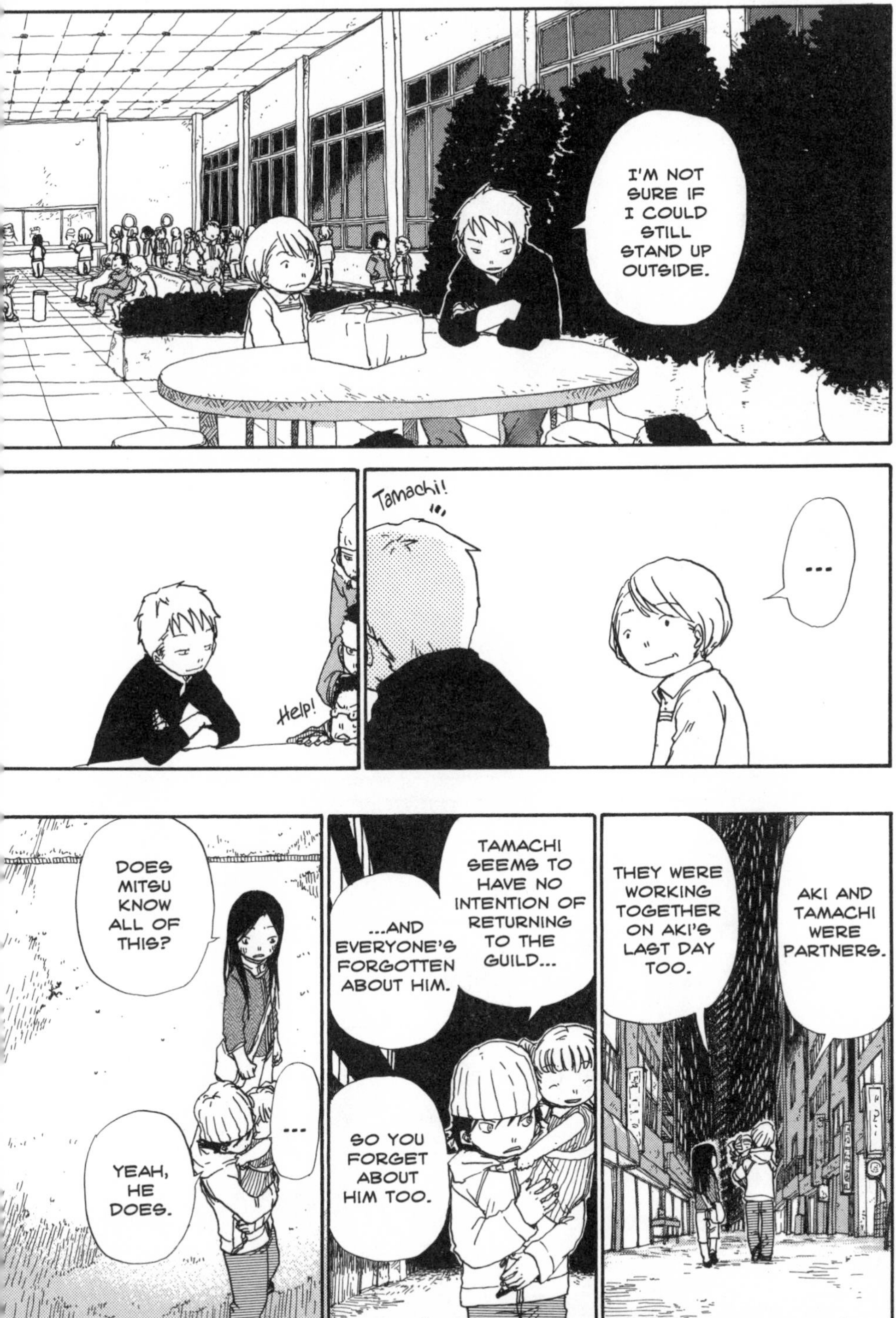
I'M NOT SURE IF I COULD STILL STAND UP OUTSIDE.
Tamachi!
...
Help!
AKI AND TAMACHI WERE PARTNERS.
THEY WERE WORKING TOGETHER ON AKI'S LAST DAY TOO.
TAMACHI SEEMS TO HAVE NO INTENTION OF RETURNING TO THE GUILD...
...AND EVERYONE'S FORGOTTEN ABOUT HIM.
SO YOU FORGET ABOUT HIM TOO.
DOES MITSU KNOW ALL OF THIS?
...
YEAH, HE DOES.

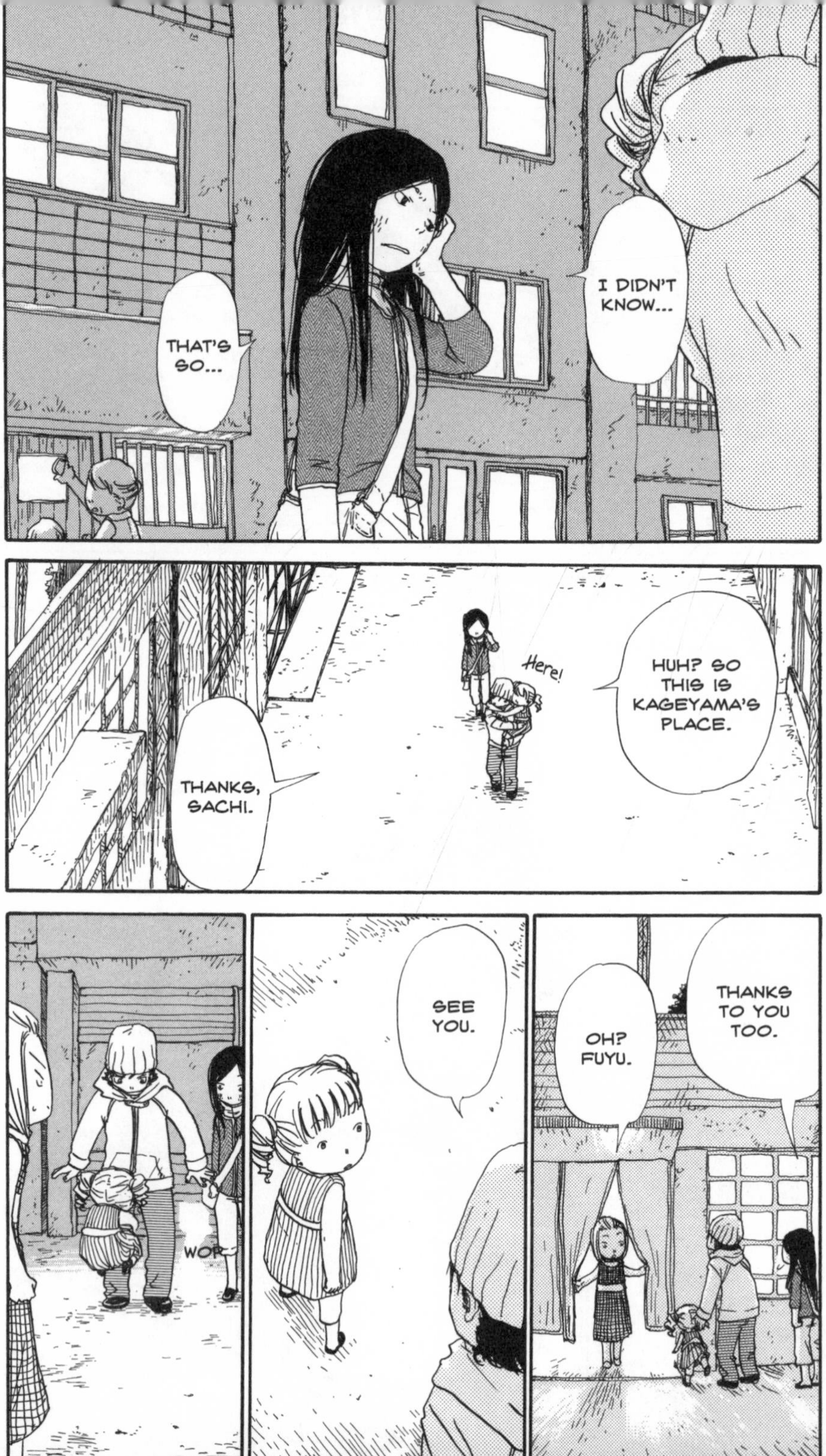
I DIDN'T KNOW...
THAT'S SO...
HUH? SO THIS IS KAGEYAMA'S PLACE.
Here!
THANKS, SACHI.
THANKS TO YOU TOO.
OH? FUYU.
SEE YOU.
WOP

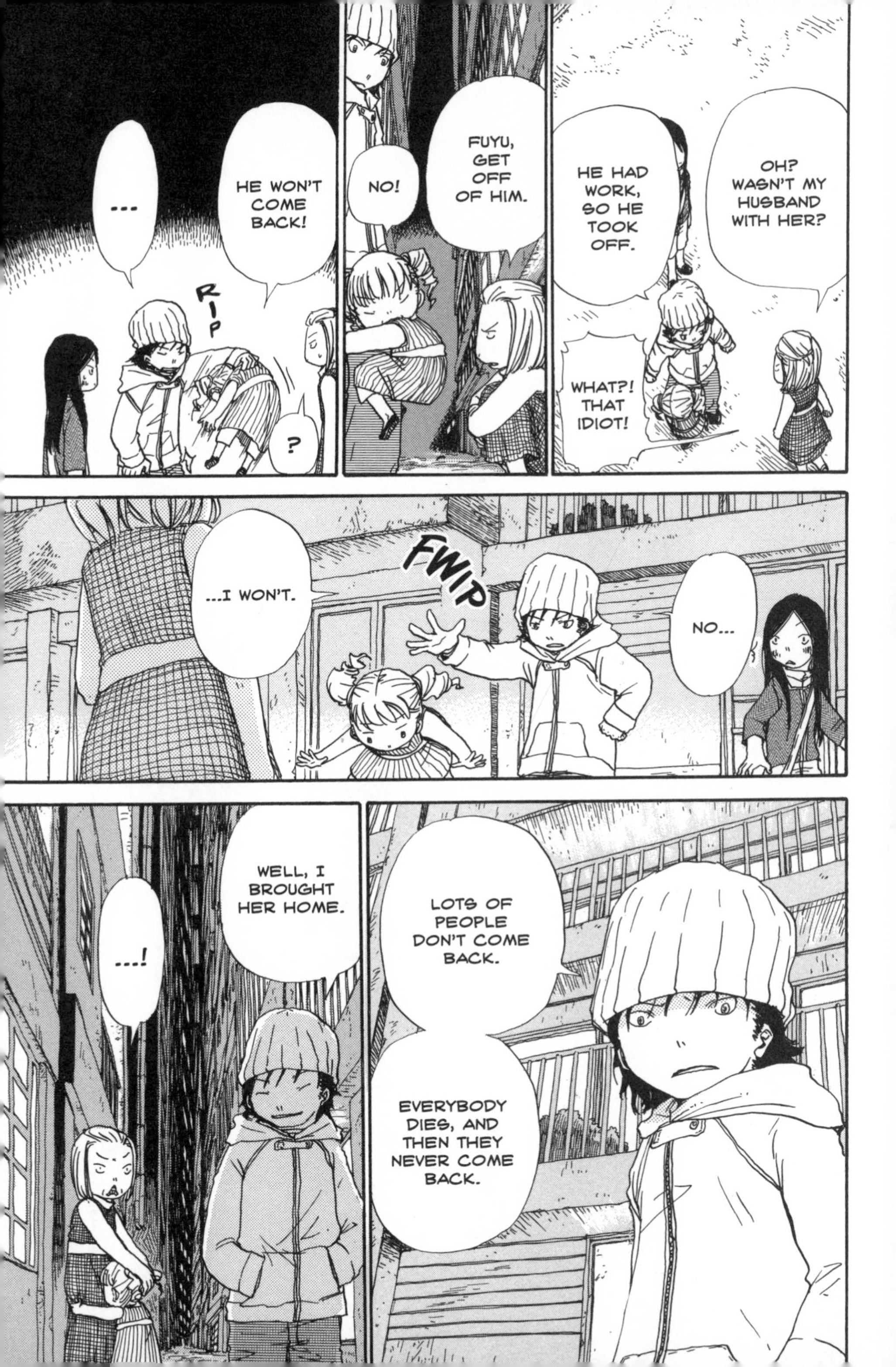
OH? WASN'T MY HUSBAND WITH HER?
HE HAD WORK, SO HE TOOK OFF.
WHAT?! THAT IDIOT!
FUYU, GET OFF OF HIM.
NO!
HE WON'T COME BACK!
...
RIP
?
NO...
FWIP
...I WON'T.
LOTS OF PEOPLE DON'T COME BACK.
EVERYBODY DIES, AND THEN THEY NEVER COME BACK.
WELL, I BROUGHT HER HOME.
...!

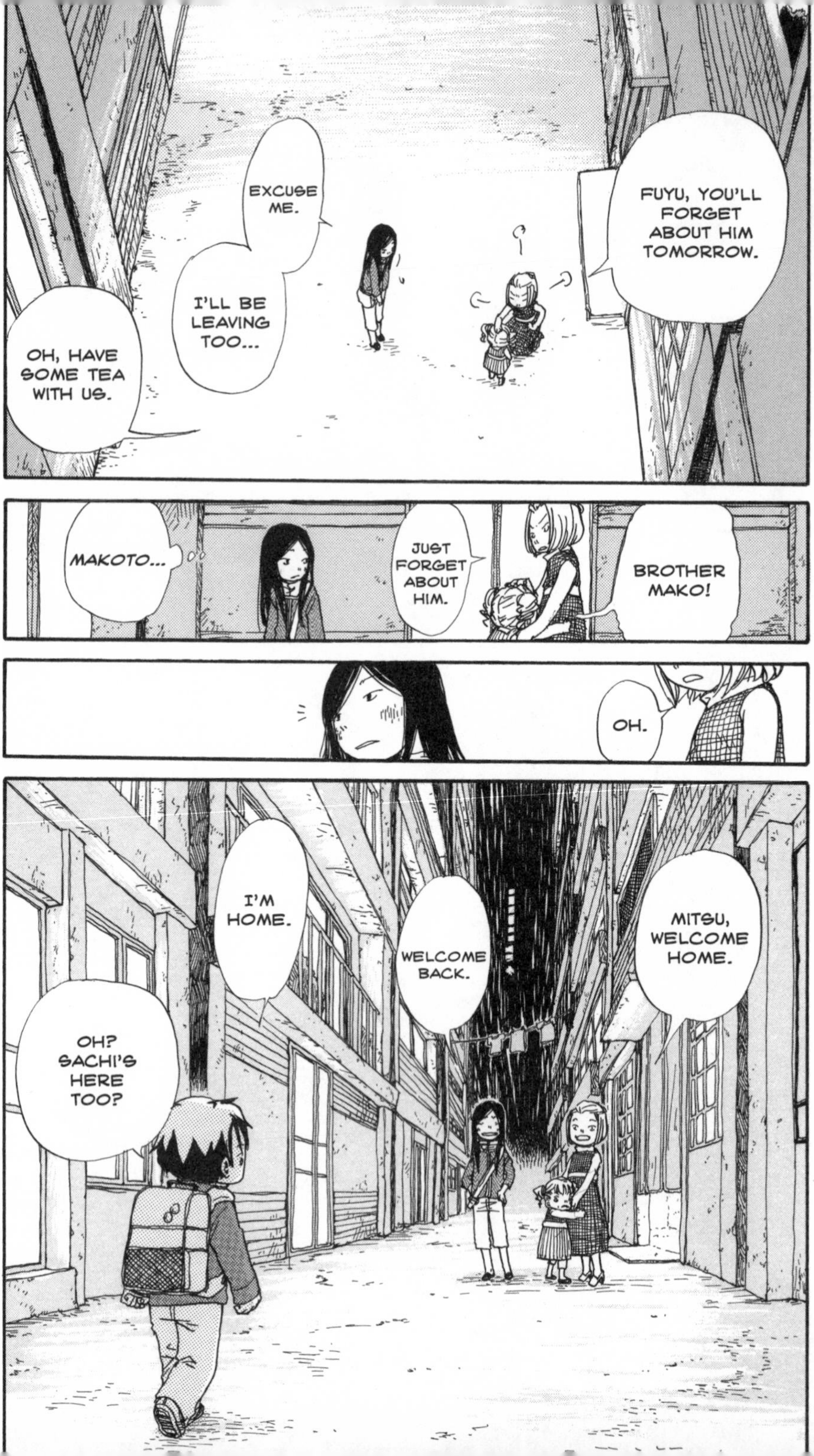
FUYU, YOU'LL FORGET ABOUT HIM TOMORROW.
EXCUSE ME.
I'LL BE LEAVING TOO...
OH, HAVE SOME TEA WITH US.
BROTHER MAKO!
JUST FORGET ABOUT HIM.
MAKOTO...
OH.
MITSU, WELCOME HOME.
WELCOME BACK.
I'M HOME.
OH? SACHI'S HERE TOO?

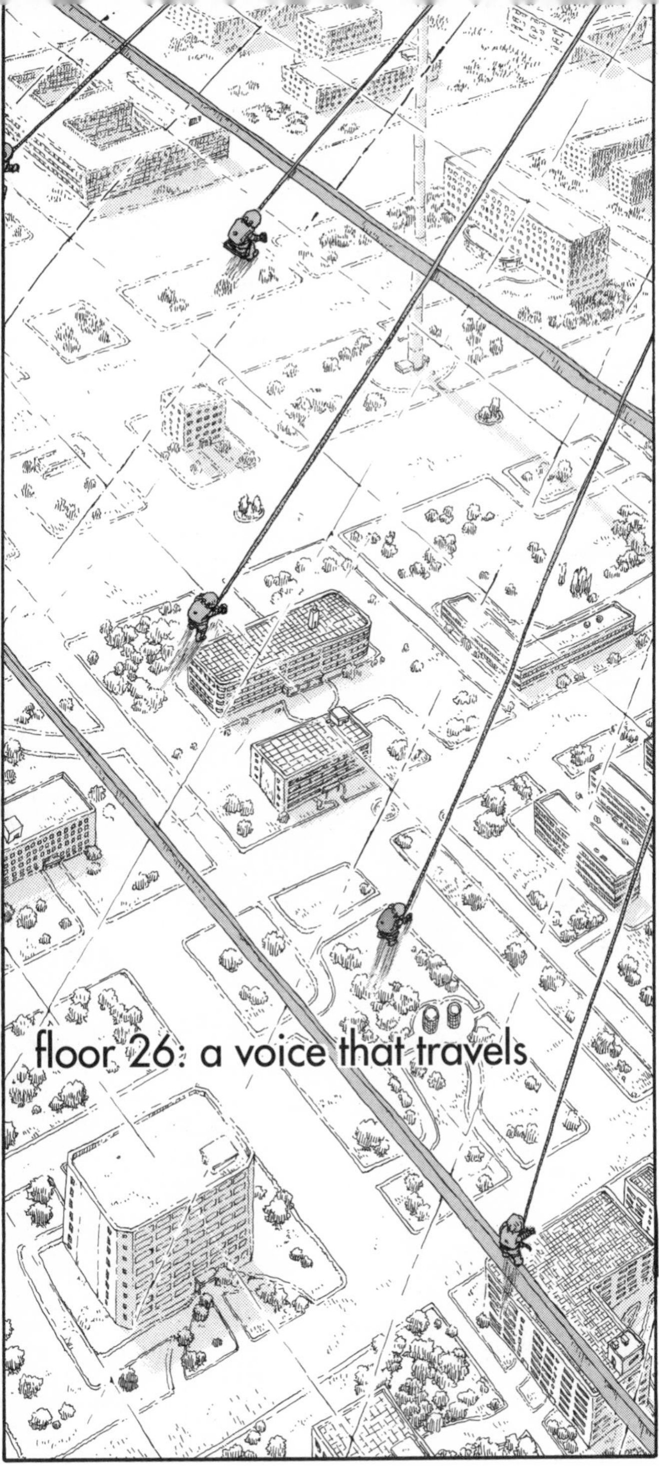
floor 26: a voice that travels

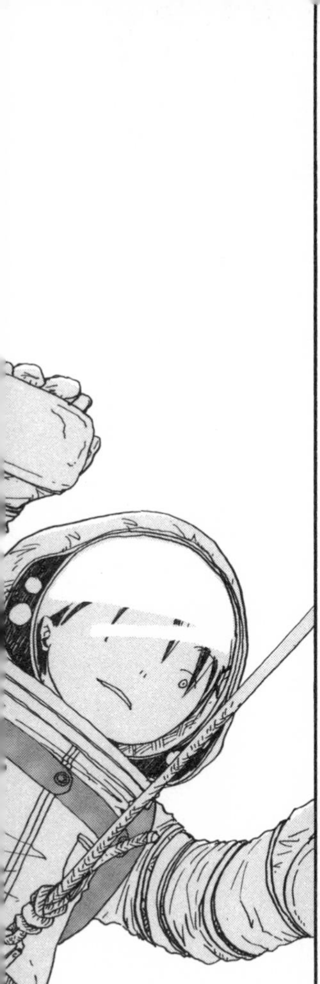

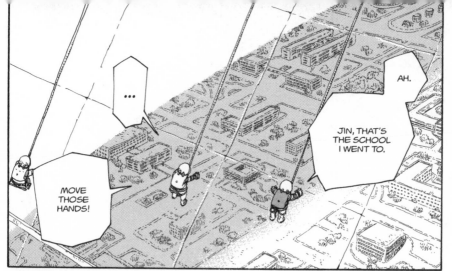

AH.
JIN, THAT'S THE SCHOOL I WENT TO.
...
MOVE THOSE HANDS!
THE MIDDLE LEVELS ARE IMMENSE...
I USED TO COME HERE EVERY DAY.
HM? MITSU, YOU MISSED A SPOT.
CLEAN IT WELL.
NOOOO!
TOK
TOK
GOD, I'M TIRED.
THE MIDDLE-LEVEL WINDOWS ARE ENDLESS. IT'S NOT WORTH THE MONEY.
BUT I ENJOYED ALL THAT SPACE.

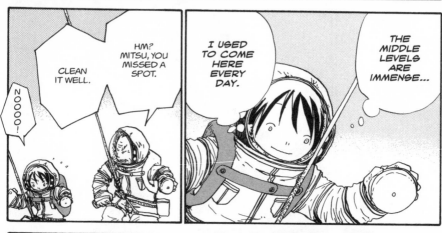

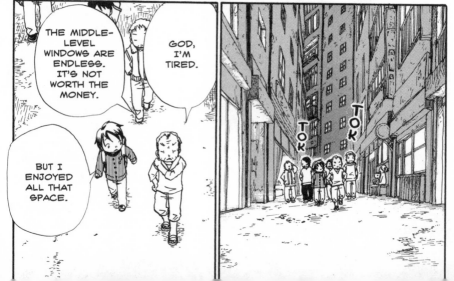

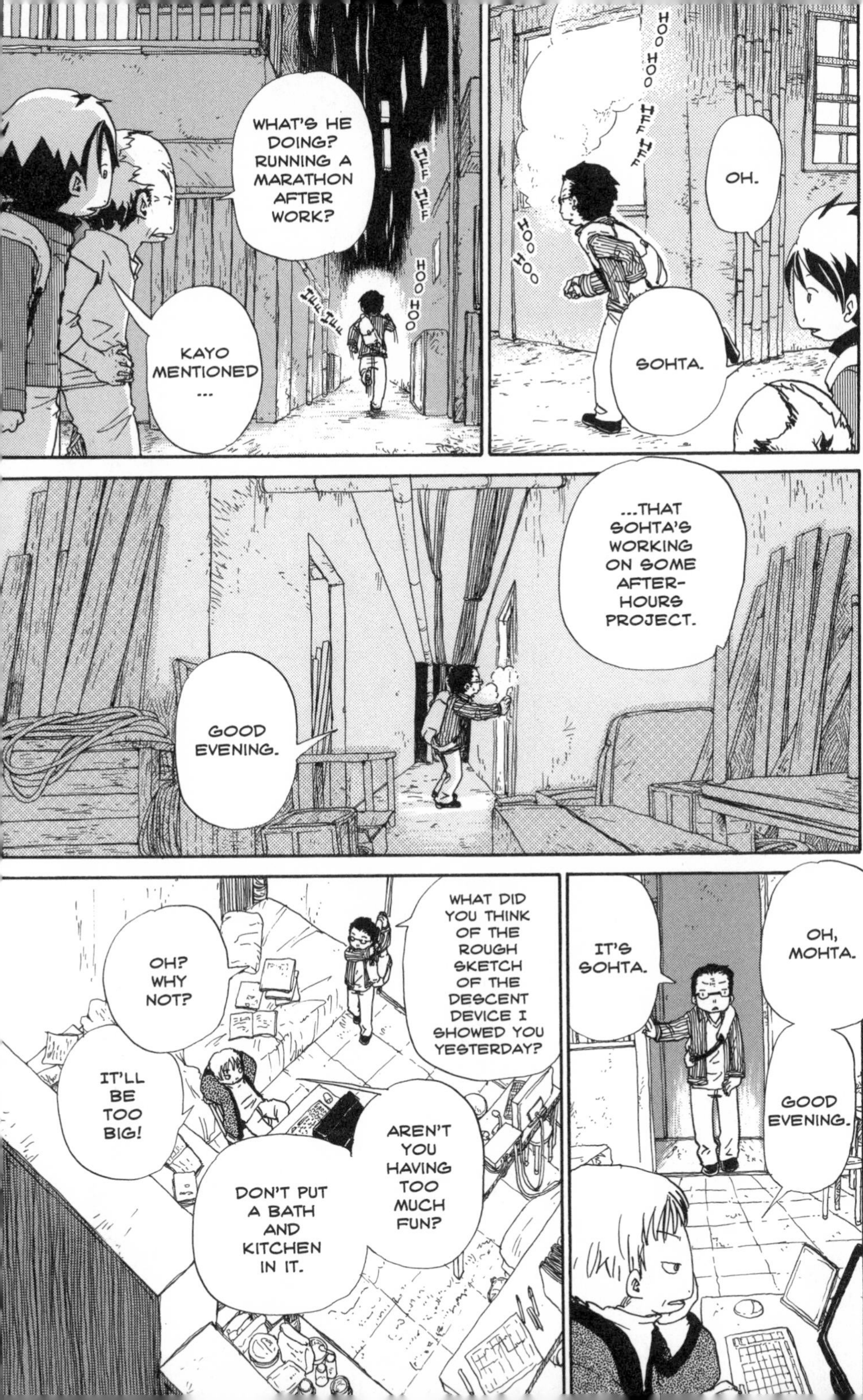
HOO HOO
HFF HFF
HOO HOO
OH.
SOHTA.
WHAT'S HE DOING? RUNNING A MARATHON AFTER WORK?
HFF HFF
HOO HOO
KAYO MENTIONED ...
...THAT SOHTA'S WORKING ON SOME AFTER-HOURS PROJECT.
GOOD EVENING.
OH, MOHTA.
IT'S SOHTA.
GOOD EVENING.
WHAT DID YOU THINK OF THE ROUGH SKETCH OF THE DESCENT DEVICE I SHOWED YOU YESTERDAY?
OH? WHY NOT?
AREN'T YOU HAVING TOO MUCH FUN?
IT'LL BE TOO BIG!
DON'T PUT A BATH AND KITCHEN IN IT.

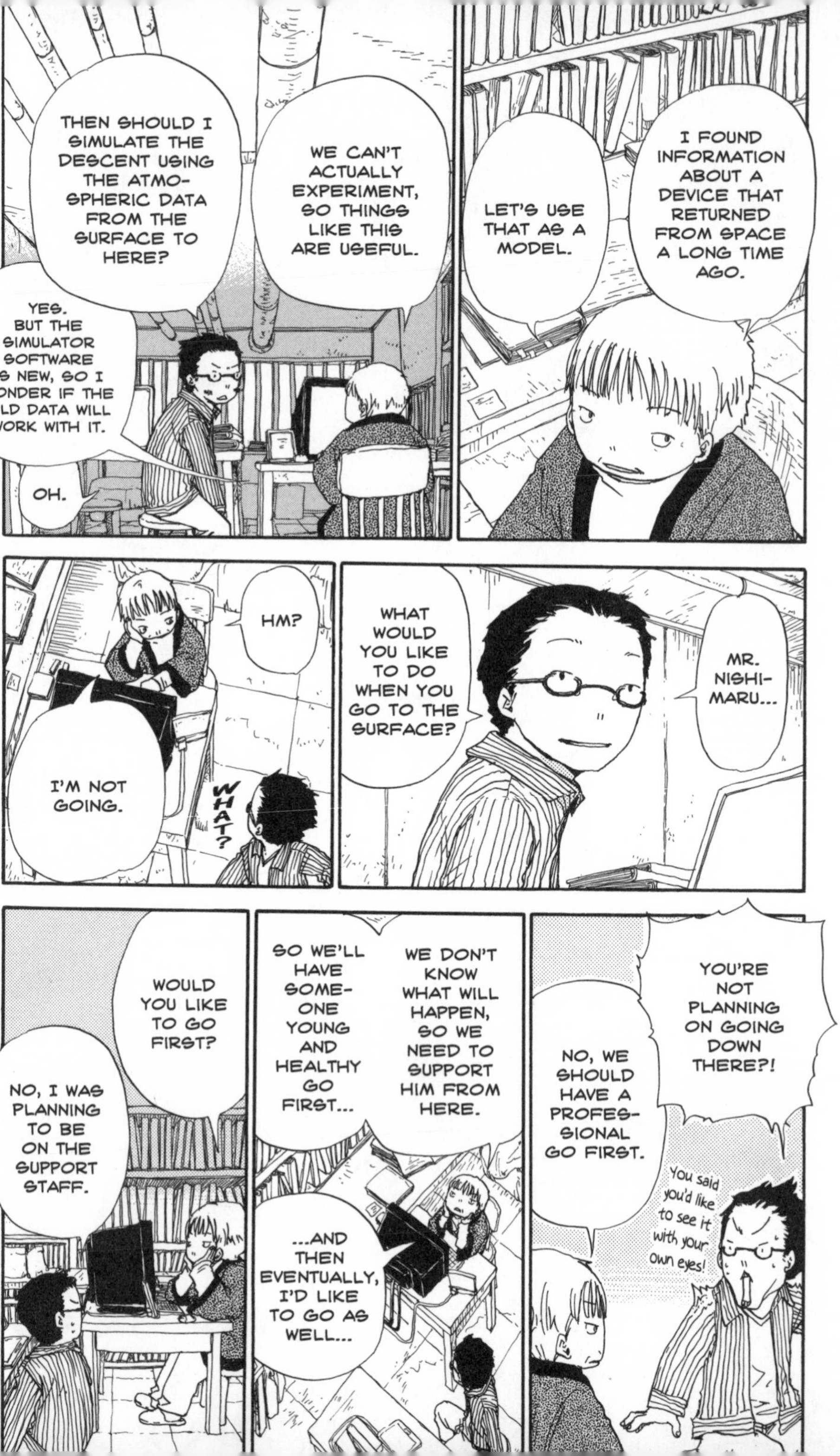
I FOUND INFORMATION ABOUT A DEVICE THAT RETURNED FROM SPACE A LONG TIME AGO.
LET'S USE THAT AS A MODEL.
WE CAN'T ACTUALLY EXPERIMENT, SO THINGS LIKE THIS ARE USEFUL.
THEN SHOULD I SIMULATE THE DESCENT USING THE ATMOSPHERIC DATA FROM THE SURFACE TO HERE?
YES. BUT THE SIMULATOR SOFTWARE IS NEW, SO I WONDER IF THE OLD DATA WILL WORK WITH IT.
OH.
MR. NISHIMARU...
WHAT WOULD YOU LIKE TO DO WHEN YOU GO TO THE SURFACE?
HM?
I'M NOT GOING.
WHAT?
YOU'RE NOT PLANNING ON GOING DOWN THERE?!
NO, WE SHOULD HAVE A PROFESSIONAL GO FIRST.
You said you'd like to see it with your own eyes!
WE DON'T KNOW WHAT WILL HAPPEN, SO WE NEED TO SUPPORT HIM FROM HERE.
SO WE'LL HAVE SOMEONE YOUNG AND HEALTHY GO FIRST...
...AND THEN EVENTUALLY, I'D LIKE TO GO AS WELL...
WOULD YOU LIKE TO GO FIRST?
NO, I WAS PLANNING TO BE ON THE SUPPORT STAFF.

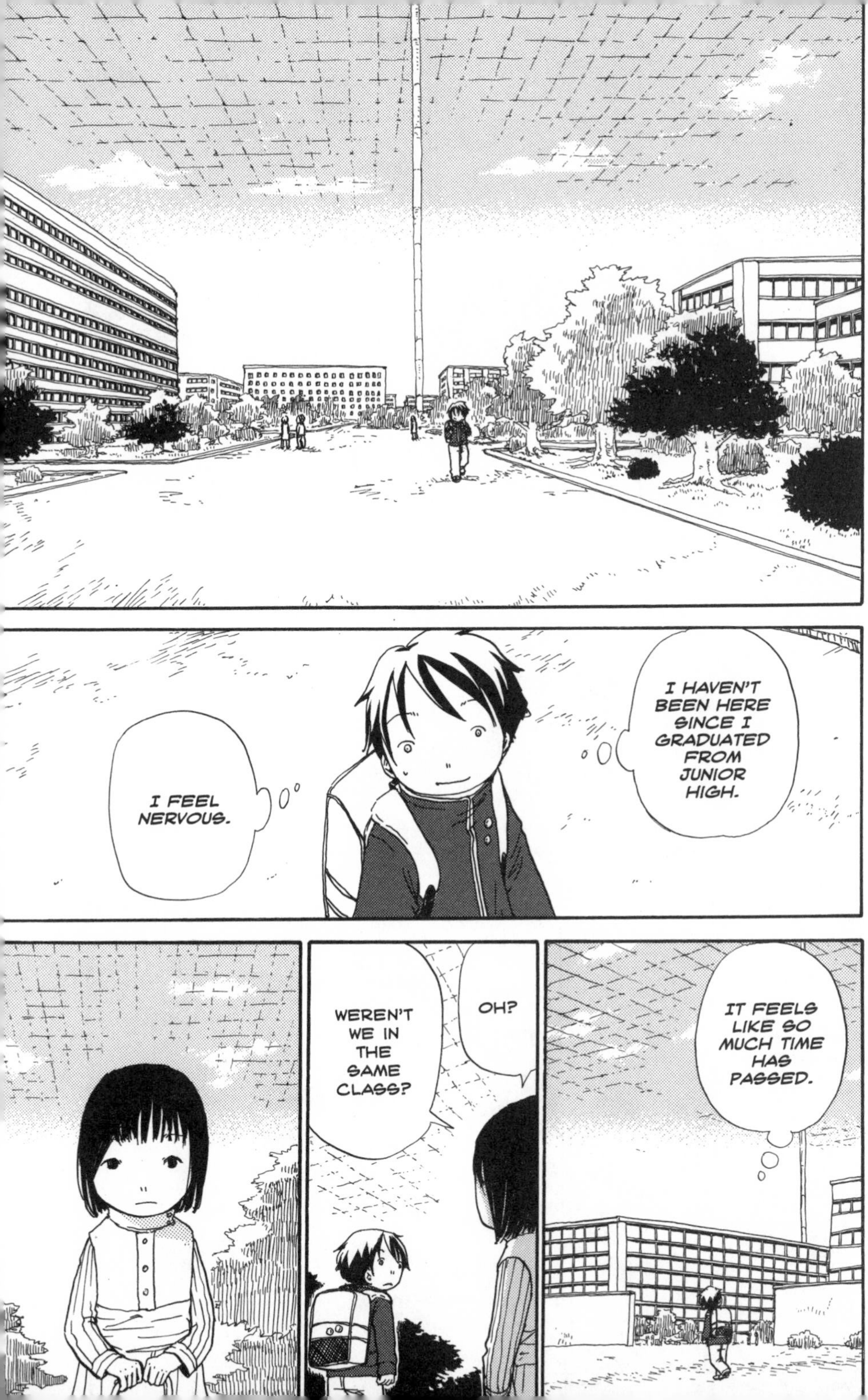
I HAVEN'T BEEN HERE SINCE I GRADUATED FROM JUNIOR HIGH.
I FEEL NERVOUS.
IT FEELS LIKE SO MUCH TIME HAS PASSED.
OH?
WEREN'T WE IN THE SAME CLASS?

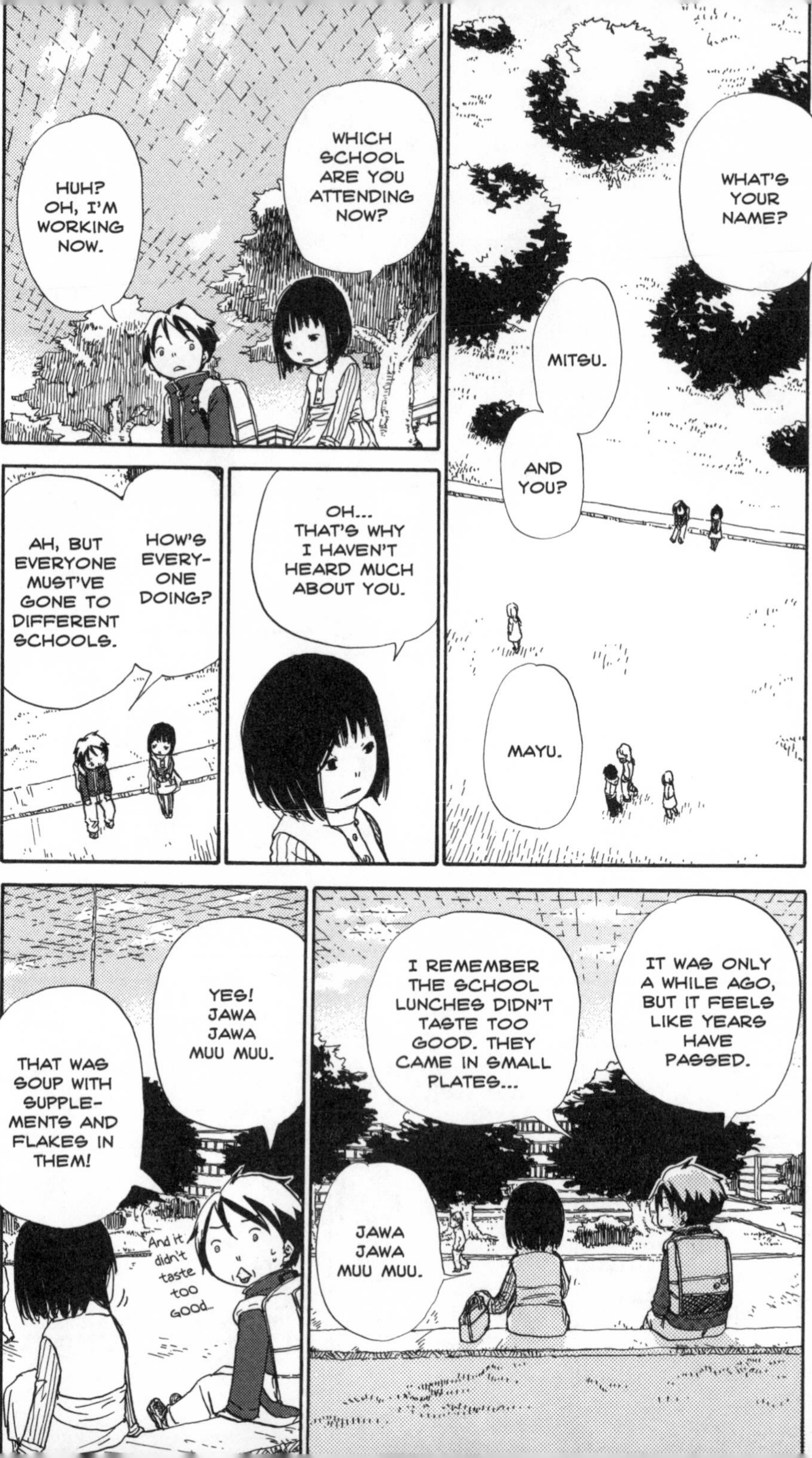
WHAT'S YOUR NAME?
MITSU.
AND YOU?
MAYU.
WHICH SCHOOL ARE YOU ATTENDING NOW?
HUH? OH, I'M WORKING NOW.
OH... THAT'S WHY I HAVEN'T HEARD MUCH ABOUT YOU.
HOW'S EVERY-ONE DOING?
AH, BUT EVERYONE MUST'VE GONE TO DIFFERENT SCHOOLS.
IT WAS ONLY A WHILE AGO, BUT IT FEELS LIKE YEARS HAVE PASSED.
I REMEMBER THE SCHOOL LUNCHES DIDN'T TASTE TOO GOOD. THEY CAME IN SMALL PLATES...
JAWA JAWA MUU MUU.
YES! JAWA JAWA MUU MUU.
THAT WAS SOUP WITH SUPPLE-MENTS AND FLAKES IN THEM!
And it didn't taste too good...

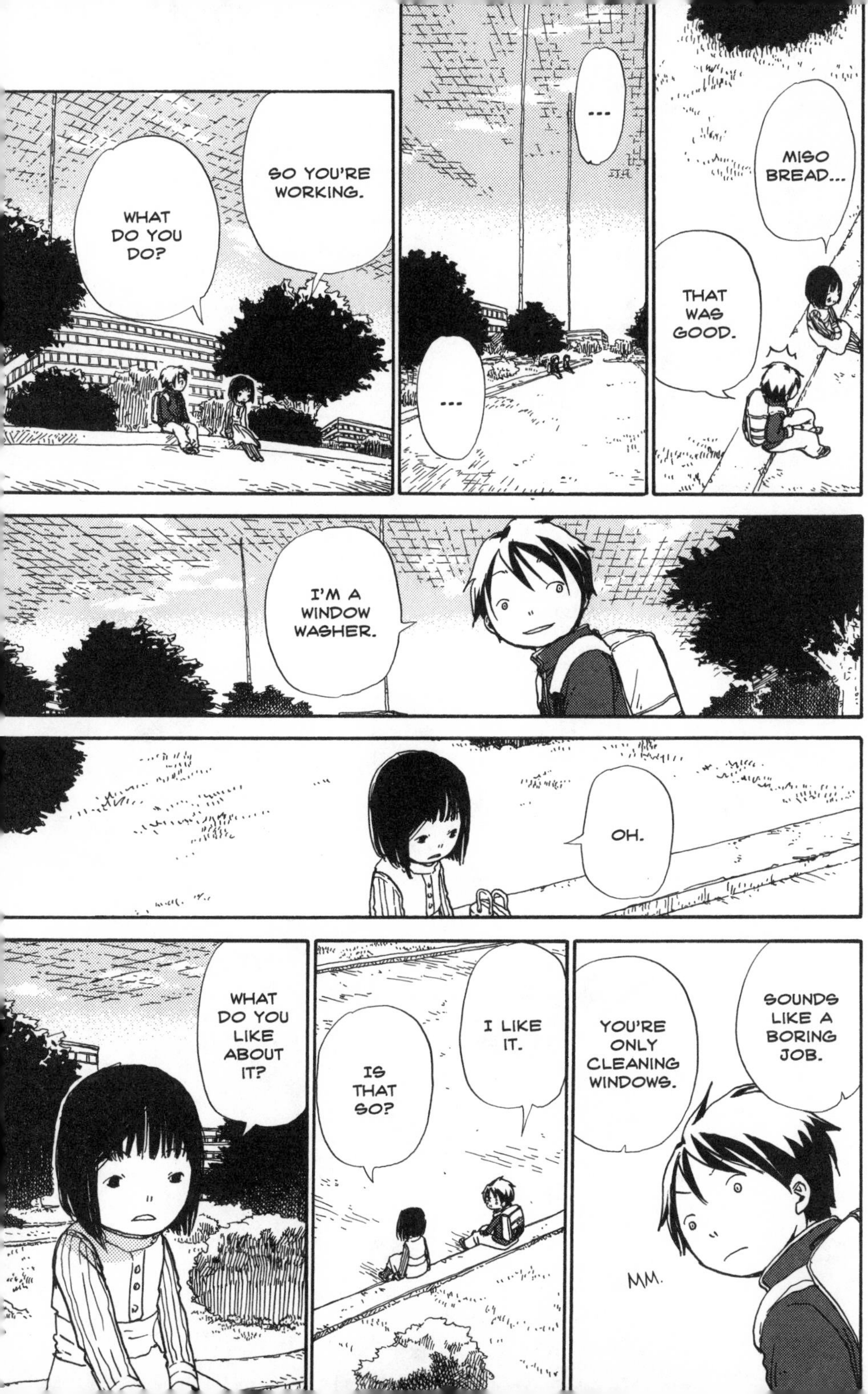
MISO BREAD...
THAT WAS GOOD.
...
...
SO YOU'RE WORKING.
WHAT DO YOU DO?
I'M A WINDOW WASHER.
OH.
SOUNDS LIKE A BORING JOB.
YOU'RE ONLY CLEANING WINDOWS.
MM.
I LIKE IT.
IS THAT SO?
WHAT DO YOU LIKE ABOUT IT?

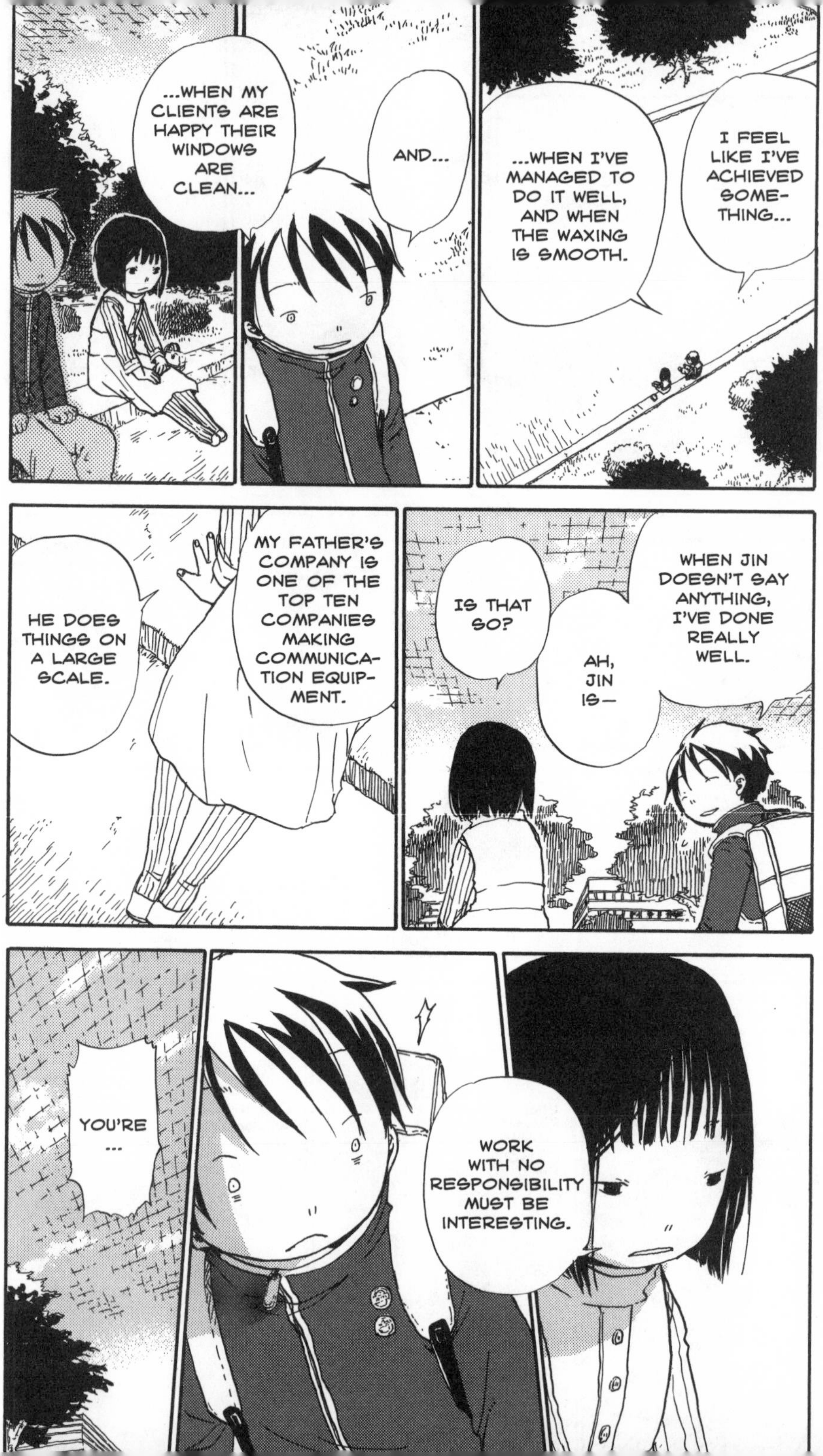
I FEEL LIKE I'VE ACHIEVED SOME-THING...
...WHEN I'VE MANAGED TO DO IT WELL, AND WHEN THE WAXING IS SMOOTH.
AND...
...WHEN MY CLIENTS ARE HAPPY THEIR WINDOWS ARE CLEAN...
WHEN JIN DOESN'T SAY ANYTHING, I'VE DONE REALLY WELL.
AH, JIN IS—
IS THAT SO?
MY FATHER'S COMPANY IS ONE OF THE TOP TEN COMPANIES MAKING COMMUNICA-TION EQUIP-MENT.
HE DOES THINGS ON A LARGE SCALE.
WORK WITH NO RESPONSIBILITY MUST BE INTERESTING.
YOU'RE ...

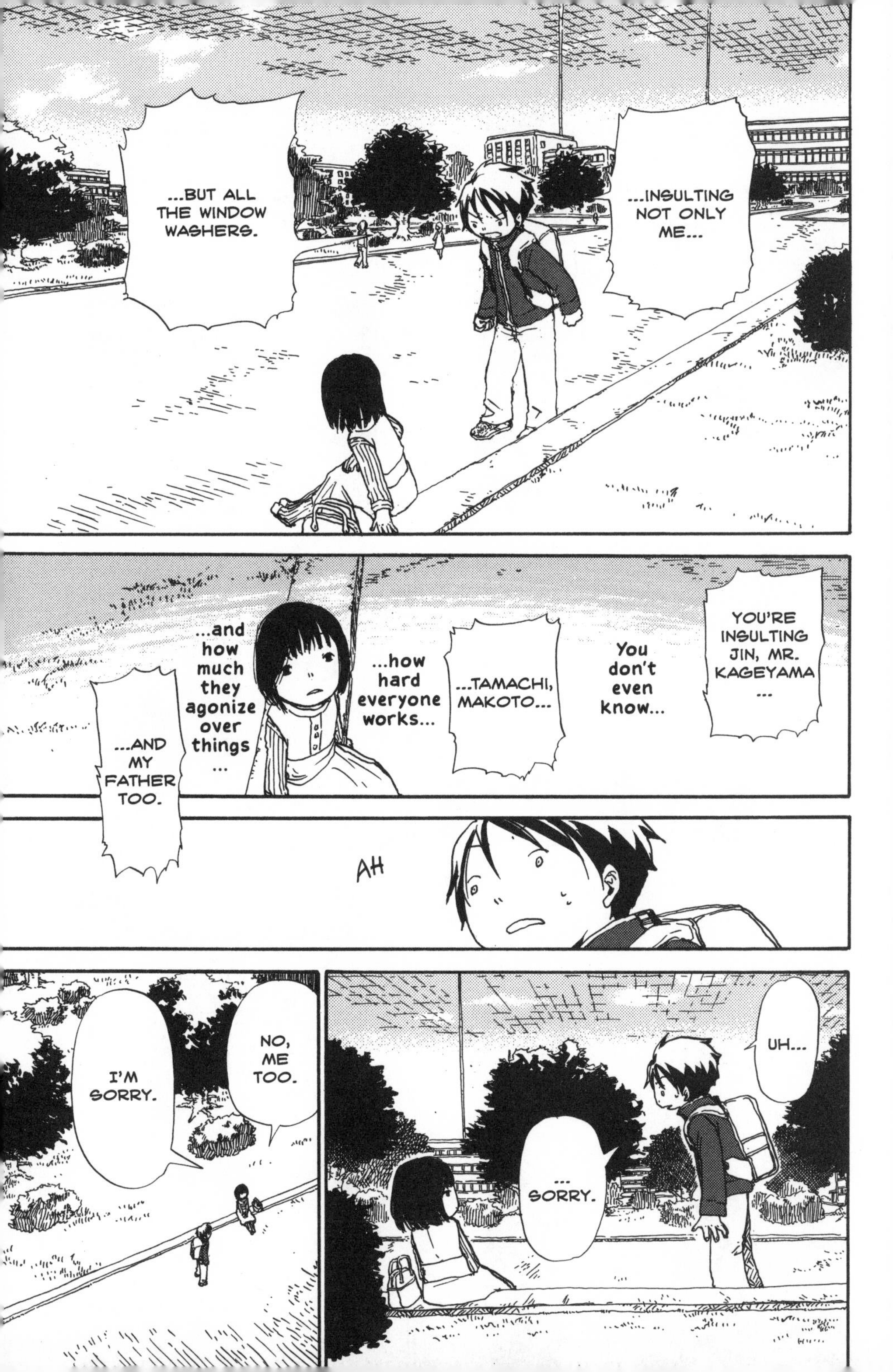
...INSULTING NOT ONLY ME...
...BUT ALL THE WINDOW WASHERS.
YOU'RE INSULTING JIN, MR. KAGEYAMA ...
You don't even know...
...TAMACHI, MAKOTO...
...how hard everyone works...
...and how much they agonize over things ...
...AND MY FATHER TOO.
AH
UH...
... SORRY.
NO, ME TOO.
I'M SORRY.

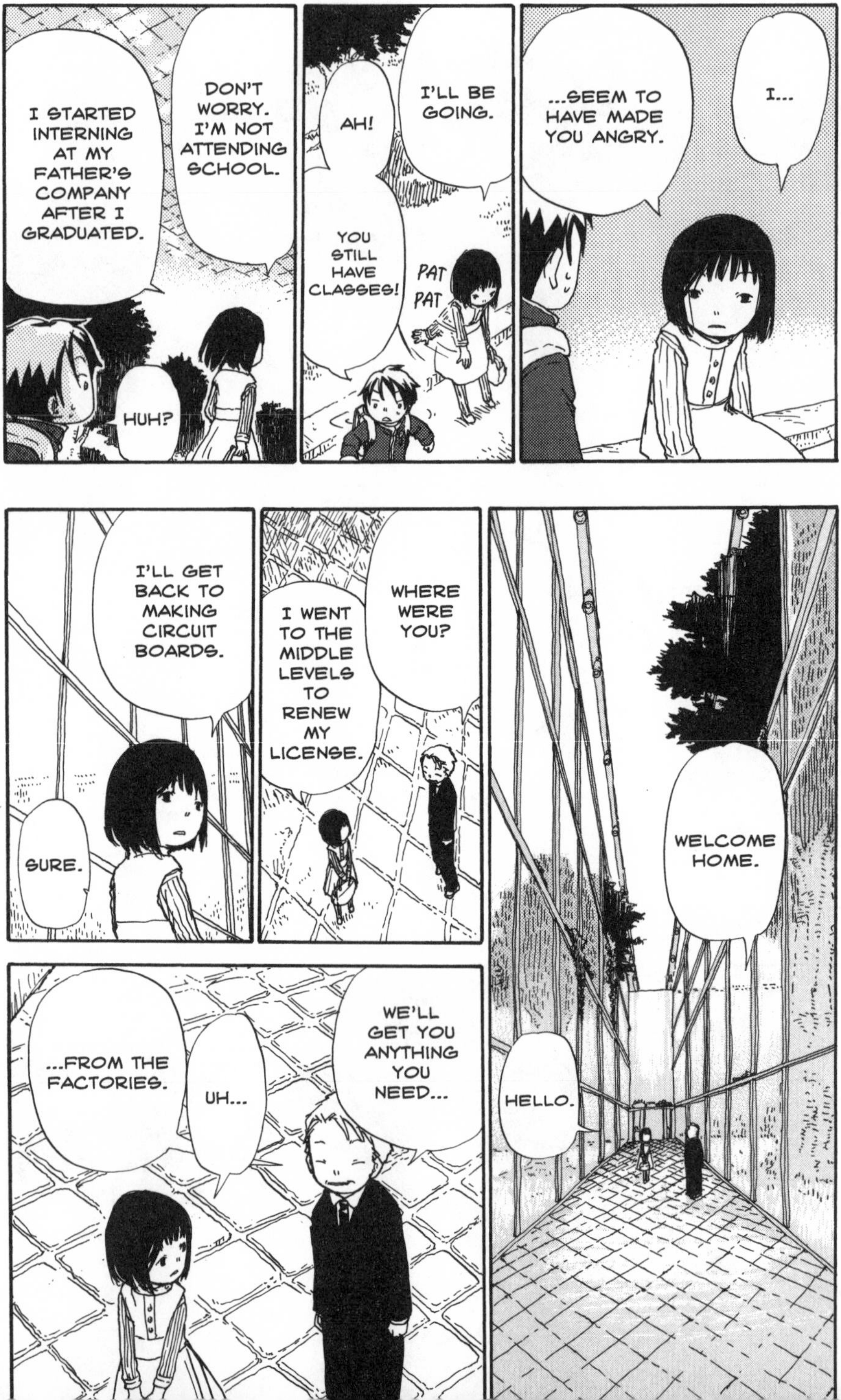
I...
...SEEM TO HAVE MADE YOU ANGRY.
I'LL BE GOING.
AH!
YOU STILL HAVE CLASSES!
PAT PAT
DON'T WORRY. I'M NOT ATTENDING SCHOOL.
I STARTED INTERNING AT MY FATHER'S COMPANY AFTER I GRADUATED.
HUH?
WELCOME HOME.
HELLO.
WHERE WERE YOU?
I WENT TO THE MIDDLE LEVELS TO RENEW MY LICENSE.
I'LL GET BACK TO MAKING CIRCUIT BOARDS.
SURE.
WE'LL GET YOU ANYTHING YOU NEED...
UH...
...FROM THE FACTORIES.

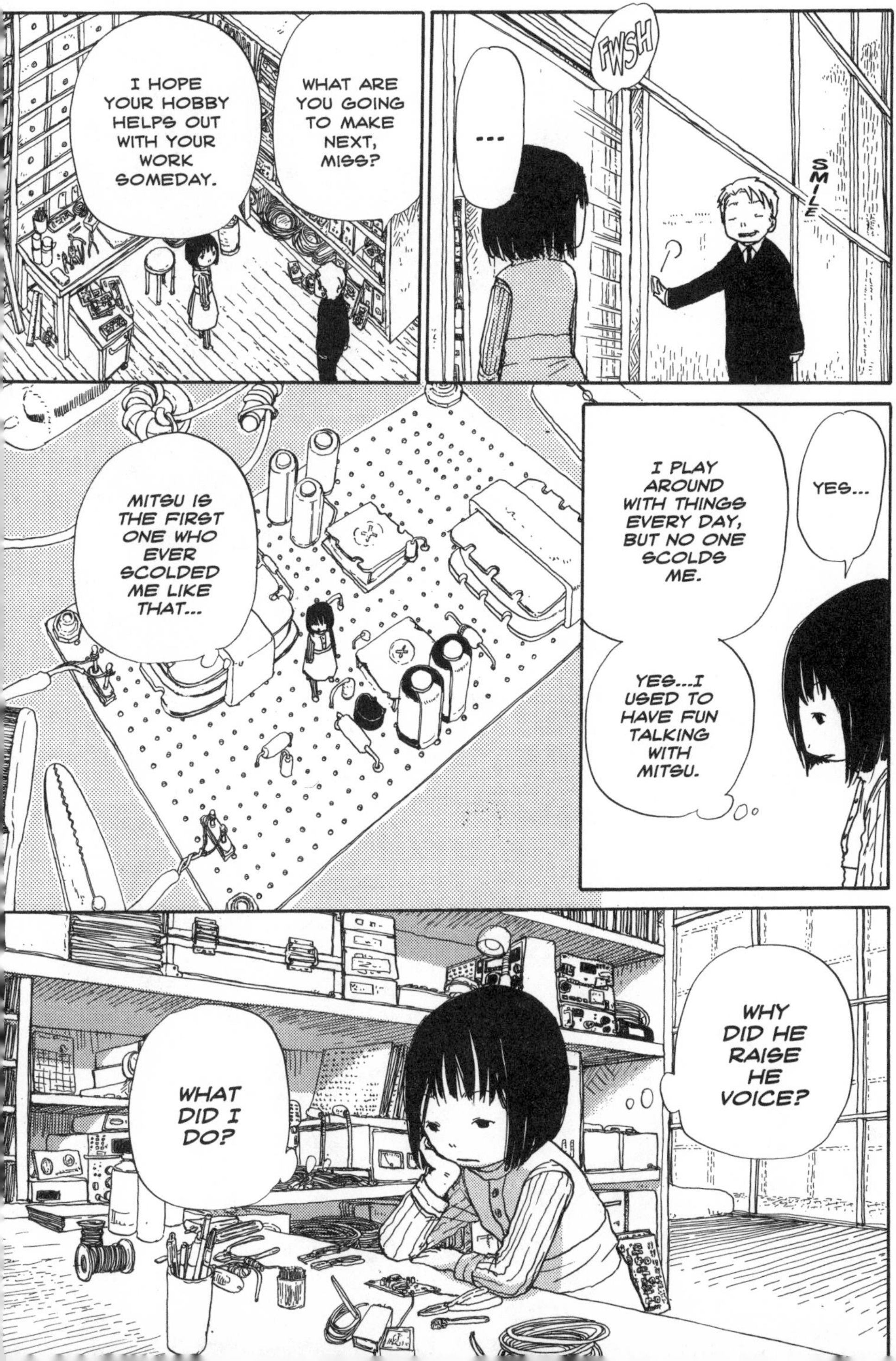
FWSH
...
SMILE
WHAT ARE YOU GOING TO MAKE NEXT, MISS?
I HOPE YOUR HOBBY HELPS OUT WITH YOUR WORK SOMEDAY.
YES...
I PLAY AROUND WITH THINGS EVERY DAY, BUT NO ONE SCOLDS ME.
YES...I USED TO HAVE FUN TALKING WITH MITSU.
MITSU IS THE FIRST ONE WHO EVER SCOLDED ME LIKE THAT...
WHY DID HE RAISE HE VOICE?
WHAT DID I DO?

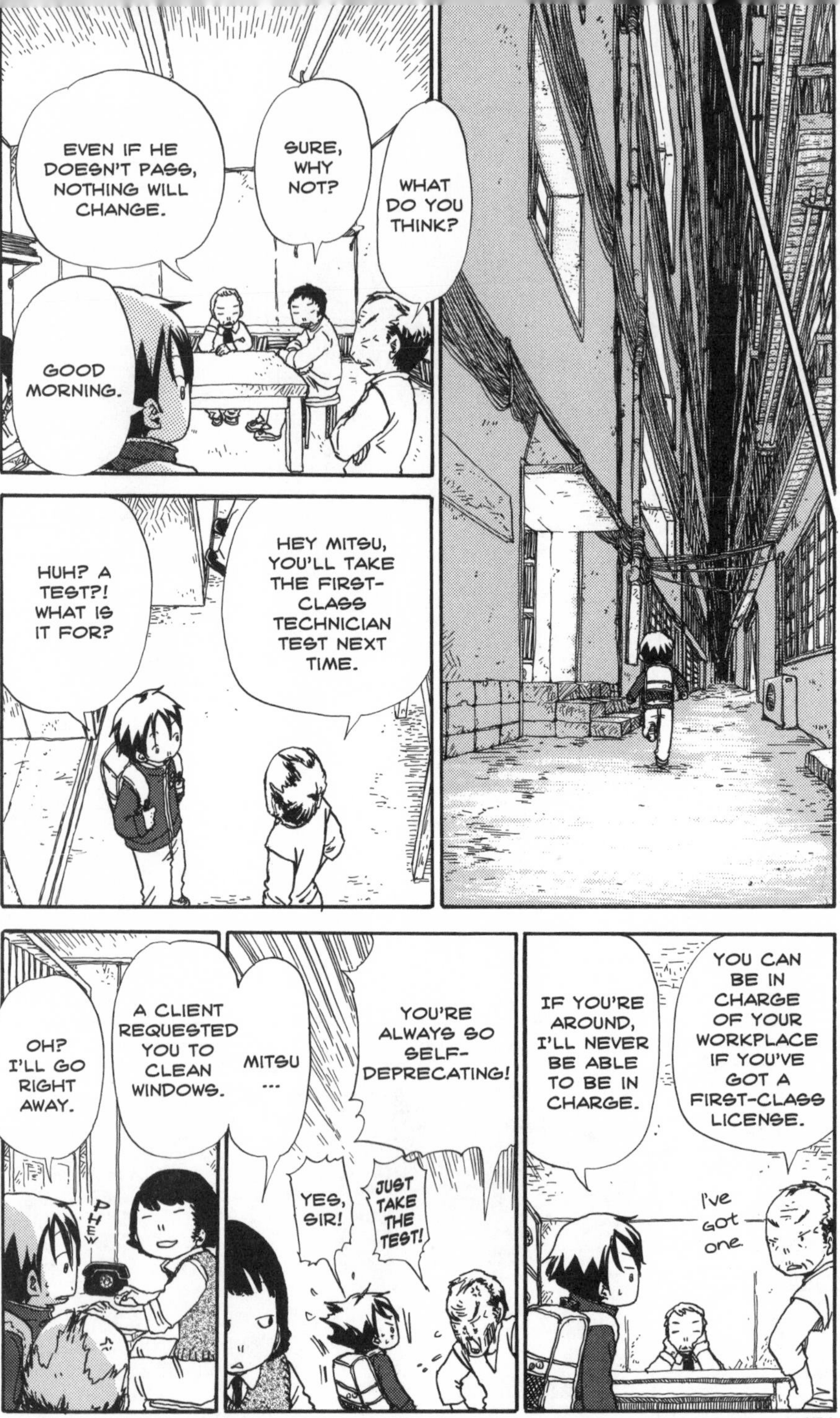
WHAT DO YOU THINK?
SURE, WHY NOT?
EVEN IF HE DOESN'T PASS, NOTHING WILL CHANGE.
GOOD MORNING.
HEY MITSU, YOU'LL TAKE THE FIRST-CLASS TECHNICIAN TEST NEXT TIME.
HUH? A TEST?! WHAT IS IT FOR?
YOU CAN BE IN CHARGE OF YOUR WORKPLACE IF YOU'VE GOT A FIRST-CLASS LICENSE.
IF YOU'RE AROUND, I'LL NEVER BE ABLE TO BE IN CHARGE.
I've got one.
YOU'RE ALWAYS SO SELF-DEPRECATING!
MITSU ...
JUST TAKE THE TEST!
YES, SIR!
A CLIENT REQUESTED YOU TO CLEAN WINDOWS.
OH? I'LL GO RIGHT AWAY.
PHEW

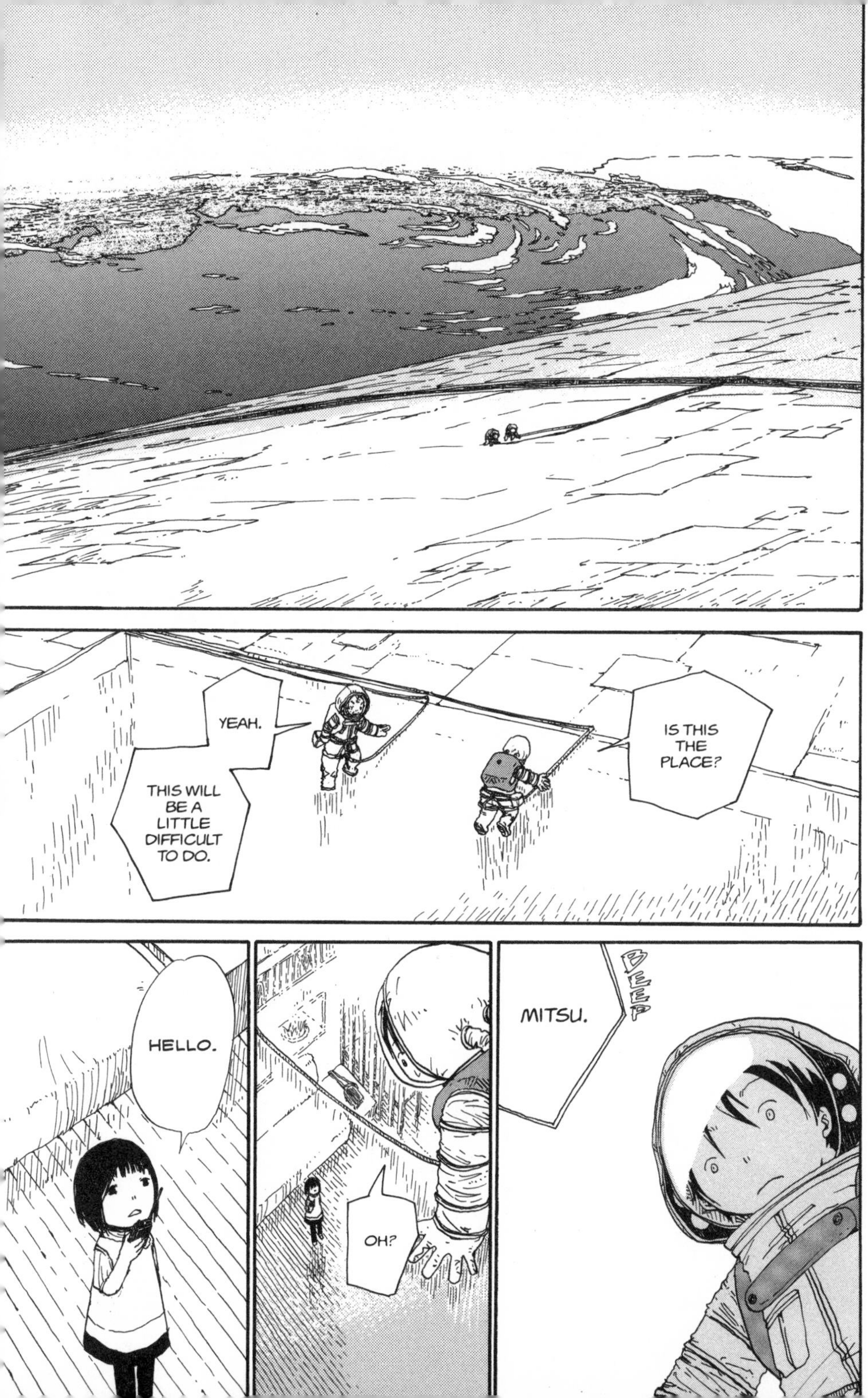
IS THIS THE PLACE?
YEAH.
THIS WILL BE A LITTLE DIFFICULT TO DO.
BEEP
MITSU.
OH?
HELLO.

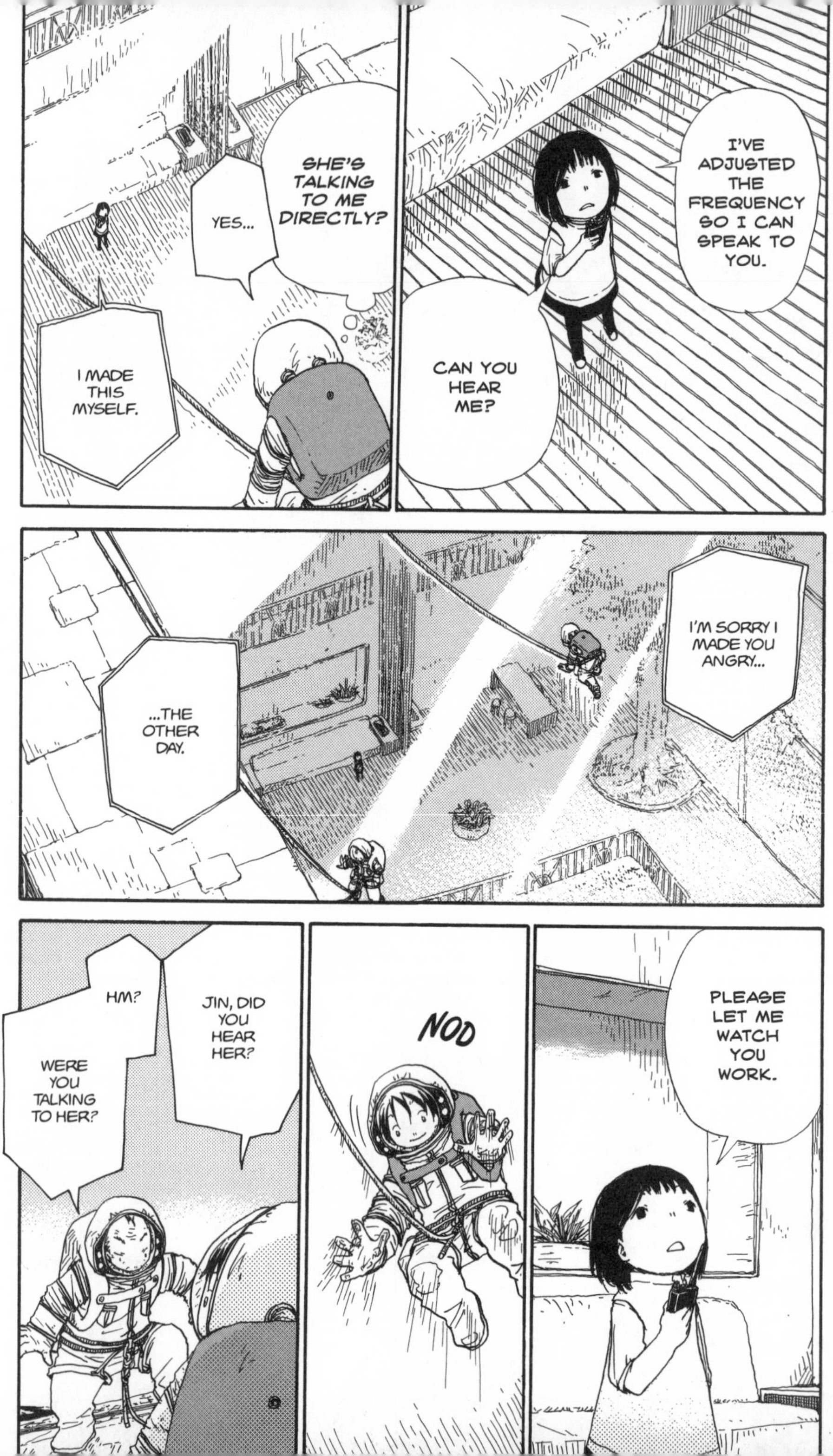
I'VE ADJUSTED THE FREQUENCY SO I CAN SPEAK TO YOU.
CAN YOU HEAR ME?
SHE'S TALKING TO ME DIRECTLY?
YES...
I MADE THIS MYSELF.
I'M SORRY I MADE YOU ANGRY...
...THE OTHER DAY.
PLEASE LET ME WATCH YOU WORK.
NOD
JIN, DID YOU HEAR HER?
HM?
WERE YOU TALKING TO HER?

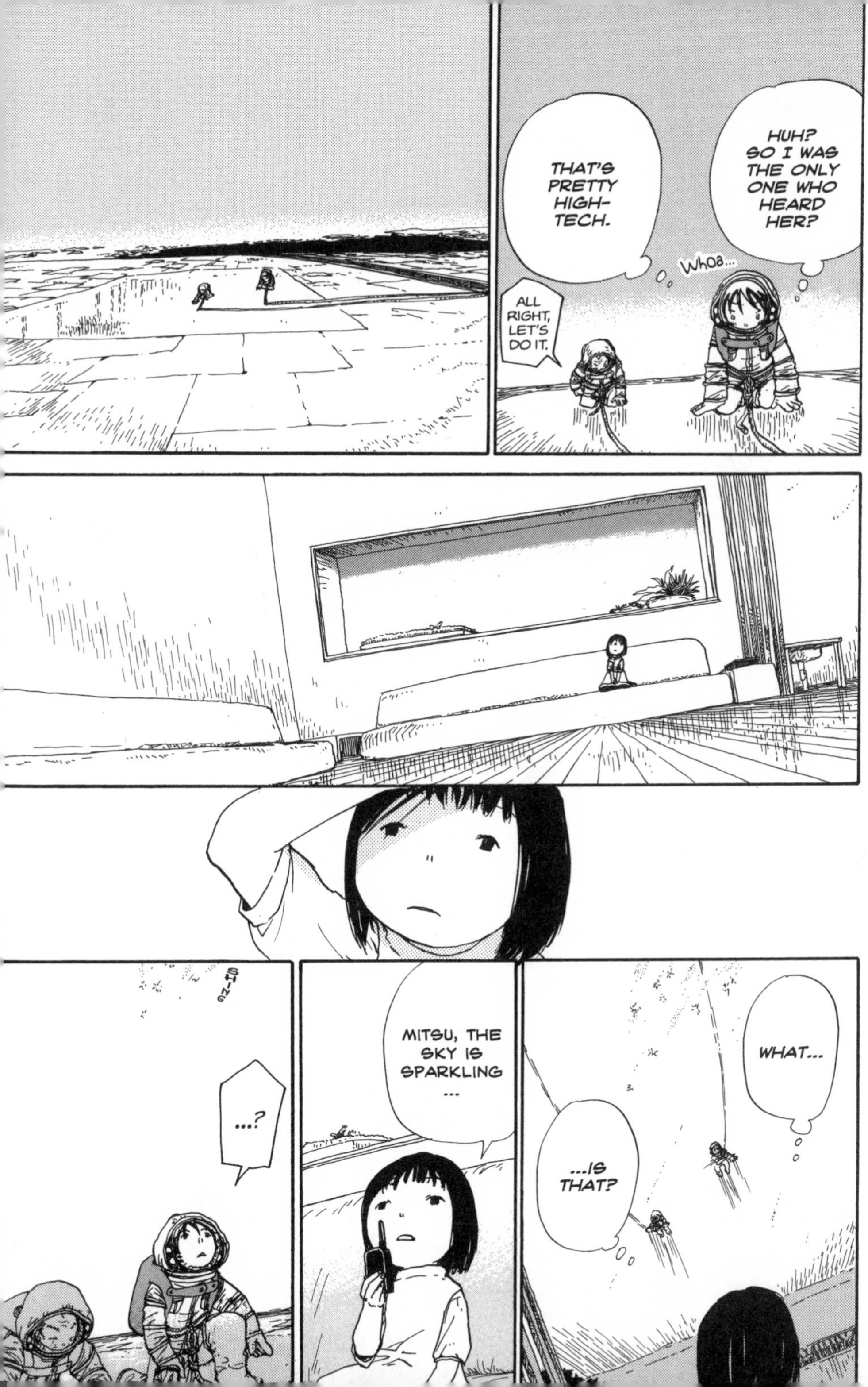
HUH? SO I WAS THE ONLY ONE WHO HEARD HER?
THAT'S PRETTY HIGH-TECH.
Whoa...
ALL RIGHT, LET'S DO IT.
WHAT...
...IS THAT?
MITSU, THE SKY IS SPARKLING ...
SHING
...?

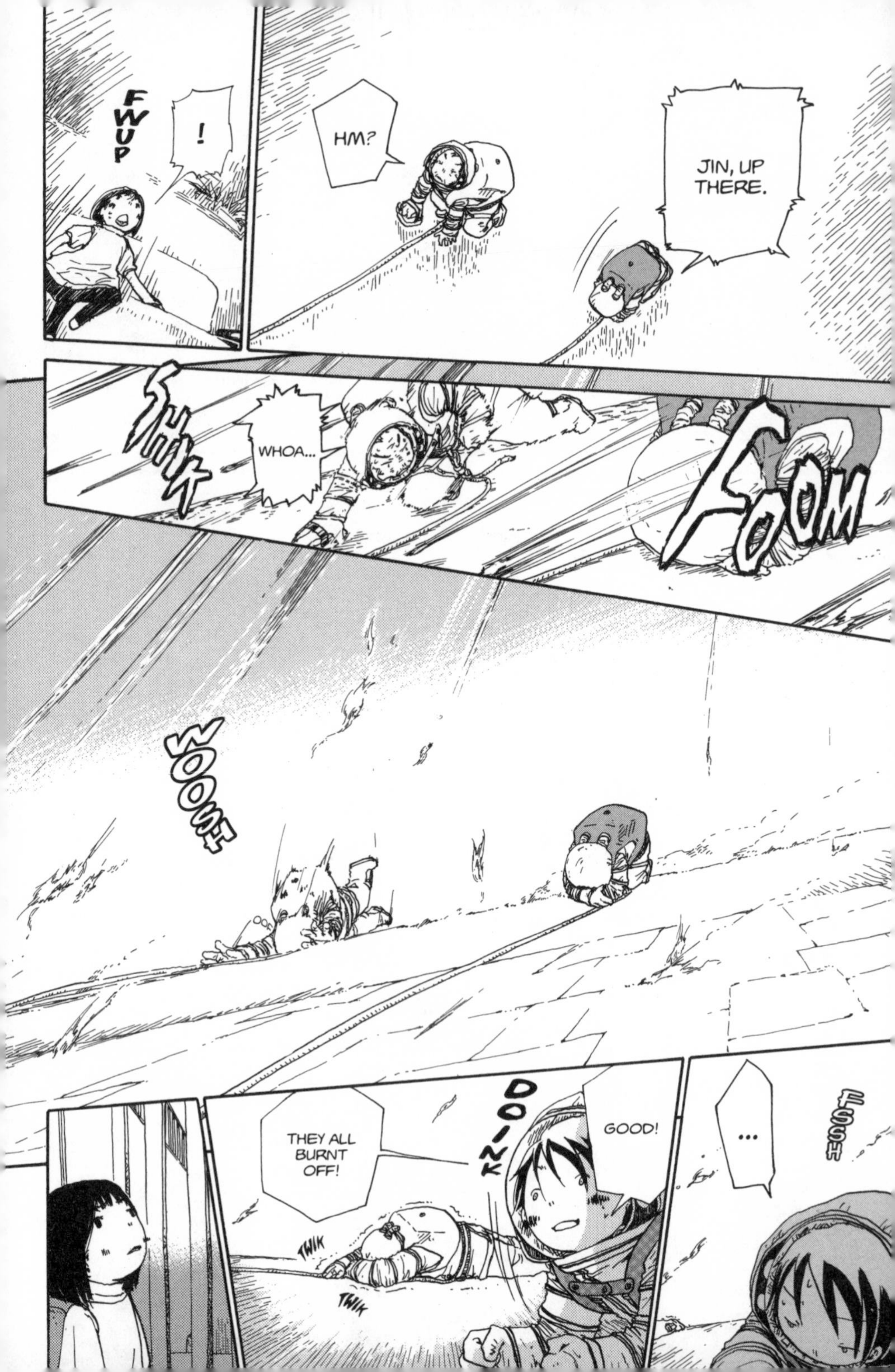
JIN, UP THERE.
HM?
FWUP
!
FOOM
WHOA...
SHUK
WOOOSH
FSSH
...
GOOD!
DOOINK
THEY ALL BURNT OFF!
TWIK
TWIK

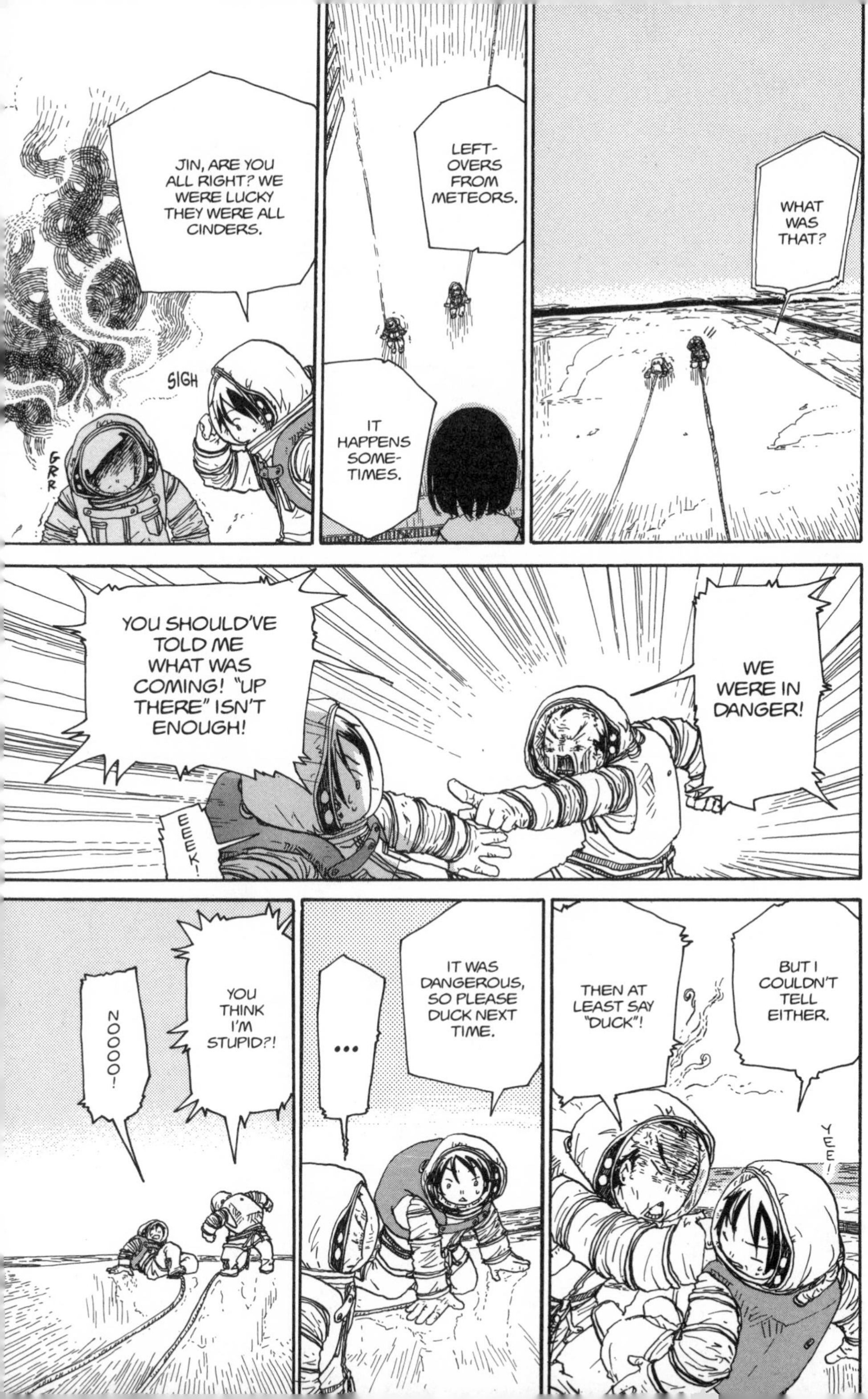
WHAT WAS THAT?
LEFT-OVERS FROM METEORS.
IT HAPPENS SOME-TIMES.
JIN, ARE YOU ALL RIGHT? WE WERE LUCKY THEY WERE ALL CINDERS.
SIGH
GRR
WE WERE IN DANGER!
YOU SHOULD'VE TOLD ME WHAT WAS COMING! "UP THERE" ISN'T ENOUGH!
EEEK!
BUT I COULDN'T TELL EITHER.
THEN AT LEAST SAY "DUCK"!
YEE!
IT WAS DANGEROUS, SO PLEASE DUCK NEXT TIME.
...
YOU THINK I'M STUPID?!
NOOOOO!

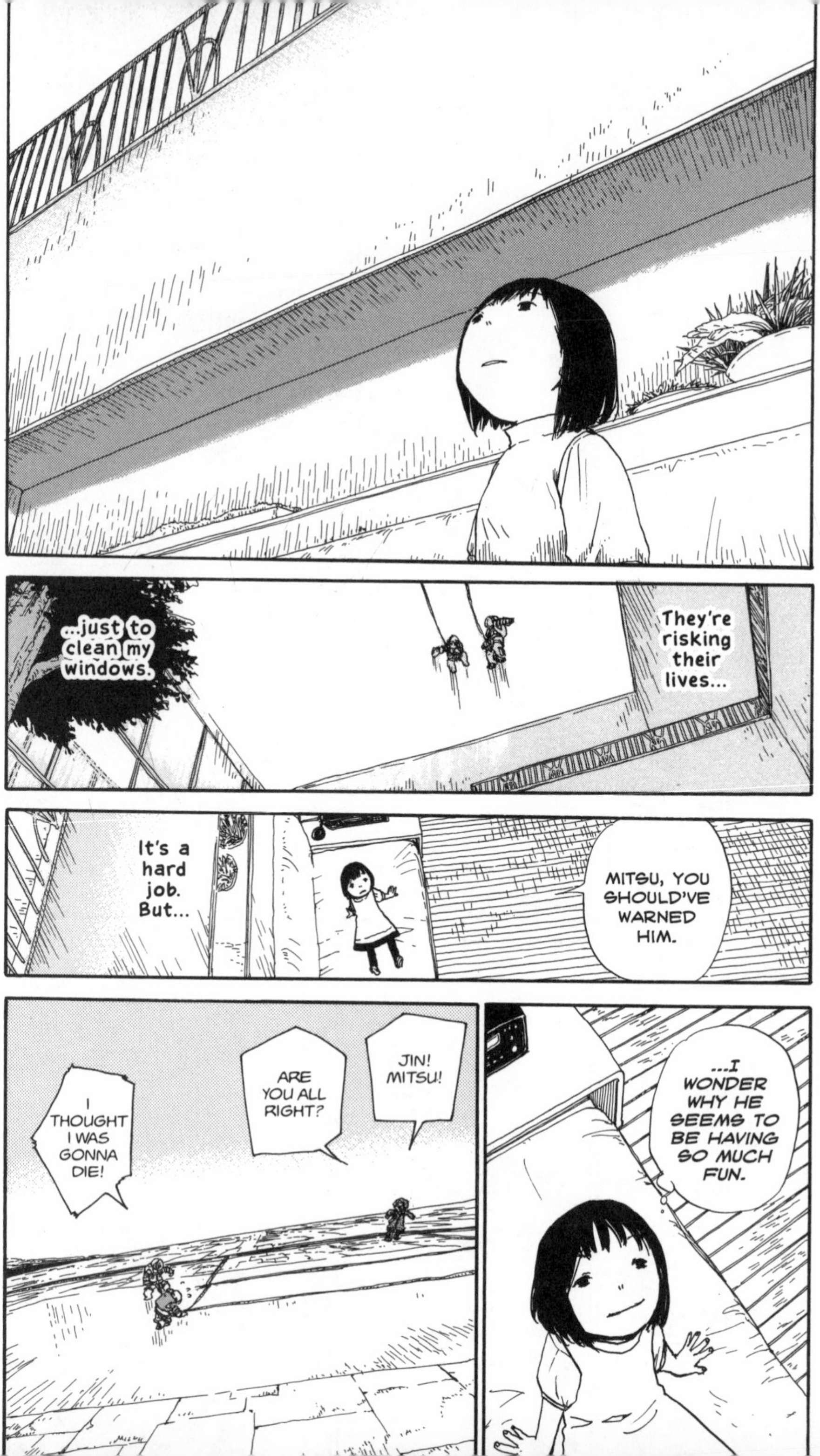
They're risking their lives...
...just to clean my windows.
MITSU, YOU SHOULD'VE WARNED HIM.
It's a hard job. But...
...I WONDER WHY HE SEEMS TO BE HAVING SO MUCH FUN.
JIN! MITSU!
ARE YOU ALL RIGHT?
I THOUGHT I WAS GONNA DIE!

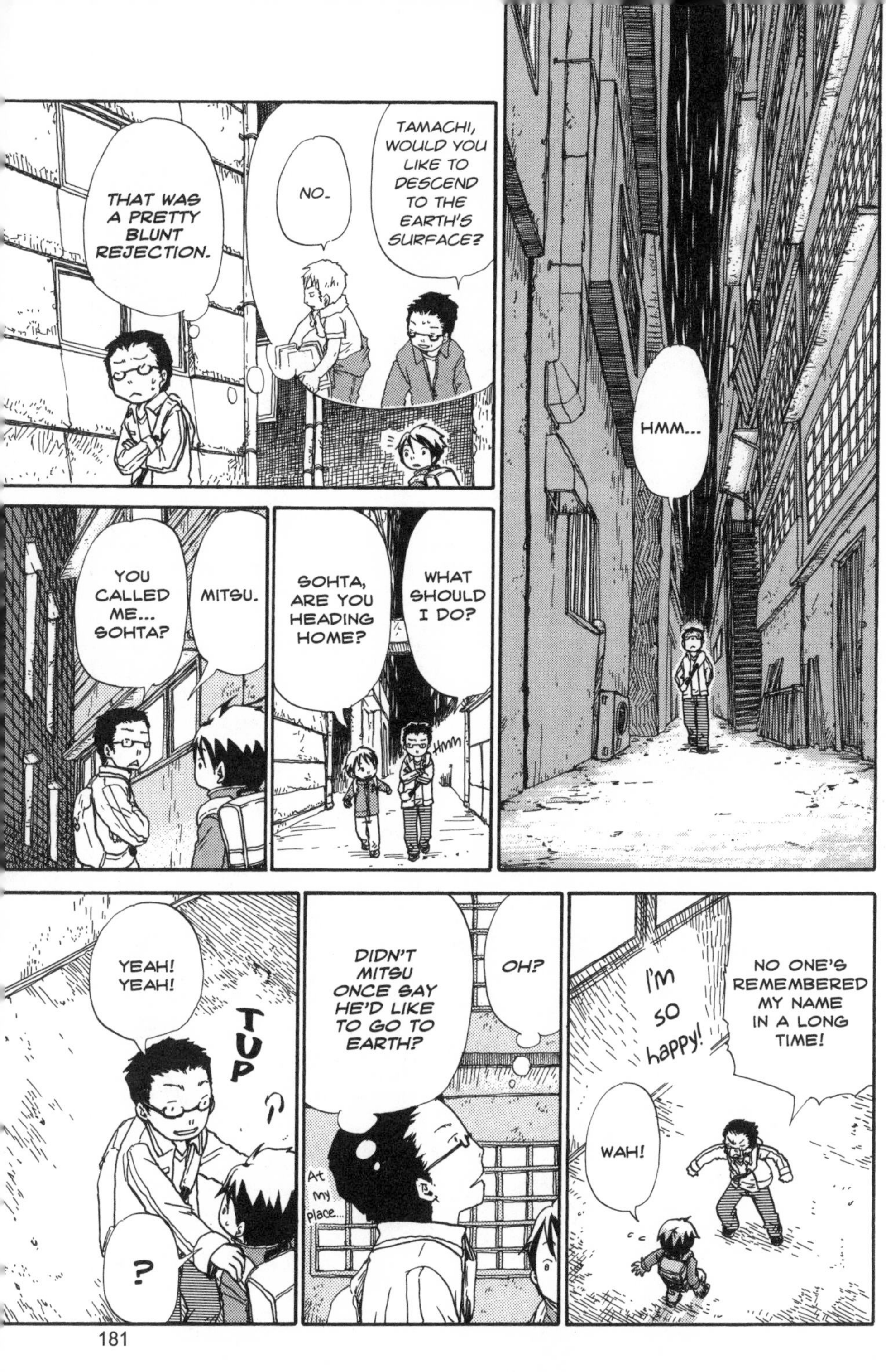
HMM...
TAMACHI, WOULD YOU LIKE TO DESCEND TO THE EARTH'S SURFACE?
NO.
THAT WAS A PRETTY BLUNT REJECTION.
WHAT SHOULD I DO?
SOHTA, ARE YOU HEADING HOME?
Hmm
MITSU.
YOU CALLED ME... SOHTA?
NO ONE'S REMEMBERED MY NAME IN A LONG TIME!
I'm so happy!
WAH!
OH?
DIDN'T MITSU ONCE SAY HE'D LIKE TO GO TO EARTH?
At my place...
YEAH! YEAH!
TUP
?

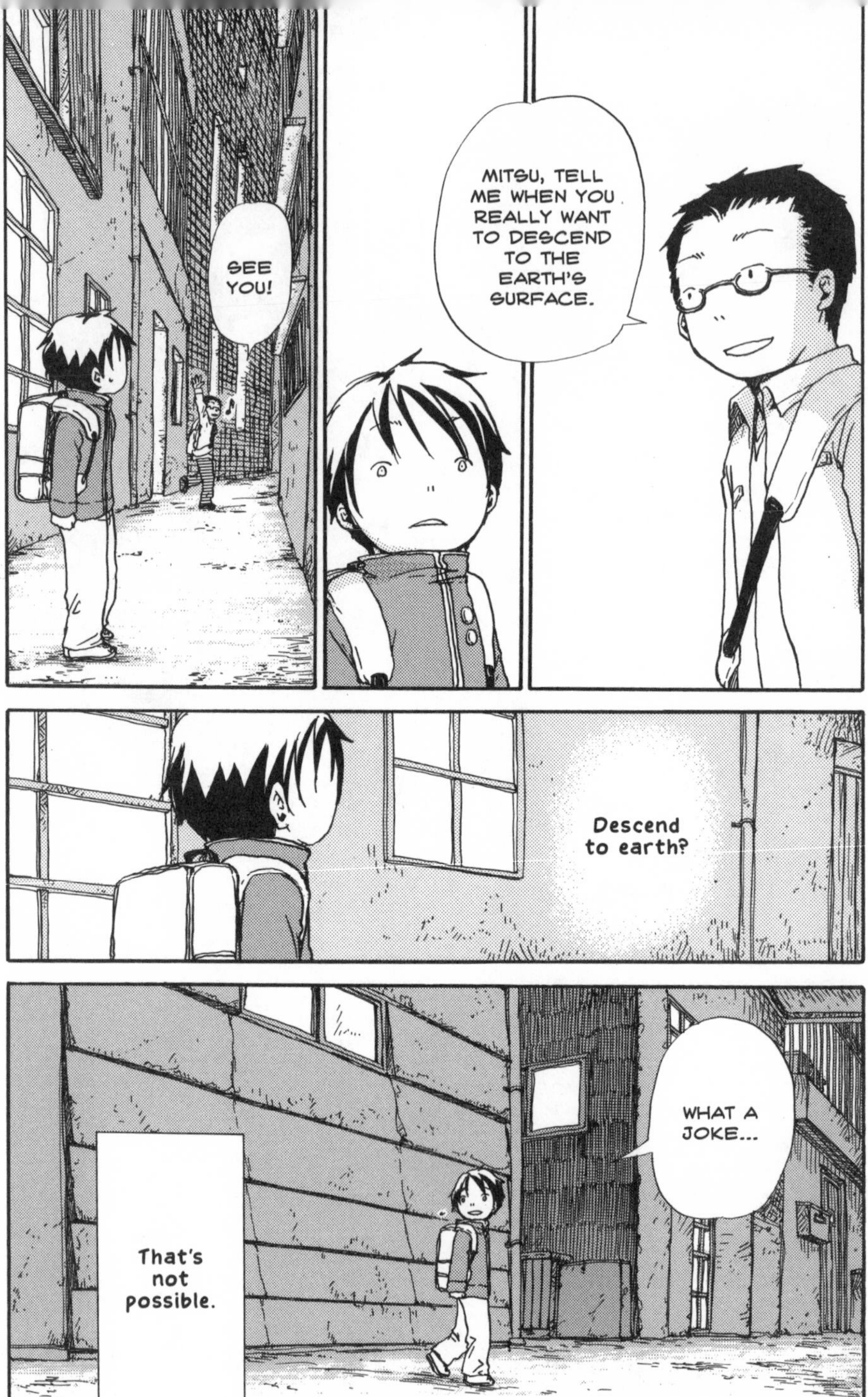
MITSU, TELL ME WHEN YOU REALLY WANT TO DESCEND TO THE EARTH'S SURFACE.
SEE YOU!
Descend to earth?
WHAT A JOKE...
That's not possible.

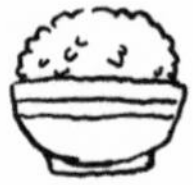

in the loft

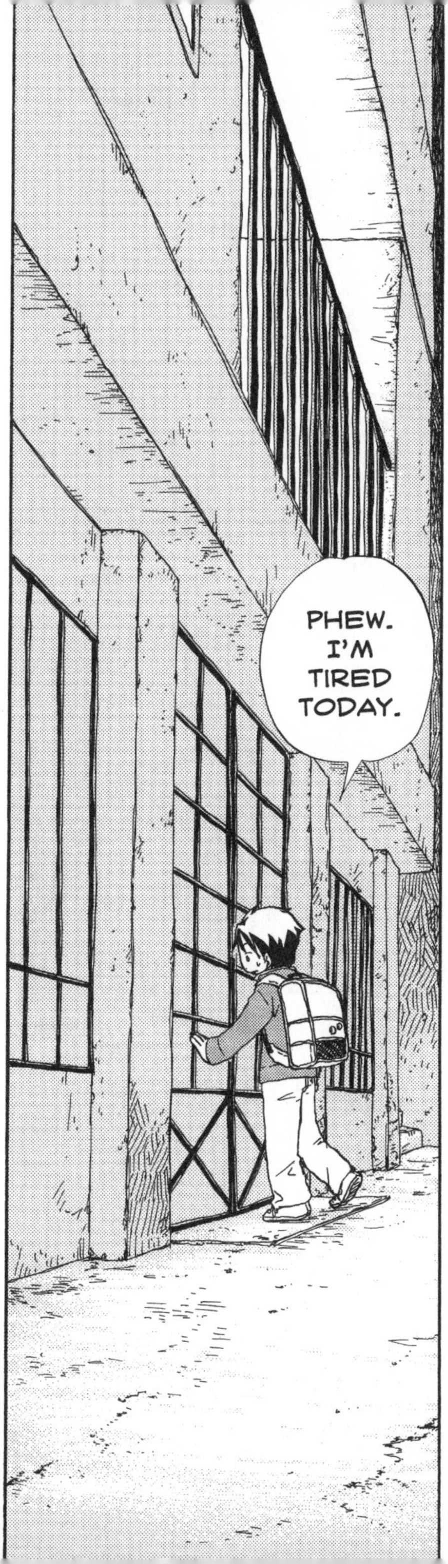
PHEW. I'M TIRED TODAY.

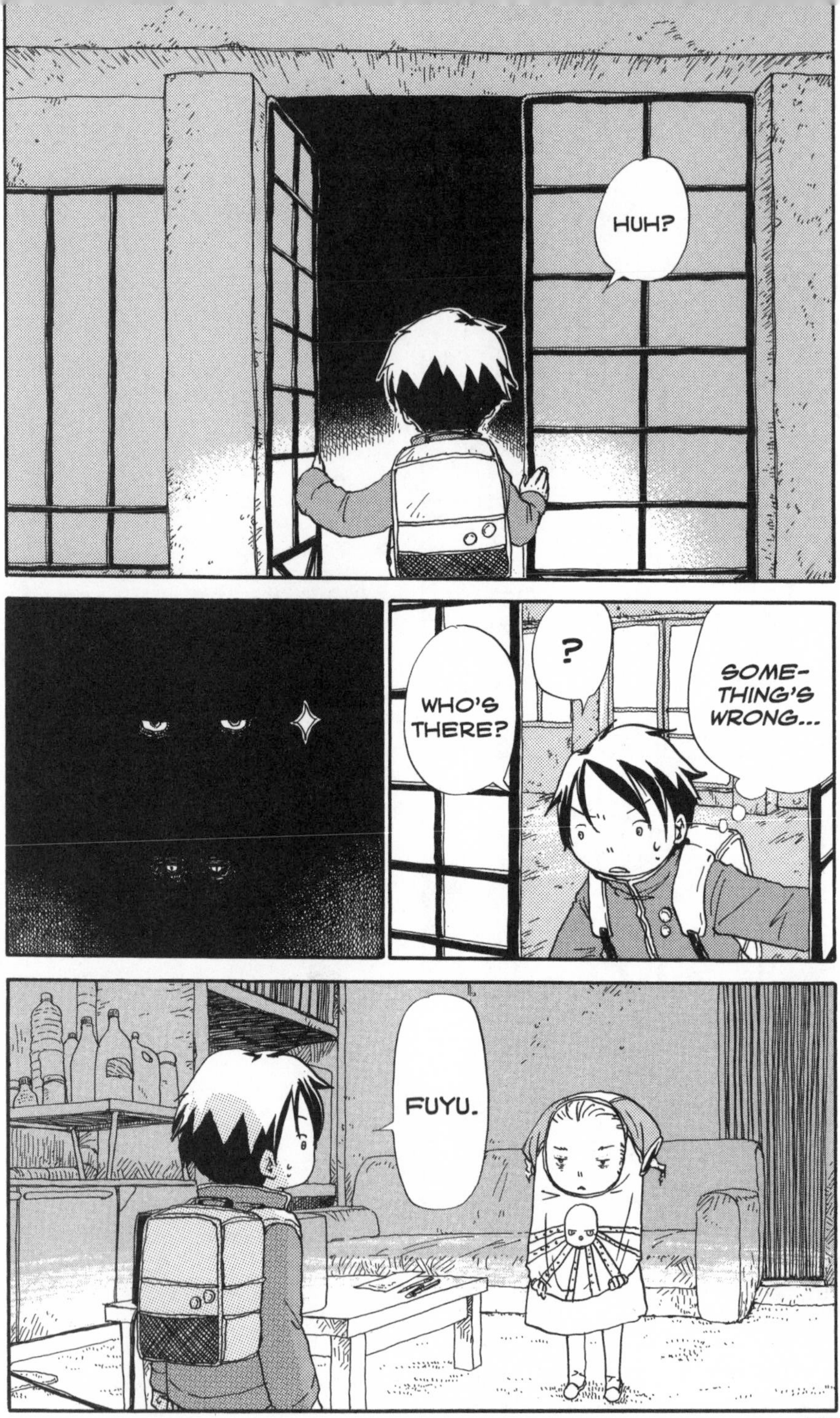
HUH?
SOME-THING'S WRONG...
?
WHO'S THERE?
FUYU.

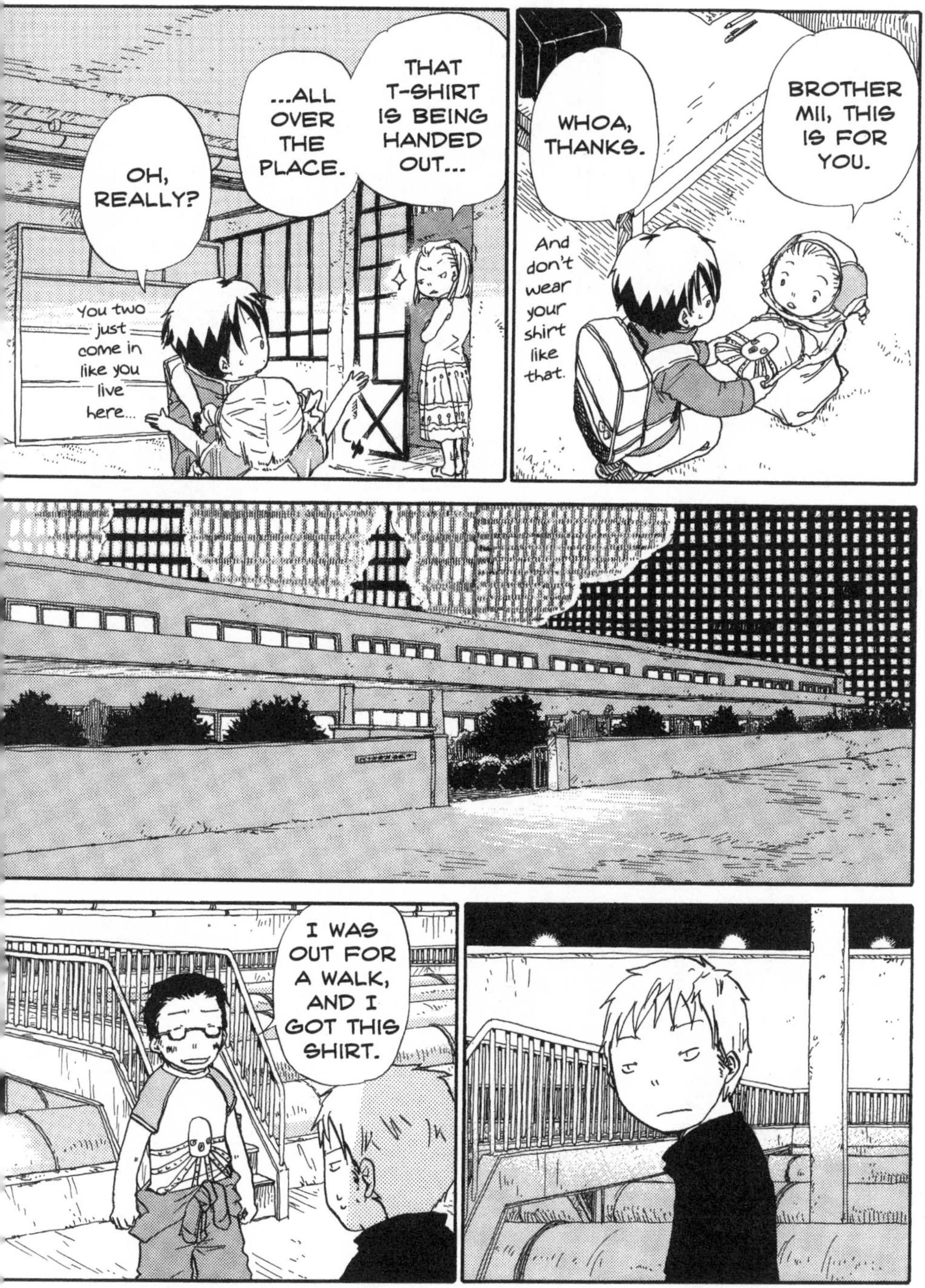
BROTHER MII, THIS IS FOR YOU.
WHOA, THANKS.
And don't wear your shirt like that.
THAT T-SHIRT IS BEING HANDED OUT...
...ALL OVER THE PLACE.
OH, REALLY?
You two just come in like you live here...
I WAS OUT FOR A WALK, AND I GOT THIS SHIRT.

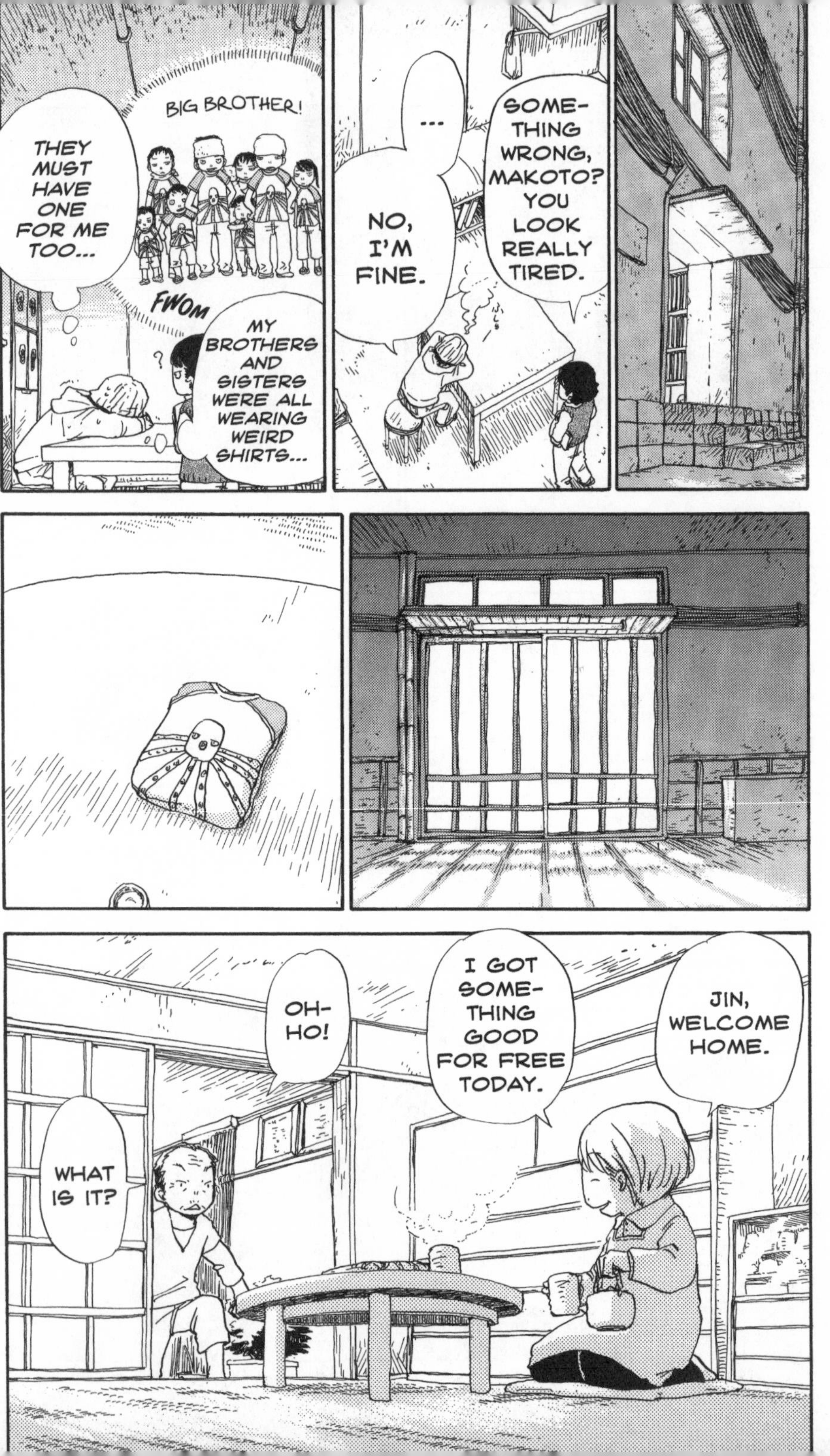
SOME-THING WRONG, MAKOTO? YOU LOOK REALLY TIRED.
...
NO, I'M FINE.
BIG BROTHER!
THEY MUST HAVE ONE FOR ME TOO...
FWOM
MY BROTHERS AND SISTERS WERE ALL WEARING WEIRD SHIRTS...
JIN, WELCOME HOME.
I GOT SOME-THING GOOD FOR FREE TODAY.
OH-HO!
WHAT IS IT?

THANKS! TO HIDEKI EGAMI, MAMI HIRAI, MEGUMI KASAI, FUMIKA, KINOZUKA, JUNKO, AND TO YOU, FOR READING.

THE END OF SATURN APARTMENTS 3

In the Next Volume

Washing windows on a space colony
hovering 35,000 meters above the
Earth is a dangerous job. Mitsu, a young
window washer, knows this all too well.
His father fell off the Ring System in
an accident. Now, Mitsu's coworker
Kageyama collapses on the job. Trying
to save Kageyama, Mitsu inadvertently
endangers his life. In recovery,
Kageyama learns that exposure to UV
rays has taken a toll on his immune
system. He's forced to choose between
his job and his health.

saturn apartments

SATURN APARTMENTS
Volume 3
VIZ Signature Edition

Story and Art by **HISAE IWAOKA**

© 2006 Hisae IWAOKA/Shogakukan
All rights reserved.
Original Japanese edition "DOSEI MANSION" published by **SHOGAKUKAN Inc.**

Design of original Japanese edition by Kei Kasai

Translation/Tomo Kimura
Touch-up Art & Lettering/Eric Erbes
Design/Yukiko Whitley
Editor/Daniel Gillespie

Printed in Canada

Published by VIZ Media, LLC
P.O. Box 77010
San Francisco, CA 94107

10 9 8 7 6 5 4 3 2 1
First printing, May 2011

VIZ SIGNATURE
www.sigikki.com

www.viz.com

YOU'RE READING
THE WRONG WAY

SATURN APARTMENTS IS
PRINTED RIGHT TO LEFT IN ORDER
TO PRESERVE THE ORIGINAL
ORIENTATION OF HISAE IWAOKA'S
GORGEOUS ART. PLEASE TURN THE
BOOK OVER AND ENJOY.